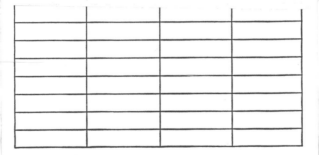

Praise for *Impossible Cure: The Promise of Homeopathy*
by Amy Lansky (R.L.Ranch Press, 2003)

"An introduction to homeopathy that stands out from the rest."
—DR. JOSEPH MERCOLA, Mercola Newsletter

"Amy Lansky is a skilled guide to the world of homeopathy."
—LARRY DOSSEY, MD, Author: *Healing Words*

"The finest general introduction to homeopathy I've yet read...This book should be read by everyone interested in homeopathy, from the rank beginner to the seasoned professional. It has something new in it for everyone."
—JULIAN WINSTON, Former Editor: *Homeopathy Today;*
Author: *The Faces of Homeopathy*

"We have never had this kind of response to an introductory book."
—GREG COOPER, Minimum Price Homeopathic Books

"One of the best introductions to homeopathy I've seen. Two thumbs up for *Impossible Cure: The Promise of Homeopathy.*"
—MICHAEL CASTLEMAN, Author: *The New Healing Herbs*
and other consumer health books

"An accessible guide to one of the most mysterious of healing arts."
—WAYNE B. JONAS, MD, Director, Samueli Institute; Former director, Office of Alternative Medicine, NIH

"This book may very well contribute to the transformation of homeopathy from the ugly duckling of medicine to the swan that it deserves to be."
—LIA BELLO, RN, FNP, CCH, Reviewer for *Homeopathy Today*

ACTIVE CONSCIOUSNESS

AWAKENING THE POWER WITHIN

Amy L. Lansky, PhD

R.L.Ranch

Press

Portola Valley, California

For more information, please contact: R.L.Ranch Press, 4119 Alpine Road, Suite A, Portola Valley, CA 94028. Telephone: 650-851-2927. Fax: 650-851-9095. E-mail: info@ activeconsciousness.com. Also visit *www.activeconsciousness.com* to find out more about the content of this book and ordering information.

Although the author and publisher have exhaustively researched all sources to ensure the accuracy and completeness of information contained in this book, we assume no responsibility for errors, inaccuracies, omissions, or any inconsistency herein. Any slights of people, places, or organizations are unintentional.

Special note to reader. Although this book includes several exercises and methods for self-development and empowerment, it is not meant to give specific recommendations of psychological, medical, or other advice. Nor does it make any warranties or guarantees of any sort that any information in this book or on *www.activeconsciousness.com* will produce any particular physical, emotional, or other result.

Permissions. Special thanks to the following publishers for their permission to include quotations from the following books: Excerpts from *In Search of the Miraculous: Fragments of an Unknown Teaching* by P.D. Ouspensky, copyright 1949 and renewed 1977 by Tatiana Nagro, reprinted by permission of Houghton Mifflin Harcourt Publishing Company; Permission granted from New World Library (*www.NewWorldLibrary.com*) for excerpts from *The Power of Now* by Eckhardt Tolle; Permission granted from New World Library (*www.NewWorldLibrary.com*) for excerpts and figure concept from *The Mandala of Being* by Richard Moss; Celest Pearsall for interview quote of Paul Pearsall; Inner Traditions Bear & Company (*www.InnerTraditions.com*) for *Science and the Akashic Field* by Ervin Laszlo; Hay House (*www.hayhouse.com*) for *The Amazing Power of Deliberate Intent* by Esther and Jerry Hicks; Thomas Walker (Roaring Fork Limited) for a quote from *The Force Is With Us: The Conspiracy Against the Supernatural, Spiritual, and Paranormal*; Rudolf Steiner Press for quotes from *Anthroposophy and the Inner Life* by Rudolf Steiner (1931); Permission granted from H.J. Kramer / New World Library (*www.NewWorldLibrary.com*) for excerpts from *Personal Power Through Awareness* and *Living With Joy* by Sanaya Roman; Energy Psychology Press for use of the EFT statement; Exercises and training materials generously provided by Gary Sherman and Ellen Miller (*www.creativeawareness.com*).

ISBN-10: 0-9727514-5-9
ISBN-13: 978-09727514-5-2
Library of Congress Control Number: 2011906014

FIRST PRINT-ON-DEMAND PRINTING—2011

Interior and cover design by Melanie Haage
Cover image of the Orion Nebula courtesy of NASA and the National Space Science Data Center
Illustrations and figures by Max Rubin
Author photo by Jennifer Dungan
Exercises inspired by material developed by Gary Sherman

Life is a complex web of beginnings
Branching like a tree of possibilities.
Splendidly intricate, yet elegant and clear.

Take each step through the garden path,
Smell each rose as it blooms,
Cut each stem when it's time,
And when you look back, don't be surprised—
For that may be changing too.

You and every atom
Awake or slumbering in the fog of sleep,
Are required and embedded in this picture of God.

Savor each hour and each day
As an experiment in creation.
Trip from moment to moment
Exploring the frontier.
Feel free as you travel
The paths of Consciousness.

TABLE OF CONTENTS

FOREWORD

A NUMBER OF YEARS AGO, I WAS TEACHING A CLASS ON HOW to bring meditation practice into daily life. I had been a teacher of meditation and self-awareness for over twenty-five years and was teaching the course at a learning center in Palo Alto I had co-founded. That night, I was speaking to the class about how important it is to shift the focus of one's attention from observing and monitoring outer behavior to giving attention to one's state of being in the moment. This shift, I was saying, requires that we reorganize ourselves into a new experience of how we hold the two obvious facts of our experience; we are a subjectivity inhabiting an objective world. A woman raised her hand and I expected a question. Instead she began a short but cogent comparison between what I was saying and its relationship to software and hardware in the world of computer science.

That same evening, while I was discussing the difference between attention and thought, she raised her hand again. This time she gave additional context to my statements by explaining their parallels to similar ideas in the Kabbalah, the esoteric text of Judaism. This was my introduction to the mind of Amy Lansky.

I didn't know then that my first encounter with Amy in the classroom was only a snapshot of the scope and breadth of her interest in and knowledge of the study of consciousness. Her new book, *Active Consciousness: Awakening the Power Within*, now makes this transparent. Applying her skill as a research scientist, she gathers and distills her knowledge from a multitude of sources, taking her reader for a ride through mathematics, physics, religion, metaphysics, philosophy, energy medicine, and mysticism. Covering both Western science and the spiritual science of the East, she shows us through contemporary research that coming to terms with the nature of consciousness is of paramount importance. She never loses sight of the proposition that it is our state of consciousness that is ultimately responsible for the quality of our lives and the world we inhabit.

The knowledge accumulated by others is often our starting place when we approach a new path of learning. It was so for me thirty years ago, when I accidentally picked up a book on Zen Buddhism left on a chair in my living room by someone. I do not know whether it was accident or *synchronicity*—something that Amy also addresses in this book. What I do know is that it helped infuse me with a new possibility for being, and I began to search out and read all I could about states of consciousness. If I'd had Amy's book at the time, it would have saved me a lot of effort in tracking down the source materials I was hungry for, and would have pointed me in directions I did not know existed. Most of all, though, her book would have given sanction to my desire to expand the boundaries of my consciousness, giving this desire context and thus granting me permission to proceed.

The more I read, the more I began to understand that I had to be an explorer and come to rest within myself to find what I was seeking. Amy arrives at this same conclusion when she formulates her concept of *active consciousness* and turns her narrative toward how to achieve it. Active consciousness becomes her method for entering experience with the conscious intent of discovering what lays beneath our normal everyday perception of who and what we are. She offers a simple yet direct way of exploring and becoming aware of the layers of subtle experience that we find when attention is turned inward and the journey of self-discovery begins. Borrowing from a number of sources, she provides easy yet profound awareness exercises that will guide the student of active consciousness into their inner world of self-experience. Some of these practices she shares from my own work—exercises that I have formulated over my years of teaching that have been successful in introducing thousands of people to their inner life and the subtle energies that comprise it.

Concluding her book with a call to consciousness, Amy exposes her larger concern; our method for knowing is irrevocably tied to what is known. We must go beyond materialism and its technological perspectives and step more directly into the experience of self, beyond man as physical machine and into the spirit that animates and gives meaning to each of our lives.

Individuals, society and the planet itself are suffering. To meet the challenges of the future we must find our way to the center of ourselves. This is the place within each of us where new creativity, vision, and inspiration are waiting to be released and made available for the collective good. This new creativity can then be fashioned into new models for being—a process of conscious evolution that lies at the heart of consciousness and is one that we all can participate in. I believe that Amy Lansky has given us a wonderful book that will find its place in this future she is calling forth and inviting us to join.

Gary Sherman
Originator of *Perceptual Integration* and
Co-founder of the *Creative Awareness Project*
February 2011

PREFACE

LIFE IS FULL OF CHOICES, AND SOMETIMES THEY TAKE US TO unexpected places. When I was working as a research computer scientist in Silicon Valley, I never would have guessed that I would eventually become an author of a book about homeopathy, and after that, a book about awakening humanity to a new level of consciousness. And yet, the forks in the road of my life have led me here.

Probably the first step that took me down this path was the one I describe in Chapter 1—when I was inspired by a TV show to think more deeply about the nature of reality and the possibility of higher dimensions in space. That inspiration eventually led to my writing an exploratory paper on the subject in 1996, "Consciousness As An Active Force."[1] Ten years later, I was hit by another unexpected moment of clarity in the middle of a board meeting for the National Center for Homeopathy. One of my colleagues had suggested that I tackle a time-consuming role within the organization. My reaction was swift and jarring—so much so that it took me by surprise. "No!" I said. "I have to write another book!" Suddenly a new possibility had appeared before me—a vision of turning my paper about consciousness into a book—and I sensed there was no other choice but to pursue it.

When such moments of sudden insight and inspiration hit us, they do tend to take us by surprise. It's as if a hidden hand or a small voice is nudging and guiding us along. Usually, though, we don't listen. We may hear the voice, we may feel the hand toying with our hearts, and we may even ponder the messages they impart to us. But most days, we simply move on, swept along in the stream of daily life. When we *do* listen, though, those moments are the ones that can change everything.

My aim in writing this book is to help enliven this mystery of life for as many people as I can. Throughout the ages, mystics and sages have taught us that by engaging in a process of self-development, we can learn to cast our hopes and dreams before us, and in response, the hidden hands and small voices of another realm—or of a deeper part of ourselves—jump in to guide us. We only need to learn to feel them and listen to them.

To fully engage with this process, we must first cast off the blinders that block us from considering such possibilities. Then we must learn to quiet the internal and external voices that constantly burden and distract us. As we do, we will find that we are gradually *waking up*—to a new aspect of ourselves and to an expanded view of what the universe is really all about. And as more of us collectively decide to do so, we may find that the world not only survives the troubling times that loom before us, but flourishes as never before.

Decide for yourself. All I ask is that you engage with this book as earnestly as you can. Play with the ideas and exercises that I present and make the effort to become more aware and awake. Make the commitment to practice and experiment a bit each day and see what you discover. Finally, if you *do* find something worthwhile in these pages, please let others know about it. Tell others about this book and about the magic you have found.

Remember: the collective power and potential of active consciousness is truly infinite. Together, we can create a much better world.

Amy L. Lansky, PhD
Portola Valley, California
January 2011

ACKNOWLEDGMENTS

FIRST AND FOREMOST, I MUST EXPRESS MY GRATITUDE FOR MY husband, Steve Rubin. He sat beside me the day I watched that fateful episode of Star Trek, and walked beside me each step of the way as I made my slow transition from computer scientist to homeopath to consciousness-awakener. He has always believed in my dreams and inspirations, never flagging in his role as my number one cheerleader, my first and last book reader, my confidant, and my partner in life. In his essence, Steve is a calm and wise soul who simultaneously anchors and buoys me up in the sometimes rocky waters of life.

Next come my sons, Izaak and Max Rubin. Both played a role in the creation of this book—Izaak as a reader, and Max as illustrator. More importantly, though, my sons are my teachers, my students, and my friends. Our journey together has been a precious one for which I am eternally grateful.

Next come my teachers—the people and events that sparked my own process of waking up. The most influential among them were Gary Sherman and Ellen Miller, whose teachings I describe at length in this book. Gary and Ellen are the best kind of spiritual guides—not gurus, but fellow travelers who share what they have learned and support those who decide to walk with them for a while. Gary's striking humility and wisdom and Ellen's shrewd insight and deep compassion are inspirational to all of their students.

Of course, other people, places, and things have also guided me. Most notable among influential books were the transformational series written by Sanaya Roman, Ouspensky's book on the teachings of Gurdjieff, Barbara Brennan's teachings about the energy body, and a book called *The Fourth Dimension* by Rudy Rucker, which I discovered in a remote corner of an esoteric bookstore in the early 1980s. I also cannot omit the inspiration of science fiction, like the TV shows

Star Trek and *Battlestar Galactica*. In fact, it was the amazing soundtrack of the latter, written by Bear McCreary, that was playing in the background much of the time I was writing this book.

My early spiritual awakening as a child was triggered by the mysterious aura of the old Temple Emanu-el in Buffalo, New York, and the beauty of Muskoka, Ontario. Various psychotherapists over the years then expanded my perception and prodded me to examine and dissect my own stories. Finally, many kinds of alternative therapies enabled me to wrestle with and sometimes overcome my own ego-based fictions of the mind. The most significant was Homeopathy, whose underlying philosophy is a critical aspect of my understanding of the world. I am eternally grateful for its profound healing power, which has repeatedly helped me and the rest of my family.

I am also grateful to those who were involved in the production of this book. Readers who provided invaluable feedback include: Denny Brown, Sally Clark, Innesa Lagen, Ellen Miller, Bernard Mont-Reynaud, Dean Radin, Mark Rosen, Izaak Rubin, Steve Rubin, Rupert Sheldrake, Gary Sherman, Oonagh Taeger, Russell Targ, Michael Temkin, Bob and Ramsay Waterman, and Chris Wellens. I also want to express my gratitude for the help of my talented book designer, Melanie Haage (who also designed my first book, *Impossible Cure*), copy-editing by Phyllis Filiberti Butler, and the fabulous work of my illustrator (and son) Max Rubin.

Acknowledgement is also due to all of my friends and family who have supported me from near and far. They include (but are not limited to): Jennifer Dungan, Sally Ahnger, Chris Wellens, John Melnychuk, Sally Clark, Richard Pitt, Bertha Philyaw, Deborah Olenev, Liz Martin Landau, Marsha Berger, and my fellow students who study with Ellen Miller and Gary Sherman.

Finally, I want to especially remember my mother, Jeanette Lansky, who passed away in 2010 at age 94. The years in which I wrote this book were also the ones in which she faced her decline and death—a process that deeply influenced me and my writing. Her support and love of me was and still is a comfort. She is deeply missed.

PART I

A FORK IN THE ROAD

"Know Thyself"

—SOCRATES

"If you come to a fork in the road, take it."

—YOGI BERRA

CHAPTER 1

⤳

INNER SPACE:
THE ULTIMATE FRONTIER

SOMETIMES A VOYAGE OF DISCOVERY BEGINS IN THE MOST UNEXPECTED of places. For me, it all began with an episode of Star Trek.

In January of 1993, my husband Steve and I were watching the first installment of the popular science-fiction television series, *Star Trek: Deep Space Nine*. As a computer scientist working at NASA, I'll admit that I was a natural-born Trekkie. This particular episode told the story of humans and aliens living on a far-flung space station near a planet called Bajor. Much to their surprise, the station crew accidentally discovers a wormhole—a distortion in the spatial fabric of the universe. By passing through it, they find that they can travel to the furthest reaches of the galaxy in seconds.

Soon, the station commander, Benjamin Sisko, is confronted with an alien species living within the wormhole's strange hyper-dimensional expanse. Rather than being confined to the three-dimensional universe we humans are familiar with, the wormhole aliens have access to a *fourth dimension*—literally an extra dimension in space. As a result, they can jump between two locations in our world, no matter how distant, as if they were stepping into the next room. They can also transcend the human experience of time. Rather than perceiving it like we do, as a step-by-step progression that leads only from the past to the future, the aliens are able to visit the distant past and every one of our possible

3

futures in the blink of an eye. This allows them to see and understand the entire scope of human existence as an instantaneous whole.

Using these unique abilities, the wormhole aliens enable Sisko to revisit his past and come to terms with his wife's death. They also show him his potential future role in the fate of nearby Bajor. In fact, Bajoran spiritual seekers have developed portal-like devices that allow them to communicate with the aliens too. Like Sisko, they have found that catching a glimpse of the entire scope of their lives can serve as a path to enlightenment—one that enables greater clarity, insight, and wisdom.

Somehow, this story grabbed me in a profound way. Rather than tossing it aside as pure science fiction, I lay awake into the wee hours that night wondering if it also contained a kernel of scientific fact. What *are* space and time? Could a fourth spatial dimension actually exist? And if we could access it, what would we find there?

This book will take you on a voyage of discovery—to the realms of *inner* space. It is a journey that weaves the strands of many pieces of knowledge together—from scientific results about paranormal phenomena to higher-dimensional models of reality, from the mysticism of enlightened masters to powerful forms of alternative medicine. By assembling this information together as a coherent whole, I hope to convince you that abilities typically relegated to science fiction or fantasy might actually be possible. In fact, not only may we be able to sense our possible futures, but we might also be able to *mold* them—through powers of conscious creation, or what I call *active consciousness*. Another important goal of this book is to kick-start your own process of personal transformation so that you can develop these abilities for yourself.

From Robot Consciousness to Cosmic Consciousness

Of course, you may be wondering how a former NASA computer expert could entertain ideas like these! It's true that my views about human consciousness are unusual for a person with my background.

As a researcher in computer science and artificial intelligence for over twenty years, I was known for my work on a variety of computer systems that tried to mimic human reasoning abilities.[1,2] For instance, I built artificial agents that "perceived" as well as "reasoned" about their environment and took actions as a result. Despite or perhaps *because* of my expertise in this area, I am alarmed when scientists and philosophers equate consciousness with simple forms of awareness, or even with more complex forms of reasoning. The natural result of this equation is to find computers capable of consciousness, or perhaps even worse, to view humans as complex machines![3]

To me, computers are simply complex tools, no more conscious than cars or telephones. And artificial intelligence is just that—artificial. In fact, rather than subscribing to the notion of machine-as-human or human-as-machine, my years as a computer scientist were the period in my life when I became increasingly drawn to the metaphysical. I grew to believe that much more exists than meets our limited awareness, and that the universe is not the mundane three-dimensional mechanistic place that it appears to be. Today, I understand that it is filled with energy fields and forces that scientists have yet to measure. And it is through an examination of our interaction with these energies that I believe humanity will ultimately develop a more accurate understanding of what consciousness is and of our true inner power and potential.

A DOORWAY TO ENLIGHTENMENT

Where are these energies and forces and how can we access them? The answer is that they lie *within* you. Just as the Bajorans on Star Trek used portals to contact the wormhole aliens, I believe that each one of us possesses our own personal portal to enlightenment—a doorway that leads to higher dimensions of space and time.

When I first began reading about this subject back in 1993, I was surprised to discover that many physicists do consider four or even more spatial dimensions to be a scientific possibility. Indeed, because the existence of more than three spatial dimensions is necessary for recent scientific theories (such as *string theory*) to be correct, an acceptance of their existence has become fairly common among physicists over the past decade.[4, 5] I also discovered that the mathematics of higher-dimensional space has been studied and envisioned for nearly 200 years, and that it does yield the kinds of phenomena described on Star Trek—in particular, the ability to reach across time and space in an instant.[6, 7]

Imagine the possibilities! Given access to four dimensions or even higher-dimensional realms, we could sense our possible futures and weigh the alternatives that lie before us. Rather than feeling like puppets buffeted about in a chaotic world, a higher-dimensional form of awareness would allow each one of us to shape our own destiny and become an active *creator*—a master of our own fate. Could such an ability be achieved? Or is it pure fantasy?

In the *Harry Potter* fantasy book series by J.K. Rowling, a potion named "Felix Felicis" enables a power quite like this.[8] After taking it, a person is filled with joy and intuitively knows, at each moment, exactly what to do in order to reach his or her goals. For example, after Harry drinks the Felix Felicis potion, he manages to rescue his friends through a series of very improbable choices, and he does so in a state of sheer happiness, relaxation, and confidence. In the world of Harry Potter, Felix Felicis is simply considered to be a "good luck" potion. But much more profound than bestowing luck, what the potion actually does is enable someone to know exactly what to say or do in order to reach his or her desired goal. It's like a magic compass that illuminates the best path into the future—the path that allows one's desires to unfold before them.

After more reading and exploration, I discovered that abilities like these are also an intrinsic part of the belief systems of many cultures. For instance, author Michael Talbot's intriguing book, *The Holographic Universe*, describes how the Hawaiian shamans or *kahunas* believe that thoughts directly affect how the future unfolds. Because most of our thoughts about the future tend to be a jumble of plans, fears, and hopes, our lives seem equally haphazard or random. However, the kahunas believe that by gaining mastery over our thoughts, and in particular by working in cooperation with a more knowing, interior part of ourselves, we can gain control over the world and the future we create.[9]

Is there truth to these shamanic beliefs? And can they be explained scientifically—perhaps in terms of a higher-dimensional form of awareness? Can an average person—not just a trained shaman—make use of such powers in his or her day-to-day life?

I believe that the answer is: Yes. Each one of us possesses our own portal to higher-dimensional realms and capabilities. The process of developing and accessing it requires time, dedication, and sincerity, but attaining at least some form of access is definitely within reach. It is my hope that this book will serve as a guide that helps you get there.

THIS BOOK IS AN EXPERIENCE

Try to think of this book as an experience—not just one of reading, but also one of personal development and experimentation. While some parts of this book will simply provide you with information, others will ask you to try out ideas and activities for yourself. If you wish to gain the maximum benefits and effects, please engage with and practice the various suggestions and exercises as you encounter them.

I also designed this book to stimulate the different parts of your mind. Just as there are many kinds of people, each with different orientations of thought and interest, there are also many different facets of each one of us. There is the "everyday" part of us concerned with material affairs, and there is the mystical part of us that suspects there may be more going on. There is the skeptical scientist within each one of us that adopts and defends the conventionally accepted view of things, and there is the part of us that is more open and wondering. For this reason, you will find that different sections of this book address and stimulate these different parts of you. Some will appeal more to some readers than others. But my suggestion is to try and remain open to all of it, no matter who you are or where you're coming from. The net effect will be an experience that will permeate and change you.

The path of your voyage will be much like a spiral that begins in the outer world and winds inward toward the interior realms of the self. For the rest of Part I, I'll begin by describing my own journey of discovery and paint a road map of where you will be headed. Then, in Part II, you'll visit the outer world of science. My goal there is to coax you away from the typical intuitions that most of us have about how the world works—the materialistic or traditional view, where the world is seen as a clockwork mechanism devoid of meaning and mystery. To do this, I'll tell you about a range of amazing scientific evidence that indicates there may be much more going on beneath the surface of accepted reality than you might think. Not only may there be fields of energy that we are not yet aware of, but they might carry information that has meaning and purpose.

Next, in Part III, I'll describe a model of what this expanded view of reality might be all about. It incorporates ideas about higher dimensions in space and also provides a way for you to understand how active consciousness might work. My hope is that it will serve as a conceptual construct or mental model for you as you continue along your path. I believe that it also jibes with the unusual phenomena described in Part II.

Then, in Part IV, you'll move inward toward the interior realms of human experience. I'll present several esoteric systems of knowledge that describe how human consciousness and reality itself may be operating at a very deep level. These ideas were developed by mystics of the past and adopted by many ancient cultures—and are still important to many people today. You'll also learn how the scientific information described in Part II and the model described in Part III mesh with these wisdom teachings.

The rest of the book then focuses on your own process of development and evolution. Part V begins by presenting a variety of obstacles that most people confront when they embark upon the consciousness quest, and provides an overview of techniques that have been used to overcome them. Part VI then supplies many exercises and experiments for you to try out for yourself.

Of course, in order to develop active consciousness for yourself, you must *do*—not just read about it. This includes learning how to meditate and engaging in some serious introspection. For this reason, even from the very beginning of your voyage, I have sprinkled "rest stops" or exercises along the way. These are places where you can stop, play, and experiment with a variety of new ideas and techniques. They include Exercises I—V, provided at the ends of Parts I—V, as well as all of Part VI. All of this material is an amalgam of what I have learned from my own teachers and from researchers who have studied the quest for the inner self. As you proceed down the spiral path, please take time to relax and open up to these experiences. You might be surprised by what you discover! But even if you skip over them initially, please do return to Exercises I—V before you embark upon the deep inner work described in Part VI.

WE ARE ALL CONNECTED

Becoming the master of one's life and achieving one's desires is something that we all yearn for. But my true motivation in writing this book is much deeper than that. While I do wish for you to learn how to create a life with more abundance, love, and happiness, the real reason I am taking you on this voyage is to help our world survive.

Never in recorded history has there been a more urgent time—a time in which large numbers of us need to wake up and change our way of being in the world. While humanity has faced periods of crisis before, the world's population has never been so numerous and its future so uncertain. Each day our collective sense of urgency is reinforced by reports about climate change, shortage of resources, international health and financial crises, and growing cultural and political unrest. Indeed, it may be possible that all of these political, cultural, and planetary changes are linked at a deep energetic level.

Whatever our personal views on these matters may be, there's no denying that real change is coming our way. *I believe that the best strategy for meeting these challenges is for each one of us to move forward into a new way of being.* This is no time to scurry back fearfully to older ways— ways that may be comforting, but are likely no longer appropriate or sufficient. In fact, *the challenges ahead may actually enable us to reach a much better world. We just need to make it happen.*

A collective evolution into a deeper form of consciousness may be the critical ingredient that enables us to achieve this aim. As I discuss in Part II, scientific evidence indicates that collective forms of directed meditation can achieve results that exceed the sum of individual efforts. So if large numbers of us try to achieve active consciousness, we might not only be able to improve our own individual lives, but also impact the entire planet. My hope is that this book will inspire you to join this effort—a collective evolution of humanity that will transform our entire world into one of peace, abundance, and joy.

CHAPTER 2

A GLIMPSE AT FOUR DIMENSIONS

AFTER PONDERING THAT STAR TREK EPISODE BACK IN 1993, it occurred to me that the existence of higher-dimensional realities might be able to explain and enable some quite unusual phenomena. For example, paranormal abilities like *remote viewing* (the ability to "see" things that are spatially very distant) and *precognition* (the ability to "know" things that will occur in the future) would be simple if a fourth spatial dimension were actually accessible to us. Here's a quick tutorial that explains why. While it may seem a bit technical at first, please bear with me for the next few pages and gather what you can. While understanding the concept of higher dimensions is not necessary for you to benefit from this book, it *will* become clearer and easier for you to grasp, especially in Part III.

Let's start by trying to visualize a four-dimensional space. It's actually a bit tricky since we are three-dimensional creatures and our perception is tuned to a three-dimensional world—a world in which objects possess only length, width, and height. An easy way to approach this task, however, is to drop down a level and think about the difference between two and three dimensions. Then, by analogy, the difference between three and four dimensions can be better understood. This was the strategy used by author Edwin Abbott in his popular novel of the late 1800s, *Flatland*.[1] It tells the story of a Square living in a flat two-dimensional world who is "lifted up" and given the opportunity to see his world from a three-dimensional perspective.

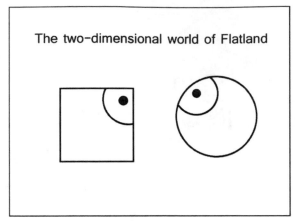

FIGURE I.1

As Abbott describes, a two-dimensional world would be much like an impossibly thin sheet of paper. That's because two-dimensional things possess only length and width. A two dimensional creature would be flat too—like the Circle and Square depicted in Figure I.1. In fact, if they had eyes, the Circle and Square would only be able to see the edges of their fellow Flatland creatures.

We humans, of course, live in a three-dimensional world, so we can look down upon Flatland and see the insides of its inhabitants. If we wanted to, we could even pick the Circle up out of Flatland and drop it down elsewhere. While hovering above its flat world, the Circle would be able to view distant locations that would normally be too remote for it to see, just as we can see vast distances while flying in an airplane. The Circle would be able to see *inside* the Square too. When we placed it back down, the Square would be mind-boggled! From the Square's perspective, the Circle would have suddenly disappeared and reappeared elsewhere, without ever having moved in a normal step-by-step fashion.

Now let's apply these same ideas, by analogy, to three and four dimensions. A four-dimensional creature would have all the same capabilities that we have relative to the Circle and Square. For example, if Mr. 4-D "lifted" one of us up into four-dimensional space—outside of our conventional three-dimensional space and time—we would be able to see distant objects or magically jump to distant locations. And remember how the Circle could see inside the Square as he hovered above, in three-dimensional space? If we could develop access to a four-dimensional form of vision, we would gain a similar x-ray-like ability to see inside three-dimensional objects. Could this be how medical intuitives "see" inside the bodies of their clients and diagnose tumors and other diseases? Are such healers accessing a four-dimensional aspect of themselves?

Now let's consider *time*. Normally, most of us think of time as the fourth dimension. But that is only a small aspect of what a fourth spatial dimension might be all about. First, consider this possibility: our conception of the passage of time might simply be our way of perceiving *change*—the transition of one three-dimensional world into another. Think about it. Would you notice the passing of time if absolutely *nothing* changed? Not even your thoughts or your body functions? Next, consider the fact that a four-dimensional universe could contain *all* three-dimensional worlds—every aspect of our past as well as everything that could occur in the future. As a result, our three-dimensional perception of the passage of time might actually be a *four-dimensional spatial object*. To understand why, let's return to the flat world of the Circle and Square.

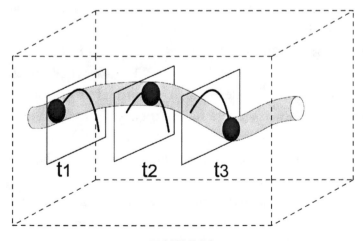

FIGURE I.2

Figure I.2 shows the Circle at three moments in time that occur from its two-dimensional perspective: *t1, t2,* and *t3*. Each slice of time is depicted as a flat sheet that indicates where the Circle is located as it makes its way along a curved path. If you stacked all of these snapshots of the Circle's world alongside one another, its movement through time would appear to us like a tube carved through three-dimensional space. In fact, we would be able to see the Circle's entire life in an instant. From our three-dimensional perspective, the Circle's two-dimensional passage through time would simply be a three-dimensional spatial object—a long meandering tube.

There's also a lot more that we could see. For example, what if the Circle decided to branch off onto a new path at some point? From our perspective, this would create a tube that veers off in another direction. In other words, from our position in three-dimensional space, we could see every path that the Circle *might* choose—*all* of its possible choices and paths. Taken together, these would appear to us like a shape composed of many branching tubes. And if the Circle could see and even manipulate this shape while hovering above Flatland in three-dimensional space, it would be able to make informed choices that enable it to better reach its goals.

Now let's bounce up again to three and four dimensions. What if *we* could gain access to a four-dimensional form of awareness that could illuminate our possible futures and guide us more easily to our goals? Perhaps this ability would feel like a special form of intuition. Is that what psychic abilities are all about? The so-called "sixth sense"? And what if hands-on healers—perhaps through some sort of higher-dimensional influence—could nudge their patients' bodies to choose unlikely but possible paths of healing? If so, miraculous cures would become quite plausible. After all, the body's tissues are always regenerating; the body we have today is not the body we had two weeks ago. Perhaps a four-dimensional form of awareness and intent could enable a sick body to follow a path into the future that manifests health instead of disease.

As I began to explore these ideas further, I was surprised to find many studies, conducted by respected scientists, that verify the existence of these kinds of abilities.[2, 3, 4, 5] I also began to read more about quantum physics and discovered that physicists do utilize higher spatial dimensions—in fact, up to ten dimensions—in their mathematical calculations.[6] Are these higher dimensions merely mathematical tools, or do they actually exist all around us, just outside our reach? In her recent book, *Warped Passages*, physicist Lisa Randall explains why a growing number of her colleagues are coming to believe that this may indeed be the case.[7]

To me, the writings of physicist-philosopher David Bohm, about a hidden "implicate" or enfolded order, unfolding into our actual "explicate" universe, also seemed to line up with these ideas.[8] Might Bohm's implicate order really be a higher-dimensional space of possibilities, unfolding into our three-dimensional universe? Is our world—the three-dimensional universe that we are all experiencing—just one of its many possible unfoldings? And could we somehow have an influence upon this unfolding process? As I pondered these ideas, the course of my life was about to change in ways that would convince me that this might indeed be the case.

CHAPTER 3

୬

A MIRACULOUS CURE

FAST FORWARD TWO YEARS. OUR FAMILY WAS FACING A LOOM-ING medical crisis. Our sons Izaak and Max were six and three at the time, and Max was having cognitive and behavioral problems that we eventually realized were symptoms of autism. This was back at the beginning of the autism epidemic, when not much was known about the condition or what to do about it. In 1994, we were advised to seek medical help, and after he was tested, Max qualified for state benefits and began attending bi-weekly speech and language therapy sessions. Of course, I began searching desperately for solutions. For instance, I began to experiment with food elimination strategies, an approach now viewed as essential within the autism community. Al-though eliminating milk from Max's diet did lead to some significant improvements—he finally gained some limited speech—his progress was slow and his behavior was becoming more classically autistic.

Thankfully, in January 1995, we were fortunate to benefit from a bit of divine intervention. While reading *Mothering*, an alternative parenting magazine, I learned about the remarkable success of *home-opathy*—an alternative medical system developed in the 1800s—in treating and even curing problems such as hyperactivity and other children's behavioral problems.[1] I was eager to give it a try. We found a homeopath in Palo Alto and Max's road to recovery soon began. Within less than a week after beginning the recommended treatment, we began to notice subtle changes in his speech and social cognition.

When Max next saw his therapist, she noticed the changes too. Even though we had not told her about our introduction of homeopathy, within just a few minutes she asked, "What did you do?"

The improvements in Max's condition were slow but steady, and after a few months were quite apparent. In fact, his pattern of improvement directly corresponded with changes in the dose of his homeopathic remedy. After nine months of homeopathic treatment, Max's speech and language therapist felt that her sessions with him were no longer necessary. In fact, she told us that she had never seen an autistic child recover like Max had. By the time he was five, two years after beginning homeopathic treatment, Max was testing above age level. And by the time he was nine or ten, Max no longer showed any signs of his former autism and remains free of all symptoms to this day.[2] Not surprisingly, this remarkable sequence of events completely changed my life and the life of our entire family. My discovery of homeopathy was a significant fork in the road—a juncture in my life that changed everything.

Shortly after we began our homeopathic journey, I bought some books about this venerable and mysterious form of healing and began to study them. I quickly became captivated. What I discovered was a hidden gem from the past that could be the answer to many of our healthcare woes today. Developed in the early 1800s by a German physician named Samuel Hahnemann, homeopathy is based on a seemingly incongruous therapeutic principle—that a disease can be cured by a substance that causes the disease's symptoms in healthy people. In fact, homeopathy became a leading medicine of the nineteenth century because of its successes in treating virulent epidemics like cholera, typhoid fever, scarlet fever, influenza, and even smallpox.[3] And here's the most mysterious part: Homeopathic remedies are made from such extreme dilutions of plant, animal, and mineral matter that they do not contain even a single molecule of the original substances from which they are derived. Instead, homeopaths believe that they carry an *energetic signature* of these substances—a claim that only today is beginning to be scientifically verified.[4, 5, 6]

By the end of 1995, as Max's problems slowly faded away, I decided to enroll in a formal program of study in homeopathy. And as it gradually became my family's primary form of medical treatment, our experiences became increasingly extraordinary. I saw fevers and flus quickly nipped in the bud, warts dry up and drop off, and my own summer allergies completely disappear after years of growing steadily worse. I began to experiment with other alternative therapies too. For instance, I learned a hands-on healing method called Reiki and found that it helped to overcome minor ailments as well as boost the curative effects of homeopathy.

Naturally, my ruminations about higher dimensions were put on the backburner during our period of struggle with Max's autism. But by the spring of 1996, when he was clearly "out of the woods," I found that my study of homeopathy and other forms of energy healing served as a catalyst that reawakened my interest in consciousness and the paranormal. Indeed, I began to suspect that the mysterious healing powers of these alternative therapies were somehow connected to a deeper and unseen reality.

Being a researcher, I decided to write a paper that described my ideas about higher dimensions, consciousness, and alternative energy medicines like homeopathy. I entitled it: *Consciousness as an Active Force*. In mid-1996, I created my first web site and put this paper on it—my first experiment in Internet publishing. Little did I suspect that this act would become another significant fork in the road of my life. Over the years, the paper became widely linked on the Internet, scores of people continued to write to me about it, and it was also eventually published.[7] It also became the seed from which this book grew.

CHAPTER 4

FERTILE SOIL

T HE TRUTH IS, I WOULD BE LYING IF I SAID I WAS A STRICT materialist when I first saw that episode of Star Trek back in 1993. I have always had a spiritual or mystical bent. Even as a child, I sensed that there was more to life than what was apparent to our five senses, and I yearned to find out what that deeper reality was all about.

Nevertheless, all of that lay dormant in me as I made my way through high school and university studying mathematics. In fact, my spiritual inclinations were barely discernable during my years at Stanford University as I worked hard to earn my doctorate in computer science. I was the only woman in my entering class, and it wasn't easy to be female in an otherwise all-male field. My focus had to be clear and intense—no time for ruminations about unseen realities! But by 1984, I had graduated, begun my work as a researcher, and had married. I could now relax enough to let my spiritual side reemerge once again.

My first job after completing my doctorate was at SRI International, the former Stanford Research Institute. In 1984, the coffee hours were abuzz with jokes about a controversial project going on at the institute—a project studying psychic phenomena. This taboo research was being led by Russell Targ, the father of an acquaintance of mine from Stanford, Elisabeth Targ. Elisabeth was a brilliant medical student who sometimes worked with her physicist father on his psychic research. While I didn't know anything about their explorations, I definitely didn't think it was deserving of my colleagues' snide derision. In fact, I suspected there was something to ESP and at times I thought I might be a bit psychic myself. Like most people, I had experienced things that made me wonder. For example, at the precise moment of my father's death from a heart attack in 1971, I was sitting at home eating breakfast. Inexplicably, I was gripped by a wave of intense nausea. Only later did I discover what had actually happened.

During the SRI coffee hours, while others joked, a friend and I would perform our own little psychic experiments; we tried to mentally "send" and "receive" numbers randomly chosen between 1 and 10. At home, my husband Steve and I experimented too. In fact, we found that if we put ourselves into a state of loving connection, our guessing abilities improved. Interestingly, recent research has proven that this method of enhancing psychic abilities does work. In particular, studies conducted by researchers of the paranormal have shown that pairs of people who are emotionally linked are better senders and receivers of mental thoughts and imagery.[1, 2]

Soon I began to explore other aspects of the paranormal as well. During my lunch breaks, I would wander the neighborhood surrounding SRI, sometimes visiting a local bookshop that specialized in metaphysical and other "New Age" subjects. I found myself drawn to books by Barbara Brennan, a medical intuitive who described her hands-on healing work and ability to see *auras*—the energy fields that she claims surround living things. I was especially fascinated by Brennan's drawings of these auras and by how she correlated a person's aura structure with their personality.[3]

In 1989, I decided to leave SRI and took a senior research position at nearby NASA Ames Research Center. I loved this new job and the people who worked there. It had a more light-hearted and optimistic atmosphere than SRI, where my work was usually focused on military contracts. At NASA, it was all about "Space—The Final Frontier," and most of my colleagues were Trekkies too! But at times, it was hard to balance children, marriage, and a challenging career. At one point I began to see a counselor who directed me to a series of books by Sanaya Roman.[4,5,6,7] These "channeled teachings"—information supposedly transmitted from a spirit-being to a human receiver—were transformational for me. Although I didn't buy into the notion of channeling at the time, the information in these books was pivotal to my spiritual development. Indeed, when I read them now, I realize that a great deal of their content formed the foundation for this book.

Years later, in February 1995—shortly after my discovery of homeopathy—I took my spiritual quest a bit further. Spurred on by my fascination with Barbara Brennan's work, I decided to attend a weekend workshop with her in San Francisco that promised to awaken our psychic and intuitive healing abilities. I'll never forget one exercise we tried that weekend; we were encouraged to use our energy bodies to "touch" something at a distance. Several hundred of us were sitting in an immense ballroom with the lighting dimmed; the ceiling was at least forty feet above us. With my eyes closed, I stretched my arm upward and distinctly "felt" a cold pipe with my "energy hand." When I opened my eyes, I was flabbergasted to see that my hand did indeed point directly at one of the only pipes barely visible in the ceiling above me.

The workshop also included sessions during which we practiced hands-on healing upon one another, and forums in which Brennan channeled teachings from spirit guides. By the end of the weekend, I must admit that I was beginning to feel a bit put-off by all the guru-worship going on. But I was also intrigued by what I had learned and experienced. Over the course of the workshop I had reached such an expanded state of awareness that I felt almost drugged. As I drove home from San Francisco, I decided that all of this was either complete bunk or some extremely powerful stuff. Either way, I had two small children at home, including one struggling with autism. So now wasn't quite the right time for me to explore this realm much further. That would have to wait.

When I look back on those years, I realize that I had begun to explore alternative forms of healing long before I heard the word "homeopathy." For instance, during the summer of 1993, nearly a year before Max's problems really became obvious, I took an eight-week course on *Chi Gong* at a local Palo Alto community center. Chi Gong is a type of Chinese meditative exercise that fosters health by strengthening and cleansing *chi* (or *qi*)—the body energy that is believed to form the underlying framework for the physical body. During the eight weeks of the class, I practiced daily and really began to feel effects. I felt stronger and actually began to sense the flow of chi in my body—a kind of wave-like tingling sensation. At one point, the teacher challenged us to see auras around our hands. I seemed to be the only one in the class who could vaguely detect something.

Each week, the Chi Gong teacher also used the class as an opportunity to drum up some business. After a few weeks of hearing about how we should come in to his clinic to have our "channels cleared," I decided to give it a try. I arrived one afternoon and was asked to lie on a table, fully clothed, in a room with several other people undergoing the same treatment. About ten minutes later, as one of the assistants gently rubbed my back, I felt a sudden surge of energy well up inside me—an orgasmic rush that went from the base of my spine up to the top of my head and out my extremities. It was truly mind-blowing. I left the clinic rattled by what had happened, and soon afterwards, fell sick with a flu-like illness. I never returned because I feared that some kind of harm had been done to me.

Now I realize that I had likely undergone a *Kundalini experience*—an awakening of chi at the base of my spine. Such experiences are much sought after by spiritual seekers and are supposedly able to create deep shifts in consciousness. And perhaps this did indeed occur. Soon thereafter, my life underwent some very significant changes—my explorations into higher dimensions and the paranormal, my discovery of homeopathy, and ultimately, my writing of papers and books about these subjects. That experience at the Chi Gong teacher's clinic may have been another significant fork in the road.

CHAPTER 5

>

WHAT IS
CONSCIOUSNESS?

JUST AFTER I WROTE THE INITIAL DRAFT OF MY PAPER ABOUT
higher-dimensions and active consciousness in early 1996, I decided to test the waters and attend a conference on the subject. I had
no idea what to expect, but I mailed in my registration and flew to
Tucson, Arizona in April to attend "Tucson II—Toward a Science of
Consciousness."

Very soon after arriving, I could see that there was a split among
the attendees. Most of the speakers were academics convinced that
consciousness is a mere byproduct of the brain and its complex syn-
aptic activity. On the flip side were people presenting posters in the
large exhibit hall. These were the people with "way out" ideas like
mine—ideas about higher dimensions and manifesting change in
the outer world by utilizing the mysterious and intangible power of
consciousness.

At one of the opening sessions, a raging debate took place between
these two factions. The "consciousness equals brain" position was argued by people like philosophers Daniel Dennett and Patricia and Paul
Churchland. They claimed that, not only is there no duality between
mind and body, but there really is no "mind" at all—there is *only* body.
To them, we are all simply robots fulfilling our biological programming. They also claimed that there is no life after death, there is no
soul or free will, and there is no consciousness other than the awareness

23

we gain with our bodily senses and the processing of our brain tissues. Any feeling that there is more, they said, is merely a delusion. In *Conversations on Consciousness*—an excellent set of interviews of top academic consciousness researchers, many of whom were speakers at Tucson II—hard-liner Dennett states, "I think the idea of a soul is a curious fossil trace of the desire to treat ourselves as absolute." [1]

Another topic that came up repeatedly at Tucson II was the notion of the "hard problem" versus the "easy problem." The so-called "easy problem" involves figuring out how the activity in our brains results in the sensations and thoughts that we all experience. The "hard problem," in contrast, is concerned with finding an explanation for *subjective experience*—for example, the experience of beauty. Since each person has a different internal response to such things, can subjective experience also be explained strictly in terms of brain activity?

Materialists like Dennett do not believe that subjective experiences are any different from objective ones; it's all the result of brain activity. David Chalmers, the philosopher who coined the terms "hard problem" and "easy problem," has a different view. While there may be correlations between brain activity and conscious experience, Chalmers claims that, "No explanation solely in terms of brain processes will be such that we can deduce the existence of consciousness from it." [2] Although he does believe that consciousness ends at death, Chalmers sees it as a fundamental property of the universe, just like space, time, mass, and charge. As a result, it cannot be reduced simply to brain firings. And the fact is, there *have* been near-death cases in which people have accurately remembered experiences that occurred while they were "brain dead." [3] If these people were "conscious" when their brains were not functioning at all, perhaps Chalmers is right.

Another lively topic of debate at the conference was the hypothetical question of "zombies," originally posed as a thought experiment by philosopher Todd Moody. [4] Moody asked, can there be human zombies who behave just like we do, but have no deeper consciousness? During the debates, Dennett asserted that this question was irrelevant because there is no difference between us and zombies. We *are* zombies, he said, because there is no such thing as deeper consciousness. Of course, this led to many jokes at the conference. People poked fun at Dennett by saying—"Well, you may be a zombie, but *I'm* conscious!"

One person who locked horns with Dennett during a particularly memorable evening session was computer scientist Jaron Lanier. I had met Lanier years before at Stanford. Known for coining the term "virtual reality," Lanier has worked for years creating simulated computer environments in which people are hooked up to video, audio, and other high-tech gadgetry in order to create realistic computerized experiences. Given his fascination with the human-computer connection, I was surprised to see Lanier boldly stand up and criticize Dennett's views. Lanier warned everyone that there was too much idolization of computers and artificial intelligence. While computers can be programmed to do many amazing things, he argued, they do not possess consciousness. His own personal experiences had taught him that there was definitely a dividing line between men and machines.

"Aha!" I thought. Here is another computer scientist who, like me, has come to believe that humans are decidedly more than just machines.

Actually, I believe that the philosophers and scientists who view consciousness as a mere side effect of a computer-like brain are getting their analogies all wrong. Computer scientists know that there's more to computing than hardware. And the brain itself is just that—a piece of biological hardware. Even a kindergartner today knows that a computer isn't anything without *software*—the programs that run on it. Of course, materialists will argue that the analog to software is the "information" stored within the brain. When synapses fire, they argue, it's analogous to software "executing." But the real question is: *who writes the software?*

In the case of a computer, a human programmer must ultimately reside outside the machine. That's why my former field of research was called *artificial* intelligence. A computer's intelligence is artificial. Even though programs can be designed that "learn" to create new knowledge and even to create new programs, ultimately a programmer must exist outside the machine. So if the brain is just a computer, the ultimate "programmer of the brain" may need to reside outside of it too.

I believe that this mysterious programmer of the brain is the true locus of human consciousness. In other words, consciousness is the *creator* of our brain activity, not the other way around. Here's another analogy that has often been used to make the same point. Consider the television sitting in your living room. Believing that consciousness is a byproduct of the brain is like believing that the show you watch on TV is a byproduct of your TV's circuitry. On a superficial level this is true; the program you watch on TV can be correlated with the activity of the TV's circuitry. But as we all know, what is shown on TV is actually received from a transmission that originates *outside* the physical device. And ultimately, this transmission is created by a higher intelligence— the people writing, acting, and filming a television show.

As it turns out, the existence of an entity outside the "brain computer" is also implied by a mathematical law called Gödel's Theorem. This law states that certain types of knowledge cannot be derived within a closed computational system. Since we humans possess this kind of knowledge, it can be argued that our brains cannot possibly be closed computational systems either. As mathematician and consciousness researcher Roger Penrose says, "[T]he Gödel argument tells us that we are not simply computational entities; that our understanding is something outside computation."[5] While parts of our human experience may indeed be the result of the execution of "brain software," Gödel's theorem implies that there must be something else going on outside the brain as well.

Personally, I believe that this shadowy programmer of our brain is a kind of energy or force—otherwise known as the soul, the spirit, or the higher, deeper Self. This energy encompasses and interacts with our brain and body and is the force that truly runs the show. And not only might it have a broader and deeper view of reality—perhaps even a higher-dimensional view—but it might also be what gives us our sense of free will.

THE SPECTRUM OF CONSCIOUSNESS

Actually, many of the arguments about consciousness in academic circles stem from a lack of consensus about what the word "consciousness" means. Each researcher seems to have a different definition or assumption about this mysterious concept. I like to think of these various interpretations of consciousness as a spectrum that spans a range of qualities along at least two axes (see Figure I.3).

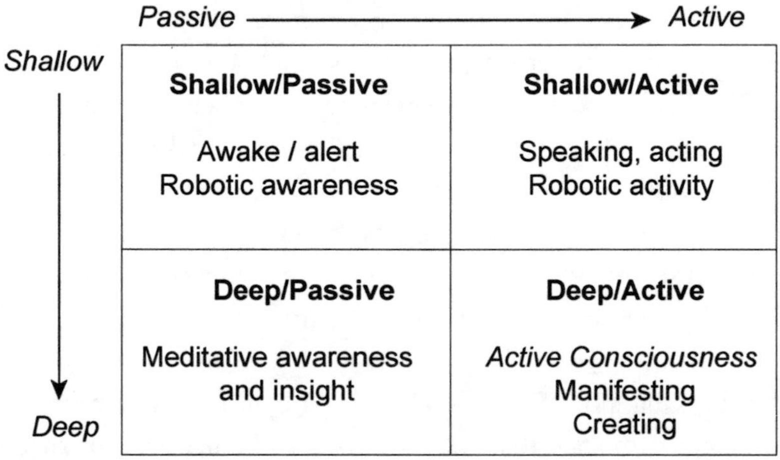

Passive ⟶ Active	
Shallow/Passive Awake / alert Robotic awareness	**Shallow/Active** Speaking, acting Robotic activity
Deep/Passive Meditative awareness and insight	**Deep/Active** *Active Consciousness* Manifesting Creating

(Shallow ⟶ Deep on the vertical axis)

FIGURE I.3

Along one axis lay various depths of consciousness, ranging from *shallow awareness*—what we typically feel when we are alert or awake—to *deep awareness*—a more profound form of being or knowing. The other axis deals with how consciousness manifests itself: from the *passive* reception of information (such as information picked up by our senses) to *active* forms of consciousness, which can cause change in the external world.

Of course, passive observation can cause measurable changes in the world too. That is one of the important and profound lessons of quantum physics—that a simple act of observation can create change in the quantum field. As a result, the assumption that science can ever be truly "objective" is, at least at the quantum level, inherently false. If the world can be affected by the power of our gaze, everything must be intrinsically interconnected.

Nevertheless, there are more explicit forms of action that consciousness can create as well. For example, there are the things each of us consciously "do" to create change—speaking, moving, etc. This mundane or shallow form of conscious action lies in the upper right quadrant of Figure I.3. In the lower right quadrant, however, lays the possibility of deep active consciousness—or what I will simply call *active consciousness*. This fourth quadrant is a primary focus of this book.

As I see it, there are at least two ways active consciousness might operate. The first works much like Harry Potter's Felix Felicis potion: *a deep form of awareness is used to determine what action to take at any point in time in order to reach a desired goal.* In essence, this type of active consciousness functions like a light in the darkness. It illuminates a path before us so that we can see more clearly and make the right choices at the right time. I'll call it *manifestation.* For example, through a series of correct choices and actions, we might manifest the job of our dreams or find the perfect parking spot. While no miracle takes place in order for these things to happen, the fact that we can produce the perfect sequence of actions that yields the desired result is miracle enough.

Another type of active consciousness is similar, but subtly different. I'll call it *creation.* In this case, we use active consciousness to enable something much more improbable to occur. We carve an unusual path out of the sea of infinite possibilities that lie before us and somehow we make the unlikely more likely. For example, we might create a path of healing for our body, even though the probability of this happening is miniscule from a conventional medical standpoint. Or, as I will describe in Part II, we might coax the behavior of an otherwise random mechanical device to act in a way that obeys the dictates of our intention. In other words, when we *manifest*, we produce an unlikely outcome from a series of fairly likely occurrences. But when we *create*, we produce unlikely occurrences too.

Of course, there is a third possible axis that is also relevant to the spectrum of consciousness: the one ranging from *individual* forms of consciousness to ones that are *collective*. And when you think about it, the power of a deep, active, collective form of consciousness could be extremely profound. That is the kind of power that would be unleashed if more and more of us embark upon the quest to evolve and deepen our own individual levels of consciousness. But for now, let's focus on individual forms of deep active consciousness, and see where that might lead.

CHAPTER 6

❧

THE ROAD TO ACTIVE CONSCIOUSNESS

I F WE TAKE CONSCIOUSNESS TO BE MERELY A SHALLOW PHENOMENON —being awake rather than asleep, or being alert rather than knocked out—then, yes, perhaps we humans are merely biological robots. A robot can be programmed to be "aware" of its environment and to create change through action. The sensors of a robot can be programmed to "see," "hear," "touch," store observations as "memories," and even react in ways that mimic emotions and feelings. A robot can also "reason" about its memories and take meaningful actions in response. In fact, artificial intelligence programs exist that could, at least in very limited settings, pass the Turing Test (named after famed mathematician Alan Turing)—that is, fool a human being into thinking that they are dealing with another human being rather than a computer.[1] So, in a sense, robotic zombies *can* be created. And if consciousness is merely shallow awareness, then perhaps we are all robot zombies too.

Even one of the most esoteric of mystics, G.I. Gurdjieff, thought humans operated like machines most of the time.[2] The trick, he said, was to break free of this state of being and become something more— the complete humans we were meant to be. Gurdjieff was a controversial figure of the early twentieth century who traveled and taught throughout Europe, Russia, and the Middle East and drew thousands of followers to his methods for achieving deeper states of awareness. By following what he called "The Work"—a rigorous program of meditation, exercise, and self-reflection—Gurdjieff believed that humans could be freed to exceed their biological programming. If Gurdjieff and Daniel Dennett met today, they would probably agree that most people are nothing more than robot zombies. But Gurdjieff would also claim that each one of us has the potential to access and embody the "programmer" of our zombie brain too.

Of course, there weren't any computers in the early 1900s, so Gurdjieff didn't talk about robots or zombies. Instead, he used the following analogy. Imagine a horse-drawn carriage carrying a passenger, with a hired driver sitting on the outside (see Figure I.4). The carriage, Gurdjieff said, is analogous to our body and brain—the physical mechanism of our existence. The horse is also part of this working system, but represents the emotional aspect our being. The driver is then seen as the analog of the ego or shallow consciousness—all of the chattering thoughts that we live with day to day.

Gurdjieff also used the driver to represent the false identity that most of us use to define who we are—the various stories we tell about ourselves. Such stories include roles we play, like "spouse," "child," or "worker"; emotional or physical problems we identify with such

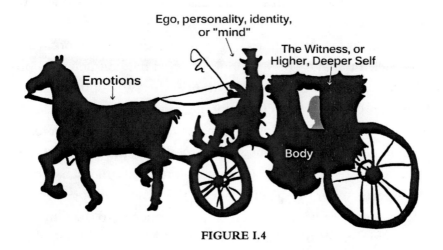

FIGURE I.4

as "alcoholic" or "cancer survivor"; and identifications with certain national, ethnic, or religious heritages. In other words, the carriage driver is the face we present to the world: "I am a male, Christian Englishman, a police officer and father of two children, who suffers from arthritis, alcoholism, and a loveless marriage."

The important thing to realize about this driver, however, is that he (or she) usually believes that he is the only one in charge of the horse and carriage. He also doesn't let go of the reins very easily! What he has completely forgotten is that there is a passenger *inside* the carriage. The goal, Gurdjieff said, is to get in touch with this passenger and pay much less attention to the chattering driver. This interior passenger has been called the Real "I" or the Witness. Mystics like Sri Ramana Maharshi call it the Self, the Heart, or "I Am".[3] It is this passenger sitting inside the carriage of our being that is our true nature, our true Self—the Self that possesses the wisdom and power of active consciousness.

So was Gurdjieff right? Is there somebody or something sitting inside the carriage of our existence? And do we all have the potential to transcend shallow consciousness and open up to the deeper Self within us? Depth consciousness is certainly the aim of spiritual seekers and mystics. As described in Ouspensky's landmark book about Gurdjieff, *In Search of the Miraculous*,[4] there are many paths that can lead to it. One involves undergoing arduous physical trials—the so-called "Way of the Fakir." Another involves the development of deep emotional devotion, which Gurdjieff called the "Way of the Monk." A third method utilizes an intense introspective investigation of the mind—the "Way of the Yogi."

However, Gurdjieff taught that there is yet another way—what he called the "Fourth Way." This involves developing a deep awareness of all three elements of the outer self—the body, the emotions, and the mind. By distinguishing, clarifying, and intensifying each of these distinct aspects of our being, and then by finally integrating them together in a conscious way, Gurdjieff taught that access to the inner Self could be achieved. While the Fourth Way isn't easy to follow, it also doesn't require us to go off and live in a monastery or cave. As a result, it's also much more accessible to seekers like you and me. And that's a good thing, because now may be the first time in human history when it is imperative that more of us attempt to pursue this path.

IT'S TIME TO WAKE UP

Let's face it, our lives are in a frenzy. Most of us find it difficult to live in a mindful, peaceful way anymore. Every summer my family spends a few weeks at a cottage on a lake in Canada. When we return to Silicon Valley, we can hardly believe the pace of life here. Soon, we forget the peace of our summer vacation and resume the desperate struggle to keep up—with the traffic, the information overload, the commitments, the cost of living, and the inflated materialistic expectations.

Even though each of us may feel like it's our own fault that we're drowning in this maelstrom, the truth is, few people were designed to live this kind of existence. Two hundred years ago, when life was more slow-paced, perhaps it was easier to find and rest in the present moment, even if day-to-day life was a struggle. Today, despite the availability of more leisure time for many people, our days are increasingly filled with anxiety, mind chatter, and distractions. It's hard to escape it.

In the early 1900s, Gurdjieff said that most people operated like mechanical slaves of the forces around them. How much more so is this true today! We live like robots marching to the tides that surge around us—the media, the government, advertising, wars, political chaos, family dynamics, the demands of school and work, and the various cultural expectations heaped upon us. If we use only our "brain minds"—our shallow consciousness—to navigate, we quickly find ourselves caught up in unending planning, evaluation, and execution of our daily lives. But if we could somehow access our deeper Selves—the wiser passengers inside our respective carriages—we might be able to achieve and become so much more. We could become happier, more peaceful, and less afraid. And we could devote more of our leisure time to exploring the realms of conscious creation and manifestation.

Attaining this kind of creative mastery requires many things. One is acknowledging and then truly believing that *you,* not someone or something outside you, *determine what your emotions are, what your thoughts are, and what actions you take.* In other words, you really *are* the master of your carriage. You can choose what you are thinking and feeling, not just passively react to what is going on around you. It just takes practice.

Of course, when you first succeed in feeling the presence of the Self, it might only be for a fleeting moment. Over time, though, you can learn to invoke it intentionally. Eventually, as you begin to achieve this state of being more often, you will find yourself riding the waves of chaos much more easily. The benefits are numerous: greater vitality, joy, compassion, harmony, and a reduction in stress, fear, and anxiety.

I know this may sound impossible. After all, we have all been conditioned to live in a different way. Nearly every waking moment, our chattering minds focus on what's going on outside of us or on our own unique "story lines"—for example, how people annoy us or are unfair to us. Since our emotions seem to naturally respond to this mental patter, it isn't surprising that we come to think we have no choice but to become depressed when bad things happen, annoyed when we believe we are slighted, or filled with fear and anxiety when the world seems dangerous and chaotic. We also believe we have no other option than to try and control it all with more planning, more mind chatter, and more activity. In fact, our families and our society train us to live this way.

How do we usually cope? One strategy that many of us use is to suppress or evade our feelings and thoughts with entertainment or drugs. But that only works for a short time. Reactive emotions and thoughts are a natural part of shallow consciousness and cannot be escaped, because they are a part of being human. Using Gurdjieff's analogy, the horse of your carriage (your emotions) is still a horse; nothing is going to change that. So becoming the master of your carriage isn't about replacing fearful or anxious feelings with hopeful or confident ones. Nor is it about conquering or suppressing your emotions—something you cannot and should not do. Instead, it's about accepting who and what you are—a being that includes your carriage, horse, and driver, but also the true master of the carriage: your Self. Once you have done so, you can work on developing the ability to *transcend* troublesome emotional and mental habits. With commitment and practice, a more skillful way of being slowly becomes possible. And the more you work at it, the easier it becomes.

Gurdjieff likened the process of becoming fully and deeply conscious to one of *waking up*. The problem is, most of us don't realize that we're asleep. We move through our lives on autopilot. We really *are* robot zombies most of the time. We think that when we are sleeping we are unconscious and that when we wake up, we become conscious. But from the standpoint of mystics like Gurdjieff, our normal waking state *is* sleep. Becoming deeply conscious is then the *true* awakening— waking up to a reality with less suffering and with a greater power to create the future we desire. As he said, when men are told they are sleeping,

> "[they] take it simply as a form of speech, as an expression, as a metaphor. They completely fail to understand that it must be taken literally... Man's possibilities are very great. You cannot conceive even a shadow of what man is capable of attaining. But nothing can be attained in sleep... [T]his is the reason why he can never make use of all the powers he possesses and why he always lives in only a small part of himself."[5]

In a way, the quest for the deeper Self is about freedom—gaining the ability to become the masters of our own fates. When we are asleep, we are more easily prey to others. In fact, we become predators too because of our lack of awareness. As spiritual teacher Eckhardt Tolle writes, "It is true that only an unconscious person will try to use or manipulate others, but it is equally true that only an unconscious person *can* be used and manipulated."[6] The key to waking up and becoming truly free, then, is to focus on where our intelligence and power truly originates: the inner Self. As Gurdjieff said:

> "Without self-knowledge, without understanding the working and functions of his machine, man cannot be free, he cannot govern himself and he will always remain a slave, and the plaything of the forces acting upon him. This is why in all ancient teachings the first demand at the beginning of the way to liberation was: '*Know thyself.*'"[7]

CHAPTER 7

✢

A PATH EMERGES

WHILE I WAS AT THE TUCSON II CONFERENCE IN 1996, I happened to run into an old acquaintance of mine—Elisabeth Targ, the daughter and colleague of psychic researcher Russell Targ. For the rest of my visit there, I spent time with Elisabeth and her coterie of friends, many of them physicians interested in studying psychic phenomena, the healing power of prayer, and shamanic medicine. It was a fascinating few days, and I managed to get some feedback on my new paper about consciousness as well.

I came home from Tucson excited about the emerging field of consciousness studies. But I was worried that it would veer off in the wrong direction. Like Jaron Lanier, I feared it would be overtaken by academics discussing neurophysiology or computer-based analogies for human consciousness. Unfortunately, this has largely been the case. An examination of the experiences of mystics, shamans, and meditators, and a serious exploration of the wisdom of our world's ancient cultures and religions has been left, for the most part, on the outer edges of academic discourse about consciousness. For instance, although some researchers have worked with the Dalai Lama to investigate what happens to Buddhist monks when they meditate, they have been more interested in recording the monks' brain waves than their insights. That's a shame, because while gaining a deeper understanding of the human brain is a worthy endeavor, I believe there is so much more to be found.

After I completed my paper, "Consciousness as an Active Force," I tried to have it published. As I suspected, it was too "way out" for academic journals and too technical for more informal publications. I settled for publishing it on my web site, and as the Internet grew, interest in my paper grew as well.

Time passed. I continued my homeopathic studies and, in 1998, gave up my work in computer science altogether. My new goal was to write a book about homeopathy's healing power. The result was *Impossible Cure: The Promise of Homeopathy*, published in 2003.[1] Over time, it became a best-selling introductory book on homeopathy and has gotten the word out to the autism community as well. I like to think of it as my own product of manifestation!

However, in 2005, I felt the call to move on to something new. My return to an exploration of consciousness began when I learned about a new form of healing called *EFT*—Emotional Freedom Technique.[2] Developed by engineer and self-help author Gary Craig, the technique involves repeating specific types of affirmations while tapping on a sequence of acupressure points. Using it, people have achieved some astounding results—from losing long-standing phobias to healing intractable medical conditions. While it can be extremely helpful to work with an EFT practitioner, the technique can also be easily learned and used on oneself or others.

For a while I experimented with EFT on my own. Eventually, I decided to seek out a practitioner in the Palo Alto area named Ellen Miller. After a few sessions with her, I learned much more about the technique and how to use it. But something much more profound came out of that experience; I learned about the work Miller does with her psychotherapist/teacher husband Gary Sherman on developing deeper states of awareness. Meeting Miller and Sherman was another significant fork in the road for me.

Soon, I began to take a series of classes on what Sherman calls *perceptual integration*. This unique blend of teachings and exercises, based on Sherman's thirty years of study in meditation and awareness techniques, enables his students to develop and integrate deeper forms of awareness into their daily lives. I believe it also implements Gurdjieff's Fourth Way, because it helps students become more aware of and integrate their physical senses, emotions, and thoughts, as well as develop more subtle energetic forms of perception. The net effect is a gradual development of a more graceful, powerful, and peaceful way of being in the world.

After a couple of years of study with Sherman and Miller, I began to realize that the time had come to write a new book. My goal was to blend my ideas about higher-dimensional active consciousness with Sherman's practical techniques for awakening and utilizing it. This book is the result of that effort.

Now don't get me wrong. I am no guru and I have not reached enlightenment. But I am much better off than I used to be. I have less anxiety, I worry less, and I'm less fearful. I am more in charge of my emotions and my thoughts, and I am less reactive to the world around me. I can turn my mind chatter off fairly easily after just a few minutes of meditation, my connection to my inner Self is clearer, and the guidance I receive is more accurate. So my message to you is: *If I can do this, so can you.*

Many of us exercise our bodies each day to stay in good physical shape. I believe that if we also devoted a small portion of time each day to exercising our consciousness—even as little as fifteen minutes a day—we could begin to move toward our full human potential. The goal of this book is to help you start this process.

CHAPTER 8

STonic

START EVOLVING—NOW

IF YOU HAVE EVER EXPERIMENTED WITH MEDITATION, YOU ALREADY
know that an important goal of any meditative practice is to focus your awareness on the current moment—the *Now*. Normally, we
spend most of our time ruminating about the past or planning and
worrying about the future. But the Now is where your true power
lies. As teacher Richard Moss writes:

> "[T]hat's where we'll find the juice of life and the truth of who
> we are and why we are here... When our awareness is rooted in the
> present, we access our higher emotional potential—empathy, com-
> passion, and forgiveness. We experience greater oneness with a vast
> field of awareness that far transcends our limited personal realities.
> We begin to touch the Source, to drink from a fountain of alive-
> ness and intelligence in which we perceive each moment's innate
> wholeness and to which our natural response is a sense of gratitude,
> wonderment, and implicit trust in life's goodness."[1]

I believe that the Now is also the gateway to active consciousness.
It is from this vantage point that we can develop our ability to bring
the non-physical into the physical world, to coax Bohm's "implicate
order" into the realm of our three-dimensional lives.

Of course, "now" is also important in another sense—because *now*
is the perfect time for you to begin your own process of self-development and join others in the consciousness quest. Why? Because the

very future of humanity may be at stake. Indeed, there is a lot of evidence that growing numbers of people are taking up this call. More and more books are being written about creative intention, manifestation, meditation, and the coming world changes. Movies have begun to touch upon these themes too. People may sense that a change is underway, and their growing interest in meditation and deeper forms of awareness may be a form of preparation. As Moss writes, "At this evolutionary moment, humankind is wavering between fear and love, focusing on survival and yet beginning to touch the infinite potential of being."[2]

Of course, a feeling of impending change can be difficult emotionally. Many, if not most of us, react by escaping into a world of distracting and addictive entertainment or drowning our anxieties in material possessions and food. Another natural reaction is to fearfully cling to older, more traditional ways. The hope is that the slower-paced, more structured forms of the past can be recreated. We also seek security within our various groups or clans, be they religious, familial, or regional. While participating in community *can* be quite positive and helpful, it is important to remember that it is counterproductive if it is accompanied by an increased distrust and hatred of others. The world cannot afford to become more insular and divided as it is also growing more populous and intertwined. If humanity is to survive the coming times, we need to learn to get along better, not worse.

Rather than becoming overwhelmed or growing pessimistic about the increasing speed and complexity of our lives, it might be helpful to remember that humanity has always learned to adapt and survive and we can do so once again. Indeed, mystics have always emphasized that a process of growth and change comes most easily if we surrender to it rather than struggle. The idea is to untwist and relax our spiritual selves rather than impose a change through brute force. So let's put our fears behind us, reawaken our intrinsic child-like wonder—which is, after all, the best posture for growth—and examine where we might be headed.

THE STRUCTURE OF EVOLUTION

In his book *A Brief History of Everything*,[3] philosopher Ken Wilber discusses how people, cultures, and the universe tend to evolve. At each new step of development, the forms or ideas of an earlier time become subsumed by new, more powerful forms and ideas. Wilber argues that four fundamental types of evolution tend to occur side by side:

1. The evolution of the outer world of things.

2. The evolution of the outer collective world of political and social structures.

3. The evolution of the internal psychological and spiritual world of the individual.

4. The evolution of the collective internal world of culture and religion.

These four parallel strands of evolution can be understood as the cross-product of two aspects: the external versus the internal, and the individual versus the collective (see Figure I.5).

I have found Wilber's model of evolution to be extremely insightful and clarifying. For one thing, it goes beyond the conventional scientific

	Internal	External
Individual	**Evolution of the Self** Psychological Spiritual	**Evolution of Individual Things (Scientific Evolution)** Material World
Collective	**Evolution of the Collective Internal** Culture Religion/ Spirituality	**Evolution of the Collective External** Social and political structures

FIGURE I.5

notion of evolution and embraces the importance of the interior realms—the evolution of the self, culture, religion, and spirit. It also emphasizes how the four spheres of evolution affect one another. For example, our evolving political structures influence, and are influenced by, our cultural and spiritual beliefs. The evolution of particular individuals can also lead to profound cultural and religious changes (think of Jesus, Buddha, Abraham, or Muhammad), or can influence political structures (think of the Founding Fathers of the United States). Human society's cultural and political evolution may also be impacting the global climate and thus affecting the evolution of the Earth itself.

Is it possible that the growing planetary changes will also cause evolutionary changes within us? With less space, food, and resources for humanity, our illusions of insularity will quickly fade away. Soon, we will be forced to wake up to the reality of overpopulation, over-consumption, and the truth of our interconnectedness. Will we react by moving into chaos? Will widespread disaster result in a "de-evolution" to earlier periods of human history? Or, will we respond by evolving our individual selves, our culture, and our political structures in a positive way?

Wilber also points out that evolutionary steps tend to be met with resistance. As a result, it is no surprise when skeptics pounce upon any challenge to the dominant scientific world-view. This has always been the case—from the jailing of Galileo for his claim that the planets revolve around the sun, to today's attacks on scientists who explore psychic phenomena or alternative methods of healing.[4] Of course, resistance to political, cultural, and religious evolution can be even more intense. That may be why we are experiencing so much war and political tension in the world today. Ironically however, this resistance can also serve as the catalyst that eventually enables evolutionary steps forward to occur.

WHERE WE'RE HEADED: THE STAGES OF EVOLUTION

From an evolutionary point of view, where are we now and where are we headed? Wilber claims that most of the cultures and political structures on Earth today are at what he calls the *Concrete Operational* stage. Developmentally, this is similar to the stage of late childhood, just before puberty, when children realize that they have to consider the feelings of others in their group. People in societies at this stage create and obey rules and laws and try to adhere to the conventions and beliefs of others. Their problems include feelings of alienation or worries about "fitting in." Cultures at this stage tend to be ethnocentric or tribal in identity, and political structures tend to be nationalistic. One key sign of this stage of development on Earth was the rise of the democratic nation-states during the nineteenth and twentieth centuries.

Wilber calls the next stage of evolution *Formal Operational*. Developmentally, this stage is like the teenage years—idealistic, introspective, post-conventional, and thought-based rather than concrete. In 2001, Wilber estimated that, culturally and individually, about ten percent of Americans had reached this stage. It is characterized by a more world-centric or global viewpoint, rather than one that is focused on the needs of one's own group. The Internet has certainly been a catalyst for the development of this stage, and indeed, technological changes have often triggered evolutionary leaps for humanity. Before the information age, the world was only connected by the slowly moving "circulatory system" of physical travel—boats, cars, trains, and airplanes. But now that we are all instantaneously interconnected by the digital "nervous system" of the Internet and by various media transmitted by satellite, most of us are beginning to realize that we all live together on one small planet. Media phenomena like YouTube and Facebook may seem escapist on the surface, but they are also manifestations of everyone trying to connect to one another—trying to feel part of a global community.

Of course, problems arise at this stage of evolution as well. Without a strong connection to a local group, world-centric individuals may experience feelings of dissociation and lost identity. Global citizenship doesn't provide enough social context for most people, at least not yet. It is also important to point out that a "global economy" is not necessarily a sign that a society has achieved the world-centric stage of evolution. There is a big difference between recognizing the entire world as one's community, and being engaged in an economic system that just happens to be global in scope, but applies the same tribal, exploitative strategies based on caring only for one's self or one's group. In a truly world-centric economy, everyone on the planet would be viewed and treated as a neighbor.

Naturally, there is resistance to the emerging world-centric stage of evolution. Most places—including the West—are still very tribal in their ways. Consider, for example, continuing nationalistic expressions of xenophobia and unwillingness to cooperate on global issues like climate change and arms control. In some societies, we are even witnessing attempts to return to stages of evolution that preceded the tribal stage. For example, this can be seen in countries that are attempting to disempower and re-subjugate women. As Wilber points out, cultural evolution has always been accompanied by a gradual blurring of the distinctions between the sexes. That is why the development of the nation-states of the nineteenth and twentieth centuries was accompanied by the development of women's education, suffrage, and ownership of property.

As we reach the world-centric stage and beyond, gender roles will blur even further. Not only will men and women reach greater forms of parity, but sexual distinctions may begin to blur too—something we may already be witnessing as homosexuality becomes increasingly accepted and the issue of gay marriage comes to the forefront. These changes are frightening to many. But as Wilber points out, the momentum towards evolutionary progress is extremely strong and usually prevails.

There are also a small number of people moving on to the next stage of evolution. After adolescence comes adulthood, with a focus on service to others and transcendence of the personal. Wilber calls this the *Vision Logic* stage. It is a stage of synthesis and integration of the components of the self. Rather than being identified with the body, mind, or emotions, individuals at this stage achieve an inner or higher knowing. External cultural and political structures tend to have less meaning or significance to them. On the downside, such people may experience feelings of dread or meaninglessness. Without cultural, political, or even personal stories to identify with, they may ask themselves, "Who am I? What am I? What is real?"

Inevitably, the answer will be found by continuing to evolve—to stages that very few humans have achieved: the *Transpersonal* stages, where the line between the individual and the environment becomes blurred. People who reach these stages of development deeply realize that each of us is truly, not just figuratively, One—one with nature, one with each other, one with God. This is a realm where few have gone, and where psychic phenomena, spiritual forms of healing, and the use of consciousness to create and manifest reality may be commonplace. Is it possible that we could reach a time when this kind of consciousness is the norm?

One thing is certain: more of us must attain at least the world-centric stage if we are to survive. As long as we are unable to look beyond the welfare of our own group, it will be impossible for us to collectively change our behavior and take on the challenges coming our way. Rather than succumbing to media hype and fear mongering and viewing the coming times as an impending calamity, I think it is more productive to view them as an opportunity. The Hopi Indians, for example, believe that we are now leaving the Fourth World of Destruction and entering the Fifth World of Peace. So *now* may indeed be the perfect time for each one of us to take the leap and focus on our own process of evolution.

Gurdjieff said, "[T]he evolution of humanity can proceed only through the evolution of a certain group, which, in its turn, will influence and lead the rest of humanity."[5] He called this group the *conscious nucleus*. Wilber has also argued that such groups can create a tipping point that allows a culture to enter the next stage of evolution. I believe that now is the time for more of us to join and surround this nucleus, in ever-increasing numbers. As most spiritual teachers argue, true evolution requires us to consciously make the choice to change and grow. It is my hope that this book will convince you to make this choice, and that it will also help you to achieve its aim.

On the next page you will move on to Exercise 1. Please be aware that the majority of the exercises in this book emanate from the teachings of Gary Sherman. I encourage you to visit his websites to learn more about his work: *www.becomingselfaware.com, www.creativeawareness.org,* and *www.deepening.com.*

EXERCISE 1

BEING PRESENT IN OUTER SENSATION

It is time to begin your journey of awakening!

Before I describe the first exercise, let me begin by reminding you that the exercises in this book form a progression. Please take the time to play with each one as you encounter it. I recommend reserving at least fifteen minutes each day for practice, and trying each exercise at least three times before moving on to the next.

To achieve active consciousness, there are many components of yourself that you need to become more aware of. One way of mapping these components is shown below.

OUTER WORLD	INTERNAL WORLD	DEEPER SELF
Outer senses	Internal body senses	Subtle senses
	Emotions	Deeper emotions
	Thoughts	Deeper thoughts

In this first exercise, we will begin by exploring the realm of the *outer senses*. Personally, I find this activity fun and relaxing. Try it when you are sitting in traffic or waiting in line at the supermarket. You might be surprised by the experience!

During this exercise you may notice:

- Heightened sense abilities—for example, greater visual and hearing acuity.

• A feeling of relaxation as you take your focus off your internal world (with its mind chatter and emotions) and rest in outer sensation.

STEP 1. Settle into the Now: "Feet. Seat. Back."

This basic step should be taken at the beginning of every exercise or meditation. With practice, you will be able to settle in just a few seconds. To begin, you should focus on this step for a few minutes.

Sit in a comfortable upright chair with your feet firmly on the floor. Place your hands palm down on your thighs. Keep your eyes **open**.

• Focus your attention first on the sensation of your feet on the ground. If you are wearing socks or shoes, feel them. Feel your feet and their connection to the ground or floor.

• Next focus your attention on your seat—the sensation of your buttocks sitting on the chair.

• Then, focus your attention on your back—the sensation of your back against the chair.

• Now, let the body relax into these three areas of sensation.

If at any point you find that you are wandering into mind-chatter or emotions, simply re-settle by thinking "Feet. Seat. Back." and bring your attention back to the sensation of your feet, seat, and back.

STEP 2. Focus your attention in outer sensation for about ten minutes.

With your eyes open and remaining settled in your body, focus your attention on the outer world. Be curious and have fun. Look at things but do not "think" about them. Just look at an object's shape, texture, color. It may be a flower, a lamp, a tree, or a crack in the wall. You do not need to stay focused on a single object. Look at anything you want and move your attention around, but try to rest your attention on each object for at least five or ten seconds.

Similarly, take time to listen to the sounds around you. Do not "think" about them—just listen to them. Move your hearing attention slowly around your environment.

Remember, try not to think about what you are seeing or hearing, just see and hear. You will know you are getting somewhere if you start noticing any of these things:

- A sensation of stillness or space.

- A feeling as if you are moving toward objects or as if they are moving toward you.

- A heightened visual sense. For example, your perception of light might become intensified. If you are very deeply in this state, you might also begin to notice a fog or haze, which may be the perception of auras.

- A heightened sense of sound. For example, if you are doing this exercise outside, you may notice how pervasive the sound of traffic is, or you may experience the sounds of nature more deeply—birds, insects, the breeze, etc.

Here are some other ideas to play with while relaxing in outer sensation:

- Can you become "one" with an object? Can you sense the feeling of "being" a lamp or a tree?

- As you see and hear, do you feel any inner sensations in your body?

Do this exercise (and all exercises in this book) in a spirit of playfulness. There is no right or wrong experience. If your attention wanders (which it will), just settle again using "Feet. Seat. Back." You will find that the exercises in this book become easier the more you try them. Have fun!

When you are done and return to your normal mode of awareness, you may literally feel the return of your normal mind chatter and emotions. This is an important clue—because it helps you realize that your thoughts and emotions are not *you*, only a part of you. You can turn them on and off at will, just like you did during this exercise.

PART II

THE MYSTERY THAT SURROUNDS YOU

"Because institutional science has become so conservative, so limited by conventional paradigms, some of the most fundamental problems are either ignored, treated as taboo, or put at the bottom of the scientific agenda. They are anomalies; they don't fit in." [1]

—*RUPERT SHELDRAKE*

"Reality is merely an illusion, albeit a very persistent one."

—*ALBERT EINSTEIN*

OPEN YOUR MIND...

THE SCIENTIFIC EVIDENCE SUPPORTING THE EXISTENCE OF
paranormal phenomena is so vast that it is amazing it is largely ignored. This state of affairs reminds me of the story of the island natives
who cannot see the large sailing ship approaching them, because it just
doesn't fit into their reality. Whether it be an islander who has never
confronted the outside world, or a modern scientist with a narrow and
rigid mindset, anyone who has a vested interest in maintaining the
status quo will tend to shut out that which "doesn't fit in."

Of course, if now is the time for more of us to take an evolutionary leap forward and acknowledge the truth of such mysteries—mysteries that reveal a deep and pervasive interconnectivity between all
things—it may also be time for mainstream scientists to do so as well.
Indeed, a growing number of popular books have been written in
recent years that describe the mounting scientific evidence for a variety of unexplained, yet apparently commonplace phenomena in our
world. These include psychic experiences like precognition, remote-
viewing, psychokinesis, and distance healing with prayer.[2, 3, 4, 5, 6, 7]

Many researchers also believe that these unusual phenomena have
a relationship with mystical experiences described by a variety of religious traditions and esoteric systems from the past.[8, 9] A possible link
to ancient knowledge should not be viewed in a dismissive way, however. Rather than reverting to pre-scientific ways of thinking, what
today's scientists of the paranormal are trying to do is enable a meeting of science and mysticism. After all, both science and mysticism
are trying to describe the same underlying truth—the truth about
how our world really operates. By taking frontier science more seriously, humanity may finally be able to develop knowledge that transcends and incorporates all previous thought systems, both scientific
and mystical.

My goal in Part II is to introduce you to some of these results. Rather than replicating what other writers have so ably done, however, I'd just like to loosen up your mind a bit. Think of it as a "mind-expansion massage." Hopefully, it will relax you enough to consider new ways of participating in and playing with your own universe. Then, in Part III, we'll begin to explore how you can do just that.

CHAPTER 9

)r

SILICON VALLEY MEETS
DIAGON ALLEY*

Y OU MIGHT THINK THAT THE STANFORD INDUSTRIAL PARK—
a place normally associated with high-tech companies—would
be the last place on Earth to find experiments investigating psychic
phenomena. However, in the mid-1990s, Microsoft billionaire Paul
Allen started a research laboratory called Interval Research, sand-
wiched between companies like Hewlett Packard and Varian, that did
just that. After my husband Steve left his job at Apple Computer in
1998, he began working at Interval on computer graphics, virtual
reality systems, and some other interesting projects—including one
led by Dean Radin, one of the world's leading researchers on psychic
phenomena.

Given my budding interest in consciousness, I couldn't believe
that it was my husband—and not I—that got to work on a day-to-day
basis with Dean Radin. But because of this remarkable confluence
of events, I got to know Radin and his colleague, Russell Targ, on a
personal level. I also got an up-close look at some of the software that
Steve developed for them.

One particularly memorable experiment involved testing the human power of *precognition*—the ability to sense something that will occur in the future.[1] After being hooked up to a variety of instruments
that measure heart rate, skin conductivity, and the like (the kinds

---

* The magical portal city in the *Harry Potter* series's fictional London.

of instruments used in lie-detector tests), test subjects were shown a random sequence of images. Some of these images were calming or neutral—for instance, an image of a flower, spoon, or a house. Other images were highly disturbing or arousing, depicting graphic sex, violence, or gore. In fact, in order to heighten the effect of the provocative images, they were accompanied by extremely harsh or grating sounds.

Naturally, the test subjects did physically react to the images and sounds in the expected way. Calm images were soothing, and disturbing images and sounds caused high levels of agitation. But that wasn't the interesting part of the experiment. Astonishingly, the subjects also tended to react just *before* they were shown an image. Thus, even though the pictures were selected at random, the test subjects' bodies responded in a content-appropriate way *in advance*. In fact, these reactions occurred even before the computer had selected an image!

As it turns out, this experiment was a successful replication of other, similar experiments, and more have been conducted since that time.[2] Steve would come home and tell me about these amazing results. He would also describe the rigor and precision that Radin expected from the computer code—making absolutely certain that the randomness of image selection and that the recording and timing of image selection, image display, and body measurements were absolutely unquestionable.

If this study was correct, our natural intuition about cause and effect—that our eyes and ears must see or hear something before we can react to it—is called into question. Indeed, this study showed that human precognitive abilities can occur on an unconscious level. While the test subjects in Radin's study did not *consciously* react until after they saw an image, their bodies did indeed react earlier. If we are all picking up this kind of information on a subconscious level, what else might be going on beneath the surface of our accepted reality?

This experiment was by no means an isolated case. The normally assumed constraints of space and time have been broken in a long string of psychic experiments, many of them funded by the U.S.

government. These investigations into the paranormal began in the 1970s, in an effort to catch up with similar studies being conducted in the Soviet Union. The results were impressive enough for the CIA to continue funding research of this kind for many years.

Back in 1987, just before Steve and I began our voyage of parenthood, we decided to take one last exotic vacation. We chose a photography tour of China and amazingly, one of the people on our trip was George Pezdirtz—the man in charge of funding Russell Targ's psychic research at SRI—the research I alluded to in Chapter 4. Because of this interesting coincidence, I got to hear about Targ's results straight from Pezdirtz, instead of them having them filtered through the mocking laughter of my SRI colleagues.

One of Targ's experiments with his SRI collaborator, physicist Harold Puthoff, tested the paranormal ability called *remote viewing*. Remote viewers are gifted individuals who are able to "see" target destinations from vast distances. In the SRI experiments, talented viewers like Pat Price, Ingo Swann, and Joe McMoneagle were given latitude and longitude coordinates of distant target sites and were able to sense what was located at them. In one experiment, the contents of a secret military installation in the Soviet Union were drawn in detail by the viewer and later ultimately verified.[3]

Targ and Puthoff's remote viewing experiments also violated the normal constraints of time. A typical experiment went something like this. First, a viewer was isolated and monitored while a target location was chosen at random from a large set of possible locations. Then another participant traveled to the target and, at a specified time, the viewer "sensed" their location and reported their impressions by drawing the target on paper. Amazingly, not only could gifted viewers describe and draw distant targets in fair detail, but their ability to do so was not affected by time; they could "see" distant targets in real time (the present), but they could also sense targets that were selected and visited in the past or in the future. Somehow, they possessed a psychic sense that could transcend both space *and* time.

How can we understand this? Perhaps one explanation is that re-mote viewers are somehow able to "lift" themselves out of their bod-ies, or access a part of themselves that is not confined to their physical bodies, and travel through space and time to the target location. This phenomenon is similar to so-called "out-of-body experiences" (OBEs) that have been studied scientifically too. In his book, *The Holographic Universe*, Michael Talbot reports that OBEs have been reported through-out history and in most cultures. They usually occur when a person is in an altered state of awareness—such as during meditation, anesthesia, or when undergoing a severe body stress such as trauma. The person suddenly notices that they are floating above their body and can move to other locations. In fact, about 20% of people report having an OBE at some point in their lives.[4]

One might chalk these experiences up to dreams or hallucina-tions, but repeatedly it has been verified that people having an OBE do accurately view something that they would not be able to see us-ing their physical bodies. For example, Talbot talks about the case of a hospitalized woman who left her body and saw a tennis shoe in an obscure location on the roof of the hospital. The shoe's location was later verified and the woman's detailed description of it was accurate as well. Indeed, some individuals are particularly skilled at producing intentional OBEs and a few of them have been tested in laboratory settings. Gifted subjects were even able to "fly in" and view objects in a laboratory from across the country.[5]

Generally, remote viewing and OBEs are passive experiences—the viewer "sees" but doesn't "do." But if a person experiencing an OBE can travel to remote places and times, could they cause changes there as well? How *active* can these paranormal experiences be? Can a person utilize deep forms of active consciousness to cause unlikely, yet noticeable, changes in the physical world too? As it turns out, these kinds of abilities have also been demonstrated.

Consider, for example, the power of *psychokinesis*—the ability of the mind or "psyche" to move or affect physical objects. One famous example is the purported ability of Israeli psychic Uri Geller to bend spoons. In fact, it was Russell Targ's controversial experiments with Geller that provoked all of the joking at the SRI coffee hours.[6]

A more subtle form of psychokinesis, however, has been demonstrated repeatedly in thousands of controlled trials at the Princeton Engineering Anomalies Research laboratory. Over a two-decade period, Princeton researchers Robert Jahn and Brenda Dunne worked with hundreds of volunteers to demonstrate that humans do indeed have the ability to affect the behavior of random output devices, including electrical, mechanical, optical, and acoustical devices.[7] Somehow, the test subjects were able to steer these devices so that their output was no longer random at all. Indeed, could psychokinesis be another possible explanation for Dean Radin's precognition results? What if Radin's subjects didn't sense what they were going to see, but instead, *caused* the computer to select the harsh or calm image that they were anticipating?

Either way, these and other results from similar experiments on psychic phenomena indicate that much more is going on beneath the surface of accepted reality than we might think. And it might have a lot to do with a kind of subtle interconnectivity that links all of us and everything else in the universe together.

CHAPTER 10

ENTANGLEMENTS

IN THE EARLY 1900S, THE NEW FIELD OF QUANTUM PHYSICS BEGAN to turn up some pretty mind-boggling things. It appears that at subatomic levels of reality—levels that are even more minute than electrons, protons, and neutrons—particles can have effects upon one another at great distances without any known means of communication between them. Somehow, at the quantum level, the normally assumed constraints of time and space simply no longer apply.

Nearly a century has now passed since these strange phenomena have become known. Nevertheless, most of us have not admitted this information into our everyday intuition about how the world works. Indeed, many scientific fields, like biology and medicine, do not account for the weird habits of the subatomic realm either. Despite this disinterest, however, there is growing evidence that such phenomena do play an important role in our day-to-day lives. Little by little, the wisdom of shamans and sages is beginning to emerge from the closet of dismissed nonsense into the light of confirmed scientific reality.

For example, one of the things that quantum physicists have discovered is that weird violations of space and time tend to occur in cases of *entanglement*—when the energies of two objects become intertwined. For instance, once two quantum particles come into contact, they continue to influence each other, even after physical contact or communication between them has become impossible. In fact, these influences are instantaneous. Up until recently, it has always been assumed that this kind of phenomenon can occur only in the sub-atomic realm. But recent physics experiments have shown similar behavior cropping up at atomic and molecular levels too.[1,2]

Of course, as many of us intuitively know, humans can also get entangled, and not just in a romantic way! There is some aspect of us, and perhaps of all living things, that can get tangled up with the energy of others. For instance, researchers of the paranormal have repeatedly demonstrated that individuals who are emotionally connected to one another are more psychically connected as well. This holds true even if the individuals are initially strangers and have simply spent some time meditating or connecting with one another. Jahn and Dunne's experiments with random output generators, for instance, found that connected couples could influence the machines' outputs better than individuals working alone. Somehow their emotional connection enhanced the power of *psi*—the force that is said to underlie psychic phenomena.

One of Dean Radin's most recent experiments in this realm, conducted with researcher Marilyn Schlitz at the Institute of Noetic Sciences in California, was nicknamed the "Love Study."[3,4] It was specifically designed to test the power of human entanglement. Many studies of this kind have used electroencephalograms (EEGs) to demonstrate that the brains of two people can become synchronized or "entrained" under various circumstances. For example, even if a couple is isolated from one another, their brains often register the same reactions if one of them receives a stimulus such as a mild electric shock or an exposure to flickering light—but only if a prior emotional connection has been established between them.[5] Studies have also shown that the deeper the emotional connection between two people, and the more intense their motivation for success in a psychic connection, the greater the impact of entanglement.

Taking a lead from these results, Radin and Schlitz recruited couples with a high motivation for intentional connection: one of them had to be suffering from cancer. The experiment then tested the power of one partner to transmit healing energy to the other. The group was divided into two sub-groups—one set of couples that received additional training designed to increase their psychic connection, and one that did not. A third group of healthy couples also participated as a control group.

Radin and Schlitz designed their training program for the first group of couples based on past research results in the field. It included: training in meditation (which has been shown to aid in healing and also to create more coherent brain waves and biophoton emissions—the subtle light given off by the body); training in the Buddhist practice of empathy and compassion—the ability to develop a deep understanding of the pain of others and to transform this compassion into a force for healing; and instruction on how to enhance belief and confidence in the psychic connection. During the actual trials, the couples were thoroughly isolated from one another behind solid steel, double-walled, electromagnetically shielded enclosures that also blocked all sound. Nevertheless, several correlations were found in the couples' body measurements.

The experiment proceeded as follows. "Senders" were instructed to transmit healing for a period of ten seconds whenever they were signaled with an image of their partner on a television screen. Because the timing of these visual signals was randomly generated and because the "receivers" were not told how long senders would be focusing their healing intent, there was no way for them to know when these transmissions would occur or how long they would last. Nevertheless, correlations were found between the members of each couple in all three trial groups while healing intentions were transmitted—in skin conductance, heart rate, blood flow, respiration, and brain waves. The correlations were definitely the strongest, however, in the first group of trained couples.[6]

Given the outcome of this study, experimental results about the effectiveness of prayer to promote healing are not surprising.[7] Perhaps the best-known studies of this kind analyzed the effect of prayer on hospitalized heart patients. Even though the patients did not know that they were being prayed for, and even though the prayers were offered by complete strangers at distant locations, most of the studies found prayer to be helpful. For example, in one meta-analysis, 75% of 227 prayer studies showed a positive impact.[8] There is definitely a reason why congregations of every denomination set aside time to pray for their sick members!

But these uncanny connections are found not only among humans. There is also evidence that they may exist among other living things, such as dogs, birds, and insects. Biologist Rupert Sheldrake has been studying such phenomena for years. He is well known for his theory of *morphic fields*—hypothetical fields of energy that instantaneously connect members of a species across space and time. In his book, *The Presence of the Past,* Sheldrake argues that such fields are also what truly determine the structure of living things.[9] Thus, it isn't simply the genetic code that determines the way our bodies look and grow—it's also the energetic morphic field, which Sheldrake believes our genes decode and implement. Using the analogy mentioned in Chapter 5, the morphic field is essentially the "TV transmission" that is picked up by the "TV circuitry" of our genetic material.

Among the wide-ranging pieces of evidence that Sheldrake presents for the existence of the morphic field is the fact that similar evolutionary steps have occurred among animals in far-flung regions of the planet—something that would be extremely unlikely if evolution were driven solely by local random mutations. Sheldrake also surmises that the morphic field could explain uncanny connections that have been observed between pets and their owners.[10] For example, he has studied how dogs tend to prepare for their owner's arrival each day—at just about the time when the owner leaves work to return home. This has been shown to be true even when the owner comes home at random times. Somehow the connection between a pet and its owner creates an entanglement that allows the transmission of such information to occur. Indeed, morphic fields might also explain all those apocryphal stories about dogs that are able to find their families, even after they have moved thousands of miles away.

Another example of this phenomenon can be seen in the behavior of homing pigeons. These amazing birds were critical carriers of information in past war efforts because of their uncanny ability to come home to roost, even when their roost is moved to unpredictable locations. Up until now, these abilities have never been explained in a conventional way. The only plausible explanation provided thus far has been Sheldrake's morphic fields.

Of course, if some kind of energy field does enable information to be exchanged between connected or similar things, what could be more connected than the various parts of our own bodies? Most of us have heard of "phantom-limbs"—sensations such as pain, heat and cold that amputees feel. From a conventional medical standpoint, these sensations are explained neurologically—that is, as being the result of severed nerve endings. But this explanation has not been borne out in practice. Phantom pain can occur in paraplegics and in people who have lost the portion of their brain that would register this information.[11]

In his book *Seven Experiments that Could Change the World*, Sheldrake relates several anecdotes that seem to indicate that phantom sensations may actually be coming from the severed limb itself. For instance, one man who kept his amputated finger in a jar in a heated basement began to feel extreme cold in his phantom digit. When he went to investigate, he discovered that the basement window had been broken, just inches away from the jar. When the amputated finger was moved to a warmer location, the sensation of coldness in his phantom disappeared.[12]

Esoteric views of the human body might also be able to explain phantom limbs. Many alternative medical systems focus upon an invisible "energy body" that transcends and interpenetrates our physical form. The first layer of this energy body is called *chi* (or *qi*) in Chinese medicine, *prana* in Ayurveda (traditional Indian medicine), and the *vital force* in homeopathy. It is considered to be the fundamental lattice upon which the physical body is built. Esoteric philosophies, like those of Rudolf Steiner and G.I. Gurdjieff, call this first layer of the energy body the *etheric body*. They also describe three additional layers—the *astral, mental,* and *causal bodies*—which I will describe in detail in Part IV. If any of these energy bodies truly exist, then perhaps an "energy limb," existing on the etheric or higher levels, remains connected to the energy body of an amputee, even when their physical connection has been severed. In other words, it is the "energy limb" that serves as a conduit of communication between an amputee and his or her amputated limb.

Amazingly, it may even be possible that our physical organs remain in communication with their energetic counterparts after death. In his book *The Heart's Code*, researcher Paul Pearsall explores some intriguing phenomena that occur in cases of heart transplants.[13] Many organ recipients report that their personalities change after a transplant and begin to conform to those of their donors—including the development of new food cravings and personality quirks. Even memories have been transmitted in this way. For instance, one patient "remembered" information that enabled his donor's killer to be arrested. Could this information be stored in the donated heart itself? Or does it lie within the heart's energetic counterpart, which remains in communication with other energetic aspects of the donor, even after death? An interview of Pearsall reported that, because of his findings, he grew to believe that:

> "... the soul, at least in part, is a set of cellular memories that is carried largely by our hearts. Predictably, such views have met with opposition in the medical world. But in his view, the implications of his theories—that the heart 'thinks,' cells remember, and communication can therefore transcend the boundaries of time and space—are too important for him to dismiss." [14]

CHAPTER 11

THE FIELD

"There is not only matter and energy in the universe, but also a more subtle yet real element: information… [that] connects all things in space and time—indeed it connects all things *through* space and time."[1]

—ERVIN LASZLO

IF THE BONDS THAT LINK QUANTUM PARTICLES TOGETHER ACROSS space and time can be felt in the domain of living things, they may also interconnect everything else going on around us. Even inert substances like minerals might be able to communicate with one another. As it turns out, this has actually been demonstrated. Crystals that are very difficult to grow in laboratory settings become increasingly easy and quicker to grow as more and more laboratories manufacture them—even when the labs are very distant from one another and do not share any personnel or data.[2] It's as if a piece of information is remembered each time a new crystal is generated, and that information is made available to all such crystals in the future.

Indeed, there is a growing body of evidence that suggests there is more coordination and correlation of phenomena in the universe than would be possible if the universe were as random and disconnected as most scientists assume. Philosopher and systems theorist Ervin Laszlo, in his book *Science and the Akashic Field*, discusses how this unexplained coherence is popping up in nearly every domain— from the cosmic realm of galaxies to the minute realm of subatomic particles, and everything else in between.[3] For example, scientists are uncovering unexpected forms of uniformity in the cosmos. As far as we can determine, background radiation is the same everywhere, and all known galaxies have developed in the same way. Since no accepted form of communication can exist between these distant galaxies—even light cannot travel fast enough—what is causing all of this coherence if evolution is just a matter of chance?

The answer is that some kind of informational field must be allowing communication to occur. To fulfill this role, Laszlo proposes the *Akashic Field*, whose name he chose in deference to the ancient Indian concept of the Akashic Chronicle—a record of all that has ever happened and all that is yet to come. He suggests that this field creates a kind of interconnectivity or coherence in our universe, which may even link it to prior universes that preceded it.[4] Sounds a bit like the morphic or the psi field, doesn't it?

A UNIFIED FIELD?

Of course, it's possible that the Akashic Field, the morphic field, and the psi field are all one and the same thing. Some scientists believe that these proposed fields are also related to the controversial *zero-point field* (ZPF), a concept that emerged in late twentieth-century physics. The ZPF can be understood as a quantum field created by energy passing between subatomic particles. It is also sometimes called the "unified vacuum" because it supposedly fills the vacuum of space. Its name derives from the fact that this field continues to exist at absolute zero, the temperature at which all accepted forms of energy are thought to be impossible.[5]

Up until now, there have only been four force fields that are widely accepted by modern physicists: the electromagnetic field, gravity, and the strong and weak nuclear forces. However, it has long been the quest of modern physics to find a *unified field*—one that could be used to explain all the others. This would enable the four known fields to be seen as special cases of this one underlying unified field. The zero-point field was first proposed as a theoretical construct to help model such a field. More and more, however, the ZPF is coming to be viewed as an actual field, thanks to growing experimental evidence.

One of the people active in this area of research is Harold Puthoff—the same man who worked on paranormal experiments with Russell Targ at SRI. Puthoff and his collaborators have shown that inertia, gravity, and mass can all be explained in terms of charged particles in the zero-point field. The ZPF has also been used to account for the stability of electrons in their orbits around the nucleus of an atom and the stability of planets in their orbits around a star. Mathematical physicist Hartmut Mueller has proposed the concept of density pressure waves in the ZPF to serve as the carrier of light, and as the fundamental basis for the gravitational, electromagnetic, and strong and weak nuclear forces. Increasingly, scientists are also coming to believe that the ZPF might be a carrier of *information*. In particular, tiny vortices within the ZPF pressure waves may encode the states of particles and transmit that information throughout the field, just as the ocean's waves carry information about what has passed through them. As Laszlo writes:

> "There is no evident limit to the information that interfering vacuum torsion waves can conserve and convey... [T]hey can carry information on the state of the whole universe... When many things move simultaneously in a waving medium, be it the ordinary sea or the extraordinary vacuum, that medium becomes modulated: full of waves that intersect and interfere... The modulation of the sea's surface... carries information on the ships that created the disturbance... [O]ne can deduce the location, speed, and even the tonnage of the vessels by analyzing the resulting wave-interference patterns... In the vacuum... there are no forces or things that could cancel or even attenuate waves... [T]he wave memory of the universe may be eternal."[6]

When we consider that the space between the atoms of our apparent world is, relative to their size, as vast as the vacuum of outer space, we can begin to understand that the zero-point field might actually encode all of our day-to-day reality. Thus, in the realm of the ZPF, everything might be connected and informed by everything else in a fundamental way. In fact, our intentions and thoughts might create measurable changes in the ZPF too.

Consider, for example, a fascinating set of experiments performed by Stanford University material science professor William Tiller—a world expert on the science of crystallization who has also spent decades researching paranormal phenomena. In 1997, Tiller decided to put his two fields of interest together to see if he could "charge" a simple physical device with human intentions. First he created the device—a box containing quartz oscillators and some erasable, programmable read-only computer memory. He then chose his experimental subjects: fruit flies. Here is how his experiment went.

First, while they were in the presence of his device, Tiller instructed a group of meditators to hold a specific intention about the flies' physiology that would speed up fruit fly development and increase their robustness. An identical device, not impregnated with these intentions, was used as a control. The experiment was then carefully double blinded; the two boxes were labeled and wrapped so that their identity would not be known, and were shipped to a laboratory in Minnesota 1500 miles away, where the experiment was completed. The results were mind-boggling. Over an eight-month period, thousands of larvae and adult flies were exposed to the devices. The boxes imprinted with the intentions apparently caused the larvae to develop fifteen percent faster than normal, and once they matured, these flies were not only healthier, but their descendants were too![7, 8]

Tiller also imprinted devices with other kinds of intentions. For example, in one set of experiments, intentions were directed toward affecting the pH of water—either upward or downward. All of these experiments were successful. However, in the midst of his work, Tiller discovered something even more amazing. After repeating the experiments over a period of several months, the effects became stronger and manifested more quickly—just like in the experiments with crystal formation. After investigating the laboratory environment for anomalies, Tiller discovered that the temperature was going up and down in a regular way—in fact, these rhythmic fluctuations were not affected by air conditioning, heating, the opening of doors or windows, or the presence or movement of people. He also found the same kinds of fluctuations occurring in the lab water's ability to conduct electricity.

Tiller realized that these environmental fluctuations provided evidence for a possible mechanism—a change in the very nature of the physical fields within the room. He repeated the experiments in different rooms and the same effects began to appear once enough experiments had been carried out. He then tried changing the environment, and found that the removal or addition of objects stopped the oscillations for a while, but they eventually reappeared. In fact, they continued even when the imprinted devices were shielded in Faraday cages and aluminum foil. However, after the imprinted devices were removed entirely, the oscillations slowly decayed.

Suspecting some kind of magnetic effect, Tiller decided to check the magnetic field of water in the room. He found that exposing the affected water to the south pole of a magnet would create a huge increase in its pH, but exposing it to the north pole of a magnet caused its pH to not only decrease, but its fluctuations to slowly decay. This meant that, by using repeated *focused intentions*, Tiller had created a magnetic monopole—a magnet with only one pole—something that governments around the world have spent billions of dollars trying to do.[9,10] Amazing!

CHAPTER 12

➤

WHEN YOU HAVE THE RIGHT VIBE, IT'S NOT A COINCIDENCE

A NOTHER WAY MANY HAVE EXPLAINED THE INHERENT interconnectivity of our universe is in terms of a *hologram*.[1] I distinctly remember the first time I saw this type of device in action—at the Haunted House at Disneyland. By projecting two-dimensional laser-light images of a woman's head and creating an interference pattern between them (much like the ocean-wave interference patterns described in Chapter 11), an eerie three-dimensional image of the woman's head was produced inside a glass jar. Today, of course, holograms are embedded in many common objects—from credit cards to children's toys. One of their amazing properties is that *every tiny piece of a hologram includes the interference pattern that can generate the entire image.* Thus, it doesn't matter how much you chop a hologram up; each tiny piece can create the same 3-D effect.

What some researchers have now proposed is that the zero-point field also encodes our three-dimensional reality holographically—that is, in terms of interference patterns. Moreover, because each tiny piece of the ZPF encodes the whole, this information is available everywhere, instantly. Indeed, just as the three-dimensional image of a woman's head at Disneyland was created from two-dimensional projections, the ZPF's encoding of information about our universe may yield a *four-dimensional* product. Is there some part of us—perhaps a higher-dimensional, energetic part of us—that has access to this information? Some neuroscientists do believe that memory and vision are stored in the brain in a holographic way.[2] Are our brains and energy bodies three-dimensional storage and access devices that can interact with higher-dimensional projections of the zero-point field?

One piece of evidence for the holographic nature of the zero-point field (and of the psi, Akashic, and morphic fields) is that they all share a common feature: sensitivity to *similarity in vibration*. For instance, if a holographic image has many different holograms embedded within it, shining a laser of a specific frequency upon it will cause only those holograms made with lasers of the same frequency to stand out. That's because things with the same vibration naturally resonate and reinforce one another—just as two violin strings at the same pitch resonate with one another. This property of resonance has been used to explain how each of us might interact with these mysterious fields. For instance, one might reasonably ask: if the zero-point or Akashic fields encode everything that has ever happened, and if we humans have access to it, why aren't we aware of all of this encoded information? The answer, Michael Talbot suggests, is that people pick up only that with which they personally "resonate." In other words, each individual's resonant frequency, determined by their life experience, physical body, and energy body, limits what they can perceive.

Rupert Sheldrake agrees. His theory of morphic resonance also depends upon similarity in vibration. Members of the same species, being "on the same wavelength," are able to tap into information that pertains uniquely to them. And while members of an entire species might be able to tune into a fairly broad spectrum of frequencies (think of Carl Jung's notion of the *collective unconscious* that humans supposedly tap into),[3] smaller, more tightly connected groups—such as members of the same family or loving couples—resonate in more focused zones of vibration; they have access to their own "private frequency." In fact, Sheldrake goes even further and suggests that morphic fields can explain how human memory operates. Instead of being stored in our brains, he suggests that memories are stored in the morphic field. Our brains then pick them up via resonance, like radios tuning to their own private stations.[4]

The existence and importance of similarity in vibration has also popped up in psi experiments. For example, individuals gifted at psychokinesis—the ability to affect physical objects with the mind—have described the experience as a feeling of resonance with those objects. A fascinating body of evidence has also been uncovered by Dean Radin and his colleague Roger Nelson at Princeton's PEAR lab. As mentioned earlier, researchers at PEAR found that connected couples can influence random event generators (REGs) more effectively than individuals working alone. Because of this phenomenon, Radin and Nelson decided to test for even larger field effects by using these random devices as "antennae." First they placed REGs at events where people were all focused on the same thing and therefore "vibrating" similarly—for example, at music festivals, religious events, and even at the Academy Awards. The results were as predicted; these venues did indeed cause the machines' outputs to deviate from the norm.[5, 6]

Then, in 1997, they decided to place REGs at fifty locations all over the world, run them continuously, and see if they could pick up on major world events. The results were astounding. Over the next ten years, Radin and Nelson studied the machines' reactions to 205 major world events and discovered that they did indeed respond to events that were intense on a global level—especially those that were tragic. The most striking effects occurred in response to the events on 9/11, which caused the largest daily average correlation between the machines' outputs. Even more amazing, this correlation became noticeable a few hours *before* the first of the twin towers was hit![7, 8, 9] An instance of collective precognition?

Whereas world events less horrific than 9/11 probably evoke more varied vibratory responses in people (and therefore do not resonate and amplify each other as well), truly frightening events tend to evoke a more common, coherent response. As this study showed, when nearly all of the people on Earth "got onto the same wavelength" on 9/11, even machines noticed. One important question to ask is: how can we use this phenomenon to *help* humanity? What if we could all get together and create a shared intentional vibration to *heal* our planet?

SYNCHRONICITY AND FIELDS OF MEANING

Similarity in vibration has also been used to explain the phenomenon of *synchronicity*—"coincidences" of seemingly unrelated events that share a common meaning. A typical example of synchronicity is when the beloved clock or watch of an individual breaks or stops at the precise moment of his or her death. Another well-known illustration of this phenomenon was described by psychiatrist Carl Jung, the originator of the notion of synchronicity.[10] One of Jung's patients was recounting her dream about a golden scarab beetle when he heard a rapping on the window. When he opened it, a rose chafer beetle—the insect most similar to a scarab in Jung's region—flew into the room. Jung quickly put two and two together. He realized that the mythological meaning of the scarab—an ancient Egyptian symbol for rebirth—was highly pertinent to his patient's problems. And this was also the reason why the insect had appeared in waking life.

Both of these examples of synchronicity demonstrate a key point— the universe may not be operating like a cold, meaningless machine after all. Instead, the reality we experience each day may be flooded with *fields of meaning*. One field might embody the horror and violence of 9/11. Another field might be associated with a hope for rebirth. Each field of meaning has a particular vibration to it, and objects, individuals, emotions, dreams, and events with similar vibrations will tend to resonate with one another and then co-occur. This is what creates synchronicities. In fact, various theories of quantum physics *require* the existence of synchronicities.[11]

Similar ideas also underlie Jung's notion of an *archetype*—an idea, concept, or quality with a distinct meaning and significance, which is often represented as a mythological figure.[12] For example, in ancient Egypt, the scarab beetle symbolized the archetype of rebirth. Other archetypes are "the warrior," "the explorer," "the nurturer," and "the destroyer"—each of which is also the subject of many human myths.

Rather than just being abstract concepts or ideas, however, Jung believed that archetypes *actually exist* and that we interact with them through dreams, the collective unconscious, and synchronicities. Greek philosopher Plato also believed in the existence of archetypes, which he called *forms*. Along the same lines, consciousness researcher Stuart Hameroff has proposed that *qualia*—the qualities or sensations of things, such the "redness" of a flower or the "equanimity" conveyed by a piece of art—are also vibrational patterns in the "fundamental granularity of space-time geometry that makes up the universe."[13] Do archetypes, forms, and qualia actually exist as fields of meaning within the zero-point, morphic, Akashic, or psi fields? And do these distinct fields of meaning interact with us through synchronicities?

Think about it. There may be another fundamental mechanism at play in our universe besides cause and effect. Most of us think that everything that occurs in our world is due to some causal mechanism. A causes B causes C. However, *synchronicity*—the co-occurrence of events within the same field of meaning—*may be another fundamental reason why things tend to happen.* Many things in life that we think are due to cause-and-effect or mere coincidence may actually be due to synchronicity.

Here's an example that occurred while I was writing this book. My husband Steve and I had long admired Rupert Sheldrake's work on morphic fields but had never met him. To us, he was a brilliant scientist living far away in England. However, in September 2008, just as I was working on the section of this book that describes his work, Steve got word that Sheldrake would be giving a talk at his research laboratory at Sun Microsystems. Now please understand; talks about things like the morphic field are not commonplace in computer research labs. In fact, Sheldrake's talk was poorly attended. But it just so happened that one of the lab's researchers had met Sheldrake in Scotland and had invited him to speak the next time he was in our area. When Steve heard about Sheldrake's visit, he asked if I could also attend, and we both received an invitation to have lunch with him the next day. Before I could even finish writing about Rupert Sheldrake, I was sitting and having lunch with him!

Here's another illustration. We usually assume that our emotional states are caused by external events that happen to us. We believe that we get upset because we have lost a job or become elated because we have won some recognition or prize. While this may be true much of the time, what if our emotional states also *enable* events to occur via synchronicity? For example, we have all experienced days when nothing goes right, or when several similar mishaps occur one after the other. What if our emotional state is *enabling* these events, rather than the other way around? Periods of "bad luck" may simply be times in which we have entered a particular field of meaning—a field that resonates with our emotional state—and the annoying things that occur may simply be part of that field as well. The next time things start breaking around your home, stop and ask yourself: does your emotional state resonate with a "broken" field of meaning? Perhaps one way to end such a string of events is simply to take charge, change your frame of mind, and leave this field of meaning behind you. Try it!

CHAPTER 13

A MEANINGFUL CURE

THE POWERFUL INFLUENCE OF SIMILARITY IN VIBRATION HAS ALSO made its way into healing. In fact, it is the very foundation of *homeopathy*—an alternative medical system originally developed in Germany in the early 1800s. The word "homeopathy" literally means *similar* (homeo) *suffering* (pathy), and practitioners of homeopathy choose medicines for their patients based on a principle of cure called the *Law of Similars*. This principle can be described as follows:

> *If a substance is shown experimentally to cause a specific pattern of emotional, physical, and behavioral symptoms in healthy test subjects, then that substance can be prepared so that it can cure individuals suffering from the same pattern of symptoms.*

In other words, homeopathy is the science of healing based on similarity of vibration. The Law of Similars essentially says: "likes cure likes." Bring two things of like vibration together—a remedy and a patient—and the effect will be a cure of the patient's disease.

Here's a simple illustration. We all know the common effects of drinking coffee: wakefulness, a mind full of thoughts, excited happiness, acute senses, and sometimes heart palpitations and diarrhea. These symptoms are manifestations of the vibration of coffee, and coffee imparts these qualities to those who drink it. Now, if a patient comes to a homeopath seeking help for chronic insomnia, and their insomnia is characterized by an overactive mind, excitement, acuteness of the senses, heart palpitations, and diarrhea, it is likely that the homeopath will prescribe *Coffea Cruda*—a remedy prepared from coffee. That's because this patient manifests the same vibrational qualities as coffee. And if the remedy is truly homeopathic to the patient—that is, if coffee's symptoms match his or her overall emotional, mental, and physical state—it has the potential to completely cure their insomnia, not just palliate it as a sleeping pill would do.

Of course, the most controversial thing about homeopathy is not the Law of Similars, but the way in which homeopathic remedies are made. The process, called *potentization*, involves a sequence of steps in which a substance is repeatedly diluted and vigorously shaken. In fact, for most remedies, these dilutions are so extreme that they do not contain even a single molecule of the original substance! Nevertheless, homeopaths have found that the higher the dilution, the more potent a remedy can be. They believe this is possible because the *energetic signature* of a substance is captured by the potentization process. In other words, potentization enables the innate vibrational quality of a substance in nature to be unleashed and harnessed. It is this vibration that evokes the symptoms caused by a remedy, and it is also this vibratory signature that enables the remedy to cure a similar vibratory state in a patient. *Like vibrations cure like vibrations.*

The healing principle of "likes cure likes" was first mentioned by the father of medicine, Hippocrates (460–370 BC). It was also explored in the Middle Ages by alchemist and physician Paracelsus (1493–1541). However, it was German physician Samuel Hahnemann (1755–1843) who developed methodologies for analyzing patient symptoms, preparing homeopathic medicines, and applying them successfully. This homeopathic method is outlined in Hahnemann's treatise, the *Organon of the Medical Art*,[1] which is an important textbook for practitioners to this day.

Since Hahnemann's time, homeopathy has become the second most widely used health modality in the world—a testimony to the truth and power of the Law of Similars. Homeopathic treatment has enabled the cure of almost every disease—from acute illnesses like cholera, typhoid, and influenza, to serious chronic diseases like asthma, arthritis, and autism. And consider this: The Law of Similars may also be a fundamental property of the zero-point field.

WATER: A POTENT CARRIER OF INFORMATION

Although homeopathy has been the target of skeptics and critics since Hahnemann's time, open-minded scientists are finally beginning to get an inkling of how the remedies might be working. Recent studies have shown that the encoding of information in homeopathic dilutions is not about their chemical composition; it's more about the bonding structures between the molecules within them. Apparently, the shaking process (also called *succussion)* performed during homeopathic potentization is the critical step that develops these structures.

In 2007, a prominent researcher in the field of structured water, Professor Rustum Roy of Pennsylvania State University, showed for the first time that extreme homeopathic dilutions are not mere water, but highly structured arrangements of water molecules. In fact, various types of instruments in Roy's laboratory were able to pick up the distinct signatures of different remedies, even at levels of dilution in which no remedy substance likely remained.[2] Homeopathic experience has shown that these unique signatures can then be transmitted to dry pills, and that the power and distinct effects of these pills remain stable indefinitely if they are stored properly. In fact, remedies prepared by homeopaths in the 1800s are known to still be effective today.

Interestingly, the potentization process can be used to capture the energetic signature of *any* substance, not just those used to make homeopathic remedies. This has been shown repeatedly by several independent scientists in replicated studies. For example, consider the work of Jacques Benveniste, a French physician and medical researcher in the field of immunology who helped discover platelet-activating factor in 1972. Unfortunately, Benveniste's career was set upon a rocky course when a colleague encouraged him to study the phenomenon of potentization. His first paper about the subject described how antibodies of immunoglobulin E (anti–IgE) could be potentized beyond Avogadro's number (the point at which it is unlikely to find a single molecule of a substance remaining in a dilution) and still cause substance-specific effects.

When Benveniste published these results in the prestigious journal *Nature* in 1988,[3] he came under a barrage of attacks that lasted for the rest of his life. But perhaps this wasn't surprising. Benveniste's work had essentially shown that any drug could be potentized and still remain effective. That means that billions of doses of any drug could be produced for pennies—information that drug companies would spend a fortune to attack and suppress. And in fact, there is evidence that a world-wide campaign to discredit homeopathy has been funded by the pharmaceutical industry for this very reason.[4]

Despite the attacks on Benveniste and his subsequent loss of government funding in France, he continued his work and came up with even more astounding results. Because he suspected that the potentization process conveys an electromagnetic signal into the water of a dilution, he developed an apparatus that could digitally record it. He then transmitted this signal electronically—via E-mail—to a distant laboratory, and had it "replayed" into water there. Amazingly, the resulting water caused the same effects as the original substance.

Benveniste eventually conducted several blinded experiments using this protocol. He published a paper in the *Journal of Clinical Immunology* in 1997 that described one such experiment, in which a specific antigen was potentized, recorded, E-mailed to Chicago, and replayed into water in a Chicago laboratory.[5] This water did indeed cause antigen-specific effects on isolated guinea pig hearts. I saw Benveniste present this paper at Stanford University Medical School in 1999. The large lecture hall was standing-room only, but the audience was politely incredulous.

Of course, Benveniste's new results in what he called "digital biology" were even more mind-boggling and threatening than his original paper in *Nature*. Not only could billions of doses of a substance be prepared cheaply using potentization, but its signature could be E-mailed and imprinted into water essentially for free. Benveniste often compared himself to Galileo—tormented by his critics, but unrelenting in his pursuit of scientific truth until his untimely death at age 69 in 2004. Despite the fact that other initially-skeptical scientists have successfully replicated his work,[6,7] acceptance of Benveniste's work remains for the future. Perhaps, with the growth of a new consciousness in the scientific community, that future will arrive sooner rather than later. Indeed, in 2009, some new research conducted by Nobel prize winner Luc Montagnier confirmed the same kinds of effects that Benveniste described.[8]

Despite the skepticism of most scientists, the amazing power of water to encode fields of meaning has certainly captured the general public's imagination. Consider the immense popularity of a New York Times bestseller by Masaru Emoto, *The Hidden Messages in Water*.[9] In it, Emoto claims that specific words, music, or thoughts can affect water in a directly visible way—in the form of ice crystals, which he photographed. Thoughts and words like "love" and "gratitude" enabled beautiful crystals to be formed. Thoughts like "I hate you" or discordant, disturbing music formed ugly, irregular crystals.

Whether or not Emoto's claims are correct, the effectiveness of homeopathic remedies and the work of scientists like Rustum Roy, Jacques Benveniste, and Luc Montagnier do demonstrate that water possesses a unique quality—the ability to pick up and transmit specific energetic signatures of physical substances. This is something that the founder of homeopathy, Samuel Hahnemann, discovered in the early 1800s, and it is something that we should all think about, since our bodies are largely made up of water. Water is life. And water may also play an important role in connecting us to the fields of meaning that surround us.

THE MEANING OF DISEASE

The power of potentization is indeed one of the landmark discoveries of Homeopathy. It provides us with a method for capturing the energetic signature of any substance in nature. But perhaps even more significant is homeopathy's therapeutic principle, the Law of Similars—because it says something specific about how fields of meaning operate and interact. There may even be a direct relationship between the Law of Similars and synchronicity.

The late psychiatrist Edward Whitmont was a student of Carl Jung and eventually became a homeopath. In his book, *Psyche and Substance*, he speaks at length about the relationship between homeopathy and synchronicity.[10] Psychiatrists have long known that patients sometimes alternate between specific physical symptoms and specific mental or emotional symptoms. In fact, when mental symptoms are present, physical symptoms often vanish, and vice versa. This phenomenon is an illustration of the fundamentally psychosomatic nature of disease—that disease manifests in both the psyche (mind) and soma (body). Even more fascinating, however, is that the symptoms of a patient's physical disease often reflect or symbolize the nature of their psychological disease. Thus, it may be no accident when emotional irritation leads to a "pain in the neck," or being "pissed off" leads to kidney problems.

Homeopathy and other holistic medical systems have long recognized that disease is a body-mind affair. That is why each patient manifests a unique pattern of mental, emotional, and physical symptoms—a pattern that is an outward representation of his or her vibratory state. As Whitmont points out, each homeopathic remedy is also associated with a vibration. Indeed, the catalog of symptoms associated with the approximately 1000 homeopathic remedies is essentially a catalog of the vibratory patterns that humans can manifest. The Law of Similars then states that bringing together the vibratory pattern of a patient and the similar vibratory pattern of a remedy can be curative. The reason this is true, Whitmont suggests, is synchronicity:

> "[W]ith mental and physical symptoms synchronistically, not causally, related, one may substitute for another and appear to be able to cancel it. Thus we get a first glimpse of an understanding how illness and 'similar' drug energy, as synchronistic entities of the same 'field' sharing a functional likeness, may perhaps substitute for another and thereby functionally cancel each other."[11]

In other words, homeopathic remedies are curative because they share the same synchronistic field as a disease and therefore can replace it within a patient's body. Hahnemann proposed essentially the same explanation in the early 1800s for the operation of his remedies upon what he called the *dynamis* or *vital force*—the energetic etheric field that encompasses the physical body.

The fact that homeopathy has worked for millions of people for 200 years says a lot about the power of the Law of Similars. But it also says something about fields of meaning and their relationship to us in disease and in health. Just as the dream of the golden scarab said something meaningful about the psychological state of Jung's patient, holistic practitioners recognize that each person's unique manifestation of disease is not merely the result of genetic inheritance or the accidents of life—it is a reflection of a field of meaning vibrating at the core of their being.

PARANORMAL MEDICINE?

Before I leave the subject of homeopathy, a couple of other phenomena witnessed in the homeopathic world are worth mentioning. Because they border on the paranormal, they are rarely openly discussed. Both tend to occur during *provings*—the homeopathic drug trials. The object of these trials is to see what pattern of symptoms a substance will create in healthy volunteers. Today's provings are conducted using modern techniques like double-blinding and placebo controls. Thus, some test subjects (called *provers*) are given placebo while others are given the actual remedy. Since the trials are also blinded, neither the provers nor their supervisors, who collect symptom information, know who has been given a real remedy or a placebo, nor the identity of the substance being tested. Nevertheless, the following kinds of phenomena have been observed during many trials.

First, it has been noticed that the moment a prover forms the intention to participate in a proving, they often begin to experience

symptoms that are later found to be characteristic of the remedy—
long before the trial actually begins. While this doesn't happen to all
provers, it happens frequently enough to be noteworthy. By simply
intending to join a remedy trial, a prover may enter into the field of
meaning of the remedy substance. Just as paranormal phenomena often defy the normal constraints of time and space, the fields of meaning created by homeopathic remedies may as well.

The second remarkable thing about provings is that the symptoms developed by provers often directly reflect the nature of the substance from which a remedy is made. This is most obvious in the
case of remedies made from animal substances. There are dozens of
such remedies, including those made from a variety of mammal milks,
snake venoms, and insect poisons. In nearly every case, the symptoms
evoked by these remedies reflect the nature of the animal itself.

Consider, for example, the blind proving of *Androctonus* conducted
in 1985. Even though the provers did not know that they were taking
a remedy made from scorpion venom, they developed the following
kinds of symptoms: overconfidence; contemptuousness and defiance;
lack of feeling and cruelty; quarrelsomeness and deceitfulness; the delusion that they were about to be assaulted and a malicious desire to
injure others; suspiciousness; a lack of impulse control; anxiety and
fear that is ameliorated by walking around; aversion to company; and
a feeling that one is alone or separated from the world.[12]

Notice how evocative many of these symptoms are of scorpions—
violent, cruel, and antisocial. Indeed, this remedy has been effective
in treating patients with serious mental illness. In my book about homeopathy, *Impossible Cure*, I describe the case of one man who, thanks
to Androctonus, experienced a cure of severe allergies and headaches,
as well as a significant lessening of arthritis, high blood pressure, and
diabetes. The man was an avid hunter, obsessed with guns and knives.
He told his homeopath how he would wait until his prey came to him
and how he could sense and communicate with them. Interestingly,
scorpions also let their prey come to them, and they can accurately

detect their victim's location by sensing their vibrations. After taking Androctonus, this hunter was not only alleviated of his physical problems, but he also became much less interested in his extensive collection of weapons.[13]

Think of it. The process of potentization may provide us with a method for accessing the very essence of the natural world. Just as Merlin the Magician showed the future King Arthur what it was like to be a fish or bird, a prover who takes a potentized remedy may learn what it's like to be a scorpion, a dolphin, a flower, or even a mineral! As all of the stories and studies described in Part II have demonstrated, our entire universe may be intricately and intimately interconnected through vibration and meaning.

Two hundred years ago, devices like cell-phones or televisions were unthinkable. Today, we should not be so sure that there aren't other unknown and unthinkable forms of energies and fields surrounding us. If we all could just open our minds a bit, we might get some clues about how these fields and energies might be used to create the future we desire for ourselves and for the rest of humanity.

EXERCISE 2

❖ ❖ ❖

BEING PRESENT IN INNER SENSATION

In Exercise 1, we played with the world of outer sensation, especially the sensations of hearing and seeing. In Exercise 2, we will continue to play with sensation, but will turn our focus inward. What sensations can you feel within your body? You might be surprised by what you discover if you take some time and pay attention to this inner realm.

Exercise 2 can also be a very important tool for discovering physical holding patterns that may be creating health problems for you. By noticing such patterns and releasing them, you may be able to find relief from a variety of aches and pains as well as emotional problems. Don't forget: health is a mind/body affair. The sensations of your physical body are intimately connected to and even symbolic of your thoughts and emotions. As a result, internal body sensations can be a gateway and navigational tool for accessing many aspects of yourself and for discovering meaning in the process.

During this exercise, you may notice the following kinds of things that are normally below the radar of your awareness:

- Tension or pain in certain areas of your body.

- Postural habits that lead to discomfort.

- Sensations associated with particular emotions or thoughts.

STEP 1. Settle into the Now: "Feet. Seat. Back."

With your eyes open, follow the instructions for this step that were given in Exercise 1.

STEP 2. Focus your attention on inner sensation for 10-15 minutes.

Close your eyes and begin to focus on the world of sensation within your body. Begin by continuing with "Feet. Seat. Back." and focus more deeply on the sensations in your feet, seat and back. You can always return to "Feet. Seat. Back." if you become lost in thought or distracted.

Now, while maintaining a state of detachment and simple observation, notice physical sensations within your body. Feel the wind and the sensation of clothing on your skin. Feel sensations in your hands, arms, legs, chest, or face. Can you feel your heart beating? Notice your breathing. You may experience sensations of heat, cold, expansion, and tingling. If outside noises occur, just let them pass through you with a sense of detachment.

Next, notice if there are any points of tension or pain within your body—for example, in your neck, chest, abdomen, or back. Try to stay neutral and just observe. Acknowledge any sensations with a feeling of love and acceptance of yourself.

If any emotions arise, notice what sensations they produce in your body. Try to focus only upon these physical sensations and not on the "story" content associated with an emotion. Confine your attention to body sensations. Try not to "think" about what you are sensing—just sense.

You may also notice that sensations, tensions, holding patterns, or postural patterns slowly begin to shift. Just let your body instinctively relax or reposition itself; let your sensations evolve. Observe what happens with a feeling of detachment and love.

If you find a particular sensation difficult, try the following:

- Intentionally put a slight smile on your face.
- Internally recite the Emotional Freedom Technique (EFT) formula: "Even though I have this <sensation>, I deeply and completely accept myself."[1]

Here are some more things you might play with while relaxing in inner sensation:

- If you hear noises outside, do they create inner sensations within you? Can you sense the "energy" of a noise within your body?

- If you notice that a particular emotion is associated with an internal sensation, what happens if you "morph" this sensation? For example, if an emotion manifests as tension in your chest, what happens if you breathe and relax this tension? Do you feel better emotionally as well?

Most of us think that emotions are the same as thoughts—that is, mental words and images. But the truth is, emotions are more related to internal body sensations. The next time you become upset about something, try to distinguish between your thoughts about the circumstance and the internal body sensation of the emotion. Where is the sensation located? What does it feel like? Part of the process of conscious evolution is to learn to recognize, differentiate, and gain mastery over these different aspects of your being. You may find that, by dissipating the physical sensation of a troublesome emotion, you not only relieve the emotion but gain greater clarity of thought too.

Finally, remember to perform this exercise (and all exercises in this book) in a spirit of play and fun. There is no right or wrong experience. If your attention wanders (which it will), just settle again using "Feet. Seat. Back." You will find that these exercises become easier the more you try them. Have fun!

When you are done and return to your normal state of awareness, you may literally feel the return of mind chatter, emotions, and physical holding patterns and sensations. This is an important clue—because it tells you that these thoughts, emotions, and sensations are not *you*, they are only a part of you. You can change them at will, just as you just did during this exercise.

PART III

THE CHOICE POINT

At each moment of time—the Now—you stand at the gateway to an infinite number of possible futures in higher dimensional space. This gateway is the Choice Point.

Some of these futures are more likely to occur than others. If you do nothing, one of these probable futures will play itself out in a fairly predictable, even mechanistic way.

But as a conscious being, you also have the ability to affect how the future unfolds. Your experience of this ability is the sensation of free will.

One of the ways you can exert a force upon this unfolding is to use explicit action. Another way is through the subtle force of active consciousness, which allows you to enable unlikely unfoldings to occur.

CHAPTER 14

FORCES AND FIELDS

IN PART II, I DISCUSSED A VARIETY OF FIELDS THAT HAVE BEEN proposed to describe a deeper realm of activity within our universe: Sheldrake's *morphic field*; the *zero-point field (ZPF)* proposed by some physicists; the *psi field* studied by researchers of psychic phenomena; and Ervin Laszlo's *Akashic field*. Even the great physicist Nikola Tesla, in a 1907 paper entitled "Man's Greatest Achievement," mentioned the Indian notion of Akasha when he talked about an "original medium, a kind of force field, [that] becomes matter when prana, cosmic energy, acts on it, and when the action ceases, matter vanishes and returns to Akasha."[1] I believe it is likely that all of these fields are one and the same, or at least highly related to one another.

But what exactly *is* a field? According to the *Columbia Encyclopedia*, a field is a "region throughout which a force may be exerted." Back in the 1800s, chemist and physicist Michael Faraday developed this concept in order to explain the mysterious properties of magnets. People at the time were perplexed by the way magnets could exert instantaneous forces upon metal objects when nothing seemed to be transmitted between them. Faraday hypothesized that magnets are *always* emanating an influence or force; we just can't see it. And because a magnet's sphere of influence—its magnetic field—is ever-present, it seems to exert a force instantaneously, without any form of physical contact or obvious mode of transmission.

Here's another example of the field concept. The gravitational field is the realm of influence of gravity—the force that enables the Earth to hold the moon in its orbit, that holds the planets in their orbits around the sun, and that pulls us down when we jump into the air. Two other fields that have been discovered by science are associated with the forces that help to hold atoms together—the strong and weak nuclear forces.

Interestingly, fields can also be related to one another. For example, the magnetic field is related to the electric field because electricity can be used to create a magnet and a magnet can be used to create electricity. For this reason, the two fields are actually considered to be aspects of the same field—the electromagnetic field. As mentioned in Chapter 11, an important question in modern physics is whether all fields are, in fact, interrelated and aspects of a single underlying field—a *unified field*. If so, this field would form the foundation for all the others. And one interesting thing about the existence of such a field is that, for the various physics equations to work out mathematically, at least ten spatial dimensions would be required.[2]

So how does consciousness fit into all of this? If you think about it, *consciousness might also be viewed as a field—a region in which the force of consciousness is exerted*. For example, when we become "conscious" of something—when we feel aware, when thoughts pop into our minds—perhaps we are receiving and processing information arising from the field of consciousness. Just as we perceive the gravitational field as a feeling of weight or as the sensation of falling, perhaps "awareness" is our sensation of the consciousness field.

Things might go in the other direction as well. Not only may we feel the effects of the consciousness field, but we might also be able to exert our own forces upon it. In other words, *not only may we be receivers of consciousness, but we may also be generators*. Just as a magnet can both create a magnetic field and be influenced by the forces of other magnets, consciousness may be both a field we are affected by and an active force that we can exert. Instead of being puppets buffeted about by the field of consciousness that surrounds us, we may all be active participants in a grand ballet of energy, exerting our own active forces of consciousness into the mix.

Of course, from the standpoint of quantum physics, much of this is old hat. It is already accepted by physicists that, at the subatomic level, everything is a set of probabilities or potentialities affected by awareness. Even a simple act of observation—or, indeed, an *intention* to observe[3]—can cause changes in the subatomic realm. A quantum particle in several simultaneous states of "possibility" becomes jelled into a single reality when we exert the power of our gaze. In fact, if particles behave in a certain way once we decide to measure them, it is almost as if we are creating them or as if they are cooperating with our desires. But few of us believe that the mere act of forming an intention could have an observable effect on our day-to-day lives.

Perhaps we are wrong. The experiments with random event generators described in Chapter 12 certainly support the possibility that our thoughts and intentions can cause observable changes in the world. Another set of experiments, conducted by researchers on the effects of transcendental meditation, found that if enough meditators work collectively, the amount of violent crime in a city can be lowered for extended periods of time.[4, 5, 6] The truth may be that our beliefs and intentions *do* affect our collective reality in profound ways all the time; we just don't realize it. Researchers have found, for example, that when doctors dispense pills that they believe will work, the pills work better; and when they dispense pills that they do not believe will work, they don't work as well. This is true whether or not the pills are placebo or medicated, whether or not the doctors know what they are actually dispensing or have come into contact with their patients, and even whether or not the patients are human. It's often the intent or belief of a doctor that matters the most.[7]

Of course, a general acceptance of consciousness as an active force that affects our day-to-day lives would turn our view of reality completely on its head! No wonder skeptics denounce every study that proves the reality of paranormal phenomena. Just as it has been true in the past, when revolutionary ideas are proposed or even scientifically proven, the knee-jerk reaction is to try and protect the status quo. First skeptics claim that such results are incorrect or poorly developed. If that fails, they claim fraud or delusion on the part of the investigators. I remember hearing about a skeptic who said that they would never accept that homeopathy works, no matter how many excellent studies were done. Homeopathy was simply "impossible." That is exactly what Galileo's contemporaries said when he told them that there were moons orbiting around Jupiter. The existence of these moons was simply "impossible," so they refused to look through the telescope to see them.

Thankfully, there *are* some sincere scientists who are willing to open up their minds and at least take an honest look. Rather than fearing for their careers or the collapse of an accepted world-view, scientists who are brave enough to explore the paranormal or alternative forms of medicine know that the highest good lies in expanding the frontiers of human knowledge. For this, they are willing to risk challenging the "party line."

So if we *do* accept the possibility of an active force of consciousness, how might it operate? That's where higher spatial dimensions might come into play.

CHAPTER 15

⟩⟨

A RADICAL HYPOTHESIS—
CONSCIOUSNESS IN
HIGHER DIMENSIONS

"We may have very good reason for saying that we are ourselves beings
of four dimensions and we are turned toward the third dimension with
only one of our sides, i.e., with only a small part of our being."[1]

—P.D. OUSPENSKY

IN CHAPTER 2, I BEGAN TO EXPLAIN THE NATURE OF HIGHER
spatial dimensions. In this chapter we'll dive deeper into this mind-
boggling realm as I describe my own model of consciousness and how
the force of active consciousness might be operating within it. But
first, I'd like you to reorient yourself a bit.

Try to think of this chapter as a thought experiment—a mental
exercise in exploring a radical hypothesis. As it turns out, such experiments are a recognized way of expanding knowledge. The approach is
called the *hypothetico-deductive* method of inquiry.[2] Instead of inferring
a scientific hypothesis from experience, the hypothetico-deductive
approach proposes a new theory and then tries to determine whether
observations line up with it. Many great scientists, like Newton and
Einstein, used this technique to create new breakthroughs in scientific
thought and vision.

Note, however, that this approach is quite different from what is
used in most scientific endeavors. For example, one guideline that is

often used in artificial intelligence is the requirement that a computer only make use of information that can be derived from what it already knows. In general, much of conventional science operates in the same way. It's "safest" for scientists to limit the horizons of their research to that which can be derived from accepted knowledge. But it can also be stifling. True revolutions in science require us to puncture these limits and explore beyond what is accepted or known. As philosopher Paul Feyerabend said, "The consistency condition which demands that new hypotheses agree with accepted theories is unreasonable because it preserves the older theory, and not the better theory."[3] So embark upon a "far out" thought experiment with me and try to leave your doubts behind for a few minutes. Let's see what we can discover.

THE FOURTH DIMENSION

Let me begin by saying that when I say "higher dimensions," I'm not talking about figurative realms populated by mysterious beings. I'm literally talking about higher *spatial* dimensions. Just as a two-dimensional universe can be understood as a flat surface, and just as we ourselves live in three-dimensional space with objects possessing length, width, and height, a four-dimensional universe would actually be a space with one extra spatial dimension. While it's easy to visualize other ways of adding a "dimension" to our reality—for example, a dimension of *time* would add a timestamp to each object, and a dimension of *color* would add a color—getting our brains to wrap around an extra spatial dimension is quite difficult.

And why limit ourselves to four dimensions? If a fourth spatial dimension truly exists, it stands to reason that even higher spatial dimensions might as well. Maybe the true reality of God's creation is infinite dimensional. Personally, I think so. But for now, let's just try to grasp the fourth dimension. The existence of just this one extra spatial dimension would help to explain the paranormal phenomena described in Part II, and could also help us understand the power of active consciousness.

It turns out that a fascination with the fourth dimension was a fad of the late 1800s. This was the era in which mediums, like today's television medium John Edward, were quite popular. It was also the era in which *spiritualism* emerged, an American religious movement focused on communicating with the spirits of those who had passed away. Scientists of the time proposed the fourth spatial dimension as a way of explaining spiritist phenomena. Ultimately, however, nearly all the mediums of the 1800s were debunked as frauds and as a consequence, speculation about the fourth dimension fell into disrepute as well. But perhaps we should not have been so hasty to throw the baby out with the bath water.

As mathematician Rudy Rucker points out in his book, *The Fourth Dimension*,[4] the first philosopher to discuss the possibility of a fourth dimension was Immanuel Kant (1724-1804). The idea of spirits as four-dimensional beings was then popularized by Johann Carl Friederich Zollner (1834-1882), an astronomer at the University of Leipzig. The first true theoretician of the fourth dimension, however, was British mathematician Charles Hinton (1853-1907), known for his work on visualizing the geometry of higher dimensional space.[a] In addition to his mathematical work, Hinton also wrote a series of science fiction books, such as *What is the Fourth Dimension?* and *A Plane World*,[b] which focus on realms with different dimensionality than our own. He also believed that higher spatial dimensions could be used to prove the inherently unified nature of the universe.

Hinton came up with a variety of ways to help us understand the fourth dimension and its properties. One was the strategy I used in

---

[a] An interesting side note: Hinton was married to Mary Boole, whose father George Boole was the founder of mathematical logic and Boolean algebra — an important foundational mathematics for computer science. Mary's mother, Mary Everest Boole, was a serious devotee of homeopathy, and the Everest family (yes, the world's highest peak, Mt. Everest, was named after Mary's uncle) often traveled to France to be treated homeopathically by Dr. Samuel Hahnemann himself.

[b] A *plane* is the mathematical term for a two-dimensional space.

Chapter 2: examining the difference between two and three dimensions and then, by analogy, grasping the difference between three and four dimensions. Here's another illustration of this technique.

If you take two flat two-dimensional surfaces and intersect them in the context of three-dimensional space, what do you get? The answer: a line, which is a one-dimensional object. To understand this, just imagine taking two sheets of paper and intersecting them. By analogy, if you take two three-dimensional spaces and intersect them in the context of four-dimensional space, what will you get? The answer: a two-dimensional space—a flat surface. That means, if there were another three-dimensional world floating out there and it happened to overlap and intersect with us, the region of overlap between our two worlds would appear to us like a flat, impossibly thin sheet of paper (see Figure III.1). Could this be an explanation for the phenomenon of ghosts? Are ghosts simply ephemeral two-dimensional visions of beings in another three-dimensional world? That's what Zollner proposed in the mid 1800s.

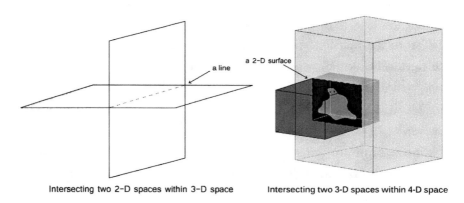

Intersecting two 2-D spaces within 3-D space   Intersecting two 3-D spaces within 4-D space

FIGURE III.1

Here's another puzzle. When you think about it, a two-dimensional surface cuts three-dimensional space into two regions: the region on one side of the surface and the region on the other side. Just imagine an infinitely large piece of paper floating in space; half of our universe would fall on one side of the paper and the rest would fall on the other side. In the same way, a three-dimensional space would cut the world of four dimensions into two regions: one half on one side, and one half on the other side (see Figure III.2). Hinton called these two sides of the four-dimensional universe *ana* and *kata*.

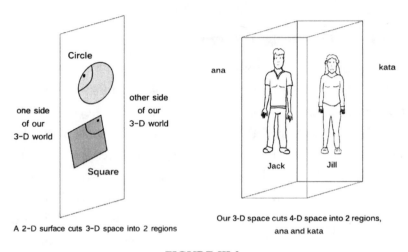

A 2-D surface cuts 3-D space into 2 regions

Our 3-D space cuts 4-D space into 2 regions, ana and kata

FIGURE III.2

By using the notion of ana and kata, we can easily visualize many interesting things about the fourth dimension and its relationship to our three-dimensional reality. In particular, a four-dimensional creature would have amazing and seemingly omniscient abilities to us, because he or she would be able to view or enter and exit our three-dimensional world from ana or kata.

Imagine Mr. 4-D. He would be able to see inside our bodies just as easily as we could see inside the Circle and Square, because he could stand outside of our three-dimensional world (in ana or kata) and look in on us. He would also be able to see points in our universe that are extremely distant, and tell us about them. And just as we could tie a rope between the insides of the Circle and Square, Mr. 4-D could invisibly connect the insides of Jill to the insides of Jack by hiding a rope in ana or kata. Finally, because every moment of our past or future is also just another three-dimensional world in a sequence of three-dimensional worlds existing in four-dimensional space, Mr. 4-D could see our past and all of our possible futures, just as the Star Trek wormhole aliens could. In fact, Mr. 4-D could even see three-dimensional worlds that have nothing to do with our own reality.

PHYSICS AND HIGHER DIMENSIONS

Of course, speculation about higher dimensions is nothing new to physicists; they have considered the possible existence of four or more spatial dimensions for a long time. For example, between 1907 and 1915, Einstein developed the theory of *general relativity*, which states that gravity exists because a large mass causes three-dimensional space to bend within the fourth dimension. This is easy to visualize if you drop down into two dimensions. What if the mass of a large Circle caused the flat world of two dimensions to bend around it in three-dimensional space? Just imagine bending a large piece of paper around the edges of the Circle. That would cause everything near the Circle

A massive circle bending 2-D space around it

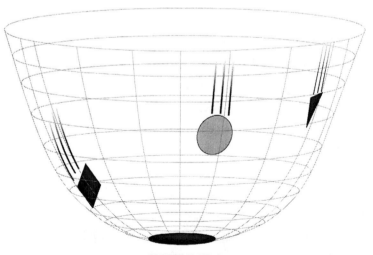

FIGURE III.3

to fall toward it (see Figure III.3). In the same way, bending three-dimensional space around massive bodies like planets would cause nearby objects to fall toward them. Voila! Gravity.

And what about wormholes, like the one in *Star Trek* that connected distant parts of the galaxy? Things like that aren't just science fiction fantasies. Physicists believe that three-dimensional space might be bent so heavily by the mass of a black hole that the fabric of the universe folds back on itself, causing one part to intersect with another, thereby creating a portal between them. To see how this could happen, just imagine bending a sheet of paper so much that two distant points on it touch.

In 1972, physicist John Wheeler took these ideas even further. He proposed the theory of *geometrodynamics*, which hypothesized that matter not only caused geometrical distortions in higher dimensional space (causing phenomena like gravity), but that matter itself *was* the result of distortions in higher-dimensional space. Today's *string theory*, a candidate theory for a unified field, postulates something similar—that all known forms of matter are actually manifestations of energy vibrating in the realm of ten or more spatial dimensions. Indeed, more and more physicists are accepting the reality of higher spatial dimensions, because they *must* be real if string theory and other proposed theories in quantum physics hold true. As Harvard physicist Lisa Randall points out in her book, *Warped Passages*,[5] these higher spatial dimensions may simply be so tiny that we cannot detect them yet. Or they might be infinite in size, but elude us because they are curved. So in spite of the fact that they are not yet apparent to us, widespread scientific acceptance of higher dimensions may be just around the corner.

One question that still begs to be answered, though, is: What kind of access can *we* have to the fourth or higher dimensions? Even if our bodies are stuck here in three-dimensional space, is there a four-dimensional aspect of ourselves that we're simply not aware of? Ouspensky, Gurdjieff's student and chronicler, thought so. In fact, he felt that the primary goal of Gurdjieff's teachings was to help us access our higher dimensional selves. As Rudy Rucker writes, "For Ouspensky, the fourth dimension was not only a spatial concept but a type of consciousness, an awareness of greater complexities and higher unities."[6] Thus, rather than trying to contact other beings in the fourth dimension, perhaps our real goal should be to tap into our *own* four dimensionality. Indeed, I believe it is from this higher dimensional perspective that we may be able to exert the deep power of active consciousness—the ability to navigate and influence the unfolding of our three-dimensional lives.

THE BRANCHING TREE

> "At the deepest level, our world can be regarded as a
> pattern in infinite-dimensional space, a space in which we
> and our minds move like fish in water."[7]
>
> —RUDY RUCKER

In Chapter 2, I began to give you an idea of how the unfolding of our three-dimensional world might be seen from the perspective of the fourth dimension. In particular, a complete human life—every activity of the inner and outer physical body—would simply appear as an eternal shape or object in four-dimensional space. In fact, from a four-dimensional perspective, the human experience of time would be irrelevant; our entire existence would just be one big four-dimensional Now. As Meister Eckhart, a philosopher and theologian of the Middle Ages, said, "Time gone a thousand years ago is now as present and as near to God as this very instant." [8]

So if our lives are simply eternal objects in four-dimensional space, what determines their shape? That's when things get interesting. At each point in time *we make choices*. Do we walk left or right? Does our body repair itself or does it descend further into disease? At each instant, we choose one from a potentially infinite number of possible futures that lie before us. And while it may seem that only one future is chosen at each point in time, perhaps all of the other possible choices and futures exist in four-dimensional space too. If so, then our many *potential* lives—from a four-dimensional perspective—would look like a vast branching tree of possibilities.

Interestingly, this idea was hypothesized by physicist Hugh Everett in 1957.[9] In the quantum realm, particles exist in many simultaneous states until they are observed and become "solidified" into a single state. To us, these quantum choices seem random. Everett proposed, however, that there really is no randomness at all. Each and every one of the possible choices for a particle actually exists—*in another parallel world*. We ourselves perceive only one choice—the one that takes place in *our* world. But Everett asserted that the others choices exist too—in other worlds. Indeed, parallel versions of ourselves exist in those other worlds too, and they witness the particle resolving into other possible states. Mind boggling! It sounds like science fiction, and indeed, many science fiction stories have been written based on this idea. But what if it's science fact? I believe that this conception of our universe may also be the basis for how active consciousness might operate.

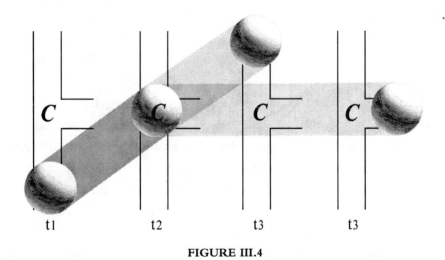

FIGURE III.4

Let's begin to consider this mind-bending idea by simply imagining a single point of branching. Consider the world of a three-dimensional ball, depicted in Figure III.4. The ball begins, at time *t1*, at the bottom of a road. When it arrives at point *C* (which occurs at time *t2*), the ball must make a choice. Does it move along the branch moving to the right, or does it continue moving upward? In one future reality, the ball has moved up at time *t3*. In another future reality, it has branched to the right at *t3*, creating a fork in four-dimensional space.

Let's call *C* a *choice point*—a point in space and time at which the Now splits into two or more possible futures. In order for this split to occur, some force must be exerted. If this does not happen, there may be only one possible future—the one that would play itself out according to the mechanistic laws of nature. For the ball, this might be the future in which it continues moving upward, in a straight line. But if some kind of force, intention, or will is brought to bear at point *C*, the Now will split into more than one possible future, like a branching tree. And when we humans exert such a force upon our own lives, we experience the sensation of *free will*.

Of course, people usually make rather mundane choices at choice points. We might choose to move our arm or walk to the grocery store. But at times the actions we take can be much more subtle—like when our thoughts affect the behavior of a random event generator. *What I would like to propose is that this more subtle kind of force is what underlies the power of active consciousness.* I'll call it the *C-force*. And just as the experiments with random event generators showed, a person's use of the C-force can influence not only his or her own life, but can also affect the unfolding of the greater reality around us. As a result, each and every one of us helps to create a much greater collective reality—an infinitely complex shape in four-dimensional space. Indeed, even if we took into account every tiny mechanism already understood by conventional science, the influence of our collective use of the C-force would be beyond our imaginations! In fact, it might even be possible that our influence extends *beyond* four dimensions. If so, we humans—seemingly three-dimensional creatures—may have creative potential that we have only just begun to tap into.

CHAPTER 16

٭

THE PROCESS OF ACTIVE CONSCIOUSNESS

"[Y]ou are not separate from the Non-Physical; you are an extension—a Leading Edge extension—of that Non-Physical energy. You are not here on planet Earth trying to get back to what is Non-Physical, but instead, you are summoning the Non-Physical outward to where *you* are. And in that summoning, *All-That-Is* expands, and your summoning is the reason for the expansion." [1]

—ESTHER AND JERRY HICKS (THE TEACHINGS OF ABRAHAM)

THE LAST CHAPTER'S DISCUSSION OF HIGHER DIMENSIONS WAS fairly esoteric and theoretical. Now let's get a bit more practical. After all, my goal is to enable you to use the force of active consciousness in your own life.

When I chose the term C-force, I used the letter "C" intentionally—because it serves as a reminder of several important aspects of this force: Consciousness, Choice, and Creativity. Using the C-force—the force of active consciousness—you can make beneficial choices that take you down desired paths in life. You can create new and unlikely paths as well. Either way, harnessing the power of active consciousness will enable you to make the improbable much more probable and become an active creator of your own destiny. Let's examine this process now in more detail.

As discussed in Chapter 5, one way in which the C-force might be used is through the process of *manifestation*. In this case, you enable an

105

unlikely combination of otherwise mundane events to occur so that a desired goal comes about. For example, let's say that you would like to get a desirable parking spot near a restaurant. The restaurant might be in the middle of a busy city where parking spots are hard to find, but finding the perfect spot at just the right time could definitely happen. Everything just needs to be coordinated correctly: the choices made by the person who parked in the spot before you, the route you choose to drive, the timing of the lights as you are driving, and so on. By invoking the power of active consciousness (using the method I will describe in Chapter 18), these fortuitous choices and events could be enabled.

Or let's say that you would like to find a new job with better pay. You've been stuck in a rut for a long time and can't figure out how to leave your current job situation. Through the process of manifestation, however, it may be quite possible that a sequence of events could occur that leads you to your goal. Perhaps a bout with the flu forces you to take a couple of weeks off from work. As a result, your quirky boss decides to lay you off. Now you've been forced to leave your job. The following week, a long-lost friend calls you unexpectedly. She tells you about an acquaintance who needs to hire someone with your exact qualifications—the dream job. With this connection, you get the new job with ease.

Another way the C-force might operate is through the process of *creation*. In this case, a bit more magic is involved because much more unlikely (but still possible) unfoldings occur. Whereas manifestation is about enabling an unlikely *combination* of events to occur, creation is more about enabling more unlikely choices and events to appear in the first place.

For example, let's say that you suffer from chronic eczema. Given the natural tendency of the body to recreate itself in the same way, it is most likely that your skin will continue to suffer from this condition. You might apply some cortisone cream, which chemically forces the body to suppress the eczema, but the innate tendency for your skin to develop eczema has not gone away. The next time you experience a period of anxiety or come into contact with an allergen, the eczema flares up.

But remember this: your skin is always sloughing off and regenerating. The outer layer of your skin (the epidermis) is replaced every month. There is a *possibility* that your skin could regenerate without this problem and that it would never return again. It's not very probable, but it *is* possible. Similarly, it is *possible* that a cancerous tumor could be broken down by the natural defenses of the body without the use of poisonous chemotherapy or toxic radiation. It's not very probable, but it *is* possible.

I believe that the C-force—the force of active consciousness—can be used to create such improbable but possible choices for the body. For example, a patient could use the power of active consciousness to enable their skin to regenerate without eczema or their cancerous tumor to be broken down and absorbed. Such medical cases of "spontaneous remission" do occur. Because doctors cannot understand or explain them, they sweep them under the rug by saying that their original diagnosis was mistaken or that the cure was an unexplainable fluke. But what if more of us could tap into this kind of healing through the C-force—the *Cure* force? It would be wonderful! We could be spared many toxic medicines and expensive medical bills too.

In fact, "energy" medicines like homeopathy, acupuncture, and hands-on healing may make this particular application of the C-force substantially easier to achieve. That's because they operate not only on the physical body, but also on a subtler aspect of our selves—what is often called the "energy body" (a subject that will be a primary topic of discussion in Part IV). By helping to dislodge problems within this invisible realm—a realm that most alternative medical systems view as the true origin of disease—such treatments vastly increase the probability that the physical body will be able to create a healthier future. As a result, they also make healing applications of the C-force easier to achieve.

Here's a simple illustration. For many years, all the expert help of my homeopaths could not cure my athlete's foot. Each summer, our vacation in the moist lake region of Muskoka, Ontario would trigger another bout of itchy feet. I'd try to cope, but ultimately the itching became too intense and I would suppress the problem with foot powder. And just as predicted by homeopathic theory, my repeated suppression of athlete's foot each year led to a worsening of the problem.

However in 2008, when I returned home from Canada resigned to another month of anti-fungal powder, my homeopath recommended a new remedy for me. That night, I slept without being awakened by itchy feet for the first time in weeks. Over the course of the next three months, my athlete's foot slowly disappeared. First, the acutely itchy pustules turned brown and healed. Then, the more intransigent tinea rubrum, a mocassin-like hardening of my soles, slowly peeled off and healed. My skin regenerated without athlete's foot, and without my using foot powder! Amazing.

Interestingly, that summer I had also targeted my active consciousness meditations on my athlete's foot. Perhaps these meditations, coupled with the help of the new remedy, enabled my skin to choose a healing path into the future. These meditations may also have enabled my homeopath to choose a better remedy for me. Thus, through the combined use of active consciousness and homeopathy, I had finally managed to cause a fungus-free future to unfold.

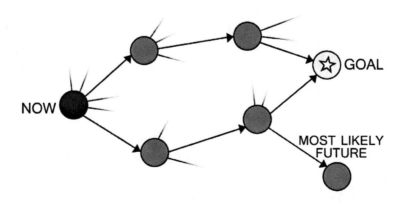

FIGURE III. 5

So how does this fit within with the four-dimensional model described earlier? Let's look at some diagrams to find out. In Figure III.5, I use circles to represent choice points and arrows to indicate possible futures that emanate from them. Let's say that you are currently at NOW. The circle labeled GOAL is a future that you'd like to reach—say, one in which you have a new job. The circle labeled MOST LIKELY FUTURE is the most likely or probable outcome—the one in which you stay at your current job. As the diagram illustrates, you can reach your goal in at least two ways—either by choosing or creating a new path right now (branching upward immediately), or by doing so a little later on. For instance, right NOW, you might decide to quit your job. Or you might create an improbable future—through creation—where a freak accident or illness ultimately leads to you being laid off. By using active consciousness to enable new choices to appear and to help you make the correct choices over time, you may find that you are ultimately led to your goal of a new and better job.

Now let's consider my story about athlete's foot. Figure III.6 depicts how I acquired athlete's foot (represented by the broken outer circle) and how it's 99% likely that I'll continue to have this problem indefinitely.

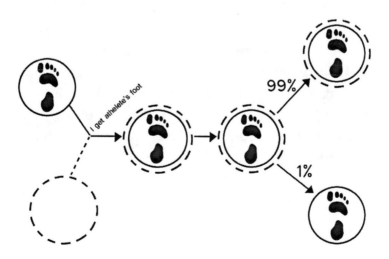

FIGURE III.6

However, as depicted in Figure III.7, by taking the correct homeo-pathic remedy, I make it only 25% likely that this condition will con-tinue and 75% likely that it will be cured. This increases the chance I can then use active consciousness to enable my body to choose a future without itchy feet.

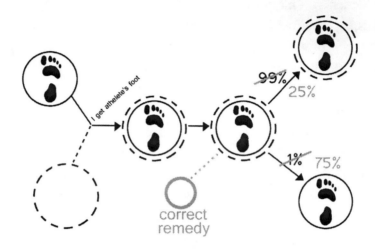

FIGURE III.7

In many ways, it's all about possibilities and probabilities. Even if something is improbable, it can still be possible. And if it's possible, the force of active consciousness—the C-force—can play a part in making it happen. Using manifestation, you can make the right choices at the right time and, through an unlikely combination of such choices, you are led to your goal. Using creation, an unlikely choice appears before you; you just need to take it. In the next chapter, we'll consider this issue of possibility versus probability a bit more deeply.

CHAPTER 17

✦

THE FORCE IS WITHIN YOU

"The future [is] composed of 'crystallizing possibilities'." [1]

—INGO SWANN

"Perhaps the mind can influence the probabilities of happenings which are 'probabilistic,' not rigidly determined in advance." [2]

—RUPERT SHELDRAKE

PROBABILITY IS ALL ABOUT THE LIKELIHOOD OR CHANCE THAT something will happen. In contrast, *possibility* is a more cut-and-dried affair; something is either possible or it's not. As it turns out, probability and possibility also have a lot to do with the process of active consciousness.

If you think about it, the probability of something occurring is usually determined by larger encompassing factors—the circumstances that surround an event. The possibility of an event, however, is usually determined by smaller intrinsic factors—the mechanisms at lower levels of detail that combine to make it happen. For example, it is certainly *possible* to get a parking spot on a busy street, but it might be *improbable* because of larger issues like population density or time of day. Similarly, it might be *improbable* that you can get a better job because of the state of the economy. It's certainly *possible* though, because of the small daily occurrences that could make it happen. The way philosopher Ken Wilber puts it, "The lower [holon] sets the possibilities of the higher; the higher sets the probabilities of the lower." [3]

So what's a *holon*? The term "holon" was first coined by writer Arthur Koestler to refer to "an entity that is itself a *whole* and simultaneously a *part* of some other whole."[4] For example, a hydrogen atom is a holon and so is an oxygen atom, but when two hydrogen atoms and one oxygen atom combine, they become part of another holon— a water molecule. Similarly, the individual cells of your body are holons, which in turn may be part of the larger holon of your circulatory system, which is then part of the holon of your complete physical body. Indeed, your physical body might be part of an even larger holon—the one that includes the various layers of your energy body.

Holons can also be conceptual. For example, cultures, nations, economies, religions, and levels of consciousness can also be viewed as holons. According to Wilber's theory about how the universe evolves, when physical, cultural, political, and spiritual forms of evolution occur, it's because larger holons are created that incorporate and transcend the holons that comprise it. For example, democratic government is a holon that evolved from monarchy; while a democracy may have a single head of state like a monarchy does, this position is elected rather than inherited.

As part of his theory, Wilber outlines a range of qualities and properties that holons tend to manifest. One is the principle that I just mentioned about possibility and probability: that encompassing holons determine the probability of events, while component holons determine their possibility. For instance, because of the way individual skin cell holons regenerate, it's *possible* that athlete's foot could be replaced by healthy skin. But because of the encompassing skin–system holon and its interaction with a fungal holon, this occurrence may be *improbable*.

So how does this relate to active consciousness?

The secret to making a desired outcome more probable is to create a new higher-level holon that includes the desired outcome.

Do you want a future without athlete's foot? Then create a new holon—a foot with healthy skin. Do you want a future with a better job? Create a new holon for your future that incorporates the best job you can imagine. In other words, envision and create that future, rather than believing your employment situation is hopeless. Do you want a world at peace and free from pollution? Create that holon too. *But how do you create a holon? And is it even possible?*

If you doubt that you have the power to create or manifest anything, consider this: even animals can use the power of active consciousness to bend reality to their will. In her book *The Field*, Lynne McTaggart describes how baby chicks, simply by desiring the presence of a mother, were able to affect the behavior of a randomly moving machine. A French scientist named René Peoc'h created a "robot mother hen" (a mobile version of the random event generators or REGs used in the experiments described in Chapter 12) and 'imprinted' it on the chicks soon after they were born. It was then left to roam freely outside the chicks' cage. Amazingly, Peoc'h found that the mobile REG was moving toward the chicks more than it normally would, given random chance. Somehow, the chicks' collective desire to be near their "mother" was having an effect on the behavior of an otherwise random device![5,6]

Naturally, it's not just that the chicks wanted something. We all want to be well, we all want to have a great job, we all want comfort and love, and we all desire world peace. Simply wanting something can't be enough. Where we humans differ from chicks, however, is in the complexity of our thoughts, emotions, and desires. While human beings definitely benefit from the power of our conventional thought processes—learning from the past and projecting possible outcomes into the future—it is our typical jumble of thoughts and beliefs that can also derail the potential of active consciousness.

Here's an example. As you drive home from work, you might plan out a route based on past traffic patterns and today's errands. But when you get stuck in a traffic jam, your body is flooded with irritation.

Your mind wanders to the annoying things your boss said today. This brings up repeating "stories" about your life that you have come to believe: "No one respects me"; "I'll never succeed"; "Life is unfair." Now your stomach hurts because you've become angry and frustrated. This reminds you of the meal you need to cook for your family. You begin to worry that the grocery store will run out of your favorite dessert by the time you get there. And on it goes. The problem is, your life is influenced by this jumble of thoughts and emotions. No wonder the universe seems so chaotic and random! Not only are you projecting a cloud of randomness around you, but so is everyone else.

Luckily, manifesting and creating aren't that easy. Otherwise, all of our worst fears would always come true. The holons of nature, culture, and the physical world tend to have very strong habits, and as a result, things work out mostly as expected. But if we really could see the collective effect of all of our consciousnesses upon the world, things might not seem so random at all—just incomprehensibly complex.

Naturally, almost no one can become a perfect master of their thoughts and emotions. But if we could become *more* aware of these processes and get *more* in touch with a deeper, more focused form of consciousness, we might be able to bring about our desires a bit more often—just as the baby chicks did. It's just a matter of practice and using the right technology.

And don't forget: the chicks focused their desires for "mother" together as a group. Because collective active consciousness is even more powerful than individual active consciousness working alone, the chicks were able to be even more effective. Similarly, if more of us could get together and focus our collective active consciousness on desirable goals for Earth, the effects could be truly awesome. So let's get started!

CHAPTER 18

FOUR STEPS TO ACTIVE CONSCIOUSNESS

"Consciousness is technology—the only technology that exists."[1]

—*DANIEL PINCHBECK*

THIS CHAPTER DESCRIBES WHAT I BELIEVE TO BE ONE RECIPE FOR active consciousness. In many ways, it is similar to techniques described by others—for example, those found in the Abraham teachings channeled by Esther Hicks.[2] It incorporates four key elements or steps, each of which I've labeled with a catch phrase to serve as a reminder or mnemonic device for you: *NOW+; PURE GOAL; LET GO*; and *CHOOSE JOY*.

1. **NOW+**: Focus your attention on the Now and then enter a state of open-heartedness and compassion—a state that I call NOW+.

2. **PURE GOAL**: While in NOW+, embody your goal— both in content and feeling. Truly be in the goal state— without harboring any doubt.

3. **LET GO**: Once you leave NOW+ and resume life as usual, let go and trust that your goal will come to pass. Continue to release all doubt.

4. **CHOOSE JOY**: As you go through your day, stay in contact with NOW+ as much as possible—especially when you

need to make a choice. This enhanced state of awareness will enable you to use your deeper emotions as a guide. A calm feeling of happiness or joy will indicate that you are on the right track. A contracted state of unhappiness provides a sign that you are veering off course. Choose joy and you will head in the right direction toward your goal.

These four steps may sound easy, and with practice and some effort at self-development they can be. But at first you will probably have some difficulties. *Keep at it.* As you do, your ability to harness active consciousness will improve bit by bit. And as it does, you will notice that you are achieving your goals more often. The only way to succeed is to keep trying.

So why these four steps? Let's return to the four-dimensional model described in Chapters 15 and 16 to see why NOW+, PURE GOAL, LET GO, and CHOOSE JOY make sense.

NOW+

All meditative practices and most wisdom traditions stress the importance of training oneself to get into the Now. One reason is that deep active consciousness emanates from this vantage point. Recurring every instant of your life, the Now is a constant opportunity to exercise active consciousness and direct your trajectory through four-dimensional space. In other words, *the Now is the Choice Point.*

Unfortunately, for most of us, the Now usually passes us by. We may be awake and we may be thinking, but we aren't paying any attention to the Now. Instead, we tend to project many possible paths into the future, as if we were planning out a chess game. Or we spend a lot of time dwelling on the past, reviewing the things that we've done or said: "Why did I say A instead of B?" "What if I had done X instead of Y?"

Because of these tendencies, we literally become lost in our possible futures and mired in the past. Who knows? We may even be projecting an energetic part of ourselves down these trajectories in four-dimensional space without realizing it. And as we scurry back and forth between the past and the future, our bodies are subjected to their emotional residues—the sorrows and regrets of the past, and anxieties about futures that may never come to pass.

While we're busy doing this, of course, we're not enjoying the present. We don't truly see and feel what's happening right Now. As a result, we are missing precious moments and losing opportunities to manifest and create. Indeed, because we aren't consciously sensing our feelings and intuitions in the Now, we are also losing access to information that could help guide us. That's why the road to active consciousness begins with learning to rest in the Now. And once you get there, reaching NOW+ —the state of open-heartedness and com-passion in the Now—is fairly easy. Simply ask for it.

One way to move from Now into NOW+ is to bring beloved family members, friends, or pets into your awareness. By evoking lov-ing and compassionate feelings for those you truly hold dear, you will begin to sense what the state of NOW+ feels like in your body. Then, you will be able to call it up much more quickly and easily. Personally, I find that once I am in the Now, simply putting a smile on my face gently pushes me into NOW+. The exercises in this book (especially Exercise 4 at the end of Part IV) will also help make NOW+ much more accessible to you.

I believe NOW+ is a primary gateway to active consciousness be-cause it provides access to deep forms of intuition and information about what is possible. It is an expanded state of being that enables you to tap into the passenger inside your carriage—your deeper Self. This Self is the wise and compassionate soul that resides within you. It understands much better than your ego or your personality what your goals are and how to achieve them in a way that truly serves your needs. The Self also has a broader or higher-dimensional view of things. When you are in the Now, you are free, like a blank slate. But when you are in NOW+, you are tapping into the deeper wisdom and power of the Self.

PURE GOAL

"There is a substantial difference between the words 'believe in your dreams' and actually being in vibrational alignment with your dreams. Your words are not your point of attraction—but your vibration is."[3]

—ESTHER AND JERRY HICKS (THE TEACHINGS OF ABRAHAM)

As the Hawaiian shamans say, your thoughts tend to manifest and create the future. So if you really want to bring a new state of being into your life, you must learn to evoke its energy or vibration as completely as you can. Try to remember this: Even if you spend a lot of time visualizing a better future, if you are also harboring doubts, those doubts can cancel things out. The same thing goes for your fears. President Franklin Roosevelt was truly wise when he said, "The only thing we have to fear is fear itself." Or consider the words of Jamie Sams and David Carson when they describe what Native American wisdom has to say about Rabbit—the animal totem that represents the archetype of Fear:

> "...Rabbit medicine people are so afraid of tragedy, illness, disaster, and 'being taken,' that they call those very fears to them to teach them lessons. The keynote here is: what you resist will persist! What you fear most is what you become."[4]

In other words, if you truly want to bring a desired goal to you, enter NOW+ and truly *embody* your goal. Feel its vibration. Experience it fully—*without fears and doubts*. Create a holon or larger reality that encompasses your goal. Why? Because when you are in PURE GOAL, it's as if you are lighting up that desired reality out in four-dimensional space. This light helps you reach your goal by illuminating a correct path to it, perhaps via intuitive feelings that you notice along the way. Just as shining light of a particular frequency upon a hologram highlights those components that were made by lasers of the same frequency, being in the state or vibration of PURE GOAL helps reinforce and strengthen improbable paths that can lead you there.

LET GO

"By letting it go it all gets done. The world is won by those who let it go.
But when you try and try, the world is beyond the winning."

—LAO TZU

Of course, it's impossible to stay in NOW+ and PURE GOAL all the time. Once you reenter your normal state of awareness, the voice of your chattering mind and the pull of your emotions will tend to take over. Doubts and fears will resurface. While these wayward thoughts and feelings will probably have less impact than those emanating from NOW+, they may still lead you astray. At the very least, they will diminish your ability to take advantage of intuitive feelings that could help guide you.

That's why it's very useful to simply tell yourself: *Let go.* Try not to get attached to an outcome. Attachments contract your emotional state and create more doubt and worry. Instead, have confidence and trust. Rather than pushing or forcing, let things flow and follow your day. The Abraham teachings described by Esther and Jerry Hicks are full of techniques for dispelling fears and doubts and letting go. One catch phrase they often use is: "Turn it over to the Universal Manager."[5] The idea is that once you've entered PURE GOAL, simply thank the Universal Manager (essentially, the deeper Self that is always working for you in the background) and let go in the knowledge that things will be taken care of.

CHOOSE JOY

So you've entered NOW+, envisioned and experienced PURE GOAL, and LET GO. What's next? Obviously, things must happen that bring you to your desired destination. Your use of active consciousness in NOW+ might have created new paths and possibilities for you and might even have increased the probability that you will follow them, but ultimately, the "everyday you" must participate in the process as well. Opportunities will arise, but will you take them? Or will you just sit at home and watch TV? And how will you know what's a genuine opportunity? After all, sitting at home and watching TV might actually be the right choice. You might get that fateful call from your friend that leads you to your new job. Or a TV show might provide some new insights that lead you to a cure for your health problem or suggest a new career direction for you.

Here's where intuition and inner guidance come in. Remember Harry Potter and his good luck potion, Felix Felicis? After taking it, Harry just knew, with a feeling of real joy in his heart, exactly what to do to reach his goal. The trick is to realize that even when you aren't consciously aware of it, your inner Self is always sitting in the carriage of your being and can provide guidance to you. You just have to be still, peek inside the carriage, and ask for it. It's really all about achieving a state of *relaxed alertness*—an ability to flow through your day, while remaining aware of signals and intuitions coming from the Self.

Luckily, these signals aren't hidden or obscure; they can be found within your body. Observing them can be as simple as tuning in to happy joyful feelings or to more negative sensations like contraction or lack of ease. Call it your sixth sense. In other words, making productive choices—CHOOSING JOY—is really a matter of learning to be aware of these intuitions and developing an ability to distinguish between genuine information and feelings that are simply the fears or hopes of the ego. It just takes a bit of practice.

The best way I've found to CHOOSE JOY is to seek the guidance of the Self while in a state of NOW+. Not sure whether to go to a party or stay home? Get into NOW+ by using the meditative techniques suggested in this book. Then, bring the choice into this relaxed state of awareness. Does going to the party create a sense of calm or joy? Or do you feel a sense of anxiety and apprehension? Let these feelings be your guide. You may also get other types of information while in NOW+. Listen to this inner wisdom and you will likely achieve much better results for yourself.

Why does this work? As the Hickses point out in the Abraham teachings, your emotional state is like a measuring device that senses the difference between the guidance of the Self and what you are actually doing. They call it the *emotional guidance system*. Using Gurdjieff's analogy, when the wise passenger inside your carriage doesn't like where the carriage is going, it lets the horse and carriage (your body) know it, by creating unpleasant feelings of contraction. But when your carriage is on the right track, you'll feel a quiet peace and confidence, even if outer circumstances seem less than ideal. Things will just seem more "right."

Of course, this doesn't mean that every time you feel unhappy, you're on the wrong track. Your worries and anxieties might be your ego talking—the carriage driver pulling on the reins or whipping the horse. Or you may simply be replaying old stories about your past or projecting unnecessary fears about the future. There's also a big difference between the quiet joy of the Self and states of happiness or ecstasy brought about by drugs or entertainment. That's why it helps to "check in" with your Self by entering NOW+. With practice, you can make these distinctions more easily.

Finally, before I conclude this chapter, let's consider a perplexing question: *Can active consciousness be used for destructive purposes?* In my view, the ability to utilize active consciousness for harmful goals will be diminished by an important factor: people who dwell in contracted, negative states will inherently have a hard time getting into NOW+ and focusing their power of active consciousness. Indeed, if they *were* able to achieve NOW+, their contracted states would likely diminish, and so would their desire to use active consciousness maliciously.

Indeed, if you think about it, the perpetuation of evil in our world occurs *because* people have lost touch with their deeper Selves. As Gurdjieff said:

> "People are machines... And the unconscious activity of *a million machines* must necessarily result in destruction and extermination...You do not yet understand and cannot imagine all the results of this evil. But the time will come when you will understand."[6]

Gurdjieff said these prescient words as World War I was brewing. After the horrors and wars of the twentieth century, and given the ongoing social, political, economic, and environmental woes that we face today, perhaps the time that Gurdjieff spoke of has finally come. More and more of us are beginning to realize that learning to meditate and getting in touch with our higher wisdom may provide the best pathway towards leaving our robotic selves behind and creating a much better world.

CHAPTER 19

❧

HOW DOES IT WORK?

CAUSATION PLUS SYNCHRONICITY

HOW DO THE FOUR STEPS OF ACTIVE CONSCIOUSNESS ACTUALLY work? What is the *mechanism* that brings you to your desired goal? One clue is a phenomenon that many people who practice these methods have noticed: *Periods in which unlikely but beneficial things occur tend to be accompanied by increased synchronicities.*

Remember, a synchronicity is an event in which meaningfully re-lated, but causally unconnected things occur at the same time. If the achievement of envisioned goals tends to be accompanied by an in-crease in such phenomena, then the mechanism of active consciousness might have something to do with synchronicity as well. Perhaps, by following the steps NOW+, PURE GOAL, LET GO, and CHOOSE JOY, each of us affects the consciousness field in such a way that mean-ingfully-related things co-occur and meaningfully-related people con-nect. These useful synchronicities then help bring us to our goals.

Many people have also reported that synchronicities tend to have a *numinous* quality to them—a kind of aura of mystery or of the divine. If you can try to remain alert for this feeling of numinosity, it can be another sign that you are moving in the right direction.

I have some excellent examples of synchronicity in my own life and I bet you do too. Synchronicities are often involved when you find the perfect job or when meet your life partner. I'll never forget those few days in Pittsburgh when I first met my husband Steve. By a series of sheer "coincidences," we were introduced at a conference that I normally would never have attended. That period was also suffused with a numinous quality that I will always remember and cherish.

It all began with some unusual circumstances that led me to go to Pittsburgh in the first place. On a whim, my PhD advisor decided to apply a research technique that she had developed to a problem outside her normal area of expertise. She wrote up her results and submitted them to a conference in Pittsburgh. After the paper was accepted for presentation, however, she discovered that it would be difficult for her to attend. So she decided to send me in her stead—the first and only time this ever occurred. The next thing I knew, I was off to Pittsburgh to give my first conference talk.

While I was there, I hung out with a Stanford professor I knew named Forest. As we ate lunch one day, we began talking about a man at the conference who I found intriguing. For some reason, this discussion triggered a precognitive thought in Forest's mind—about a completely different man. Inexplicably, he said to me, "Oh, I could tell that you were in love with Steve." "Who's Steve?" I asked. "Aren't you going out with Steve Rubin?" he replied. "No. I've never heard of him. But why don't you introduce me to him tonight?" That night, at a conference reception, Forest pointed out my future husband to me, and soon we were sitting next to each other at the conference banquet.

The next day, I drove to the airport for my flight home. I had arranged to have dinner at an airport restaurant with an old college acquaintance of mine who now lived in Pittsburgh. Even though he and I had never dated, hadn't communicated in years, and had never socialized outside of our college classes, he suddenly suggested over dinner that we get married! I quickly wrapped up this awkward exchange and rushed off to my gate. And there, sitting in the gate lounge, was Steve—my *future* husband! We greeted each other casually and about a half hour later, boarded a plane for Dallas.

Then something else unusual happened. Our flight was delayed for three hours on the ground. With nothing to do for three hours and a plane that was half empty, I went over to Steve and asked if I could sit with him. By the time we landed in Dallas, we had talked for over six hours and Steve had missed his connection to San Jose. He managed to transfer onto my flight to nearby San Francisco and we continued our conversation all the way to California. We've been together ever since.

Now, what I'd like to propose to you is that useful but improbable pathways into the future can be created or made more probable through at least two mechanisms: *causality*—i.e., the usual scheme of things, in which one thing ultimately causes another; and *synchronicity*—the co-occurrence of meaningfully related events. The story that I just related includes many examples of both, and together they forged a path that led to my happily married future with Steve.

Certainly, it was not unusual that my advisor decided not to attend a conference in a research area that was of little interest to her. Nor was it unlikely that Steve and I would be on the same outbound flight from Pittsburgh. These were the result of normal causal chains of events. But why did my advisor choose to send *me* to the conference and not one of her other graduate students? Even more importantly, why did Forest suddenly think of Steve when I was talking about someone else? Or come to believe that Steve and I were already in love? Why did my old college friend suddenly ask me to marry him when we hadn't communicated in over four years and had never had any kind of romantic relationship?

I believe that the answer is synchronicity. Somehow, Steve and I had become enveloped in a *field of meaning* that was bringing us together. This field increased the chance that my advisor would choose me instead of one of her other graduate students to present her paper. Perhaps it also had some influence in causing our flight to be delayed on the ground for three hours. And in my view, nothing but synchronicity could have caused Forest to suddenly think of Steve and suggest that we were in love. To this day, I still marvel at this precognitive leap. Indeed, my old college friend may have unwittingly come under the spell of my "marital field of meaning" too!

Everything that happened to me over the course of those amazing few days in Pittsburgh was *possible*, but much of it was quite unlikely. These unlikely but fortuitous events were instances when the choice points that lay before me resulted in a *realignment*—a veering off onto an unlikely path into an improbable future. David Loye, a psychologist and futurist, calls such realignments "intra-holographic leaps" or "hololeaps."[1] One thing I can say for sure: those few days in Pittsburgh were suffused with a numinous quality. In fact, both Steve and I knew within days that we were destined to be married.

Of course, I had to use my intuition and take action too. I had to act on my impulse to suggest that Forest introduce me to Steve and to boldly ask Steve if I could sit with him on the plane. I had to make my way through a branching tree of possibilities and take the right path. But I also needed synchronicity to introduce new and unlikely paths for me. I needed Forest to think of Steve and tell me about him in the first place. And once these new paths were available to me, I needed to choose them.

Finally, *why* did this all happen? Perhaps it was my sincere yearning for a lasting relationship during the few months that preceded the conference that finally caused a marital field of meaning to form for me. I had had a long string of failed romances during my years in graduate school, but about a month before the conference, I finally decided to *let go* and not worry about my love life anymore. Perhaps I had unwittingly used active consciousness. I had applied PURE GOAL and LET GO without realizing it.

Of course, if it is true that active consciousness causes synchronicities to form, then it's not about "magic" or even coincidence—it's just a different kind of mechanism at work at a deeper level of reality. F. David Peat, a physicist who once collaborated with the late David Bohm and has made a life study of synchronicity and human creativity, has asserted that phenomena like synchronicities actually reflect the true nature of depth consciousness. As he wrote, "It is the human mind operating, for a moment, in its true order and extending throughout society and nature, moving through orders of increasing subtlety, reaching past the source of mind and matter into creativity itself."[2] In other words, synchronicities are just a natural aspect of how the world works. We just need to create and cultivate them.

RETROCAUSATION

There may be an even more surprising mechanism at work—beyond causality and synchronicity. Within the realm of four and higher dimensions, there's more than just the present and our possible futures; there is also our past. Can active consciousness affect that too?

Consider, for example, the studies that prove the power of *retrocausation*—the ability to influence something that has already occurred. One such study, designed by Lockheed Martin physicist Helmut Schmidt, enabled Princeton scientists Robert Jahn and Brenda Dunne to demonstrate that people could influence the output of random event generators when they were being recorded *in the past*.[3]

There are several other such studies, with the same basic design, described in Lynne McTaggart's book *The Intention Experiment*. In one experiment, German parapsychologist Elmar Gruber tested the ability to retroactively affect gerbil behavior.[4] First, Gruber created a device that could record gerbils running on an activity wheel. Many trials of gerbil behavior were then recorded, and each recording was copied to create an exact duplicate. Next, human subjects were asked to listen to a subset of the original recordings and to try to speed up the gerbil activity on them. Amazingly, analysis showed that the "influenced" recordings *and* their copies had a faster rate of activity on them than the control pairs of recordings. Because each of the copies remained the same as its corresponding original recording, the experiment demonstrated that the subjects had not altered the tapes that they were listening to, but rather, had influenced the recordings *when they were first made*. And the effect size of this result—a measure of statistical significance—was huge: 0.7. In fact, retrocausation studies in general have garnered larger effect sizes than studies of other psychic phenomena.[5]

What can we make of this? Can people really influence the past as well as the present and the future? Physicists have indeed begun to admit the possibility of time displacement and alterations of spacetime.[6] If each of us has some aspect of ourselves that dwells in higher-dimensional space, then perhaps retrocausation really is conceivable.

Note that retrocausation has been shown to be most effective if the targeted event has not yet been measured or observed. For example, suppose that you discover that your car is being recalled for a possible manufacturing defect. Is your car actually one of the lemons? Before you find out for sure, try to use active consciousness to influence the moment at which your car was first manufactured. Or, suppose you are going in for a test to see if you have been exposed to a pathogen. Before you do so, try to use active consciousness to influence the point in time at which this might have occurred.

Prime target moments for active consciousness experiments (both in the past and the future) have been called *seed moments*. These are junctures or choice points at which the possibilities are more numerous and the outcomes are more pliable, and thus are more ripe for influence. These moments tend to occur early on in a process, when relevant outcomes or details have not yet been observed and are therefore less "congealed." As McTaggart points out, they are much like the branches of a young plant that can still be bent easily. Choice points are also more subject to our influence if the possible choices that occur at them are somehow random or equally likely.[7]

LOOSENING THE GRIP OF THE PAST

There is also something else that we can achieve by heightening our connection to the past: improve our mental and physical health. Often our current state of being is unconsciously locked or gripped by an event that occurred long ago. By focusing our deeper awareness on that event, we may be able to free ourselves. For example, some psychological therapies, like neurolinguistic programming,[8] take patients back to traumatic events and ask them to either alter the events or "talk" to their prior selves in a consoling way. Is this merely a way to heal old psychological wounds? Or do such techniques actually enable some form of retrocausation to occur—if not by changing the actual events that took place, then by influencing our response to them?

Here are two other examples from the healing realm to consider. It turns out that when homeopaths examine the characteristics of a patient's case, the causative or triggering event for a disease is often the best guide to a curative remedy. For example, if a physical illness immediately followed a grief event, it is quite likely that a grief-related remedy will successfully cure the physical illness, even if that remedy isn't normally useful for that particular disease. Is it possible that the remedy goes in and retroactively alleviates the grief wound so that the ensuing physical disease process is dampened?

Another fascinating healing modality that may work in the same way is Gary Craig's *Emotional Freedom Technique* (EFT),[9] which I mentioned in Chapter 7. It requires a patient to tap on a sequence of acupressure points while repeating a phrase of the following form: "Even though <problem>, I deeply and completely accept myself." For instance, "Even though I have asthma, I deeply and completely accept myself."

EFT can be most effective if a patient continues to tap on deeper roots of a problem that emerge during this process. For example, after you tap on your asthma, a feeling of anxiety might come up. You should then tap on the anxiety: "Even though I'm feeling anxious, I deeply and completely accept myself." Then, a memory of an accident might arise: "Even though I was in that car accident, I deeply and completely accept myself." And so on. You'd be amazed at how quickly EFT can resolve longstanding emotional problems, phobias, and even serious physical problems. Sometimes the effect is instantaneous.

How does this work? Consider the scenario depicted in Figure III.8. By applying EFT, a person manages to retroactively dislodge a disease to the extent that they now have a 75% chance of recovery instead of a 1% chance. Like homeopathy, EFT may affect the root of a problem that occurred in the past. The consequences of healing this root can then impact the disease processes that occurred afterward.

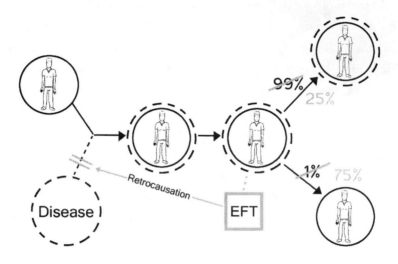

FIGURE III.8

Indeed, I believe that the actual words of the EFT formula are critical to its success. Consider the structure of the formula; it literally separates you from your problem: "Even though <problem>, I deeply and completely accept myself." *You* are not the problem. Even though you "have" a problem, you acknowledge that you still completely accept yourself. Next, by uncovering the root cause of the problem, you project yourself back to the point in time at which it began. Finally, by adding love and acceptance of yourself to that point in time—essentially being in NOW+ at a choice point—you arm yourself with the power of active consciousness. With this power, you can then influence that seed moment, alleviate the past wound, and heal its consequences too.

CHAPTER 20

DEMYSTIFYING THE MYSTERIOUS

"The world is nothing but an objectivized dream and whatever your powerful mind believes very intensely instantly comes to pass."[1]

—PARAMAHANSA YOGANANDA

I'LL NOW CONCLUDE PART III WITH A REVIEW OF THE VARIOUS
paranormal phenomena, energy fields, and mechanisms described thus
far. First, let's consider some of the fields that have been discussed: the
morphic field of Sheldrake, the Akashic field of Laszlo, the zero-point
field of modern physics, and the psi field studied by psychic researchers.
Personally, I believe that all of these fields are one and the same as the
consciousness field. The gravitational field, the electromagnetic field, and
the strong and weak nuclear fields may all be subsets or specific types of
manifestation within this deeper, unifying field of consciousness.

What about the life-force fields associated with various healing
modalities? They include: *chi* (or *qi*)—the life force field of Chinese
medicine; *prana*—the field manipulated by the Indian medicine
called *Ayurveda*; and the *vital force* or *dynamis*—the energy field of
homeopathy. Some healing modalities also associate a particular
structure with this field. For example, acupuncturists believe that
there are meridians of chi running vertically throughout the body.
In contrast, Indian systems of medicine talk about *chakras*—spinning
vortices of energy at specific locations in the energy body at which
prana enters and exits.

In my view, chi, prana, and the vital force are all one and the same, but are a subfield of the unified consciousness field. In other words, chi is not identical to consciousness. There's actually evidence for this. For instance, while psi experiments are typically not affected by distance, time, or the presence of any intervening material, experiments with chi *are* affected by distance and intervening materials such as glass. Perhaps that is why homeopathic remedies are traditionally stored in glass vials—so that their energetic fields do not interact. Baron Karl von Reichenbach (1788 —1869), a German chemist of the 1800s, called the life-force field the *odic field* or *od*. He found that od travels at a specific speed, which he calculated as being thirteen feet per second.[2] In contrast, experiments with psi uniformly indicate that its effects are instantaneous—another indicator that chi (od, prana, etc.) are not the same as psi or consciousness. Interestingly, Reichenbach also found that like poles of the odic field *attract* rather than repel (as they do in magnets). Perhaps this explains how the Law of Similars actually works; when it comes to the life-force field, likes *attract* likes.

What about the other body-energy fields mentioned in Chapter 10? Most wisdom traditions associate the human body with five interpenetrating envelopes: (1) the *physical body*; (2) the *etheric body*; (3) the *astral body*; (4) the *mental body*; and (5) the *causal body*. The life-force field (chi) is usually equated with the etheric body—the first envelope extending beyond our physical form. In contrast, the astral, mental, and causal bodies supposedly link us up to the unified consciousness field and higher-dimensional forms of awareness. I believe it is also these higher energy bodies that allow us to wield the power of active consciousness. Just as the Circle was lifted above Flatland to see his world from a higher three-dimensional perspective, I believe that we utilize our higher energy bodies to access higher spatial dimensions, have out-of-body experiences, "see" distant locations, access our possible futures, and perhaps even influence them. The parts of us that exist beyond our physical and etheric bodies may even be able to survive our physical life here on Earth. All of these ideas will be explored in detail in Part IV.

Experiment after experiment has shown that something is going on that exceeds the bounds of accepted science. And a key aspect of many of these unusual phenomena is *similarity in vibration*. Homeopathy demonstrates that a substance possessing a similar vibration as a patient's disease will heal them. The teachings of many esoteric systems indicate that being in the state of vibration of our goals can help us reach them—perhaps via a higher-dimensional mechanism like the one proposed in Chapter 15. Rupert Sheldrake's research has shown that groups of connected or similar people or animals can affect one another, even across great distances. Researchers of psychic phenomena like Dean Radin have found that "entangled" individuals have a greater power to influence one another and even mechanical devices. And meaningful coincidences or synchronicities do occur, which involve objects and people that are connected in a meaningful way. Even minerals and plants take part in this intricate ballet of unseen energy.

Consciousness does indeed have an effect upon the world around us. That is an accepted scientific fact of the subatomic realm. But experiments have also shown that the power of active consciousness can lower crime rates in cities, enhance the development of fruit flies, and affect the physical properties of a laboratory at Stanford University. The improbable is still possible. And improbable occurrences can be made more likely if we use active consciousness to enable events and pathways that exist in the higher-dimensional realm of infinite possibilities to manifest in our tangible three-dimensional world.

The next section of this book describes some even more amazing phenomena that have been observed and accepted by many people and cultures. Instead of viewing them as superstitions or hallucinations, perhaps science should consider them as uncharted territory to be explored.

EXERCISE 3

❖ ❖ ❖

DIFFERENTIATING BETWEEN SENSATION, EMOTION, AND THOUGHT

Exercises 1 and 2 focused on the worlds of sensation—first, the world of outer sensation (Exercise 1), and then the world of inner sensation (Exercise 2). By performing these exercises, you learned to settle into your body and free yourself from the typical thoughts and emotions that dominate most of your waking moments. In Exercise 3, you will now learn to notice the *differences* between sensations, emotions, and thoughts, and to realize that you have control over how you experience them. By identifying, isolating, and differentiating between these components of your experience, you can then learn to integrate them in a more masterful way.

Before we begin, please recall that at the end of Exercises 1 and 2, I asked you to notice how thoughts and emotions palpably return after experiments with pure sensation. The primary lesson was that you can intentionally disengage from your emotions and thoughts—that is, you have the ability to turn them on and off. Now, in Exercise 3, we'll play with this concept a bit more and begin exercising these "on" and "off" muscles. Also please note: Step 2 of this exercise is composed of several sub-steps. Each of these steps can be utilized as part of a separate meditation.

STEP 1. Settle into the Now: "Feet. Seat. Back."

With your eyes open, settle into outer sensation using the techniques described in Exercise 1. Once you feel grounded in your body, close your eyes and begin to focus on inner sensation (Exercise 2). Rest here for a few minutes until you feel free from inner thoughts and emotions. If you have any difficulty, keep refocusing using "Feet. Seat. Back."

STEP 2. Intentionally migrate between thought, emotion, and sensation, noticing the differences between these components of yourself and their interrelationships.

a) Emotions as sensations

Keeping your eyes closed, bring into your awareness a difficult emotion you have been experiencing. In order to do this, you will probably need to focus on the "thought story" or circumstance surrounding this emotion. However, once you feel that you have entered the emotional state, focus only upon the internal body sensation associated with the emotion. For example, you might feel a tightening of the throat or a clenching of the abdomen. As you focus more deeply on this sensation, you may find that the associated thought story disengages.

Continue to rest in this sensation and see what happens. For example, you may notice a relationship between this sensation and other body sensations. Do any of these sensations have a relationship with health problems you are experiencing? For example, if your emotion manifests as a clenching in the abdomen, do you also tend to experience gastrointestinal problems? Stick with the sensation and be curious about what happens. Breathe into it. You may find that the sensation relaxes. If it does, has your emotion changed too? During this process, certain insights might also appear. If so, take note of them.

If you do not find any relief from a difficult emotional sensation or develop any insights, just rest quietly with the sensation and keep regrounding with "Feet. Seat. Back."

Now slowly detach from the emotional situation by returning to the Now and focus solely on outer sensation. It may help to open your eyes and rest in outer sensation for a while.

b) Thoughts

Next, close your eyes and move into thought. Pick a situation from your day that does not have any emotional baggage—perhaps a neutral task that you need to get done. Think about the steps required. Notice how your mind starts to analyze and plan. You might find yourself visualizing the steps of the task, or you might think about the task using words. Notice what happens. As you are swept into thought, you may find that you are barely noticing your body sensations anymore. Remain in thought for a few minutes and observe how your thought processes work.

When you are done, return to the Now using "Feet. Seat. Back." and bring yourself back into internal or external sensation. Notice how your thoughts about the task disappear. If your mind wanders, keep refocusing using "Feet. Seat. Back." It may help to open your eyes and rest in outer sensation for a while.

c) Play with other emotions

If you would like to play further, try calling up other emotions, such as Worry, Fear, or Grief. Can you do this without using an associated story? Notice the different patterns of body sensation associated with each of these different emotions. What happens to your emotional state if you relax its associated body sensation? After you are done with an emotion, reset yourself by returning to the Now, opening your eyes, and resting in outer sensation.

d) Play with other thoughts

Try playing with different kinds of thought processes. How does thinking about a neutral topic differ from thinking about a less neutral one? Can you tell the difference between the "thought story" of a situation and the physically-felt emotion associated with it? Can you "think" about a difficult story without having an emotional response? Can you feel an emotion without thinking about a story?

Remember to return periodically to pure outer sensation using "Feet. Seat. Back." Open your eyes if it helps. As you continue to play with this exercise, try to notice what happens as you migrate in and out of thought, emotion, and sensation.

After you are done performing this exercise and return to your normal mode of awareness, you will literally feel the return of your ordinary mind chatter, emotions, and physical holding patterns and sensations. Use this experience to remind you that your sensations, emotions, and thoughts are not *you*, only a part of you. You can change them at will, just like you just did during this exercise. And always remember that these exercises should be performed in a spirit of play and fun and compassion for yourself. There is no right or wrong experience—just your own unique experience.

Finally, here is a related exercise that you might try during everyday life.

While you are listening to or talking with someone, try to notice your reaction. It might help to ground yourself by using "Feet. Seat. Back." and entering into a light state of Now. Then ask yourself, what is the quality of your reaction? What are your thoughts, emotions, and sensations? Can you distinguish between them? If you apply this exercise to both joyful and difficult situations, you may notice that joyful situations are associated with sensations of expansion, whereas difficult situations are associated with sensations of contraction. Play with these sensations and see what happens.

PART IV

TAKE A DEEPER LOOK

"Man is, in the full sense of the term, a 'miniature universe'; in him are all the matters of which the universe consists;… therefore in studying man we can study the whole world, just as in studying the world we can study man."[1]

—G.I. GURDJIEFF

CONSIDER THE PERENNIAL WISDOM OF THE AGES...

S O FAR, I HAVE PRESENTED SCIENTIFIC EVIDENCE FOR A WIDE VARIETY
of unusual phenomena and have proposed a framework that provides some sort of explanation for them. I have also described a meth-
odology for cultivating and participating in such experiences. But the
fact is, much of this information can be found in the ancient wisdom
of nearly every mystical tradition on Earth. We twenty-first century
materialists may find these kinds of phenomena to be astounding. But
if we simply took the teachings of the past more seriously—the so-
called "perennial philosophy" that springs forth from every era and
culture—we might not be so surprised at all.

I believe that at their core, all of these teachings are saying the same
thing. Perhaps they borrowed from or cross-fertilized one another. Or
perhaps enlightened individuals, whatever their origin, have always
tapped into the same knowledge embedded within the universal consciousness field that surrounds us. Each of these people then transcribed
this information in a way that reflected his or her culture, age, and
individuality. But if you throw aside the details, the overall message is
largely the same. It is this common picture of the deeper realities that
surround us that I will attempt to describe in Part IV.

Obviously, I'm taking on quite a task—trying to present a unified
view of the esoteric wisdom of so many traditions in just a few pages.
My approach will be to lay out a single coherent image that I have
formulated for myself, in the hope that it will be interesting and enlightening to you. I'll cite my inspirations and sources, but I make no
pretense of being exhaustive. I encourage each of you to then read and
investigate further on your own and expand upon this framework.
Perhaps you can build a different internal model and belief system
about this information that makes sense to you.

My sources for Part IV are quite broad. They include: the wisdom of energy-based representations of the body, such as those described in Chinese and Indian medicine and by modern teachers
like Barbara Brennan; the teachings of Kabbalah (Jewish mysticism);

Gurdjieff's teachings; the writings of Rudolf Steiner, a contemporary of Gurdjieff; the wisdom of Buddhist and Hindu masters like Sri Ramana Maharshi and Sri Aurobindo; the revelations of Emmanuel Swedenborg, a scientist and Christian mystic of the 1700s; the channeled teachings of Seth, Abraham, Orin, Bartholomew, and others; research by Stanislav Grof and other scientists about past-lives and altered states of awareness; and the experiences of people, such as the Findhorn community in Scotland, who have attempted to interact with various hidden forces of nature.

The basic structure of Part IV is inspired by that of the human energy body—the interpenetrating layers that I described in Chapter 20. Beginning with the coarsest layer, the physical body, I proceed outward toward the etheric, astral, mental, and causal layers. At each level or layer, a different universe plays itself out that interacts with different dimensions and worlds. Ultimately, the energies that operate within these higher realms descend and manifest within our physical three-dimensional world. At the same time, the things we do here on Earth ascend to be incorporated into the layers of reality beyond our own. As it was inscribed on the Emerald Tablet of Hermes Trismegistus—an ancient text that was said to reveal the secrets of the primordial substance: "That which is Below corresponds to that which is Above, and that which is Above, corresponds to that which is Below, to accomplish the miracles of the One Thing." [2]

The amazing thing is, we humans have the potential to access all of it. Through personal development and effort, we can learn to sense and manipulate not only our physical world, but also worlds at other levels of reality. And as we evolve, we come closer to embodying the divine human or *Adam Kadmon*, the Kabbalistic term for the primordial human created in the image of God.

CHAPTER 21

∿

THE BODY ESOTERIC

Let's begin by examining a commonly-accepted structure for the human energy body, depicted in Figure IV.1.

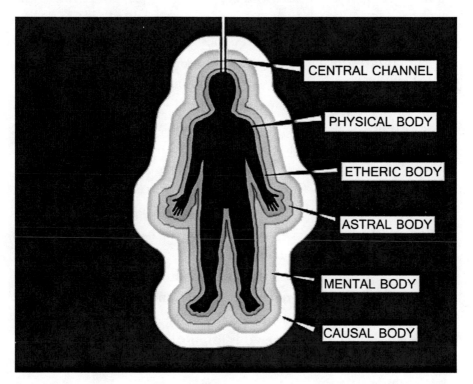

FIGURE IV.1

The complete human is viewed as including not only a physical body—the machine of our physical existence—but also a series of energy bodies: the *etheric body*, the *astral body*, the *mental body*, and the *causal body*. In addition, a *central channel* runs through all of the energy bodies and is said to be the location where interchanges occur between the energy bodies and their outer environment.

One important aspect of this structure is that, rather than being layered one on top of another, each energy body interpenetrates the bodies that precede it. Thus, the scope of the etheric body includes the physical, the astral body interpenetrates the etheric and physical, and so on. Each successive layer is also considered to be finer or more detailed in vibration than the preceding layers.

The higher energy bodies are also said to embody the more unifying or global themes of our existence. For instance, according to the teachings of Steiner,[1] which will be described in detail in Part IV, the astral and mental levels relate to themes that pertain not only to this life, but also to past lives. Because they are believed to transcend the limited three-dimensional extent of our physical bodies, the astral, mental, and causal bodies may even exist in higher spatial dimensions. For now though, let's focus on the first body that lies just beyond our familiar physical form—the *etheric body*.

The Etheric Body

The etheric body is the energetic part of us that is most accessible, and it has certainly been studied the most—especially for purposes of healing. The word "ethereal" has been defined as "light, airy, tenuous, extremely delicate or refined, heavenly, and celestial." The word "ether" has also been used historically for a hypothetical substance that occupies all of space. Given this linguistic heritage, it's easy to see why the term "etheric" was chosen for the first layer of our existence beyond physical form.

Nearly all energy healing systems around the world—including homeopathy, Chinese medicine, Indian medicine, and hands-on healing systems like Reiki—focus their attention on the etheric body.

Its substance has been called *chi* (or *qi*) by the Chinese, *prana* by the Indians, and the *vital force* or *dynamis* by homeopathy. Indeed, since the etheric body lays only one step beyond our physical form, most people can learn to feel and manipulate it. Let's try to do that right now.

A typical beginner's exercise is to try to feel the chi between your hands. Hold your hands in front of you with palms facing each other, about six inches apart. Close your eyes. Now very slowly, move your palms toward each other. Do you notice a slight tingling sensation? Or a sensation of density or pressure? Now play with this sensation by moving your hands slowly toward and away from one another. Can you notice the sensation of chi at further distances? You may even notice a taffy-like pulling sensation as the chi of your two hands meets, blends, and then pulls apart.

A focus on chi can be found everywhere in the world, but especially in Asia. For example, the aim of therapeutic exercises like Chi Gong or Tai Chi is to improve the flow and quality of chi in the etheric body. Chi is also the foundation of the Asian martial arts. Most sophisticated practitioners of disciplines like Aikido or Karate know that their power derives from the manipulation of chi, not simply the clever use of muscles, movement, leverage, or physical power. That's why a tiny martial arts master can fend off the blows of hordes of attackers. Such feats may be exaggerated or fantasized in the movies, but they also depict ancient wisdom about how the limitations of the physical world can be overcome if we tap into the more fundamental power of chi.

Of course, conventional Western medicine is all about the physical body, which is typically viewed as a vast and complex plumbing system carrying chemicals around. Gaining an understanding of and learning how to manipulate this system has undoubtedly been an astounding accomplishment of modern medicine. But how did humanity survive before modern drugs and techniques? While people, on average, did die at younger ages than they do now, a careful examination of the facts will reveal that this higher mortality rate was largely due to the impact of epidemic diseases—and that improvements in hygiene, not drugs, were the biggest factors in mitigating them. The truth is, there have always been people who lived to extreme old age, and in the past, these people depended upon traditional forms of healing that were often based on manipulation of the etheric body.

Because the etheric body operates at a finer energetic level than the physical body, it is also more fundamental, just as quantum particles are more fundamental than molecules. Indeed, the etheric body is said to be the lattice upon which the physical body is built. As a result, healing via manipulation of the etheric layer can also be deeper and more fundamental than the use of chemically-based drugs. Once problems in the etheric layer are healed, normal functioning of the physical body is also usually restored, enabling the body to repair itself. That's why medical systems like homeopathy and acupuncture can effectively treat the *root cause* of a chronic disease like arthritis or asthma and cure it, not just palliate its symptoms.

Traditional Asian medicines—most notably acupuncture—have observed that the etheric body has a specific structure. For example, acupuncturists believe that twenty meridians or channels of energy (twelve regular channels and eight extraordinary channels) run more or less vertically through the body, punctuated by hundreds of points of importance along their length. These are the acupuncture points into which acupuncturists insert their needles. Note, however, that these meridians are not the same as the physical nervous system. While meridians may run through physical organs (and, as a result, their associated points may affect these organs), the way acupuncture works is not physically based. Instead, an acupuncturist's needles affect the flow of chi. Note, too, that because the meridians run the full extent of the body and include points in the palms of the hands, the soles of the feet, and even the outer ear, stimulating acupuncture points on the foot, hand, or elsewhere can help to heal the liver, spleen, or any other organ. When it comes to the meridians of the etheric level, it's all connected!

The Indian culture has uncovered another aspect of the etheric body—the *chakras*. "Chakra" is a Sanskrit word that means wheel or disc. Located along the central channel of the etheric body, seven chakras function like spinning wheels that bring chi (or as the Indians call it, *prana*) into and out of the etheric system. The chakras are also associated with distinct functions, emotions, colors, and organs, and may be described as follows:

*   The *base* or *root chakra*, associated with the color red, affects functions having to do with instinct and survival. It is located at the base of the spinal column, in the area of the perineum between the genitals and anus. This area is also the source of *kundalini* experiences (like the one I described in Chapter 4), in which a surge of energy shoots up the central channel from the root chakra and outward through the etheric layer.

*   The *sacral chakra*, associated with the color orange, affects functions having to do with reproduction, enthusiasm, and creativity. It is located in the area of the lower abdomen, near the reproductive organs.

*   The *solar plexus chakra*, associated with the color yellow, affects functions having to do with digestion. This chakra is also considered to be the locus of personal power and can be involved in emotional problems such as fear and anxiety (which arise from a feeling of lack of power). The solar plexus chakra is located just above the navel and below the rib cage.

*   The *heart chakra*, associated with the color green, affects functions having to do with the immune system, and complex emotions such as love and compassion. It is located in the chest area.

*   The *throat chakra*, associated with the color blue, affects functions having to do with the thyroid, growth, communication, and action. It is located in the area of the throat.

- The *brow chakra*, also known as the "third eye," is associated with the color indigo. It affects functions having to do with the pineal gland, intuition, and inner guidance. It is located in the area of the forehead.

- The *crown chakra*, associated with the color violet or white, affects functions having to do with the thalamus gland, consciousness, meditation—and death. It is located at the very crown of the head and is often symbolized as a lotus with a thousand petals.

SEEING IS BELIEVING

Of course, these descriptions of meridians and chakras are highly simplified. People have been studying them for thousands of years and the knowledge that has been accumulated could fill volumes. But what I find particularly intriguing are the accounts of people like healer Barbara Brennan who claim to be able to see people's auras—visual manifestations of the etheric layer. In her books, Brennan provides colored illustrations of these auras and reports about the various phenomena she has witnessed.[2] For example, she describes how people can manipulate others by sending a cord of energy out from their solar plexus chakra (the chakra having to do with power) and invading other people's solar plexus chakras. I have experienced this feeling of invasion myself when I've been around manipulative, power-hungry people. Brennan recommends repelling these cords by creating an energy mesh with one's hands in order to protect and narrow the opening of the solar plexus chakra.

An important focus of Brennan's healing system is to improve the function of the chakras. She claims that there are chakra access points on both the front and back of the body and that these openings can malfunction in a variety ways. For instance, sometimes they are closed, sometimes they are open too wide, or sometimes they are distorted or torn. Brennan trains healers to repair the chakra openings so that they function properly. And if treatment is successful, the chakras can then begin to transmit chi into and out of the etheric body in a correct manner, and as a result, etheric and physical health will improve.

If people like Barbara Brennan can actually see auras, can cameras pick them up too? Perhaps. First, it's important to realize that many scientists already acknowledge that the body emanates light. For example, it is estimated that mammals emit one photon per cell twice a minute. In his book, *The Force Is With Us: The Conspiracy Against the Supernatural, Spiritual and Paranormal*, chiropractor Thomas Walker describes a wide range of scientific and esoteric information about this subject, including work by Stanford material scientist William Tiller, who I mentioned in Chapter 11. When Tiller studied the emission of light from the fingertips of Chi Gong masters, for example, he found that they did emit a greater amount of red and blue photons than average people do.[3] As Walker astutely points out:

> "[A]lthough great attention has been given to the chemical aspects of living things, very little has been focused on the fact that we are also creatures of light. The human body, for instance, is an extraordinarily complex network of enzymatic reactions... Photons of light are required to activate these processes... Light is the thing that keeps 'the pot bubbling efficiently'... Light is emitted just by mitosis, so growing tissues radiate with a special light of their own. Cancer cells, which reproduce at an uncontrollable rate, give off even higher radiations, something alternative health researchers have reported for decades, and suggest could be a method of identifying and destroying them. Conventional science ignores this, of course..."[4]

So do aura readers simply pick up light emissions from the physical body? Or are they actually seeing something else—the etheric level? In the late 1930s, a Russian electrician named Semyon Kirlian discovered that he could indeed photograph what seemed to be manifestations of the etheric body. By placing photographic paper between an electrode discharging a high frequency field and a grounded object, he found that he was able to photograph the object's corona discharge.

Amazingly, Kirlian's photographs of human subjects also showed flares of energy radiating from the traditional acupuncture points. He also found that healthy people and plants radiated more light than sick ones, and even more astounding, that *when a plant leaf was severed, its photograph still registered that something was there*—the so-called "phantom leaf effect." Because of this effect, many have come to believe that Kirlian photography does register traces of the etheric body, which hangs around for a while, even after the physical body has been eliminated. Indeed, while Kirlian photography has garnered mostly skepticism in the United States, it is now widely used for medical diagnostics in Russia.

ORBS—AN EXPERIMENT

Another phenomenon that has garnered quite a lot of attention recently is the ability to photograph *orbs*. If you own a digital camera, you can check it out for yourself by trying the following experiment. First, you'll need two people—a photographer and a meditator. To maximize your chance of success, take your photographs indoors and make sure that the flash goes off. Also make sure that no one enters or exits the room or moves anything around during the experiment, in order to minimize the movement of dust.

Begin by taking some flash photos of the meditator sitting in a chair. Next, both the photographer and the meditator should send out a "psychic invitation" or a genuine intention for orbs to appear. The meditator should then begin to settle and meditate, as the photographer continues to take flash photos about every thirty seconds. Continue for as long as you like, as the meditator enters deeper and deeper states of awareness. Finally, after the meditator returns to a normal state of awarenes, continue taking photos for a few minutes.

Now look at your photos. If you are successful, you will find that as the meditator's state deepens, first a few and then dozens of small spherical transparent balls will appear in the images. Sometimes they are quite subtle, so look closely. You will also likely find that as the meditator returns to normal consciousness, the orbs will also slowly disappear from view. Most orbs are pastel, transparent, gray, or ethereal looking, with a distinct border. If you zoom in on a vivid orb, you may notice a nucleus-like structure at the center. Skeptics say that orbs are simply photographic artifacts of dust particles, and it is true that stirring up dust in a room will produce numerous orb-like images. But if orbs are simply the result of dust, why would they slowly appear as a meditation proceeds and dissipate after it ends?

I first heard about orbs from friends who regularly go to Brazil to visit a psychic healer called John of God. Each successive trip to Brazil has increased the number of orbs that have appeared in their photographs—so much so that today, their photos are completely covered in orbs. You can barely make out the people and scenery! After my husband Steve and I "invited" orbs to appear in our photographs, they began to appear regularly. Indeed, looking back through old photos, including some non-digital images, we have noticed that orbs tend to appear at intense events like graduations and parties.

So just what *are* orbs? Part of me thinks that the skeptics are right and that they're just artifacts of dust. But part of me thinks that they are something more. Professor Tiller and another former Stanford researcher and NASA scientist, Dr. Klaus Heinemann, have studied the orb phenomenon and are convinced that they are not due to dust, water, or anything else that's obvious. Like me, they have also found that orbs tend to appear when they are "invited," and that they increase in number and size in spiritual settings.[5] Decide for yourself!

While it's easy to think of orbs as ghosts or entities visiting us from another realm, I have come to believe that they may actually be manifestations of some aspect of ourselves. In particular, I believe they may be what the Tibetan Buddhists call *tulpas*—embodied thought-forms. Tibetans believe that tulpas are energetic manifestations of our intent and that they possess a form of sentience. In a way, they are like living spiritual beings created by our use of active consciousness. Perhaps that's why they tend to appear at intense events like graduations. These are moments when people are taken out of their normal day-to-day mindset and become truly *awake*—and therefore create more vivid thought-forms. Indeed, perhaps that's why we also tend to remember such events so well; we create tulpas that embody our thoughts and emotions, and these tulpas continue to persist in the etheric realm. At collective spiritual events, it also makes sense that giant collective tulpas could form. And if you surf the Internet, you will indeed find many photos of giant orbs hovering over crowds of people at meditation workshops.

Orbs may also be the same as *thought balls* that have been described by people having near-death experiences, as well as by adepts having out-of-body experiences. One notable adept was Emanuel Swedenborg (1688-1772), a renowned Swedish mathematician, scientist, and inventor. In his mid-fifties, Swedenborg started to undergo a series of profound spiritual experiences, which he painstakingly recorded and published in a series of books. These works then became the basis of the Swedenborgian church. Swedenborg's abilities were taken quite seriously by those who knew him. He served in the Swedish government during that period and was called upon by the royal family as a medium. Among the many details of the afterlife and higher angelic realms that Swedenborg recorded was a description of thought balls as a mode of angelic and etheric communication. He said that they were similar to "portrayals" that he could see in the "wave-substance" that surrounded people, and described them as pictorially-encoded bursts of knowledge or ideas.[6] These accounts certainly provide further confirmation that orbs, thought balls, or tulpas are visible objects within the etheric realm.

ACCESSING THE ETHERIC REALM

Let's conclude this chapter with a discussion of what Rudolf Steiner had to say about the etheric body and how to become more aware of it. Steiner (1861–1925) was an Austrian philosopher, writer, and mystic who developed several new branches of knowledge, including: *anthroposophy* (a field of spiritual science with an accompanying form of medicine—anthroposophical medicine); *biodynamic agriculture* (a holistic method of organic farming); the educational philosophy that is the basis for today's Waldorf schools; and *eurythmy* (an artistic and therapeutic form of movement).

The underlying goal of Steiner's anthroposophy is similar to the aim of Gurdjieff's teachings—to cultivate a form of awareness outside of normal sensory experience that can lead to an objective and comprehensible experience of the spiritual world. Indeed, this motive also underlies Swedenborgianism and Buddhism. All of these disciplines claim that we simply need to train ourselves, using techniques that comprise a form of "spiritual science," in order to expand our awareness of otherwise inaccessible realms.

Like Barbara Brennan, Steiner could see the higher energy bodies, and he lectured and wrote prolifically about his experiences. In contrast to the physical body, which he described as solid, he said that the etheric realm is more like a fluid. He associated it with the color blue, water, spherical shapes, and the visual sense. As a result, perhaps it isn't surprising that we can learn to *see* the etheric realm, that orbs or tulpas are *spherical*, and that the *water*-based remedies of homeopathy are able to capture the etheric essence of substances and heal the etheric body.

Steiner said that all living things—plants, animals and humans—participate in the etheric world. In fact, he said that minerals and the Earth itself have etheric bodies too. However, he claimed that plants and minerals do not possess astral, mental, and causal bodies. Steiner taught that we can all learn to see the etheric level by developing what he called *strengthened thinking*. In particular, he said that people begin to see etheric auras when they become able to observe their own thoughts and realize that they have control over them. As he wrote:

> "Our meditation is successful when we are at length able to say: In my ordinary thinking I am really quite passive. I allow something to happen to me; I let Nature fill me with thoughts. But I

will no longer let myself be filled with thoughts, I will place in my consciousness the thoughts I want to have, and will only pass from one thought to another through the force of inner thinking itself. In this way our thinking becomes stronger and stronger, just as the force of our muscles grows stronger if we use our arms. At length we notice that this thinking activity is a 'tension,' a 'touching,' an inner experience, like the experience of our own muscular force… And in experiencing this higher man within, who is as real as the physical man himself, we come, at the same time, to perceive with our strengthened thinking the external things of the world." [7]

Perhaps now you can understand why I stressed the importance of learning to observe sensations, emotions, and thoughts in Exercises 1–3. This ability is a key to attaining deeper forms of awareness. Indeed, I've experienced the truth of Steiner's words myself. As I mentioned in Chapter 4, back in 1993, I was already able to vaguely see an aura around my hands when challenged to do so by my Chi Gong teacher. And as I have become more adept at meditation and at observing my thoughts, emotions, and sensations, my ability to see auras has increased. I'm certainly no Barbara Brennan, but I have found that if I ground myself and get into the Now, I can see vague auras around trees and people's heads, especially if there is a light background behind them. For instance, I can see a gray-bluish cloud around trees. I can also distinguish between the visual optical effect that can occur around trees in bright sunlight and a tree's actual aura. The optical effect has a bright border that echoes the exact shape of a tree. In contrast, a tree's aura appears like an amorphous cloud-like layer, with occasional wisps that extend outwards from the tree, and tendrils that reach from one branch to another.

I've also seen the aura around my fingers. Maybe you can too. Go outside on a brightly lit day, sit in a chair, settle, and meditate for a while. Now, put your two hands in front of you with your palms facing toward you and your fingertips reaching toward each other but not touching. A clear sky should be in the background. Let your eyes defocus a bit and try not to censor your experience; be open. Soon, you may begin to see a gray-bluish aura around your hands. With your fingertips about an inch from each other, notice if you can see energy cords reaching between them. For me, these cords appear light yellow or rainbow colored. Now slowly move one of your hands upwards and see if the cord reaching between your fingers "stretches" as you move your fingertips away from each other. If you can actually see this effect, it will probably convince you that you are not seeing an optical effect, but rather, some form of energy that's always there—you just don't perceive it most of the time. Indeed, when you return to normal consciousness, you will notice that these auras disappear from view.

Steiner had many other interesting things to say about the etheric body. For example, his experiences convinced him that the etheric and physical realms are tightly connected to one another. He said that while you are asleep, your astral, mental, and causal bodies can detach from your physical body, but that your etheric body always remains tethered to you. This actually makes sense, because if your etheric body is ultimately responsible for your physical health, how could you survive the night without it?

Steiner also asserted that after the physical body dies, the etheric body slowly disintegrates over a period of a few days, leaving the higher astral, mental, and causal bodies to continue onward to future lives. According to Tibetan Buddhism, this disintegrative process takes three days,[8] during which time the deceased's etheric memories—perhaps stored as tulpas or orbs—are released to merge with the larger universal etheric realm in which they remain stored for all time. As Steiner wrote,

"Between waking up and falling asleep we move about the world, receiving impressions from all sides... This world is like a deep ocean confined within us... When man sheds his physical body, this whole world is there, bound up with his etheric body. Upon this all his experiences have been impressed, and these man bears within him immediately after death... Now man's first experience, immediately after death, is of everything that has made its impression upon him... The earthly elements take over the physical body and destroy it; the cosmic ether, working... from the periphery, streams in and dispels in all directions what has been impressed upon the etheric body... This lasts some days... Man sheds his second corpse; or, strictly speaking, the cosmos takes it from him... The world gives us much and we hold it together. The moment we die the world takes back what it has given. But it is something new that it receives, for we have experienced it all in a particular way. The world receives our whole experience and impresses it upon its own ether... As human beings we are not here for our own ends alone; in respect to our etheric body... we are here for the universe." [9]

CHAPTER 22

⟩⟨

THE HIGHER ENERGY BODIES—FROM HERE TO ETERNITY

T HINGS GET EVEN MORE MYSTERIOUS WHEN WE EXTEND OUR view of ourselves outward to include the realms of the astral, mental, and causal bodies. It is these higher bodies that are supposedly able to detach from our physical selves and maintain their own, independent existence during sleep and after death. These bodies are also part of the esoteric teachings of many cultures, and remarkably, are described in very similar ways.

One system of thought that addresses the higher energy bodies is *Kabbalah*, the mystical teachings of Judaism. Based primarily on second and third century scholarship, Kabbalah is an esoteric interpretation of the Hebrew scriptures that attempts to reconcile earthly and cosmic concepts. In the Kabbalistic paradigm, the physical body (and the physical world in general) is called the world of *Asyyah*, or action. Laying beyond this day-to-day existence are the astral level (the world of *Yezirah*, or formation), the mental level (the world of *Beriah*, or creation), and the causal level (the world of *Azilut*, or emanation). Although the etheric body is not mentioned per se, according to the teachings of Kabbalah scholar Z'ev ben Shimon Halevi, each of these four worlds overlaps with the worlds that adjoin it.[1] The region where the physical and astral levels intersect is said to be where energy-based forms of communication occur within the body, and is thus likely equivalent to the etheric level. But what's the astral body all about?

THE ASTRAL BODY

> "We've known each other from other lives
> I want to see you today
> But I'll prove my knowledge of what's inside
> When I intercept you on the astral plane"[2]

> — JONATHAN RICHMAN, *ASTRAL PLANE*

According to the teachings of Gurdjieff, Steiner, Kabbalah, and other esoteric systems, the astral body is the higher emotional center of our beings. While ordinary emotions arise from the physical body and reflect the nature of the ego or personality, astral emotions reflect the emotional nature of our spirit or soul.

Gurdjieff said that the astral and higher energy bodies have to be intentionally developed and cultivated—they are not a given. In fact, he said that many people do not have them at all! As he wrote, "A man without an 'astral body' may even produce the impression of being a very intellectual or even *spiritual man*, and may deceive not only others but also himself."[3] Since nearly all esoteric teachings assert that it is only the astral, mental, and causal bodies that can survive death, in Gurdjieff's system of thought, those individuals who have not cultivated these higher bodies cannot continue on after death.

In contrast, mystical philosopher Rudolf Steiner claimed that everyone has an astral body. He also provided specific information about what the astral world was like and how to perceive it. In contrast to the watery and expansive realm of the etheric body, Steiner said that the astral realm is gaseous in nature and is associated with the inwardly moving process of respiration. Indeed, he said that it's the astral level that "inspires" us. Steiner agreed with Gurdjieff that the astral body is associated with emotions and the color red. However, rather than being visible, he said that our perception of it is in the form of a subtle kind of hearing—an inner music.

Interestingly, the notion of a subtle musical realm is spoken of in many traditions. For instance, it is sometimes called the *music of the spheres*. In Hinduism, this music is called *shabda* or the "audible life stream." In esoteric Christian teachings, the musical astral realm is called the *second heaven*. Rosicrucian teachings state that "the heavenly 'music of the spheres' is heard in the Region of Concrete Thought, the lower region of the World of Thought, which is an ocean of harmony."[4] Since it is most likely that the Rosicrucian "World of Thought" is synonymous with the *mental body* (the level above the astral body), it makes sense that the astral level—the "Region of Concrete Thought"—lies just below it.

Steiner taught that we can all learn to perceive the astral level by entering into even deeper states of meditation. In particular, once you achieve the ability to perceive your thought processes—the so-called "observer state" or "strengthened thinking," which enables one to perceive the etheric realm (see Chapter 21)—you must then turn off this thinking and enter empty consciousness. In this state of emptiness you will be awake but have no outer sensations, and into this emptiness will stream the astral realm—as *inspirations*. As Steiner wrote:

"[O]n exposing one's empty consciousness to the indefinite on all sides, the spiritual world proper enters. One says: The spiritual world approaches me. Whereas previously one only looked out into the supra-terrestrial physical environment—which is really an etheric environment—and saw what is spatial, something new, the actual spiritual world, now approaches through this cosmic space from all sides as from indefinite distances... The third or astral man who works in the 'airy' man, is apprehended not merely in pictures but in yet another way. If you advance further and further in meditation... you notice, after reaching a certain state in your exercises, that your breath has become palpably musical. You experience it as inner music; you feel as if inner music were weaving and surging through you... This is the third man. We apprehend him when we attain to 'empty consciousness' and allow this to be filled with 'in-spirations' from without." [5]

So what would we "hear" if we could perceive this astral reality? Steiner described the experience as one that makes *"time* into *space."* [6] In particular, he said that we would perceive that the astral and mental bodies *extend back through time,* and because of this, men and women always bear their pasts with them, even their previous lives. In Steiner's words, "The human being is really like a comet stretching its tail far back into the past." [7] Is this "comet" the four-dimensional "tube" of a person's trajectory through four dimensions? Steiner was certainly quite specific about what he saw and heard. For example, he said that while the etheric body extends back only until the moment of conception, the astral body's "comet" or "tube" begins at the end of one's previous life. The mental body then extends back even further—into previous lives.

Steiner also said that while plants and minerals can participate in the vast energetic sea of the etheric realm, something very different occurs at the astral level: only animals possess a *will.* The importance of the will to the astral realm may be why Steiner sometimes called the astral body the *force man.* It's the part of us that acts and creates fundamental change or form in the world. This may be why the Kabbalists call the astral level *Yezirah,* the *world of formation.* And it may be within this realm that the power of active consciousness starts to take shape—where we begin to mold the higher-dimensional world of possibilities into three-dimensional reality.

LUCID DREAMING

So what about singer Jonathan Richman's song about the astral plane, which introduced the previous section? Can he meet his beloved there late at night? According to Steiner, maybe he can. During sleep, the astral, mental, and causal bodies can detach and visit other realms. Indeed, Steiner said that some of our dreams are actually memories of these travels to other places and times. The more developed a person's higher energy bodies are, the more they will remember these dreams and the more significant they will be.

Of course, psychologists already understand that the ego or lower mind plays an important role in dreaming. According to Kabbalah, the ego resides in the area where the physical and astral bodies intersect, so an aspect of the ego is also part of the astral body—enabling it to wander during sleep and bring memories back to us about its travels. In fact, with some training, many people can gain the ability to remain "conscious" while dreaming. These so-called *lucid dreams* have become an area of scientific research,[8] and are also an objective of Buddhist meditative practices.[9]

One method for triggering a lucid dream is performed during a normal dream. A special cue is prepared beforehand that triggers recognition in the dreamer that he or she is actually asleep and dreaming. For example, dream research laboratories sometimes utilize special masks to cue dreamers with sounds or flashes of light. Another approach is to set up a personal "dream sign"—something significant or unusual that the dreamer will recognize and can use to trigger lucidity. I've managed to have two lucid dreams in this way, using the dream sign of "flying." That is, I have trained myself to become self-aware if I fly in a dream.

If you'd like to try this for yourself, first adopt the intention to say "I am dreaming" if you experience your dream sign, and suggest to yourself at bedtime that you will experience this sign. You may also find it useful to prepare a question to ask during your lucid experience if you succeed in having one. Another handy tip suggested by Stanford lucid dream researcher Stephen LaBerge is to spin around in your dream state in order to prolong lucidity and prevent waking up.[10]

From my own experience, I can tell you that a lucid dream is as vivid and memorable as any dream you'll ever experience—perhaps as vivid and realistic as waking life. In my most remarkable lucid experience, I managed to ask the question: "What is my future?" Soon

I found myself in a living room with white furniture. Looking out the window, I saw the Golden Gate Bridge in the distance. The next thing I knew, I was flying out over San Francisco Bay. The sky was overcast and the ocean had noticeably risen—the contours of the land were no longer the same. The edges of the bay were lined with hydroponic facilities used for growing food and other structures used for water desalinization. Aside from these, most of the buildings looked residential. And all during this experience, I felt a strong sensation of happiness and ecstasy. Was I actually witnessing the future, or at least, a possible future for San Francisco Bay?

Another kind of lucid dream that is harder to achieve is more like a waking dream; the dreamer goes directly from being awake into a dream state without loss of consciousness. Studies of people who are able to achieve this have reported that it is much like an out-of-body experience. For example, they report the sensation of leaving their bodies and floating above them.[11] This may indeed indicate that lucid dreams and out-of-body experiences are the result of the higher energy bodies separating from the physical and etheric bodies and traveling to other times and places.

Steiner also delineated three kinds of dreams, in ascending order of importance. The first kind of dream is simply a modification of recent waking-life experience and is a product of the ego. According to Steiner, those who have not pursued meditation or other kinds of self-awareness training will tend to have the most literal dreams of this kind. The second type of dream arises from the astral body. Its purpose is to provide useful information to the dreamer, often about his or her physical body. For example, a dream about a row of white pillars with one dirty pillar might indicate that one of the dreamer's teeth is infected. Or a dream about a blocked tunnel might represent the fact that the dreamer is having a problem with their intestines.

Finally, a third kind of dream carries the dreamer to previous lives. Steiner called these dreams *imaginative visions*. Since such dreams extend beyond the reach of the astral body (which he said extends only as far back as the period between this life and the previous life), they are likely the product of the mental body.

THE MENTAL BODY—WHERE LIFETIMES MEET

The mental body, as its name implies, is associated with a world of thought. But these are not the kinds of thoughts you and I have most of the time. Just as the astral body is concerned with the emotions of the spirit or soul, the mental body deals with deeper forms of thought—the thoughts that survive even after our physical body has died and its etheric memories have dispersed.

So what is the mental realm like? As I have already discussed, the etheric realm can be seen visually and the astral realm can be perceived as a type of sound. The mental body, Steiner claimed, makes itself known as a kind of heat. That's why he also called it the *warmth body*—a body that stores its information as a sort of heat imprint. For example, Steiner said that performing good deeds in life creates a kind of soul warmth and light in the mental body, whereas evil deeds create soul coldness and darkness. These imprints of our life's actions then accompany us from this life on to the next.

Learning to perceive the mental body requires even deeper meditative states. Steiner said that after you achieve empty consciousness and receive "inspirations" from the astral realm, the warmth body makes itself known as the cognitive embodiment of love—a kind of loving form of knowing. As he wrote:

> "[This] further stage in cognition is attained by making the power of love a cognitive force. Only, it must not be the shallow love of which alone, as a rule, our materialistic age speaks. It must be the love by which you can identify yourself with another being—a being with whom, in the physical world, you are not identical. You must really be able to feel what is passing in the other being just as you feel what is passing in yourself; you must be able to go out of yourself and live again in another. In ordinary human life such love does not attain the intensity necessary to make it a cognitive force." [12]

Perhaps this cognitive force may be what is known as *Christ conscious-ness*—a consciousness that enables you to truly feel that you are one with everyone and everything. This may also be what Ken Wilber is talking about when he speaks of the higher *transpersonal* states of consciousness.[13] When someone reaches this level, Steiner said that they also develop an "imaginal" awareness of past lives. And indeed, most esoteric traditions agree that it is the mental body that accompanies us from life to life.

There is actually a fair amount of academic research about past-life memories. Psychiatrist Stanislav Grof is one researcher who has worked extensively in this area. In his book, *When the Impossible Happens*,[14] he describes the experience of one of his patients, Karl, who had a past-life vision of a bloody battle. Karl remembered being gored by a British soldier, thrown over the ramparts, and dying on the beach below. One unusual aspect of his vision was that the terrain seemed to look like Scotland or Ireland, but that his compatriots were speaking Spanish. Karl also remembered being a priest, not a soldier, and clearly saw some initials on a ring he was wearing.

After this intense experience, Karl decided to take a vacation trip to Ireland. When he returned, he found that he had unwittingly taken eleven photos of a particular coastline. After some research, he discov-ered that on that same shore, barely visible in his photos, were the ru-ins of an old fortress that had been invaded by Spanish forces in 1580. The Spaniards had come to aid Irish rebels fighting the British, but had all been mercilessly killed, their bodies tossed over the ramparts onto the beach below. Karl also discovered that a priest had accom-panied the Spaniards and was killed along with them—a priest whose initials were identical to the ones Karl saw on the ring in his vision. Astounding![15]

Another thing Grof has found is that when past-life memories do surface, they are often connected to current life issues. It's as if a field of meaning in this life connects you to a similar field of meaning in a past life. Are we subject to such connected fields of meaning more often than we think? For instance, if you find yourself troubled one day and just can't seem to find a reason for it, it may be that an explanation can be found, not in this life, but in a previous one. Some have even suggested that relationship difficulties in this life may actually be due to a conflict with that same individual in a past life. Such relationships, recurring from life to life, are said to have a numinous quality to them—a kind of aura of mystery—especially when the people first meet. It's as if the individuals recognize one another and continue their relationship from where they left off. One famous healer who made use of such past-life material was psychic and diagnostician Edgar Cayce (1877-1945).[16] He is perhaps best known for his life readings, in which he envisioned his clients' past incarnations for purposes of spiritual healing and development.

Whether it's fact or fantasy, I can attest to the fact that revisiting past-life material can be eye opening and beneficial. For a couple of years I worked with a therapist named D'vorah who claimed to be able to sense ancestral presences and other information about her clients' past-lives. I remember one session that had a particularly profound effect on me. D'vorah sensed that I had been a priest in Eastern Europe; she could see my face and clothing, and the time period seemed to be the 1600s or 1700s. She told me that in my former life as a priest, I had developed a close relationship with the Jewish community in my town and had tried to protect them from attack and persecution. However, I was unsuccessful and felt profoundly responsible for a massacre that had occurred.

What D'vorah didn't know was that I have always enjoyed going to church and that I have a strong feeling of connection to Christian monastic music—something a bit odd for a Jewish woman of the twenty-first century. In fact, my children often tease me for watching church services on TV as I fold my Sunday laundry! All my life, I have also had inexplicable feelings of guilt and responsibility. My mother told me that even as a three year old, I would walk around the house saying, "It's all my fault." When D'vorah told me this fantastic story about my past life as a priest, I was immediately grabbed by an intense feeling of anguish and began to cry. This spontaneous and strong emotional reaction was surprising and unusual for me, and it supported my sense that there was truth to D'vorah's vision. She assured me that the Jewish townspeople from my past honored me and did not hold me responsible for the massacre. In fact, she claimed that they too were present during our session.

Happily, I have found that acknowledging this past life has successfully lessened my free-floating feelings of guilt and responsibility, and it has also helped clarify other aspects of my life for me. Skeptics would say that D'vorah's vision simply reflected a psychological complex I developed in *this* life. Perhaps. But if working with past life material is therapeutic, why not do so? Just as going back in time to a traumatic event in childhood and using active consciousness to heal the experience can be useful and effective, using active consciousness to go back even further and heal wounds from a past life might be effective too. Perhaps even more profoundly so.

DEATH AND BEYOND

So what exactly happens when we die? Nearly all esoteric teachings have pretty much the same thing to say about this universal human experience. According to psychologist Kenneth Ring, the initial stages of dying described by most traditions jibe with the accounts of individuals who have undergone a "near death experience."[17] The first thing that occurs is that the higher astral, mental, and causal bodies detach from the physical body as a unit—comprising what is sometimes called the "soul." Those who have undergone this experience report that they pass through a dark tunnel and approach a dazzling, beautiful light. They then enter a loving and peaceful realm that feels as if it were outside of time and space and possesses a kind of "celestial music" or vibrational quality—a description one might expect of an astral body experience.

Assuming that the dying person is not revived, traditions claim that over the next few days, their etheric body slowly detaches and its memories become absorbed into the general etheric field. Those who have a near death experience describe the initial stages of this process as a "life review," which is accompanied by a feeling of evaluation. Once the etheric body and its memories have completely dispersed, however, the dead person is left with only the higher emotional and mental memories stored within their higher energy bodies.

According to Steiner, the next task of the soul is to undergo another life review with higher spiritual beings. In particular, each person must come to terms with the ramifications of their actions. Did the newly deceased individual contribute to the evolution of the world or not? Did they learn and develop as they were meant to, or did they fail to achieve what was intended for them? Perhaps this is the process that some Christians call *purgatory*. It may also be what *karma* is about—coming to terms with the full implications of one's actions. Steiner writes:

> "Should we have hindered the evolution that was intended in the spiritual world, it is as if darkness were robbing us of our very existence. If we have done something in accordance with the evolution of the spiritual world, and its effects continue, it is as if light were calling us to fresh spiritual life." [18]

This process of evaluation is also described in the Seth material channeled by Jane Roberts, a talented medium whose husband recorded her messages from the entity Seth from 1963 until her death in 1984.[19] In addition to these transcripts, Roberts also wrote a trilogy of novels that explain Seth's message in a different way. In her first novel, *The Education of Oversoul Seven*,[20] Roberts suggests that each of us has a soul that is associated with several linked lives, and that the transitions between these lives is managed by an *oversoul*—a being who shepherds us after death into a period of evaluation. Our oversouls are then further managed by even higher spiritual beings. Roberts' description of oversouls and their "over-oversouls" popping in and out of different times and places made me wonder: While we live in three dimensions, is it possible that our oversouls live in four-dimensional space, and *their* oversouls live in five dimensions? Are Seth's teachings describing a hierarchy of beings at various levels of dimensionality, who manage the lives of beings in dimensions below them?

In any case, once the stage of spiritual evaluation after death is complete, Steiner claims that the deceased fully enter a spiritual world that exists between lives. Here they meet the souls of others who have transitioned before them, as well as other higher spiritual beings. At some point, perhaps under the guidance of an oversoul, each soul may then be given the opportunity to incarnate again and experience a new physical life. Incentives to return include compensating for past failures and gaining the opportunity to serve others and develop further. The cycle of reincaration then keeps repeating until a soul manages to perfect itself.

In Hinduism and Buddhism, this cycle of repeated incarnation into physical form is called *Samsara*. While we all originate in *Brahman*, the universal field, our own little piece of Brahman is called *Atman*, the deeper Self. Each time we incarnate, we are swept into *Maya*, the illusion of being. This repeats over and over until ultimately, we reach *Moksha*, the realization of our unity with Brahman. It is then that we achieve the state that God, Brahman, or the source of all-being truly meant for us. As Steiner writes:

> "Through our body we hold together what is really seeking to become 'ideal' in the universe... First we have the tapestry of memory; behind it, the mighty cosmic pictures we have 'rolled up' within us; behind this, again, lives what we have written into the world. Not until we have lived through this are we really ourselves, standing naked in spirit before the spiritual universe, which clothes us in its garments when we enter it... Our earthly memories are transient and become dispersed in the universe. But our Self lives behind them: the Self that is given us again from out of the spiritual world that we may find our way from time to eternity." [21]

CHAPTER 23

🕊

EMANATIONS FROM THE CAUSAL REALM

S O WHAT ABOUT THE LAST ENERGY BODY—THE *CAUSAL BODY*? EVEN
Steiner had little to say about this most esoteric part of the Self.
According to Kabbalah, the causal body resides within the realm of
Azilut or emanation. It is from this mysterious realm that all creation,
all form, all reality emanates. And if we actually have the tiniest bit of
access to it, then perhaps we too can participate in this divine creative
process.

The word "emanate" means "to flow out from a source." According
to Kabbalah, the *Tree of Life* is a model or structure that describes how
this emanation takes place (see Figure IV.2). The Tree is composed of
ten interconnected *sephirot* or enumerations, representing the ten at-
tributes of God:[1, 2, 3]

- *Keter* (Crown)—the divine plan, creator, infinite light, supreme
  consciousness, "I Am That I Am," unity, nothingness.

- *Hokhma* (Wisdom)—divine reality, revelation, being, or force
  created from nothingness.

- *Binah* (Understanding)—reason, repentance, capacity to take form.

- *Chesed* (Mercy)—grace, vision, love.

- *Gevurah* (Judgment)—strength, determination, intention.

- *Tiferet* (Adornment/Beauty)—symmetry, balance, compassion,
  mercy, creativity.

- *Netzakh* (Eternity/Victory)—persistence, endurance, the eternal Now.

- *Hod* (Majesty/Glory)—intellect, observation, sincerity, steadfastness, surrender.

- *Yesod* (Foundation)—coherence, remembering, ego.

- *Malkhut* (Kingdom)—physical matter, realization, accomplishment, diversity.

An eleventh sephira, called *Daat* or Knowledge, is also sometimes added to the Tree. It represents the mystical state of unification of the other ten sephirot, and has also been associated with the state of *Adam Kadmon*—the ultimate fulfillment of human potential. The sephirot

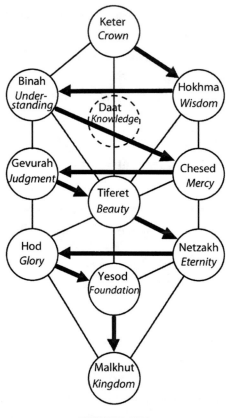

FIGURE IV.2

are then interconnected by twenty-two links, each of which is associated with one of the twenty-two letters of the Hebrew alphabet.

Needless to say, many books have been written about the Tree of Life and its various meanings and implications. The sephirot have been associated with the functions and organs of the body, the chakras, biblical characters, the planets, hierarchies of spiritual beings such as angels and archangels, and much more. Its study is easily the pursuit of a lifetime. However for our purposes, it is sufficient to understand that the Tree is used to model how reality emanates from the divine source until it manifests in our world—by proceeding through a sequence of states that begins at the top node of Keter and winds its way through the Tree until it reaches Malkhut. Also, it is interesting to note that the right side of the tree is typically associated with the active, creative forces of the "male principle," and that the left side is associated with qualities of the feminine—that which receives, molds, and structures. You might think of these two sides as analogous to the Chinese concepts of yang and yin or the Jungian psychological archetypes of animus and anima. The sephirot of the central column are then said to create balance and manifestation from the forces emerging from these two polarities.

One Bible story that is often associated with the Tree of Life is the tale of Jacob's Ladder (*Genesis* 28:12): "And he dreamed, and behold a ladder set up on the earth, and the top of it reached to heaven; and behold the angels of God ascending and descending on it." Just as the ladder in Jacob's dream was used by angels to descend from the higher realms and then to ascend again to God, scholars of Kabbalah view the Tree of Life not only as a model of how God's emanations descend into our own material reality, but also of how we can evolve and ascend—from Malkhut up to Keter—into higher states of awareness. This ascension has been the aim of students of Kabbalah for nearly 1,000 years.[4]

The notion that our reality emanates from a higher source is also found in other mystical traditions, some of which likely cross-fertilized with Kabbalah. One is Gnosticism, an early offshoot of Christianity, which teaches that a remote divinity emanates subsidiary divine beings, considered to be different aspects of the God source. These sparks of divinity then progressively emanate downward, and as they do, slowly change and become more distant in quality from the God source. Ultimately, they manifest as humankind.[5]

It is very likely that Gnosticism and Kabbalah also inspired Gurdjieff's teachings about emanation. He spoke of a *ray of creation* that proceeds from the unifying reality of the absolute and progressively splits, like a branching tree, until it reaches us humans. A discussion of the exact nature and mechanism of this ray consumes a large portion of Ouspensky's account of Gurdjieff's teachings, *In Search of the Miraculous*,[6] providing exhaustive detail about the kinds of substances and influences found at each of seven levels of reality that are formed during this process.

For example, Gurdjieff taught that the further a level is separated from the source, the more kinds of influences are felt there, and as a consequence, the more "mechanical" and less free that level becomes. He claimed that the level of everyday human reality is five degrees of separation away from the divine source and is thus relatively dense and mechanistic. However, because our energy bodies reside at higher levels in the hierarchy, they afford us greater degrees of freedom if we can learn to access them.

Is it possible that Gurdjieff's levels also correspond to spaces of different dimensionality, and that the freedom of our higher energy bodies derives from their existence in higher-dimensional space? Ouspensky thought so. Several chapters of his book about Gurdjieff's teachings are dedicated to a discussion of higher dimensional space. If Gurdjieff and Ouspensky are correct and our three-dimensional bodies are five degrees of separation from the source of creation, that would place our astral body in four dimensions (and four degrees of separation), our mental body in five dimensions (three degrees of separation), and our causal body in six-dimensional space—only two degrees of separation from source of all emanation in eight-dimensional space!

As in Kabbalah, Gurdjieff symbolically linked the levels emanating from the ray of creation with the planets, divine beings, and so forth. Two "laws" of his system, however, are particularly interesting—the *Law of Three* and the *Law of Octaves*. The Law of Three states that there are three types of principles or forces in the universe—the active or positive force, the passive or negative force, and the neutralizing force. It is easy to see how these forces map onto the "male" or right side of the Tree of Life, the "female" left side, and the balancing center column. At the source of the ray, all three of these forces are unified within the Absolute. And as the ray emanates, the three forces cause the ray to repeatedly split into three sub-rays, creating worlds at the levels below them.

The Law of Octaves, also called the Law of Seven, is even more fascinating. Gurdjieff said that it is not an accident that a musical octave consists of seven distinct notes: *do, re, mi, fa, so, la, ti*. The number seven, he taught, is a critical aspect of reality, and that's why it appears in so many forms—from the seven days of the week to the seven chakras, from the seven archangels to the seven halls of creation, from the seven colors of the rainbow to the seven rows of the periodic table. Indeed, if you don't include the eleventh Sephira of *Da'at*, there are seven levels within the Tree of Life. And if you do include *Da'at* and identify both Malkhut and Keter with the musical note *do*, you get a perfect octave. Gurdjieff also associated the seven levels of reality emanating from the ray of creation with seven states of development possible for mankind.

I could go on, describing other systems and ideas about emanation. However, the basic idea is that reality is always in a state of becoming. It's the implicate becoming explicate; it's Brahman emerging into Maya. And if the mystics are right, there is some intrinsic part of ourselves that can take part in this grand ballet and dramatically affect this unfolding process. Indeed, our goal should be to not only perfect our own lives and our own souls, but to help transform our collective reality here on Earth. As the famous Indian sage and philosopher Sri Aurobindo (1872-1950) said:

"The yoga we practice is not for ourselves alone, but for the Divine; its aim is to work out the will of the Divine in the world, to effect a spiritual transformation and to bring down a divine nature and a divine life into the mental, vital and physical nature and life of humanity. Its object is not personal Mukti [liberation], although Mukti is a necessary condition of the yoga, but the liberation and transformation of the human being. It is not personal Ananda [happiness], but the bringing down of the divine Ananda—Christ's kingdom of heaven, our Satyayuga [the era of truth]—upon the Earth."[7]

CHAPTER 24

✺

VISITS WITH OTHER REALMS

"No one can ever deny others the right to ignore the supersensible, but there is never any legitimate reason for people to declare themselves authorities, not only on what they themselves are capable of knowing, but also on what they suppose cannot be known by any other human being." [1]

—RUDOLF STEINER

THIS BRINGS ME TO THIS LAST AND PERHAPS MOST "FAR OUT" chapter of an already mind-boggling Part IV. If all I have said is true and our higher energy bodies have access to higher dimensions, and if we can also have a dramatic impact upon the unfolding of our reality, it stands to reason that there might already be some people who can wield amazing powers. And the fact is, some quite mysterious, supernatural abilities *have* been reported.

For example, I personally know followers of healer John of God in Brazil who have seen him perform painless surgeries without anesthesia. One of my friends, an osteopathic physician, shot video footage of one such operation, in which the healer removed a huge fatty tumor from a man's upper back. John of God made an incision with a scalpel, removed the tumor with his bare hands, and covered the surgery site with sterile strips. During this procedure, the patient was conscious and pain-free; he simply got up from his chair and walked away after it was complete. The video showed the entire operation in close up detail and included footage of the wound completely healed three days later, along with a testimonial from the patient. John of God is also known for performing "psychic" surgeries successfully—that is, with no physical intervention at all.[2]

Then there are the accounts of Indian gurus and adepts like Dadaji—Amiya Roy Chowdhury (1906-1992)—who supposedly manifested items out of thin air, changed water into nectar, and enabled a full-grown tree to spring out of a patch of dirt.[3] People have also been known to magically develop the stigmatic wounds of Christ and heal them just as quickly. In fact, the first reported stigmatist was St. Francis of Assisi. This twelfth century monk, as well as Therese Neumann, who died in 1962, were even able to manifest nail-like protuberances in the middle of their wounds—nails that could be pushed through to the other side of the arm.[4]

Are such things real or a hoax? If they are real, then people can manifest matter out of thin air and rearrange it according to their will. Such outcomes may exist among the infinite possible futures of our three-dimensional world. But can we mere mortals really manifest them at will? Or are these phenomena merely the product of consensual delusions of some kind?

One thing is for sure, these kinds of events have been reported everywhere on Earth. In the shamanistic societies of tribal Africa, for example, travels to other realms of existence are part of every person's life, and learning to navigate them is an important part of initiation into adulthood. In his fascinating book, *Of Water and Spirit: Ritual, Magic, and Initiation in the Life of an African Shaman*,[5] Malidoma Somé—a man who has straddled both the Western world and the world of the shamans—describes his amazing childhood. After witnessing some astounding things as the grandson of a tribal shaman, Somé was kidnapped and raised by Jesuit missionaries, who swept him into their Western view of reality. However, as a teenager, he managed to escape the mission and made his way back to his village.

Despite their initial reluctance, Somé eventually convinced the village elders to let him be initiated into the shamanic realms. There he discovered the truth of these alternate realities—where physical objects and information can be pulled out of thin air. He soon realized that his unique destiny was to bring this experience to a Western audience. After being given permission by his tribal elders to do so, Somé went on to receive doctorates from the Sorbonne and Brandeis University, and now gives seminars and retreats all over the world.

What can we make of this? In many native cultures, the bending of reality is seen as commonplace. In fact, to Somé's fellow tribesmen, our materialistic way of life is seen as narrow and childish—a kind of madness or delusion. This is exactly the way in which we view them! So consider this: What if Somé s tribe isn't backward—just aware of something different and profound? Perhaps we should find out more about it.

As Rudolf Steiner said, it's every person's right to ignore this information, but it should also be every person's right to explore it. Personally, I don't see the existence of the etheric, astral, mental, and causal realms as conflicting with science at all. Modern science has managed to competently explore our three-dimensional reality; why not try to explore this new unseen territory as well? I have found that opening myself up to these possibilities doesn't require me to abandon my rational mind; it only requires me to expand it. My advice is: *listen, be skeptical, but stay open.* There are all kinds of unexplained phenomena out there. Some are hoaxes, delusions, or can be explained in a conventional way. But others require a genuine expansion of our "normal" view of reality.

THE SPIRITUAL HIERARCHIES

Maybe it's all just a matter of developing the tools we need to access these other realms. Three hundred years ago we didn't have access to electricity and microwaves, radio and TV. Now we do. Perhaps we simply need to develop some new tools so that we can explore this new frontier—a frontier that Rudolf Steiner called the *spiritual hierarchies.* While these hierarchies were accepted in ancient times in a primitive way, now may be the time for humanity to wake up and embrace them once again—just in a different way; a way that incorporates all that we have learned in the interim.

According to Steiner, there are levels of reality "below" our own as well as those that exist "above" us. Below us lies the realm of the *elementals*—beings that animate the mineral and plant kingdoms. We unwittingly interact with them with every breath and step we take—when we ingest food, when we act in the world, even when we think or feel an emotion. Similarly, what we do and experience in our perceived reality is affected by and affects the activities of spiritual beings living in the realms above us. All of these beings are out there—they're just operating at different levels in the spiritual hierarchies.

These kinds of ideas can also be found in many cultures around the world. For example, consider the beliefs of the Australian aboriginal people about the *dreamtime*. These native people see their physical surroundings—the very landscape that surrounds them—as carrying vibrations of events occurring in other realms. For instance, the shape of a giant rock might be seen as the result of a great battle between otherworldly beings. According to Stanislav Grof, "This energy pattern, *guruwari*, or seed power, is an integral part of the terrain and lends it profound metaphysical meaning."[6] When Westerners come to a powerful spiritual place like Uluru (formerly known as Ayers Rock) and merely see it as a mountain to climb, the native people do not stop them from doing so; they just view them as foolish or insane. To the aboriginals, Uluru is a gateway between levels of the hierarchies.

The existence of parallel levels of reality might also explain other phenomena. For example, consider tales of fairies, elves, gnomes, leprechauns, and the like. Such beings are not only characters in children's stories, but they also appear in Malidoma Somé's experiences in the shamanic realms of Africa. They have also been called *nature spirits* or *devas*—elementals operating at lower levels in the hierarchies. Their role is to serve as aides to nature, nurturing the growth of plants and balancing the natural forces at work on Earth. And it is precisely through communication and cooperation with these devas that the developers of miraculous gardens like those at Findhorn, Scotland were able to grow lush tropical plants in the cold barren sands of the far north.[7]

What else could humanity achieve if we opened up more lines of communication with beings at other levels in the hierarchies? In his book *Supernatural*,[8] author Graham Hancock suggests that the very reason humanity evolved to its current level of consciousness is due to interactions with such beings. In fact, Hancock asserts that, through the use of psychedelic drugs like *ayahuasca* (a shamanic plant medicine used in South America), normal human perception can be widened so that it can perceive parallel realities that we are normally blind to. He also describes laboratory experiments with *Dimethyltryptamine* (DMT)—the active ingredient in ayahuasca—that demonstrate that, by taking the drug, human subjects can repeatedly and reliably gain access to a specific identifiable realm beyond everyday experience. Hancock suggests that it is this world and its beings that have guided humanity from the time of the cave man until today.

UFOS AND CROP CIRCLES

While I'm way out on this incredible limb, why not consider phenomena like crop circles and UFOs too? Crop circles are large, complex, geometric patterns found impressed upon field crops and sometimes in snow, sand, ice, or other vegetation. While many crop circles are admitted hoaxes created by people, some have never been explained.[9] Can all crop circles, a number of which have appeared spontaneously without any sign of human activity, be the work of nerdy graduate students with something to prove? Like the Australian dreamtime notion of the guruwari, are some crop circles manifestations of activity in other realms that have leaked into our own? Or are they transmissions from UFOs?

Most of us are aware of the numerous reports of unexplained visitors from other planets. In fact, UFO sightings have occurred all over the

Earth—some dating back centuries. One of the most dramatic events occurred in March 1997, when thousands of people witnessed a giant mile-long craft slowly making its way across the night sky of Phoenix, Arizona.[10] Many countries around the world, including several European nations, take UFOs much more seriously than the United States does— at least publicly. Several astronauts and cosmonauts, including Edgar Mitchell, Scott Carpenter, Gordon Cooper, and Victor Afanasyev, have also gone on record corroborating the existence of UFOs. In an address to the United Nations, Cooper said:

> "I believe that these extraterrestrial vehicles and their crews are visiting this planet from other planets... For many years, I have lived with a secret, in a secrecy imposed on all specialists and astro- nauts. I can now reveal that every day, in the United States, our ra- dar instruments capture objects of form and composition unknown to us. And there are thousands of witness reports and a quantity of documents to prove this, but nobody wants to make them public." [11]

Despite the fact that professing a belief in UFOs is a death knell to any professional's credibility, these astronauts were willing to go on record. So were many retired military officers who testified at a press conference organized by the Disclosure Project in May 2001,[12] and at another press conference that took place in September 2010 after the publication of a best-selling book by Leslie Kean, *UFOs*.[13] After years of keeping quiet, these military men were willing to break their security clearances and reveal what they had witnessed back in the 1950s and 1960s.

Are UFOs indeed visitations from other planets? Many claim that they carry actual beings that arrive here through inter-dimensional forms of travel. Perhaps they are making themselves more apparent to us today because they know that humanity and the Earth is at a crossroads. Another explanation for UFO phenomena was given by psi researcher Dean Radin.[14] Just as St. Francis of Assisi was able to manifest stigmatic wounds and even nails in his arms, Radin suggests that it might be humanity that is collectively manifesting crop circles and UFOs. Just as orbs may be photographable manifestations of our thoughts in the etheric realm, perhaps crop circles and even UFOs are products, not of our imagination, but of the collective power of active consciousness.

In the end, it may all be a matter of perception. Who knows what other parts of ourselves we can use to "see" and "act"? And who knows what we will experience and create when we are able to do so? Perhaps there is no hard line between our three-dimensional selves and the parts of us living in higher dimensions. After all, in the complete scheme of things, we participate in all levels of the spiritual hierarchies. What wonders will we discover as we continue to evolve and develop new and greater forms of awareness?

EXERCISE 4

❖ ❖ ❖

ENTERING NOW+ AND CONNECTING WITH THE SELF

In the previous three exercises, you learned to settle using "Feet. Seat. Back." and to explore the realms of outer sensation, inner sensation, emotions, and thoughts. You also began to learn how to better differentiate between these components of yourself and to control your experience of them. If you've been practicing regularly, you may also have achieved the *observer state*—a recognition that you are different than your sensations, emotions, and thoughts. The Observer is essentially the person sitting inside the carriage of your being—your deeper Self. Another way to think about the Self is as an amalgam of your higher energy bodies—your soul.

The goal of Exercise 4 is to spend more time experiencing this Self while in the state of NOW+. Please have a notebook ready to record any information or guidance you receive during this exercise.

STEP 1. Settle into the Now: "Feet. Seat. Back."

With your eyes open, settle into outer sensation using the techniques described in Exercise 1. Once you feel settled in your body, close your eyes and enter into an awareness of inner sensation (Exercise 2). Rest here for several minutes until you feel free from inner thoughts and emotions. If you have any difficulty, keep refocusing on "Feet. Seat. Back."

STEP 2. *Enter NOW+ and experience your Self.*

Once you feel solidly in the Now, it is time to enter NOW+. This state of being combines an awareness of the Now with open-heartedness and compassion. Here are some suggestions for achieving it:

- Call up NOW+ by simply saying to yourself internally, "open-heartedness and compassion."

- Put a slight smile on your face.

- Think about someone or something that is very beloved to you, such as a pet, child, or loved one.

- Identify with a loving person such as a grandparent or a religious figure like Jesus or Buddha.

If you are successful, you may experience the following kinds of sensations:

- A warm, expansive, or tingling sensation in your heart area.

- A feeling of energy rising from your feet up to your head and expanding outward from your chest and head.

- A sensation of calm and joy.

Rest in this state and expand it. This is the state of your higher or deeper Self. If you feel very solidly in NOW+, play with sending feelings of love, compassion, and kindness outward—first to yourself, then to loved ones, then to friends and acquaintances. You might even try sending compassion to someone you are having difficulty with. If you can do this without contracting, you will know that you are very solidly in NOW+. Finally, try to transmit your compassion outward even further—extending it to your community, city, state, country, humanity, the entire Earth, and even the universe! See what you can achieve. It will benefit you and those around you.

If you notice yourself contracting or becoming distracted by sensation, emotion, or thought, reground with "Feet. Seat. Back." and try to reenter NOW+.

STEP 3. Receive insights and guidance from your Self.

Relax and rest for a while longer in NOW+. When you are ready, form the intention to receive guidance from your Self. Stay open and receive any sensations, emotions, or thoughts that arise. Do not censor yourself. You might receive images or insights into a problem (which might include information about events from the past, or even from a past life), ideas for self-care that might be helpful, and tips about interpersonal relationships. Stay open, curious, and grateful for the guidance you receive.

Please note: If you receive thoughts, images, or emotions that are violent or negative toward yourself or others, this is your lower mind or ego speaking, not your Self. The Self always presents information that is positive and loving. If such negative information is received, it may be a good time to reground yourself using "Feet. Seat. Back." and try to reenter NOW+.

STEP 4. Return to normal awareness and record what you have experienced.

Slowly, return to your normal state of awareness. Thank your Self for its help and guidance. While you are still in a slightly altered state, record information about what you have experienced—the sensations, emotions, thoughts, and insights that you received.

Remember to perform all exercises in a spirit of play and fun and compassion for yourself. There is no right or wrong experience.

PART V

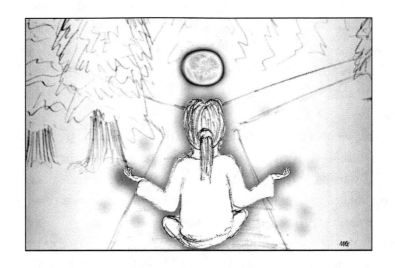

ENTER WITHIN

*"The inner voice is the voice of a fuller life,
of a wider, more comprehensive consciousness."*

—CARL JUNG

IT'S TIME TO DIVE IN...

Up until now, you've learned *about* the deeper Self: its structure according to various esoteric systems; how it might operate according to the model of active consciousness presented in Chapters 15 and 16; and scientific studies that provide indications that it may truly exist. But aside from Exercises 1—4, I haven't given you much guidance about how to get in touch with this mysterious passenger sitting inside the carriage of your being.

The rest of this book is focused on your own voyage of Self-discovery. In Chapters 25 and 26, I'll begin by describing the general contours of the road ahead, as well as some obstacles that you may encounter along the way. While confronting these roadblocks might be uncomfortable—many of them are psychological in nature—it is important that you do so in order to break through and establish solid contact with the Self.

In the second half of Part V, I'll provide a list of techniques that people from all over the world have used to navigate the bumpy road to Self-discovery—from meditation to dancing, from taking mind-altering drugs to engaging in divination practices—and why these methods can be successful, at least some of the time.

Then you'll move on to a variety of exercises. After experimenting with Exercise 5 at the end of Part V, you'll reach Part VI, a playground of activities and techniques derived from the teachings of Gary Sherman, along with some experiments based upon the method of active consciousness described in Chapter 18.

So dive in—and enjoy the waters!

CHAPTER 25

WHAT YOU ARE AND WHAT YOU ARE NOT

" 'Identifying' is one of our most terrible foes
because it penetrates everywhere."[1]

—G.I. GURDJIEFF

NEARLY ALL OF US HAVE EXPERIENCED OR HEARD OF FAMILIAL patterns of abuse. A parent, who is likely also the child of an abusive parent, fills his or her child's head with stories of self-loathing: "You're an idiot. You'll never succeed." "You're ugly—no one will ever love you." "You're a slut." "You're a bum." These stories—based, not on the truth, but on stories of pain living within the parent—accumulate like layers of wallpaper stuck to the interior of a child's mind. Their words echo at critical moments: when the child grows up and applies for a job, when they go out on a date, when they take a test at school. They are fables passed down from generation to generation, causing pain and suffering wherever they go.

Of course, stories don't have to be abusive, nor do they have to be handed down to us by our parents. Perhaps a well-meaning stranger tells a young girl, "Nice ladies wait politely until a man asks them to dance." Perhaps a teacher criticizes a student's artwork, and the student creates a story of her own making: "I'm terrible at drawing portraits. I'll never draw one again." Maybe a parent's well-intentioned nudging instills other kinds of stories in their child's mind: "I have to become a doctor or my parents won't love me"; "All of the men in my family enter the military, so I have to as well." Of course, a child might genuinely want to become a doctor or a soldier, and that's fine. In fact, many stories instill pride, courage, and feelings of belonging. They can also provide comfort and guidance when times are tough. But they are stories nonetheless. Written on the walls of our minds, they permeate our waking hours and fill our dreams at night.

Let's face it: there isn't a person alive who doesn't have stories. Every time something in the external world echoes a theme from one of them, it is reinforced. And every time we act according to the content of one of our stories, we perpetuate it further. However, a key step in the process of self-development is realizing that even if some stories are helpful, they are not *you*. They are stories that you carry around with you. If you want to discover who you truly are, you will need to distinguish between yourself and your stories.

····· YOUR STORIES ·····

One of my own stories has this theme: "Something very bad might happen suddenly to me." There were several events in my childhood that created and reinforced this story, such as unexpected outbursts of violent anger in my home and the sudden death of my father. Carrying this story around in my head, however, only served to create a kind of free-floating anxiety in me. It has also caused me to waste too much time on needless worrying and scenario planning. At some point, I even convinced myself that this story was useful, because it helped me prepare for unforeseen circumstances, protected me from inevitable disappointment, and served as a good luck charm to *avert* disaster. If

I worried enough, I told myself, I would be spared. One thing is for sure—this story has been a difficult monkey to get off my back.

Luckily, I now recognize and acknowledge that my fear of unexpected and sudden disaster is just one of my stories. I accept it and I forgive myself for having admitted it into my life. As a child I was sometimes frightened and confused, so I developed this story to protect me. Who knows? Perhaps it even accompanied me from a previous life. But now, in *this* life, I have decided to try and release it. When I hear it echo in my mind, I try to catch myself, smile, and say kindly and compassionately, "There I go again!" With a little effort at grounding in my physical body and applying some self-awareness, I am usually able to dissipate my feelings of anxiety and quell my worrisome thoughts. I return to the Now and acknowledge that I am just experiencing one of my stories. And over time, I have found that it is slowly loosening its grip on me.

Many teachers talk about the various kinds of stories we carry around with us. Gurdjieff called the process of equating ourselves with our stories *identifying*—especially when the stories pertain to roles we play in life. For example, if someone asks "What are you?", most of us will respond in a way that reflects a story of identification—with a job ("I am a writer"), a family role ("I am a wife and a mother of two sons"), or even with hobbies or ailments ("I'm a golfer," "I'm a cancer survivor"). Depending on the context, we might also cite our identification with a nationality, political party, or religion.

Most of us also associate particular emotions and thought patterns with our various roles and identifications. Have you ever felt like a chameleon? That you are many different people, acting in a different way depending on where you are or who you are with? When you are with friends, you might let it all hang out and act wild and crazy. When you are with your parents, you might recreate a petulant or clingy childhood. When you are at work, you act tough and responsible. When you are with your spouse and children, you play out the role of selfless helpmate, or strict and irritable disciplinarian. These are the various roles you play. But none of them are *you*.

The discovery of who you really are, Gurdjieff said, requires a process called *self-remembering*. It is about stripping away stories, roles, and identifications so that you can remember who you really are. One strategy is to remove yourself from settings in which you automatically assume a familiar role. As Gurdjieff wrote: "[P]ut [a man] into even only slightly different circumstances and he is unable to find a suitable role and *for a very short time he becomes himself.*" [2]

Perhaps that's why some of us travel to distant foreign lands as a method of self-discovery. As we grapple with unfamiliar situations, our stories become more obvious to us because they are now applied inappropriately in a foreign context. "You don't have coffee? I can't live without my morning coffee!" "Why are women dressing so provocatively here? That is inappropriate!" In a truly foreign context, we may also see our stories reflected back to us in the eyes of bewildered strangers who cannot understand "where we're coming from." Gradually, such circumstances force us to meet the world with a more naked, intrinsic part of ourselves.

Another benefit of immersing ourselves in new and unfamiliar ways of life is that the stories of strangers are also more obvious to us. Indeed, because foreign stories seem so odd, they help us realize that "reality" and "truth" are more relative than we usually assume—that they are, in fact, relative to culture, religion, family, and the individual. This realization helps us see that our own stories are also just that—stories. And if we gain some wisdom in the process, we may uncover a deeper, more essential part of ourselves. This *essence* is the part of us that strangers recognize, and that we ourselves recognize in strangers, no matter how alien their culture and its stories may be to us.

Of course, you don't need to travel to the furthest reaches of the planet to find yourself. You might just need to meet people who come from a completely different background than you do. While I was practicing as a homeopath for a couple of years, I had the chance to hear the life stories and perspectives of my clients. That was quite a privilege, and it also taught me that every one of us lives in a completely different world, embedded in our own unique stories. After a session with a new client, I would often drive home amazed at how our society manages to hang together, given how differently each of us sees and understands the world around us. Rather than needing to travel to a distant land, I discovered that I could learn about unfamiliar stories simply by listening to my patients.

Indeed, one way to view homeopathic treatment is as a process of uncovering the unique stories that hold a patient captive and create suffering for them. The goal of the homeopath is then to find a remedy associated with similar stories. After taking it, a patient often experiences a profound opening of perspective in both mind and body. Successful homeopathic treatment can also accentuate one's stories and create a subtle feeling of separation from them. For example, a role or behavior might suddenly seem more glaringly obvious. "Wow! I feel so nervous and I can't stop talking. Am I always like that?" "I never realized how judgmental I tend to be. No wonder people react to me the way they do!" This recognition of one's stories is an excellent beginning towards ultimately becoming free of them.

In his book, *The Power of Now*,[3] spiritual teacher Eckhart Tolle calls the truly destructive stories that imprison us the *pain body*. He associates it with the ego or personality, and stresses that it can be very hard to shake. In essence, Tolle is teaching us that the thoughts and feelings of the pain body transmit the yank of the reins and the sting of the whip of our carriage driver (the ego), who likes to remain very firmly in control. Nevertheless, the passenger sitting inside the carriage of our being is still the one who is truly in charge. And the way to reach this inner part of ourselves is by accessing the Now. Tolle writes:

> "Some people live almost entirely through their pain-body, while others may experience it only in certain situations, such as intimate relationships, or situations linked with past loss or abandonment, physical or emotional hurt, and so on. Anything can trigger it, particularly if it resonates with a pain pattern from your past. When it is ready to awaken from its dormant stage, even a thought

or an innocent remark made by someone close to you can acti-vate it. Some pain-bodies are obnoxious but relatively harmless, for example like a child who won't stop whining. Others are vicious and destructive monsters, true demons. Some are physically violent; many more are emotionally violent... The pain-body, which is the dark shadow cast by the ego, is actually afraid of the light of your consciousness. It is afraid of being found out. Its survival depends on your unconscious identification with it, as well as your unconscious fear of facing the pain that lives in you. But if you don't face it, if you don't bring the light of your consciousness into the pain, you will be forced to relive it again and again. The pain-body may seem to you like a dangerous monster that you cannot bear to look at, but I assure you that it is an insubstantial phantom that cannot prevail against the power of your presence."[4]

THE PURPOSE OF STORIES

So why do we have pain bodies and stories? What purpose do they serve? The answer is that they can help us to survive. When we are trau-matized, we usually need some form of explanation or tool in order to cope. For instance, a child might tell herself that she is "bad" and that's why her parents beat her. Facing the truth—that her parents are severe-ly flawed and even helpless—would be too horrible or threatening for a vulnerable and dependent child to accept. So concocting a story of self-blame is a way of defending herself. This and other common defense mechanisms, like *rationalization, denial,* and *projection,* have been studied extensively by psychologists, and are well-understood methods for pro-tecting the ego. They are also aspects of the *shadow,* a Jungian concept representing internal weaknesses, contradictions, and dark urges that must be brought to light in order for us to become whole.

Gurdjieff called these kinds of stories *buffers,* and said that their pri-mary purpose is to cope with internal contradictions. For example, a woman may honestly believe that she is loving and caring, and most of her day-to-day behavior may reflect this benevolent side of her nature.

But when she is in the company of certain people, this same woman might deny the humanity of another group of people because she has been told that they are "the enemy" or that they are in some way "other" and therefore harmful to her way of life. Although she may have never met one of these "others," this woman cannot consider or listen to their words or point of view, because that would mean acknowledging that she had been complicit in brutalizing them. Instead, she uses buffer stories of rationalization, denial, and projection—making excuses for her actions, denying any form of wrongdoing, and accusing the "others" of what she herself is guilty. These stories serve to protect her from facing the inherent conflict between her "loving and caring" self and her hateful and harmful words and actions. They also enable her to act in destructive ways, despite the positive aspects of her nature.

Just think about what you read in the newspaper each day about deep-seated conflicts in the Middle East or other war-torn areas, or about the demonization of immigrants and other marginalized groups, and you will quickly see that whole nations of people are busy exercising their buffers. In a way, buffers are hard to avoid. As Gurdjieff said:

> "A man is surrounded by people who live, speak, think, and feel by means of 'buffers.' Imitating them in their opinions, actions, and words, a man involuntarily creates similar 'buffers' in himself... 'Buffers' lull a man to sleep, give him the agreeable and peaceful sensation that all will be well, that no contradictions exist and that he can sleep in peace... 'Buffers' help a man not to feel his conscience." [5]

When you do start recognizing buffers, you will begin to see them everywhere. Buffers are at work when people denigrate and deny the human rights of marginalized "other" groups, like homosexuals or other minorities. Buffers also help us turn a blind eye to our overconsumption of resources—something that ultimately hurts others on the planet, including our descendants.

Unfortunately, buffers are alive and well in business and science too. They enable us to promote science and business practices that are inherently destructive. Consider the actions of scientists and companies that develop genetically-engineered plants that produce only infertile seeds—a form of agricultural greed that forces farmers to buy fertile seeds from the offending company and drives many of them into ruin and even suicide, especially in poor countries. These companies promote their products as "helping to feed the planet"—but such statements are clearly examples of rationalization and denial. Of course, most of the people who work for these companies probably have good intentions. But due to a variety of pressures and forms of indoctrination, they have developed buffers that shield them from the inherent contradiction between their intentions and their actions.

DEEP COMMUNICATION—PENETRATING THE BOUNDARIES OF STORIES AND BUFFERS

Given a planet with billions of people, each with their own stories and buffers—how do we avoid winding up in chaos? It's truly remarkable that things hang together as well as they do—and a testament to the basic goodness of humanity. Nevertheless, sometimes our stories and buffers do come into conflict with those of others. When this happens, communication becomes nearly impossible and conversations begin to resemble fortresses shooting cannons at one another.

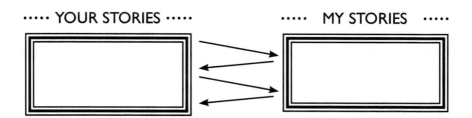

However, if each of us could free ourselves from our stories and buffers and communicate from a standpoint of *essence*—who we really are—deep and true communication could occur.

···· YOUR ESSENCE ····   ······ MY ESSENCE ······

Perhaps you can recall precious moments in your life when this kind of communication and understanding took place. Although such moments may be rare for many people, one of the byproducts of self-development is that they can occur more often. The trick is to free yourself, as much as possible, from your stories.

Of course, you might ask: what if you are sincerely trying to acknowledge your own stories and the other person is not? What if you are coming from essence, but the other person is locked behind the walls of their stories? The answer is that you must take the stance that a parent adopts with a small child. A wise parent does not take their child's temper tantrums personally; they simply exercise patience, compassion, and perhaps a little gentle discipline. It's definitely harder to adopt this kind of stance with an adult peer, but if you can, their actions and words will pass more gently through you. You will also be able to be more compassionate, because you will better understand what is motivating them. As Gurdjieff said:

> "[I]f a man really remembers himself he understands that another man is a machine just as he is himself. And then he will *enter into his position*, he will put himself in his place, and he will be really able to understand and feel what another man thinks and feels."[6]

In other words, the path to deep communication begins by recognizing your own stories and then recognizing and understanding the other person's stories too. Gradually, by assuming a more grounded, compassionate, and transparent stance—coming from essence rather than from story—you ultimately help the other people in your life to drop their stories and come from essence too.

CHAPTER 26

⌇

SELF-REMEMBERING—THE PATH TO ENLIGHTENMENT

THERE HAVE BEEN MANY TEACHERS WHO HAVE TRIED TO HELP us remember our true Self. It was the goal of Jesus to evoke the Christ consciousness within each one of us. The quest for the Self has also been the aim of Kabbalah, Sufism, Hinduism, and Buddhism. It is the basis of the teachings of mystics like Gurdjieff, Steiner, Sri Ramana Maharshi, and Sri Aurobindo. It's what the prophet Muhammad was talking about when he said that we need to surrender; it's why Jesus said we must love one another and not stand in judgment; it's why Buddha said that suffering arises because we have forgotten our true nature and have become captive to the cravings of the personality. The same message underlies the teachings of Moses and Abraham when they spoke of the unity of God and the need to follow commandments that help us maintain contact with the One-ness that encompasses us all.

All of these paths and teachings lead to the same goal: the stripping away of stories, illusions, the greediness of the ego, the vagaries of personality, and the hubris of intellect, in order to reach our *essence*—the true nature of our being. It's not easy. But in a way, it's very simple. You don't need to *add* something. You only need to remove the debris that covers up what is already there. You don't need to learn something *new*—just remember what you already know deep down inside.

As Gurdjieff said, it's all about self-remembering—the remembering of one's true nature.

Many new teachers have emerged in the past few years that are trying to bring forth this message, and the fact that more and more people are pursuing studies in meditation and other forms of self-awareness may indicate that humanity is getting closer to taking their message to heart. At least I hope so! That's why I'm writing this book. Two thousand years ago, highly evolved states of consciousness were far beyond most people's capability, so only a few enlightened prophets could lead the way. Today, as we all stand at the brink of looming planetary changes, there may be a greater number of us who can attain these states more easily.

Of course, that doesn't mean that the process of self-remembering and personal evolution is easy or effortless. If you decide to embark upon this path, part of you will resist, even if you have good intentions. But you *will* make progress if you practice on a regular basis. You also need to apply self-awareness and meditation techniques in the context of everyday life, not just on the meditation cushion. Otherwise, the lessons you learn will not permeate your experience.

Finally, remember to be patient and gentle with yourself. Try to approach the process of self-remembering in a spirit of inquisitiveness and playfulness, not one that reflexively jumps into self-loathing or blame. Remember: we're all in the same boat! When the waters get rough, just get back in and keep paddling.

WAKE UP!—TO WHO YOU ARE AND WHAT YOU'RE DOING

All the methods, meditations, exercises, and ideas that mystics have developed for gaining self-awareness are essentially ways to detach from the illusions we create when we identify with our bodies, emotions, and thought stories. These techniques help us realize what we are not, so that we can discover who we are. And when you first experience a precious moment of liberation from your habitual way of being—whether it be by turning off your mind chatter through meditation, dancing, or drumming, venturing into new forms of awareness through the use of drugs, or becoming alert to the Now by epiphany or bungee jumping—you will suddenly realize that you *can* exert some control over your awareness.

Of course, afterwards, you will likely view this experience as fleeting—as an exception, an aberration, or even as a dream. You will quickly forget about it and become reabsorbed into the normal trance of life. But the more you integrate intentional shifts of awareness into your experience, the more you will realize that you do have the ability to leave this trance behind. *You begin to wake up.*

Just as exercising your body's muscles can make strenuous activities easier to perform, the more you flex the muscle of awareness, the easier waking up becomes. You may not have a profound experience every time you penetrate the fog of everyday life. But the fog will gradually become thinner over time. Little pockets of clarity will begin to break through. Your overall experience of life will slowly change, and gradually you will not only wake up but self-remember. When you do, you will rediscover a part of you that lies beyond personality, ego, and stories. This is the deeper Self that accompanies you from life to life—your essence. And if you manage to live your life from the standpoint of this essence most of the time, you will have reached enlightenment. *So how do you get started?*

Recognize That You Are Asleep

First, acknowledge that, deep within, you are already perfect, healed, and complete. Next, recognize that most of the time you are "asleep." That's really what Exercises 1—4 were all about—helping you notice that there's more going on beyond the normal trance of daily life (a state of "waking sleep"), and that you also have control over this experience. When you see that you can alter or influence the flow of your thoughts, emotions, and sensations, you begin to realize that these experiences are not *you*. And by learning to settle into your body and be in the Now—to simply *be*—you will have taken your first step towards "waking up."

Here's another way to think about it. Much of the time your thoughts, feelings, and sensations wander around like a perpetual stream of randomly branching associations. Even when you're performing a task like cooking or driving, this associative process is always going on in the background. Stop for a moment, quiet yourself, and notice how this is the case. This is the normal trance of life. However, nearly all of us have also experienced peak moments when we're "in the zone" and our attention is focused and controlled. Time stops. We are in the Now. We feel more "awake." What if your life experience could be like that more often? That is your goal. Indeed, it is these peak moments that we often remember most vividly. That's because we experience them from the vantage point of the deepest part of our being—our inner Selves.

Notice Your Stories

Once you've learned to get into the Now, at least for a short period of time, your next step is to see more clearly, from the perspective of the Now, what you're doing when you're "asleep." For example, you may notice that many of the thoughts chattering away in your head are stories of your own creation. Do these stories really match your current experience? Or are they residues of the past? What assumptions do you make about the world or other people that aren't actually supported by what's going on? For example, do your stories cause you to be jealous or suspicious when it is totally unwarranted? Do they fill you with unnecessary fears and worries? Once you realize and acknowledge that you are simply acting out or responding to your stories, the next step is to notice when these stories are triggered. Try to catch yourself and say to yourself with compassion, "Oh! There I go again." If you succeed, you will become more awake and will have further cleared the fog of sleep.

Be Proactive, Not Reactive

The next step is to begin to exert some control and insert a new kind of experience into your life: *to be proactive rather than reactive.* Most of us think we have no choice but to react to the things that happen to us. We believe that our emotions and thoughts work like physical reflexes and that we have no control over them. But if during a meditative exercise you were able to intentionally evoke troubling emotions and thoughts, and then just as easily remove them, you will soon realize that this reactivity is not cast in stone. You *do* have some control. And when you apply these same techniques in your day-to-day life—especially when you're experiencing difficult emotions—you may find that you can become more of a master of your experience than you thought was possible.

Of course, your goal is not to suppress your feelings and thoughts. That would be counterproductive and even harmful. Instead, try to become the *director* of your experience. For example, when I become fearful just before a trip (a common pattern for me), I try to notice my fears, acknowledge them, and choose new thoughts and emotions that evoke a wonderful, exciting, and carefree travel experience. In other words, I try to consciously direct what I feel and experience, rather than simply allow my stories to dictate it. When we succeed in becoming the director of our experience, we are acting more from the vantage point of our inner Selves.

Pay Attention to Feedback

Once you've achieved some periods of being in the Now, have become more aware of your stories, and have even managed to direct your experience via contact with the Self, how will you know if you are on the right track? Are your feelings of Self-awareness just another delusion of the ego? Luckily, there are feedback mechanisms that can help guide you: *Your everyday sensations and feelings let you know how you are doing.* As mentioned in Chapter 18, this is what the "emotional guidance system" of the Abraham teachings are all about.[1]

First of all, when you are genuinely spending more of your time in a state of Self-remembering, you will also find that you are more in *alignment* with what's going on around you. Your emotions, thoughts, and sensations will line up and there won't be as much tension between what you believe and desire and what you experience. You will also sense greater clarity, ease, and expansion. Even when difficult things arise in the external world, you will be better able to cope and regain a sense of equanimity. In addition, you will have better access to active consciousness and will be able to tune in to the subtle information and guidance of the Self that is helping you manifest and create.

Interestingly, this state of being also promotes health and can even serve as a veritable youth tonic! As Eckhart Tolle writes, "[I]f you inhabit the inner body, the outer body will grow old at a much slower rate, and even when it does, your timeless essence will shine through the outer form, and you will not give the appearance of an old person."[2] The power of meditation to keep the brain young has even been verified scientifically, with improvements in memory recall, concentration, and verbal fluency measured after only eight weeks of a daily twelve-minute meditation. Physical changes to the brain have also been measured, such as added thickness in the gray matter associated with learning and motor skills.[3]

In contrast, when you are *out* of alignment, you will get a different kind of feedback. Your thoughts will be overrun by stories. Your body will experience sensations of contraction, and your emotions will be dominated by periods of unhappiness and suffering. These are signals that you should meditate more often, get back into the Now, and get in touch, as much as possible, with your Self. The outer circumstances of your life may remain difficult for a while, but your efforts to self-remember and use active consciousness will enable you to cope better. And in time, your outer circumstances will also gradually improve and come back into alignment with your beliefs and desires.

GENUINE VERSUS DISTORTED OR ARTIFICIAL FORMS OF SELF-REMEMBERING

Unfortunately, there are times when we can deceive ourselves about our state of awareness. We may believe that our insights are genuine, but in end, they may simply be the products of our stories or delusional thinking. I have sometimes heard it said that people with serious mental illness are tapping into genuine higher states of consciousness. My experience with my own schizophrenic brother makes me highly doubtful that this is the case. While psychotic people may, at times, be truly perceiving different aspects of reality, the extent to which their lives are dominated by suffering indicates that their perceptions are not arising from a clear form of self-remembering.

I also believe that the use of drugs to achieve altered states of awareness does not yield the same kinds of long-term psychological and practical benefits as attaining such states with more natural methods of self-development. While a drug experience can open a door and help someone see what's possible, it is an artificial means of entry that cannot be sustained without compromising the physical and energy bodies. And when a drug experience is over, a return to ordinary life is inevitable. Don't forget—it is during our ordinary lives that we need to manage our stories and live from essence.

In the end, there are no short cuts. The quest to genuinely self-remember requires conscious effort and regular practice. The rest of this book is all about tools and exercises that can help you achieve this aim.

CHAPTER 27

ॐ

METHODS AND TOOLS FOR ACCESSING NON-ORDINARY STATES OF AWARENESS

"We go deeper into the physical to reach the infinite."[1]

—DANIEL PINCHBECK

FOR THE REST OF PART V, I WILL DESCRIBE A LIST OF TECHNIQUES that have been used for achieving deeper or altered states of awareness. While I recommend beginning with the exercises provided in this book, the following "tool kit" of strategies may also be interesting and useful to consider.

MEDITATION

The most common method used to gain access to the Self is meditation. And the initial goal of any meditative practice is to still the chattering mind and get into the Now. Needless to say, most people find this difficult to do using will power alone. Instead, the easiest gateway is through the body—for example, by focusing on sensations like "Feet. Seat. Back." or by training one's concentration on the breath. Another common technique is to focus one's senses on an object like a flower, on a sound like a bell, or to recite a mantra—a repetitive thought statement, preferably with symbolic meaning. For example, repetitive prayers like recitation of the Rosary are essentially mantras.

Personally, I find the use of "Feet. Seat. Back." to be extremely simple and effective. It's quick too. By focusing on the sensations of my feet, seat, and back, I can immediately establish a connection with my body that envelops and grounds me. The still, ever-present sensation of the body—which is always in the Now and possesses a deep and rich way of knowing—provides each one of us with a reliable and speedy gateway to the Self.

Another wonderful aspect of using body sensations to get into the Now is that they are available to you whenever and wherever you are—in line at the supermarket, waiting at a traffic light, or while walking in the woods. With practice, you can even attain a level of body awareness while you are speaking or listening. This makes the use of body sensation especially valuable, since our goal is to integrate deeper states of awareness into our everyday lives.

So what happens when you meditate? In Chapters 21 and 22, I suggested that you literally tap into your higher energy bodies. By starting with a focus on the sensations of the physical body, you slowly integrate the sensations of the etheric, astral, mental, and even causal bodies, and from there access other realms.

Even on a purely physical level though, scientists have shown that meditative states can create measurable changes in the brain. Many books have been written about this subject and whole conferences have been devoted to it. Using electroencephalography (EEG), for example, researchers have shown that there are at least five types of brain activity, ranging from the slowest to the fastest in frequency: *delta* (deep sleep); *theta* (the state that spans dreaming to pre-sleep drowsiness); *alpha* (a state of relaxation); *beta* (a state of active concentration or busy, anxious thinking); and *gamma* (a highly focused state of awareness and deep insight).

While meditators often spend much of their time in alpha or theta, advanced practitioners spend most of their time in gamma. They also manifest the highest degree of synchronization or coherence in their brain waves. The gamma state has also been shown to yield the best results in psi experiments and distance healing abilities.[2] In fact, studies conducted by researchers Richard Davidson and Antoine Lutz at the University of Wisconsin, in cooperation with the Dalai Lama, have demonstrated that seasoned meditative practitioners register the highest gamma waves ever recorded.[3] They also showed that meditation can improve mental health and physical well-being, stimulating the parts of the brain associated with joy. Even beginners showed positive effects, including enhanced immune function, after only eight weeks of regular meditation.[4]

DRUGS

Humanity has also used a variety of drugs to achieve altered states of awareness. Indeed, many cultures have sanctified their relationship with plant hallucinogens like ayahuasca, peyote, anhalonium, datura, iboga, and psilocybin. As mentioned in Chapter 24, Malidoma Somé's tribe used such plants as part of their initiation ritual into unseen realms, and so do many other indigenous peoples.[5] In the West, drugs like LSD (initially used as a therapeutic aid for mentally ill patients), ketamine (an anesthetic with the unusual property that it does not cause unconsciousness but rather, a separation of consciousness from the body), and DMG (the primary active ingredient in ayahuasca) have also been used to access alternative realms of experience.

HYPNOSIS AND VISUALIZATION

Another method of triggering an altered form of awareness is *hypnosis*, a method of inducing the state associated with theta brain waves. Experiences with therapeutic forms of hypnosis have shown that suggestions delivered to subjects in the hypnotic state can help them make desired changes in their lives. One reason may be that the hypnosis process is similar to the steps of active consciousness—relaxing into the Now, embodying a goal state, and letting go of doubt. Tapping into the theta state for purposes of healing is also the aim of a therapeutic technique called *Theta Healing.*[6]

Another similar technique, *visualization*, works essentially the same way as hypnosis. During visualization exercises, subjects go into a relaxed state (in this case, the alpha state) and imagine themselves attaining a desired goal such as improved health or winning a race. In recent years, visualization has even become an important tool for elite athletes. In fact, studies have shown that merely visualizing weight training can build muscles half as well as doing real exercise![7]

PUSHING BODY LIMITS TO ACHIEVE TRANCE STATES

The word "trance" is derived from the Latin "transire"—to cross or pass through. By pushing the boundaries of normal bodily functions, people have found that they are sometimes able to cross over into a new and different realm of experience. As Stuart Wilde says in *The Art of Meditation*, "In order to awaken to a brand new existence including multiple-dimensions described by theoretical physicists, trance states kindly show us the escape hatch."[8]

People have pushed the limits of their bodies in a variety of ways in order to achieve this goal. Fasting, sweat lodges, drumming, chanting, dancing, and other forms of rhythmic movements have all been used to shift from a normal state of awareness into an altered state. Indeed, extreme sports like bungee jumping can have this effect too.

Trance states can also be induced by listening to rhythmic sounds. For instance, armies have long used the repetitive sound of drumming to enable troops to overcome their fear; just think of the fife and drum corps of the Revolutionary War, or the Scottish warriors marching off to war accompanied by the sound of the bagpipes and drums. Today, a whole new industry has sprung up around technologies that use sound to affect the brain in new ways. A quick surf on the Internet will turn up products that claim to deliver the experience of psychedelic drugs or the synchronization of brain waves through the use of sound.

Of course, other sensations of the body can be stretched to the limit as well. Gurdjieff, for example, stressed that habitual body postures keep us captive, and that in order to break free, we must not only become more aware of these postures, but experiment with changing them. As he said:

"Every race... every nation, every epoch, every country, every class, every profession, has its own definite number of postures and movements... A man is unable to change the form of his thinking or his feeling until he has changed his repertory of postures and movements." [9]

To aid in this process, Gurdjieff used what he called the "Stop" exercise. He would ask his students to move about, and at an unpredictable moment, would call out: "Stop!" His students were then required to remain perfectly still and not move their bodies, eyes, or facial expressions. Invariably, they would be caught in a posture that they were completely unfamiliar and uncomfortable with. "In this unaccustomed posture he is able to think in a new way, feel in a new way, know himself in a new way. In this way the circle of old automatism is broken." [10]

Another way of pushing body limits is through controlled breathing. For example, a technique developed by Stanislav Grof, called *Holotropic Breathwork*, utilizes intensified breathing similar to hyperventilation, and couples it with music, body work, and expressive drawing. Participants in Breathwork sessions have reported a variety of experiences, including hallucinations, spontaneous postural changes that aid the flow of body energy, surfacing of suppressed memories such as birth traumas (that were later verified), recall of past-life material, out-of-body experiences, and feelings of connection with the collective unconscious. [11]

NEAR-DEATH AND OUT-OF-BODY EXPERIENCES

Other bodily circumstances can also create experiences like those afforded by meditation, trance, or drugs. For instance, as mentioned in Chapter 9, near-death and out-of-body experiences triggered by trauma can be associated with a feeling that one's consciousness has separated from one's body. In Chapter 22, I also described how lucid dreaming can afford a similar experience.

GROUPS AND LOCATIONS

One important aspect of many awareness-building techniques is that they are often performed with other people. This is no accident. As verified by researchers like Dean Radin, psi effects are nearly always enhanced when a group of people is working together towards a common goal.[12,13] That's why people tend to meditate together, drum together, chant together, and pray together. When a group of people is on the "same wavelength"—when they become entangled and enter into a similar state of vibration or coherence—the results of their efforts become noticeably amplified. I have experienced this myself. When I meditate in a group setting, especially with a group that I have meditated with before, it is noticeably easier and quicker for me to enter into a very deep meditative state.

Studies have shown that location matters too. In particular, when meditation occurs in a particular location repeatedly, that location becomes "conditioned" over time so that effects are enhanced. As described in Chapter 11, this was even demonstrated scientifically by the instruments in Professor Tiller's laboratory at Stanford University. Repeated trials of his experiments with meditatively-imprinted devices literally created physical alterations within the lab. Perhaps that's why places of worship often carry a certain aura about them. When large groups of people meditate or pray in the same place on a regular basis, that place becomes more and more powerfully conditioned. But even if you're meditating on your own, doing so in the same location each day will serve to enhance and intensify your experience.

SYNCHRONICITY TOOLS

Tarot cards, I Ching coins, Rune stones, tea leaves, a pendulum, or even the pages of a spiritual book can also be used to access information from the Self—through a practice called *divination*. The art of divination involves utilizing a random process, like the draw of a card or the throw of coins, to gain information and guidance. How can this possibly work? It's all about synchronicity. If you take seriously the fact that fields of meaning manifest themselves through unlikely but meaningful "coincidences," then divination tools provide a means to access them.

Personally, I have successfully used I Ching coins, Native-American medicine cards, and the random selection of book pages with quite profound results. Each morning, if I don't have to jump out of bed for some reason, I try to spend some time meditating and contemplating my coming day. While in an open and loving state, I choose one among several spiritual books at my bedside and then randomly open to a page. Here is a typical experience that I recorded in November 2006.

At the time I was having difficulty with a friend who I felt was unfairly attacking me. I decided to perform a meditation similar to the one I will describe in Exercise 5. First, I entered NOW+. Then, I brought the problem into my awareness. Soon, I felt a tightening in my chest area, but I was able to relax it and regain equanimity. Next, I received guidance that my friend's behavior was due to her own fear and that all I had to do was make myself transparent to her aggressive energy so that it could pass through me. Finally, I selected one of Sanaya Roman's books, *Personal Power Through Awareness*, to ask for further guidance. I randomly opened to page 106, where I read the following:

> "The ability to accept other people for who they are is a great challenge, and as you master it, so do you give that gift to yourself. If someone is yelling at you or talking in a tone of voice or a way that sparks anger, defensiveness, or sadness in you, begin sending him love telepathically. Bring yourself to a peaceful center and relax your breathing. As you send him love, do not expect him to quit yelling or respond in any way. Know as you send this love you are raising *your* vibration. Soon, either he will change or you will find that you are no longer creating situations where others are angry at you." [14]

Well, how perfect and apt was that? Apparently, my meditation had enabled me to enter into a field of meaning appropriate to this situation, and synchronicity had "caused" me to choose that particular book and page. This kind of thing happens to me so often now that it no longer seems like an incredible "coincidence." In fact, just as locations can become conditioned by repeated meditative use, certain objects can as well. Thus, a specific deck of cards, a set of coins, or a book may, over time, become more and more useful as a divination tool.

SHOCKS

Some people have a hard time "waking up" no matter how much they meditate. For these individuals, a spiritual alarm clock may be necessary—what Gurdjieff called a *shock*. A shock is something, somebody, or an event that rattles a person's carriage so much that they finally become better able to question their stories and assumptions. It might be a challenging illness or a traumatic physical or emotional event. Or it might be something that occurs on a more global scale, like economic collapse or war. It might simply be a "peak moment"—an astounding athletic success, a transformative musical or theatrical experience, a sexual escapade, or a miraculous "near miss" brush with death. Whatever it is, a shock has to have enough power to thrust the individual out of their normal state of awareness and create a lasting impact. It has to create an epiphany—a transformative experience.

I had one such experience in London during a holiday vacation in the summer of 1976. I was a young woman of twenty that day, as I ventured out see Speaker's Corner in Hyde Park—a plaza where people are free to step up on soapboxs and speak their minds. Soon after emerging from the London Underground, I found myself listening to two such speakers standing side by side—one Israeli and the other Palestinian. I looked closely into their eyes and listened carefully to their impassioned words.

At the time, I was seriously considering immigrating to Israel and spending the rest of my life there. I had naturally assimilated the Israeli point of view and had a strong distrust of Palestinians. But somehow, for the first time in my life, I could clearly see that each man was speaking his own truth. The Palestinian was not lying and what he was saying wasn't easy for me to hear. This was a shocking and revelatory moment for me. In an instant, I realized that I had been culturally conditioned to hear and believe only one side of a very complex and painful story. The truth was not black and white but a speckled composite.

That event had a profound and lasting effect on me. I gave up my plans to immigrate to Israel and have not returned there since that day. Over the years, many Jews, Israelis, and Palestinians have come to the same realization that I did back in 1976. Like me, they have come to understand that the only productive path forward in the Middle East will be one based on mutual acknowledgement and reconciliation. Unfortunately, however, the vast majority of people on both sides of the Israel/Palestine struggle are still embedded in their stories and buffers and have a long road to travel before true peace can be found.

So what happened to me? I experienced a shock that penetrated my buffers and broke up some well-entrenched stories. Interestingly, it also occurred while I was overseas and far away from my normal day-to-day routine. But did this experience collapse *all* of my stories? Did I suddenly become enlightened at age twenty and develop a permanent link to my deeper Self? Of course not. But the fog cleared and I woke up a bit more.

TEACHERS

For many of us, it is a teacher who precipitates a shock and makes the wake-up call that finally shakes us awake. It might be a guru or a priest. It might be a friend, relative, or an enlightened stranger. Whoever it is, a true teacher is someone who will be honest with you and will inspire complete honesty and sincerity from you in return. They will also help you with feelings of discouragement, because they too have traveled the same path. If you do decide to study with a teacher, I encourage you to be wary of people who try to control their students. Such people are engaging in their own stories. A truly enlightened teacher will not require or desire that kind of power over others.

No Practice, No Benefit

Back in 1993, the instructor of that Chi Gong class I was taking repeatedly said something that stuck with me: "No practice, no benefit." Wise words. You cannot reap any true benefit by simply reading about something. You must experience it for yourself. The lesson is clear: You will not make progress along the path of self-development until you make that quest a part of your daily routine. You don't need to go to an expensive retreat or even have a teacher. You just need to begin where you are.

Make the commitment today to spend at least fifteen minutes each day on self-development and inquiry. Over time, you will be surprised by the results. Begin now—by reviewing Exercises 1—4, and then move on to Exercise 5 and the exercises and experiments provided in Part VI.

EXERCISE 5

❖ ❖ ❖

TAPPING INTO THE WISDOM
OF THE SELF

In the previous four exercises, you learned to settle using "Feet. Seat. Back." and explored the realms of outer sensation, inner sensation, emotion, and thought. You also learned how to achieve the state of NOW+. In Exercise 5, you will now access your deeper Self and ask for some help and guidance about a particular problem. I encourage you to use this technique any time you feel physical or emotional discomfort. Accessing the wisdom of the Self can help to ease this distress and may also provide you with some powerful insights.

Before you begin, choose something that you would like to work on. Start with something small and specific. For instance, rather than choosing "My troubled marriage," pick something specific like "My fight with Bob last night." Or rather than asking about "My health problems," select a specific problem like "The eczema on my finger." Have a piece of paper handy and jot down a short phrase that describes your problem. Then set it aside and let's begin.

STEP 1. Settle into the Now and NOW+.

With your eyes open, settle into outer sensation using the techniques described in Exercise 1. Once you feel ready, close your eyes and settle into inner sensation (Exercise 2). Rest here for a few minutes until you feel free from inner thoughts and emotions. If you have any difficulties, keep refocusing on "Feet. Seat. Back." Finally, call up the state of open-heartedness and compassion using the techniques described in Exercise 4. Enter NOW+. When you feel stable within this compassionate and loving observer state, proceed to the next step.

STEP 2. Bring your selected problem into NOW+.

When you feel ready, gently bring your selected problem into NOW+. If you suddenly find yourself overwhelmed by thought stories or contracted emotions and sensations, first observe them, settle and reground, and then internally say to yourself, "Even though I contracted, I deeply and completely accept myself." Then, try to reachieve NOW+ and gently bring your problem back into your awareness.

Once you manage to bring your problem into NOW+ and are able to maintain at least a somewhat detached observer state, try to notice the following things:

- Do you have uncomfortable sensations or tensions in your body that accompany the problem? If so, observe these sensations with detachment. Accept that a part of you is communicating through these sensations and has benevolent intent. You may also find that the sensations eventually relax.

- Have uncomfortable emotions come up? If so, notice the emotions with detachment and send loving-kindness to them. If possible, also notice their accompanying sensations. These sensations may eventually relax.

- Have stories about the problem entered your mind? Gently observe and acknowledge these stories as thoughts and send loving-kindness to them.

STEP 3. Receive insights and guidance from your Self.

Now, relax and rest for a while longer in NOW+. When you are ready, form the intention to receive guidance from your Self about your problem. Stay open and receive any sensations, emotions, or thoughts that arise. Do not censor yourself. You might receive images or insights that point to the root of your problem. These may include events from the past, or even from a past life. Stay open, curious, and grateful for the guidance you receive.

Please note: If you receive thoughts, images, or emotions that are violent or negative toward yourself or others, this is your lower mind speaking, not your Self. The Self always presents information that is positive and loving.

STEP 4. Return to normal awareness and write down what you have received.

Slowly, return to your normal state of awareness. While you are still slightly in an altered state, record any information that you received—sensations, emotions, thoughts, and insights. Thank your Self for its help.

Helpful Tips:

- With practice, you can run through a shortened form of this exercise quickly. Try it after a difficult meeting at the office, after an argument with a relative or friend, or even when you feel a cold, headache, or sore throat coming on. Take a few minutes, go to a quiet place, ground yourself, put a smile on your face, and open to receive. You might be surprised at the results!

- Create a journal to record all of your experiences with this and other exercises. A periodic review of this journal can be an important tool for self-development.

- Remember to do all exercises in a spirit of play and fun and compassion for yourself. There is no right or wrong experience.

Part VI

PLAYGROUND OF THE SPIRIT

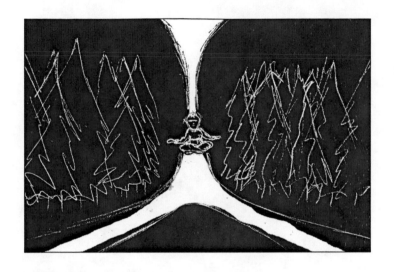

"When we begin to reside more in embodied experience,
we enter into a different relationship with ourself—
one that is creative instead of corrective."

—*Gary Sherman*

IT'S TIME TO PLAY...

If you have tried Exercises 1—5, you have already begun to build a substantial foundation for exploring the realm of the Self. Please keep playing with these exercises on a regular basis; in my studies with Gary Sherman, each one of them was the focus of many group sessions. Part VI will now provide you with many more ideas, exercises, and experiments. Of course, this material is just the tip of the iceberg. If you are serious about the consciousness quest, read more books, take some meditation classes, or find a teacher to study with. But don't forget: "No practice, no benefit!"

I will begin in Chapters 28—32 by describing exercises that, unless otherwise noted, are derived from the study materials of Gary Sherman, often using his exact words and notes. As you may recall from Chapter 7, I met Sherman and his wife Ellen Miller in 2005, and since that time, my fellow students and I have benefited greatly from their teachings on meditation, the development of deeper forms of awareness, inspiration, and creativity, and on a framework for self-development that Sherman calls *perceptual integration*. In my view, this framework has much in common with Gurdjieff's system. Its underlying goal is to help students discover the processes that govern how they think and contribute to how they feel, along with principles of attention that can enable them to better direct the content of their experience. In other words, the aim is to first "Know Thyself" and then to become the master of one's experience. For more information about Sherman's and Miller's work, please visit their web sites: *www.becomingselfaware.com*; *www.creativeawareness.org*; and *www.deepening.com*.

Part VI concludes with Chapter 33, which provides a set of active consciousness experiments—explorations in the realm of creating and manifesting in your own life. In my experience, cultivating deeper forms of awareness (using exercises like the ones provided in this book) will enhance your ability to create and manifest successfully. However, Chapter 33 will provide a few extra tips that may also increase your chances for success.

Before we begin, please take note of the General Exercise Format provided below. It applies to all of the exercises and experiments in Part VI, but especially to the exercises. It is essentially the same format as Exercise 5.

General Exercise Format:

- Settle into the Now, using "Feet. Seat. Back." or whatever technique you prefer.

- Enter NOW+, the state of open-heartedness, loving-kindness, and compassion. You may find that an easy shortcut is to put a slight smile on your face.

- Bring the content of the exercise or experiment into NOW+. Notice sensations, feelings, and thoughts that arise. Try to stick with sensation (rather than feeling and thought) as much as possible. Gently observe what comes up and how it shifts. Use "Feet. Seat. Back." to reground if necessary. If you become distressed, use the EFT formula: "Even though <problem>, I deeply and completely accept myself."[1]

- Receive, acknowledge, and take note of any information you receive from your Self while in this state.

- As you return to normal awareness and before you completely leave the meditative state, record your experience in your journal for future reference. You may also receive additional guidance and information at that time.

CHAPTER 28

❧

FACING YOUR STORIES: RELEASING THE SELF FROM THE FICTION OF THE MIND

WHAT ARE YOUR STORIES? HOW DO YOU DEFINE "WHO YOU are" to yourself and others? It is now time to develop a greater awareness of these habitual thought patterns. Do not engage with them in a half-conscious way or move away from them out of apprehension or distrust. Instead, develop a *relationship* with your stories. They are there for you and contain information for you.

Exercise: Facing and experiencing your stories.

Bring into your awareness a personal story of victimization, fear, hurt, disappointment, resentment, or resignation. Pay attention to the dialogue and pictures of your story. Notice any body sensations or feelings that arise. Notice any contractions and where they occur in your body. Notice the energy of the story. Do your feelings or thoughts further justify or validate your story? Shift into body awareness and settle with the energy and quality of your experience. Move into instead of away from your story. It is for you and contains information and knowledge that you need to know. What is it telling you?

In your day-to-day life, try to observe the degree of permission you give yourself to express this story to others and to yourself. Do you make assumptions about other people or about events in your life that are based on this story, rather than on what is actually going on in the world?

Two-person Exercise: Let a partner reflect a story back to you

If you can find a partner to do exercises with, have one person settle and enter NOW+ while the other relates one of their stories. The settled partner should try to refrain from activating their own thoughts and stories, but instead, notice body sensations and insights they receive while listening to their partner's story. Then switch roles. Afterward, discuss your experiences of each other's stories.

DO YOU HAVE A NICKNAME?

P.D. Ouspensky, Gurdjieff's chronicler, said that a nickname can be an important clue about a person's stories. In fact, he said that it can indicate what Gurdjieff called a person's "chief feature." [1]

In my early twenties, some of my friends used to call me "Amiable Amy." I even made a T-shirt for myself with the words emblazoned on it. It definitely reflected something about me—that I have a tendency to want people to like me, and as a result, that I feel I have to be nice to everyone. The truth is, I still have a hard time saying "No" to people. I have even sung the song "I'm Just a Girl Who Cain't Say No" (from the musical *Oklahoma!*) in more than one talent show! I realize now that this is just another aspect of my "chief feature." And when I think about it, my need to be "Amiable Amy" is a reflection of how I felt as a young girl who craved the approval and love of her rather formidable father. It's one of my stories.

In her channeled teachings, Sanaya Roman uses the term "sub-personality" for a story of this kind. [2] Other types of sub-personalities might be "the tough guy" or "the comedian." Her book recommends getting in touch with and evolving your sub-personalities so that they no longer hold you back. The idea is to love and honor your sub-personalities for what they have given you and how they have helped you. Once you have done this, you can ask them to evolve so that they better serve you today.

Exercise: Engage with a sub-personality. [Note: This exercise is based on one described by Sanaya Roman.³]

What is one of your nicknames? What part of your personality does it reflect? Choose this or some other aspect of your personality that you identify with. Create an image of a person that represents this sub-personality. How old and what sex is he or she? What expression do they have on their face? How do they hold their body? What sensation is created in your body when you imagine this sub-personality? Ask the sub-personality what it wants and what it is trying to do for you. Thank it for what it has given you. Slowly walk together to the top of a mountain, where you behold a broad vista, showered in light. Ask the Spirit of Light to help you both to evolve. Watch and witness how your sub-personality evolves and changes before your eyes. What does it look like now? Ask your evolved sub-personality to help you on your path of growth. Ask it to present you with a symbol that represents its newly evolved state. Integrate this symbol within you.

IT'S ALL ABOUT ENERGY

Your stories are not just living in your head. They dwell in every cell of your body and move outward into the fields of energy that surround you. They interact with all of your energy bodies and with other people's energy bodies too. In fact, much of what you are picking up each day—sensations, feelings, and thoughts—might be coming, not from within, but from the stories and energy bodies of people you come into contact with.

The next time you meet with a friend, take note of how you feel beforehand. Then notice the body sensations and feelings you experience during the meeting. Finally, check in with yourself immediately afterward. Were you in one state before the meeting and then inexplicably moved into a completely different state during and after your get-together? For example, were you happy and carefree before the meeting, but then lethargic and sad afterward? If so, consider this: Does your friend tend to be depressed? Even if your friend didn't discuss any depressing topics with you, you may have picked up on his or her energy. If so, you can choose to quickly toss off these negative emotions and sensations—because they don't really belong to you.

Here's something else to ponder. One reason why certain situations may trigger particular stories for you is that the people involved in those situations—family members, co-workers, or friends—may be holding an energetically fixed conception of you. You may literally be getting sucked into an energy story that they are projecting and holding in your presence. One solution to this problem is to enter into such situations in a more conscious way. Notice the energy shifts that occur within you and around you. Do not confront your friends and family; instead, ground yourself, acknowledge the story, and choose another state of being. See what happens. Without consciously knowing why, the other people in your life may begin to behave differently toward you.

Of course, it goes the other way too. You may be unconsciously affecting your environment and other people with your own stories about them or yourself. In fact, your stories may actually be *generating* your outer experience. Because of this phenomenon, what shows up in your life can provide extremely useful feedback to you. This information may arrive in many forms—in your interactions with other people, as events that occur in the outer world, and as body sensations. Can you think of other ways in which you get feedback about your state and your stories?

Day-to-day Exercise: Meeting your own creation.

Over the next few days, play with the idea that you are a receptor that attracts thoughts, feelings, and experiences. Practice innocence. Rather than "filling in the world" with one of your stories when a situation occurs, view the situation experimentally as a piece of feedback about your state of being. (If you do end up replaying one of your stories, just be aware that you are doing so.) Try to be graceful about receiving feedback—with maturity and less dissonance. Play with the idea that all feedback is true. Welcome it so that you can learn from it. Also, reflect on these questions while in meditation:

- What is a criticism that people have of you?

- Do you see what they see?

- What is your internal experience of this criticism? Are you resistant? Do you close down?

- How is this trait serving you? What is it trying to achieve? What is its sensation?

CHAPTER 29

>⁓

WHERE DO YOU GO
WHEN YOU'RE NOT
HERE AND NOW?

"By expanding our awareness of the ways we flee from the present and lose connection to the essential Self, we begin to 'shrink' the process of Self-avoidance and thus learn to live more consistently as who we really are."[1]

—RICHARD MOSS

YOU MAY THINK THAT YOU ARE ALWAYS PRESENT AND ALERT WHEN you're not sleeping, but you're not. Much of the time you're lost in thought. Sometimes you may even enter trance-like states—when you're listening to music, enraptured by a piece of art, or swimming laps in the pool. The truth is, shifts in consciousness are *always* taking place, even on a second-to-second basis. Can you become more aware of these shifts and make use of them?

Physician and spiritual teacher Richard Moss describes a *Mandala of Being*—a model for structuring and understanding where we're going when we're not in the Now. One axis of the mandala ranges from the past to the future. The other axis ranges between a focus *within*—on one's self (subjective consciousness), and a focus *without*—on other things or people (objective consciousness).[2]

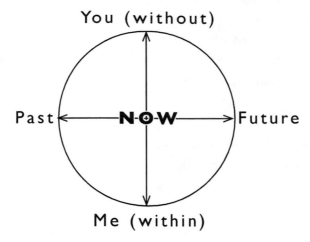

This figure is based on one from The Mandala of Being, Copyright © 2007 by Richard Moss, MD. Reprinted with permission of New World Library, Novato, CA. www.newworldlibrary.com.

Whenever you leave the Now, you are somewhere else on the Mandala. Where do *you* go? Do you tend to think a lot about the future? About what will happen at the airport tomorrow or at work next week? People who tend to focus on the future are usually worriers and planners and spend a lot of time on the right side of the Mandala. If their focus is on other people and things, they are living in the upper right quandrant. If they fret about themselves—for example, if they are absorbed in personal health worries or about what they will do or say— they inhabit the lower right quadrant.

Other people tend to spend more time in the past. For example, do you tend to dwell in regret over what you did or said, or nostalgically relive personal memories in the lower left of the Mandala? Or do you live in anger and blame over past events (the upper left)?

Wherever you are on the Mandala, if you are not at the center, you are not in the Now. And consider this: an interesting side effect of spending more time near the center is that you will become a lot happier! In fact, *it's impossible to worry, fear, or regret while you're in the Now.* Why not check it out right now? Settle using "Feet. Seat. Back." and rest in the Now for a few minutes. Then bring in a state of worry. The moment you do so, you will discover that you are no longer in the Now. And the instant you fully reenter the Now, your worries will vanish. If you experience this, you will have learned a very important lesson. It will also motivate you to visit the center of the Mandala more often.

Of course, it can be difficult to stay centered in the Now all of the time. You are always drifting. The question is, where are you going? And what takes you there? Is it one of your stories?

Exercise: Drift and shift.

Let yourself drift away from the Now. Where have you gone? Future or past? Are you focused on yourself or on others—within or without? What is the energy or feeling of this place? Next, shift back into the Now using "Feet. Seat. Back." When you are ready, pick a different place on the Mandala to visit; if you began by drifting into the future, now drift into the past, or vice versa. Where did you go? Is your focus on yourself or others? What is the feeling or energy of this place? Play with visiting other places on the Mandala and finish up by returning to the Now.

One interesting thing I've noticed about drifting from the Now, especially while in meditation, is that the focus of my eyes tends to shift unconsciously as well. See if this is also true for you; it can be a useful clue about your state.

Exercise: Baseline consciousness.

Ground yourself slightly but not completely. Let yourself enter your normal state of awareness, but try to observe yourself. Where are you? What is the feeling or tone of your state? What sensations do you experience in your body? This is your baseline consciousness, where you tend to live most of the time.

One fascinating thing about baseline consciousness is that even when the circumstances of your life improve and you have fulfilled previous dreams that you once held, your baseline consciousness will tend to remain the same. That's why even the most successful and wealthy people can still be very unhappy. Unless you proactively shift your baseline consciousness using self awareness techniques, your state of mind will most likely remain the same, no matter what happens to you.

Now let's practice drifting in a more conscious and creative way.

Exercise: Receive a movie of a wish coming true.

Come up with a wish for yourself that you would like to achieve. After settling, bring your wish into your awareness. Deliberately drift into the future and receive a "movie" of your wish coming true. Let it play for you within your mind, either as pictures or words. Mark down what you receive in your journal.

Exercise: Receive a movie about an unusual interest.

Think about one of your hobbies or interests that is somehow unusual or out of context with the rest of your life. After settling, bring this unusual interest into your awareness. Receive a "movie" about a past life in which this interest played a role. Mark down what you receive.

You might think of these "movies" as daydreams. In fact, you shift into these kinds of altered states all of the time, even when you're not aware of it. They may appear as moments of free-floating contemplation or musing. Or, they may be fleeting moments of inspiration and insight—"Aha!" moments. Indeed, your physical and energy bodies *need* to experience these kinds of states. Gurdjieff called them *impressions*, and said that they supply a kind of food to our higher energy bodies.[3] The medieval notion of alchemy, Gurdjieff said, was not about changing lead into gold, but rather, about a process of personal transformation that occurs when one "ingests" impressions while in a state of Self-remembering. Can you engage in your own personal alchemy?

First of all, acknowledge that drifts into altered states occur regularly and try to notice them when they arise. Suggest to yourself that you will experience such states, form a desire to do so, expect that they will occur, and when you do perceive them, acknowledge them. Finally, grant these experiences *validity*. Hold any impressions you receive as real and true and ascribe meaning to them. Here are some clues that indicate when you are genuinely experiencing a drift of this kind:

- a feeling of sudden calm.

- a state of relaxation.

- a feeling of joy.

- a warm energy.

- a rush of energy.

- a feeling of expansion.

- a feeling that your boundaries are dissolving or changing.

- an expectant feeling.

- a feeling that a new idea, vision or possibility is being born.

- a feeling of safety.

- a feeling of being connected and aligned.

- an experience of a new insight or perception about some circumstance.

- a new possibility for action appears that was not seen or contemplated before.

Here is one more exercise to play with, developed by Ellen Miller.

Exercise: Connecting with the Inner Teacher.

Have a pen and paper in your lap. After settling, write down a question about your growth and development. A good first question is: What is most important for my spiritual growth right now? Immediately write down whatever comes as an answer. Engage with the answer. Write for at least three to five minutes. If you feel stuck, make penmanship loops. As soon as you begin to write, you will have entered a multi-dimensional space. Write whatever you are getting, even if it isn't a response to your question. The Inner Teacher is waiting to talk to you and may take this opportunity to address something other than your question. This connection with your inner teacher is more important than the content. Date each entry. If you write in the morning, read whatever you wrote in the evening, or vice versa. Many people find that they make a better connection in the morning.

CHAPTER 30

WHAT IS YOUR
COMMITMENT?

"Everything has an idea behind it."

—GARY SHERMAN

IN THE NEXT CHAPTER, I WILL ADDRESS THE GOAL OF FEELING GOOD within yourself, no matter what's happening. But first, let's consider what tends to make us feel *not* so good.

If you think about it, *unhappiness is often the result of being out of alignment with a central commitment.* What do I mean by a "commitment"? I'm not talking about a promise you've made to attend your son's hockey game. Nor am I talking about something you think you *should* do or something you *should* care about, when you really don't. Instead, I'm talking about something that is truly important to your sense of self. And a *central* commitment is one that lies at the very center of your life—something that nothing else could interfere with if you could help it; something from which everything else in your life emanates.

For many of us, our central commitment involves our family or our children. For others, it might be work, a particular cause or hobby, or a religious practice. Although most of us are motivated by several commitments, some are more important to us than others.

Exercise: Identify your commitments.

Take some time to reflect and come up with your central or most important commitment. Next, come up with two more commitments that are important to you. For each commitment, answer the following questions. Write down your responses.

- What actions or behaviors do you take regarding this commitment? Are they commensurate with your commitment? Do they follow and support each other?

- Why does this commitment occupy such a central place in your life?

- When you hold, embrace, or think about this commitment, what do you feel emotionally and intuitively?

- How does this commitment show up inside of you in terms of thoughts, feelings, and sensations?

- How does this commitment show up in terms of your identity?

- Is there any resistance in you concerning this commitment? How do you experience it?

- List the ways you are fulfilled by actualizing and expressing this commitment.

- What intention or idea underlies this commitment?

One of the reasons why many of us feel unhappy is that we are not living in alignment with an important commitment—especially if it's our central commitment. The dissonance between our commitment and how we are living creates suffering for us. There are many ways in which this can occur:

- Our behavior doesn't line up with our commitment.

- Our commitment doesn't sufficiently motivate us to act and support it.

- Our commitment has no realistic support and is simply out of reach. For example, it might be too lofty or abstract.

- Our commitment has been sidetracked by our stories.

- Our commitment has been realized but has not been replaced by a new commitment.

- Our commitment is in conflict with another commitment.

When you experience this kind of dissonance in your life, the solution is to either modify your commitment or to change your behavior.

Exercise: Reflect upon dissonance that you are experiencing with a commitment.

Choose an area in your life in which you are experiencing dissonance or unhappiness due to the fact that your behavior is not in alignment with a commitment. In meditative reflection, consider these questions. Mark down your answers.

- What has stopped you?

- Can you confront it?

- What would you do if there were no impediments?

- How would you feel?

If you are not sufficiently motivated by your commitment or you cannot change your behavior for some reason, consider these questions and mark down your answers:

- How would you be affected if you changed your commitment to be in alignment with your behavior?

- Look at the idea underlying your commitment. Can this idea be realized by a new commitment that you can align with?

- How does this new commitment make you feel?

This last step is essentially one of reformulating your commitment so that it still fulfills your underlying idea, but you can now better align with it. This reformulation enables you to "go where your power is."

In other words, look at your fundamental ideas and intentions and reframe your beliefs and goals so that they can now take you where you want to go. This is also an important element of being successful with active consciousness, because it is hard to get into PURE GOAL and LET GO if you have a fundamental problem aligning with your goal.

Here's an example. Let's say that your commitment is to be successful at work and to be promoted to higher levels of responsibility and compensation. However, because of the nature of your job, this goal conflicts with another commitment that you hold: to be there for your family. Because of this, you experience dissonance and unhappiness in your life. You feel that you are not as successful at your job or at home as you would like. However, the *idea* behind your job commitment might be to gain respect. One possibility for you, then, would be to reframe your job commitment so that you can gain respect in another way. For example, you might discover that you can fulfill this need in a less demanding position at work or in another sphere of your life. Another possibility is that you reexamine your stories and come to better understand why you crave respect in the first place.

Of course, it's also possible that your family commitment is not as rigid as you think. Perhaps your children have grown and don't need as much time as you used to give them. Or perhaps the idea behind your family commitment is to feel close to your children, and this desire can now be fulfilled in a different way that does not conflict with your job.

Working to align beliefs, behavior, and commitments can help us to experience less dissonance in our lives. But the truth is, happiness is available to us at *any* moment—because *we* are the ones who are responsible for what we think, feel, and do. The trick is to proactively choose the states we experience, rather than constantly react to external circumstances.

CHAPTER 31

❧

FEELING GOOD

"To feel good as a conscious act is an art. To cultivate this experience in the face of the circumstances of one's life is to bring a new awareness to the moment of experience that is outside the box of our conditioned reactions. It is proactive in nature. Waiting for the moment to shape us relinquishes our own responsibility over our state of being and misses the opportunity to consciously participate in our own growth."[1]

—GARY SHERMAN

IT IS HARD NOT TO NOTICE THAT THE DALAI LAMA, THE SPIRITUAL leader of the Tibetan people and of Tibetan Buddhists worldwide, always seems to be happy. Indeed, many people ask: How can he be so happy, given the difficult circumstances of the Tibetan people? The answer is that he is a master of living in the Now and taking responsibility for his state of being. He does not live reactively, allowing his thoughts and emotions to be solely determined by what happens to him and his people. Instead, he lives proactively, choosing his state in a masterful way.

There are many benefits to proactive living, one of them being increased happiness and contentment. Other benefits include expanded perception, more harmonious relationships with ourselves and others, improved alignment with our commitments, and an acceleration in the evolution of our consciousness.

But how many of us are truly committed to feeling good? While most of us don't want to feel *bad*, few of us really believe that feeling *good* should be an important personal commitment. Indeed, many of us feel guilty or hesitant about adopting such a goal. We may believe that trying to feel good is too selfish, that we have to suffer in order to be successful, or that feeling good is a precursor to inevitable misfortune and disappointment. The fact is, however, that such beliefs are also just stories, passed down to us by our families and culture. They are also in direct contradiction with the principles discussed in Chapter 18. In particular, if you *do* genuinely feel good (that is, not by virtue of drugs or other diversions), you are more likely to be on the right path toward achieving the desires of your Self. In contrast, if you are suffering, it is very likely that you are veering off in a direction that is disconnected from your inner truth. So why not make it one of your commitments to feel good?

REACTIVE VERSUS PROACTIVE BEING

Most of us believe that our emotions are determined by external circumstances. We believe we are happy or sad because something happened or might happen, or because of what someone said or did. In essence, we believe that our state is a reaction and that we are passive receivers of our emotions. In contrast, being proactive is all about what *you* bring to the moment. It is a creative process, in which you choose to insert something into your state of being. Are you doubtful that you can be proactive and choose what you are feeling? Let's start with an exercise.

Exercise: Call up a happy feeling.

After you have settled, close your eyes and bring into your awareness something that enables you to feel happy. It might be a recent event that brought you joy, an interaction with a pet or child, a success you had at work, an ecstatic experience, a beautiful sight you beheld, or the prospect of a relaxing vacation. Rest in this state. Notice the sensations in your body. Now open your eyes and remain settled while experiencing outer sensation. Put the joyful event out of your mind and just be in the Now for a minute or two. Close your eyes again. Can you call up the happy feeling without using a story, simply by invoking the sensation of happiness? Here's another tip: put a smile on your face. See if this simple act calls up a sensation of not only happiness, but open-heartedness. It is a sensation that tells you that everything is actually perfect. Rest here as long as you like.

After you return to normal awareness, consider this: You were just able to become happy proactively. And you can choose to do this at any time. If you do, you might be surprised by the results. Give it a try in your day-to-day life with the following exercise.

Day-to-day Exercise: Enter a situation with happiness.

The next time you have a difficult task to perform or are dreading some event, try the following. First, visualize your desired outcome. Next, choose and invoke a positive feeling just before the event or task. Try to hold on to this feeling as much as possible throughout the experience. Afterward, mark down how your experience turned out in comparison with your expectation.

My husband Steve calls this the "Love Technique." Every time he has to go into a meeting with someone who he feels might be difficult or unhelpful—whether it be a co-worker or an annoying clerk—he tries to begin the encounter with a positive expectation and a feeling of love for that person. He has found this strategy to be remarkably effective in achieving his desired outcome, and it's also a much more delightful way to live life!

Of course, it's difficult to hold yourself in a happy state all of the time. Moments of sadness and irritation inevitably creep in. I'm sure this is true even for the Dalai Lama. So, your goal shouldn't be continuous happiness. Instead, try to create joy as often as you can and whenever you want to. Remember that every moment of your life is a new opportunity to reset your state to one of happiness and contentment. From this vantage point, you will be able to make better decisions, have better relationships with others, and utilize the intuition of the inner Self more effectively. You will also increase your power of active consciousness.

DEALING WITH NEGATIVE FEELINGS

Naturally, it's relatively easy to evoke happiness when you're sitting quietly in a chair at home. But what about when you have to deal with truly painful and difficult situations? What about loss and grief? What about sickness and death? All I can say is, if you can take some time for yourself when you are in the midst of these situations, you may be able to deal with them more effectively. When someone you love dies, your goal might not be happiness but rather a greater sense of equanimity. When you hear terrible news, you may be able to absorb the shock more gracefully. You shouldn't try to avoid or suppress painful emotions. Rather, try to move into and through difficult situations with greater ease. Pain is sometimes inevitable, but suffering need not be.

Utilizing the meditation described in Exercise 5—Tapping Into the Wisdom of the Self— can be very helpful in such circumstances. Bring an awareness of your difficult situation into NOW+, and from that vantage point, observe your state of contraction. Doing this might enable the contraction to relax somewhat, thereby improving your state. You may also receive helpful insights from your inner Self at that time. It is also a good idea to perform Exercise 5 on a regular basis, even during happy times. That way, you will be primed to utilize it when a real crisis does arise.

Of course, when you're caught in the middle of a difficult situation, it isn't always easy to find a time or place to meditate. Here is a shortened form of Exercise 5 that can be used as a "quickee." Even if it means running to the restroom for a few minutes to get some privacy, try this exercise when you feel out of control.

Exercise: Separate story from sensation and work with sensation.

Settle as much as you can. Repeat the EFT formula (or even better, use EFT tapping while reciting it): "Even though <problem>, I deeply and completely accept myself."[2] Now, notice the sensations in your body. As much as possible, separate your body sensations from the story running in your head. It might be a clenching in your stomach or tension in your neck or chest. Whatever it is, focus on the sensation and put the story in the background. Now, try to relax the sensation. Do not force relaxation but instead, breathe into the sensation and just be with it. Stay with it as long as you can and see what happens.

This simple exercise can have profound results. It turns out that emotions are really more about body sensations than thoughts. If you can separate the story of a difficult situation from its sensation in your body, and then work with the sensation instead, you may have an easier time regaining equanimity. From this vantage point, you may also gain some important insights that discharge the intensity of the situation.

In essence, this exercise enables you to become more separated from what is going on and take more of an *observer* stance—a stance empowered by the wisdom of your Self. It's like taking the whip out of the hand of the carriage driver (your egoic mind) for a minute, and steadying and relaxing the horse (your body) after it has gotten out of control. Afterwards, things might begin to look and feel a bit better.

BECOME A GOOD OBSERVER OF YOUR FEELINGS

Here's another exercise to try when you're feeling off kilter and have some time for meditation and reflection.

Exercise: Observe and complete a feeling.

After settling, bring a difficult feeling into your awareness. Try to keep sensation primary and thought secondary. Observe the feeling and see what happens. It has information for you. Unpack or "complete" it. For example, you might get information about other body sensations. Or the feeling might morph into another unrelated experience, feeling, or story. Images from a past-life might come up. Simply track what happens, observe it, and experience it. Keep doing this until the feeling can no longer be held in your awareness and all associations that come up dissipate. Accept any new information that comes to you. Afterwards, record what you received.

Of course, if you really want to become more proactive and less reactive, you need to become a better observer of yourself in your day-to-day life too. Here are some more exercises to play with toward that goal.

Day-to-day Exercise: Track your feelings during conversations.

This one can be challenging, but it can also be quite enlightening. During conversations with people, try to maintain a light sense of being grounded by focusing on your feet, or by using "Feet. Seat. Back." As you are listening to others, notice any feelings and sensations that arise in your body and try to track them. Are these sensations coming from within you or from the person you are with? What information are these sensations providing to you?

One useful way to think about emotions is as a form of "touch." Maybe that's why we use the same word for emotional "feeling" and "feeling" something with our hands. Some people even use the phrase "I'm feeling you" to express the fact that they are in emotional alignment with what we are saying. Similarly, when we are deeply affected by something emotionally, we say that we're "touched."

In general, there are three ways in which we are "touched" when we react in feeling:

- *Sensate*: We are touched by and react to an external event in the outside world.

- *Conceptual*: We are touched by and react to a conceptual idea, thought, or imagined scenario in our minds.

- *Energetic*: We are touched by and react to something more indefinable in the energetic field around us.

Keep these three possibilities in mind for the next exercise.

Day-to-day Exercise: Keep track of your best and worst feelings and how they arise.

Keep a notebook at your bedside. Each day before going to sleep, write down the best feeling you experienced that day, and the worst feeling you experienced. For each one, mark down whether its origin was sensate, conceptual, or energetic. Also mark down whether it was proactively generated by you or whether it was a reaction. Finally, to what degree did you accept this feeling? Record that too.

BECOME A GOOD OBSERVER OF REACTIVE BEHAVIOR

It's not just our thoughts and feelings that can get us into trouble; it's our behaviors too. One important type of behavior is talking. Having negative feelings is one thing; expressing those feelings to everyone is another. By constantly voicing our negative emotions, we spread negativity to others and magnify it within ourselves. Of course, I'm not saying that we shouldn't stand up for ourselves when it is called for. Rather, I'm saying that it is important to notice how we waste our energy by talking about and acting out our unpleasant feelings. Gurdjieff said that becoming more conscious of this kind of behavior is an absolute requirement for the evolution of the self:

"A great deal of energy is... spent on work which is completely unnecessary and harmful in every respect, such as on activity of unpleasant emotions, on the expression of unpleasant sensations, on worry, on restlessness, on haste, and on a whole series of automatic actions which are completely useless... Still further we can point to the habit of continually talking with anybody and about anything, or if there is no one else, with ourselves... [I]t is necessary to learn to economize the energy produced by our organism, not to waste this energy on unnecessary functions, and to save it for that activity which will gradually connect the lower centers with the higher."[3]

One way of becoming more aware of such tendencies is to embark on a period of silent meditation. Whether it be for a single day or for many days, deliberate periods of silence can make the innate tendency to talk acutely obvious. Indeed, Gurdjieff said that nonstop talkers are usually trying to suppress something that they are reluctant to admit to themselves. Forced periods of silence can allow these suppressed ideas and emotions to bubble up into awareness.

Aside from enforced silence, what else can we do on a day-to-day basis to help curb negative speech and behavior? In Gary Sherman's teaching, he stresses watching out for the three "C"s: *Complaint, Comparison,* and *Competitiveness.*

Day-to-day Exercise: Complaint, Comparison, Competitiveness.

In your daily life, try to notice when you are giving voice to complaints, comparing yourself or your situation to that of others, or engaging in competitiveness. If you catch yourself in this behavior, stop for a moment and try to determine what train of thought brought it up. Reflect on it and try to move away from it. You don't need to enter into a dialogue with yourself about it or feel rejecting of yourself; just consciously decide to drop the behavior.

Can you come up with a simple practice that you can perform each time you notice that you are caught in one of the three Cs? It should be something you are willing to do and that feels positive for you. Here's one that I came up with for dealing with Complaint:

1. Notice myself complaining.

2. Perform EFT tapping and the EFT formula on my complaint: "Even though <complaint>, I deeply and completely accept myself."[4]

3. Proactively focus on gratitude for the good things in my life.

Many of the exercises in Esther and Jerry Hicks' book, *The Amazing Power of Deliberate Intent*, are techniques for moving from expressions and feelings of negativity to ones of joy and empowerment. Their goal is not to instill wishful thinking, but rather, to retrain one's thought processes so that they are more positive and useful. As the Hicks emphasize, that is the only way we can bring better things into our lives, because that's how the energetic realm actually works—through resonance with like-vibration.[5]

For example, instead of dwelling on: "My old car is always breaking down," you might focus on: "This car has given me many years of enjoyment and I have had many fun times in it." Or, rather than thinking: "I'm so unhappy that I'm home sick with the flu," you could say to yourself: "I now have some nice quiet time to rest and reflect." Of course, creating better vibratory states is the way active consciousness works too.

In summary, here are a few ways to feel good, no matter what happens in your life:

• When you are unhappy, separate story from sensation and try to focus on easing the sensation.

• Proactively choose a joyful state as often as possible.

• Observe and notice your feelings as they arise and become more aware of what you're doing. Be alert for the three Cs—complaint, comparison, and competitiveness.

• Replace negative thoughts with more positive "takes" on the things in your life.

CHAPTER 32

GRATITUDE

"Have you ever noticed how much you like to be with people who
thank you, appreciate and acknowledge you?... Have you noticed how you
want to give them more? It is the same, on an energy level, with the Universe. Whenever you stop to thank the Universe for the abundance you have,
the Universe will give you more. Whenever you give thanks, you increase
the light in your aura at that very moment. You change it through your
heart, for the feeling of gratitude comes from the heart. As you give thanks,
you open your heart. Your heart is the doorway to your soul; it is
the link between the world of form and the world of essence."[1]

—SANAYA ROMAN (CHANNEL FOR ORIN)

Have you ever noticed how many prayers in the religious
liturgy are focused on gratefulness and praise for God? While
many of us have moments when we voice our complaints to God and
ask for help, it may actually be a more effective strategy to express
gratitude for what we already have. If the spiritual masters are correct,
a state of gratitude and open-heartedness is more likely to bring us
what we truly desire than all of the complaints in the world.

But how many of us take heed of this truth outside of a religious
setting? Instead, the three Cs—complaint, comparison, and competitiveness—tend to dominate many people's thinking. The following
exercises will help you to break out of this habit and to proactively
focus on more productive lines of thought. These include:

- Appreciation for what you have;

- Going with and trusting the flow of life rather than resisting it;

- Allowing yourself to have a more expansive view of what life can bring to you;

- Opening your heart towards others and becoming a source of love; and

- Opening yourself to receive and experience love that is flowing towards you.

Exercise: Expand appreciation.

At least once a day, take a few minutes for appreciation. Stop all forward momentum, both physical and mental, and settle into your body. Sense the energy within you that is always trying to go some place, get something done, or secure some future circumstance. Instead, use this momentum to expand the Now. Or rather than putting things off until something else is satisfied in the future, focus on what is happening in this moment. Try to maintain a sense of your body. Keep about sixty percent of your focus on body sensation, leaving the other forty percent for other forms of awareness. This is a good alignment. Now, select something in your environment to appreciate. It could be a friend, a pet, your home, the food on your plate, or the computer on your desk. Smile and feel gratitude.

Exercise: Nature is always in the Now.

Focus your appreciation on nature. Play energetically by sensing how the outside world (trees, mountains, sky, wind, flowers, birds, animals) helps to expand your experience of life. Line up with an aspect of nature and attune to it. Settle into your body and sense the quality of being that is evoked in you as you give your attention to this aspect of nature.

Exercise: Do you limit yourself?

The next time you feel good—whether it be joy, pleasure, peace, or happiness—notice whether you tend to impose a limit on your experience. Is there a line you can't cross? What beliefs are holding you back? Play with allowing your good feelings to expand further and further. See how far you can expand.

Exercise: Push your limits.

Think of something you would like to have happen in your life. Receive a movie of this happening. Keep expanding your movie so that it increases and improves the outcome further and further. Keep expanding it until you reach your conceptual boundary.

The last two exercises were designed to help you realize how much we tend to limit ourselves, even in our imaginations and thoughts. Societal norms and family stories can limit the scope of our creative thinking too. But if you can get into PURE GOAL and then LET GO and trust that you can achieve your soul's desire, it might actually happen!

Exercise: Go with the flow without resistance.

Most of us tend to resist the natural flow of our lives. We get in our own way. However, by not resisting, we can make it easier to align with our Self. Pick a situation or circumstance that you would like to shift or impact. After settling, imagine yourself standing at the center of a round platform and holding a diamond-like energy object. Bring the situation into your consciousness and then imagine the platform beginning to circle as you face outward. As you speed up, the diamond expands; you feel safe within its aura and a growing freedom. In this state, receive information or insight about your situation.

Two-person Exercise: Create movement.

With the help of someone you trust, have fun creating an imaginary flow or movement around an issue. Select a problem that you are working on, but feeling stuck with. Next, with your partner's help, create a story about this problem. You should begin the story by speaking for about ten seconds. Then your partner should take up where you left off and speak for another ten seconds. Go back and forth until you feel the story is complete.

These two exercises are useful because they help to move energy around an issue. And once things are moving, you're on your way—because there is an inherent intelligence to the way in which energy flows. This intelligent flow can then work to your benefit if you let it.

For example, the first time I tried these two exercises, I was feeling frustrated about my work on the board of directors of an organization that I'd been part of for many years. I just wasn't having fun anymore and was contemplating leaving. I also felt that my level of effort was out of proportion to that of others on the board, and that I was unappreciated and taken for granted. Performing the first exercise helped me realize that my frustration was causing me to close and contract my heart. The solution, I realized, was to open my heart—to love my fellow board members and to be open to who they were and what they were each trying to bring to the organization.

Performing the second exercise helped me create actual change around the issue. I began my story by describing myself sitting in frustration at the next board meeting. My partner continued with the following: "Suddenly the door to the boardroom opens and a hotel employee brings in a giant vase of roses, saying that they have been sent to me by an anonymous source." I continued: "One rose is white and the others are red. I hand out the red roses to the members of the board and keep the white rose for myself." My partner then said: "At the end of the meeting I stay behind in the boardroom and sit in reflection." I finished the story by saying: "I hear an internal voice saying: love and let go."

Not only did performing these exercise make me feel better about the organization and more willing to keep an open heart and mind, but something else quite wonderful happened. As it turns out, I had told my husband Steve about this experience and he had taken special note of it. At the next board meeting, which occurred about a month later, I was sitting with my colleagues around the boardroom table when the door suddenly opened. And in came a delivery of a dozen beautiful long-stem roses—one white, and the others red! The rest of my story unfolded just as I had envisaged—and I still have my white rose to this day.

Now, let's conclude this section with an exercise that explores the heights and depths of love. Can you send love out to the world around you—and receive it more fully when it comes your way?

Exercise: The depths of Love.

After settling, bring in the idea and feeling of love and compassion. Feel the energy expand from your chest and extend it downward toward your feet and into the ground. You may experience this expression of love as having depth, with a feeling of nurturing, understanding, and compassion. It is a soulful feeling, connected to this world and to the Earth. If you are a parent, it may evoke the deep love you have for your child. Or it may evoke an intense love for a partner, family member, or pet. Rest in this sensation. Recognize, too, the deep love that others have for you, and adopt the intention to feel and accept their love.

Exercise: The heights of Love.

After settling, bring in the idea and feeling of love and send it upward. Feel energy expanding from your chest, enveloping your head, and reaching toward the heavens. You may experience this expression of love as having a kind of peaceful lightness and joyfulness. It might feel like an outward-reaching form of compassion, which extends to your community, to your country, to all of mankind. There might also be an otherworldly quality to it. You may receive information from departed loved ones or other spirit beings while in this state. Rest here for as long as you like. Recognize as well, the joyful love that the universe holds for you, and adopt the intention to feel and accept this love on a more regular basis.

CHAPTER 33

∂⟍

EXPERIMENTS IN ACTIVE CONSCIOUSNESS: CREATING AND MANIFESTING WITH JOY

THE MEDITATIVE EXERCISES IN THE PRECEDING CHAPTERS WILL help you develop your connection with the inner Self. They will also improve your mental and physical health and the way you handle many aspects of your life. As a result, you may find that you are also able to wield the power of active consciousness more effectively. To put it another way: Once you have developed *internally*, you will be better able to manifest and create *externally*. And that's what this chapter is all about—experimenting with active consciousness in a deliberate and creative way.

I'll begin by providing some general guidelines about how to formulate fruitful active consciousness experiments. Then, I'll suggest a few experiments for you to try and will provide some helpful hints for success. But first, let's review the four steps of active consciousness discussed in Chapter 18:

- **NOW+.** Once you are settled in the Now, reach for a state of loving-kindness and open-heartedness—NOW+.

- **PURE GOAL.** *Be* in your goal state to the fullest extent possible, without doubt.

- **LET GO.** After you return to normal awareness, let go and trust the universe to help you achieve your goal. As much as possible, remain doubt-free.

- **CHOOSE JOY.** Settled in the Now, make decisions based on what seems most genuinely joyful.

GENERAL GUIDELINES FOR ACTIVE CONSCIOUSNESS EXPERIMENTS

If you think about it, the very nature of NOW+, PURE GOAL, LET GO, and CHOOSE JOY provides clues about how to formulate good candidates for active consciousness experiments:

- Since you need to enter NOW+, *choose an experimental situation where you can easily get into NOW+.*

- Since you need to achieve PURE GOAL, *choose a goal that you can fully envision and embody.* For example, pick a goal that you can easily visualize in the physical world.

- Since you need to LET GO, *choose a goal that you can pursue with minimal doubt.* While truly desiring a goal can be helpful, if it's very loaded for you, you might have trouble letting go because of anxiety and doubt. Don't forget: doubt can create the opposite effect from what you are trying to achieve. My advice is to begin with a goal that will create a positive impact for you, but little is personally at stake.

- Since you need to guide yourself using CHOOSE JOY, *choose a goal that allows you to easily make choices using CHOOSE JOY instead of intellectual reasoning as a basis for decision-making.*

Another important concept developed in Chapters 16 and 17 is the contrast between possibility and probability. In particular, I stressed that your use of active consciousness will be more productive if you select goals that are definitely *possible*, even if they're not highly probable. For example, finding a good parking spot in a crowded parking lot is easier to achieve than levitating a spoon. In addition, *manifesting*—using active consciousness to enable a sequence of ordinary events to occur—is easier to achieve than *creating*—evoking less likely occurrences out of the sea of possible futures that lie before you. In summary, here are some more tips for success that pertain to possibility and probability:

- *Choose a goal that is possible.*

- *Choose a goal whose fulfillment is affected by some random factor.* If there is some form of randomness affecting the outcome, you will have a greater chance of influencing it than if the outcome is tightly constricted by other factors.

- *Choose a goal that is far enough into the future that its likelihood has not already been predetermined.* For example, if you choose a goal like "I'll get the job" *after* you've already interviewed, you will be less likely to succeed than if you use active consciousness *before* you begin the job-seeking process, when the tree of future possibilities is more open and thus more subject to your influence.

- *Choose a goal that is not highly probable.* In particular, your goal should be improbable enough that you will be convinced that active consciousness played a role in making it happen.

- *Choose a goal that is as specific as possible and whose success can be measured.* For example, a goal like "being happy at work" is worthy, but happiness is hard to measure. Instead, select a goal about which you can definitely say: yes, I achieved that goal; or yes, I achieved that goal to a specific measurable extent.

- *Work step by step with modest goals, toward a larger goal.* Once again, smaller goals will, individually, be more specific and easier to achieve than a very grand goal that might be too vague and thus more difficult to manifest or create directly.

IDEAS FOR EXPERIMENTS

To get you started, I've developed a few active consciousness experiments that I believe meet these guidelines. As you gain more confidence, you can branch out and experiment with more challenging and improbable goals. See what experiments you can come up with for yourself!

Selection Experiment.

When faced with a situation in which you must make a fairly random choice that may impact some goal, use active consciousness to guide you. Before you enter the situation, get into NOW+ and embody PURE GOAL. Then LET GO of the outcome and make your choice using the internal sensation of JOY. Here are some sample situations in which to try this out:

- When choosing a desk in a test examination room. Enter NOW+ and the PURE GOAL of getting an A+ before you leave for the exam. Then choose your desk by sensing which one creates the most joyful feeling within you.

- When selecting a line at a supermarket, ticket counter, or at customs. Envision a quick and easy processing of your task and then choose the line that creates a sense of joy within you. Don't forget to LET GO!

- When picking the seat in a movie theater or on an airplane that will give you the best viewing or flying experience.

Travel Goal Experiment.

Select a travel goal such as: finding a great parking spot where parking is usually difficult, getting to a destination at a specific time despite traffic, or selecting specific dates for a trip that will have the best weather. Get into NOW+, achieve PURE GOAL, LET GO, and when making your travel decisions, CHOOSE JOY.

Nature Goal Experiment.

Select a goal for encounters with nature, such as seeing certain birds or other animals, or encountering specific plants.

Interpersonal Goal Experiment.

Select an interpersonal goal that you would like to occur but has never happened before, such as your spouse buying you chocolates, or your teenager voluntarily cleaning his or her room or helping out with the chores.

Health Experiment.

Choose a health goal that isn't too loaded, that you can envision with little doubt, and whose success can be measured. For example, it might be the clearing of a benign skin ailment or the healing of a friend's health problem (which might be somewhat serious for them but not as loaded for you).

Work Goal Experiment.

Choose a specific work or business goal that can be measured, such as number of products sold, timeliness of operations, or number of clients.

INCREASE YOUR CHANCES OF SUCCESS

Experiments like the ones I just described are also a focus of author Lynne McTaggart's book *The Intention Experiment*. Her book provides a plethora of information about scientific studies (like the ones I described in Part II) and stresses various factors that have been shown to increase the chance that consciousness experiments will be successful. These include the following:[1]

- *Use the same meditation space repeatedly*—for example, a particular chair—because repeated use of intention or active consciousness in the same location will condition that space so that effects are enhanced.

- *Choose a good time.* Experiments with psychic phenomena show that 1pm sidereal time (a time measurement system based on the Earth's position relative to the stars rather than to the Sun) is best. To find your local sidereal time, use the calculator provided at this website: *tycho.usno.navy.mil/sidereal.html.* Interestingly, times of increased geomagnetic activity also increase the power of consciousness. This may be one reason why scientists have noticed increased psi effects in the polar regions of the planet. See *www.spaceweather.com/rsga.html* for a forecast.

- *Experiment under favorable environmental conditions*—good visibility, low winds, and high air quality. If possible, conduct your experiments in nature, near running water, in clear sunshine, after a storm, and in the mountains. Avoid electrical appliances or electrical lines.

- *Choose a good personal time to experiment*—when you are healthy and happy.

- *If you are far from a target, a negative formulation for a goal can work best. If you are close to a target, a positive formulation works better.* For example, if your goal is to help a distant friend suffering from a fungal infection, try to focus on killing the fungus. In contrast, if you are focusing on your own fungal infection, adopt the goal of healthy clear skin.

- *If possible, formulate your goal in terms of a retro-intention*—a goal that occurs in the past (see Chapter 19 for some examples).

- *Focus on a seed moment*—a point in time in which changes are germinating and forming, rather than a moment in which an outcome is already largely determined.

- *If you have a strong need and desire for a goal, this can increase your chance of success, but only if you can manage to detach from the outcome and not harbor doubt or anxiety.*

- *Be as specific and vivid as possible about your goal*—who, what, when, where, how. Create an object or picture that symbolizes your goal that you can look at on a regular basis.

- *Work collaboratively with others to create group active consciousness.* Group efforts have been shown to create more powerful effects than working alone. For example, scientific experiments have demonstrated that large groups of meditators can positively impact levels of urban crime.[2,3] Other ideas for group efforts include trying to impact the weather, pollution levels, incidents of abuse, road accidents, or the amount of litter on streets.

BE SCIENTIFIC: RECORD YOUR RESULTS

As I've already stressed, it's important to keep track of your consciousness quest in writing. Having a journal handy for recording your personal meditation insights and your efforts at experimentation will help you to remember information that you have received, reinforce the wisdom that you gain, and help you understand and have confidence in the effects of your active consciousness efforts. For example, for each effort at PURE GOAL, you might record:

- The nature of your goal.

- The date and time.

- The location, weather conditions, or other environmental factors.

- Your state of mind.

- Any insights you receive while in NOW+ and PURE GOAL.

- Reflections about how effective you felt your effort was.

Then record something every few days about possible effects. Include notes about:

- Synchronicities that occur. These may be signs that you are on the right track.

- How well you are doing at LETTING GO.

- Times when you have used CHOOSE JOY to make a choice.

- How well you are doing in achieving your goal—that is, a record of your current measure of success.

I have also found that keeping a *dated log* of your state of health and happiness can be useful. Down one side of a sheet of paper, list qualities that you want to track such as: the status of specific physical health problems; the quality of your sleep; measures of your state of mind such as level of anxiety, stress, or worry, or level of positive emotions like joy and contentment; relationship status; and work progress. Feel free to add more items over time.

Next, along the top of the paper, list dates at regular intervals—for example, once a week. Then make a grid, yielding a box for each quality you are measuring on each date. As each date comes up, pick a number (for example, from 1 to 5, or 1 to 10) that assesses each of the qualities you are tracking. For example, you might give yourself a "3" on a scale from 1 to 10 for your level of anxiety on a particular day. As you make your assessments, cover up the assessments that you've recorded so far, so that you aren't biased by previous results. If you are indeed performing the exercises and experiments in Part VI on a regular basis, you may find that, over time, your life really starts to improve in a measurable way.

OTHER IDEAS FOR EXPERIMENTATION

Of course, there are many more experiments you can play with if you are interested in exploring the mysterious realm of consciousness. Good places to look for new ideas are the books and web sites of leading researchers in the field—Dean Radin (see *www.deanradin.com* and *www.noetic.org/research/participate/online-activities/*), Rupert Sheldrake (*www.sheldrake.org*), and Russell Targ (*www.espresearch.com*). I also recommend Lynn McTaggart's site (*www.intentionexperiment.com*). Here are a few more experiments to play with.

Plant Trimming Experiment.

If you're a plant aficionado, try out this experiment devised by my husband Steve. Take a photo of a bushy plant that you wish to trim in a few months. On the photo, clearly mark with a pen exactly which branches you intend to snip off. Make it clear that these branches will be gone, perhaps by putting an X over them, or by making a thick visible line where you intend to cut. (Note: You must ultimately snip these branches off, not just intend to.) Now, let a few months pass. Take another photo of the plant just before you do your trimming. Did the designated branches grow any differently than the other branches?

In Chapter 21, I described an experiment with photographing orbs. Here are some other ideas to try out. In all cases, be sure to record your results, including the variables you are modifying and the nature of the orbs themselves—location (for example, where they are located relative to people), size, brightness, color, and quantity.

Orb Experiments.

Are orbs—the photographable balls of light that may be manifestations of thought forms on the etheric level—affected by your thoughts or emotions? Perform the orb experiment described in Chapter 21, but focus on certain types of thoughts and emotions rather than just simply meditating. For example, experiment with different emotional states (anger, fear, sadness, happiness, gratitude, excitement, etc.) and different emotional intensities. Similarly, experiment with different types of thoughts (for example, about the present, future, or past). You might also experiment by varying the depth of your meditative state.

Another question you might wish to investigate is whether certain places or events enable more orbs to form. Take flash photos at different venues—in churches, restaurants, or lifecycle events—before, during, and after periods in which people are present. Record location, number of people present, the mood of the crowd, the events that took place, or any other interesting feature.

In Chapter 21, I described how auras can sometimes appear in one's visual field during meditations focused on external sensation. Here are some other ideas you can experiment with.

Aura Experiments.

- If you are outside on a bright shiny day, settle into the Now and gaze at the surrounding plants in a slightly defocused way. It's best to start with distant plants, like large trees, with a clear sky in the background. You may notice an optical illusion of white surrounding the vegetation that mirrors its exact structure. However, as you become fully settled, you may also notice a grayish or pastel-colored cloud surrounding a plant or tree. You are on the right track if you notice tendrils of this cloud extending from one branch to another.

- Ask to receive "impressions" from a plant and be energized by them. Stand next to a plant and settle. Extend your hands toward the plant but do not touch it. Visualize receiving energy and allow yourself to receive whatever comes. You will probably start to notice that you can smell the plant much more vividly. Then you may begin to feel a tingling energy coming through your hands and into your body. Afterward, you may feel curiously refreshed and energized.

I once did this exercise just before shopping at the supermarket for some wine. I must have had a youthful glow about me, because I got carded by the clerk—at age forty! When he looked at my ID, he was quite surprised by my age.

• When you are with a crowd of people in a quiet place like a church or library, try to see if you can settle and see auras around people's heads. This will be easier to do if there is a white wall in the background. In addition, try to align your energy with another person and see if you can receive information about their physical health or mental state. If possible, discreetly verify what you receive.

PRACTICE MAKES A MORE PERFECT WORLD

Part VI provided you with several years' worth of exercises and experiments to play with. If you make them a part of your daily life, I'm sure you will be amazed at what you discover about yourself and about your world. The question is, once you are armed with these new insights and abilities, will you join with other like-minded individuals to create a better world for humanity as a whole?

In the next and final part of this book, I'll address a variety of questions that are broader in their scope and implications. What role can each of us play in determining the future of our world? What can we learn about the consciousness of our planet? And can we humans fulfill our potential to become co-creators with the Divine?

PART VII

CHOOSE JOY

Dream lofty dreams,
and as you dream,
so shall you become.
Your vision is the promise
of what you shall one day be;
your ideal is the prophecy of
what you shall at last unveil.

—JAMES ALLEN

CHAPTER 34

✣

IT'S UP TO YOU

So now it's up to you. It's up to all of us. Will you join with others and evolve so that you can help to preserve and heal our world? As Ken Wilber points out, the odds of success are in our favor. Things, people, cultures, and political structures tend to evolve, not devolve. But can we do it in time? Or will collective inaction doom us to the fate of the dinosaurs, as the seas rise around us?

Scientists have begun to recognize that evolution often occurs suddenly—as "punctuated" or "quantum" leaps forward. As Wilber points out, when a wing evolves from a leg, the hundred or more required mutations are likely to happen all at once; otherwise, natural selection wouldn't perpetuate it—because a half-wing is of no benefit.[1] How or why this occurs is not really understood yet, but we do know that it happens.

It stands to reason then, that evolution in the non-physical realms might manifest in the same way. New forms of awareness and consciousness may suddenly emerge, become stabilized, and then just as suddenly transcend themselves to create newer forms at the next level. All evidence seems to be pointing to the fact that we may be at one of those critical times. If enough of us can take our blinders off and see what is really going on, we may also hear the growing rumbling of the evolutionary cycle gearing up for movement once again. Coming from every quarter, it is telling us that it is indeed time for us to wake up.

EVOLUTION IS INHERENT

In truth, evolution may not only be necessary for survival; it might be the way the universe works at a fundamental level. For instance, quantum physicists believe that the universe we are currently experiencing may be only one in a long string of universes, each an elaboration upon the universes that preceded it. Philosopher Ervin Laszlo puts it this way, in an imaginative rendering of a conscious universe slowly evolving towards ultimate perfection:

> "In universe after universe the plenum brings forth micro-ripples and mega-wave structures... In the next universe new and more elaborate structures appear, with more articulated reflections of the world around them. In the course of innumerable universes, the pulsating Metaverse realizes all that the primeval plenum held in potential. The plenum is no longer formless: its surface is of unimaginable complexity and coherence; its depth is fully informed. The cosmic proto-consciousness that endowed the primeval plenum with its universe-creative potentials becomes a fully articulated cosmic consciousness—it *becomes*, and thenceforth eternally *is, the self-realized mind of God.*" [2]

Physicist and mystic Amit Goswami, like Laszlo, believes that consciousness is the fundamental state of our universe and that it is in a perpetual state of evolution. Just as Gurdjieff exhorted us all to remember ourself, Goswami claims that evolution is actually "a process through which the preexistent transcendent consciousness remembers itself... until it regains its original and unconditional state of freedom." [3] The great Indian philosopher Sri Aurobindo spoke the same message:

> "But what after all, behind appearance, is the seeming mystery?... We can see that it is the Consciousness which had lost itself, returning to itself, emerging out of its giant self-forgetfulness, slowly, painfully, as a life that is would-be sentient, to be more than sentient, to be again divinely self-conscious, free, infinite, immortal." [4]

Just as the universe recreates and expands upon its previous selves, so do we. Mystics of every religion tell us that we are all bits of consciousness evolving through a repeated cycle of incarnation into material form. After each progressive lifetime, we return into the stream of consciousness, hopefully having achieved a more expanded and enlightened state. It is thus our human destiny to slowly move up the Kabbalistic Tree of Life until we reach the state of Adam Kadmon, the fully developed manifestation of humanity that God intended for us. And as we evolve ever upward, we become more aware of the energy bodies that accompany us along the way—from our physical form, to its life-sustaining etheric body, to the astral, mental, and causal bodies that have access to higher dimensions and accompany us from life to life.

Attaining such lofty realms of awareness may seem hopelessly out of reach to you. But don't discount yourself or your potential. You *can* embark upon this path and you *can* make progress.

I'm reminded of a comedy that is actually a story of cosmic evolution—*Groundhog Day*. The main character, a TV weatherman played by the wry Bill Murray, is given the opportunity to relive one day in his life—Groundhog Day—over and over again, until he ultimately reaches a state of enlightenment. In the beginning of the movie, Murray's character is egotistical, self-centered, ambitious, greedy, and uncaring about others. He is judgmental and rude to everyone he meets, and blind to the beauty around him. But he finds himself in a predicament. Each day he awakens to find himself repeating Groundhog Day once more. Just as each one of our souls reincarnates life after life in an effort to reach enlightenment and finally "get it right," Murray's character is given the difficult but magnificent opportunity to get it right in the course of a single lifetime—in fact, in the course of a single day, repeated hundreds, even thousands, of times.

At first, Murray's weatherman uses the situation to gain advantage. He teases and uses others for his amusement, knowing that there will be no repercussions. Then he moves into despair and commits suicide several times. Eventually he realizes that he has an opportunity to learn and grow from his predicament. He utilizes his endlessly repeating Groundhog Day to master a number of new skills and talents.

Finally however, Murray's character slowly moves beyond personal growth into a focus on helping and caring for others. He reaches a state of relaxed and humble joy, fully accepting himself and the people around him. He becomes fearless and loving and sees beauty in everyone and everything. And once he has reached this enlightened state, he is freed from Groundhog Day.

What a perfect metaphor! And a reminder to all of us that practice does indeed make perfect.

CHAPTER 35

🦢

TECHNOLOGY AND
THE SOUL

I BEGAN THIS BOOK BY TELLING YOU ABOUT AN EPISODE OF STAR TREK. So I guess it's only fitting that I conclude it with some lessons I've learned from another science fiction saga—*Battlestar Galactica*. This television show tells the story of the last remnants of humanity fleeing through space after its home planets have been destroyed by "Cylons"— robots that the humans themselves created. Humanity's mission is now to find a mythical planet from its distant past—a place called Earth.

But something surprising catches up with them. They discover that there are other kinds of Cylons in their midst—robots who look and act completely human. These humanoid Cylons are immortal; when they are killed, their "consciousness" and memories are down-loaded into a new Cylon body. Interestingly, these humanoid robots also seem to be evolving, gradually becoming more and more like real humans after each download. For example, they are beginning to experience dreams, and while they are in the gap between "incarna-tions," they have mystical experiences.

Is it possible that we, too, are a bit like these humanoid Cylons? Are we actually higher-dimensional creatures having a three-dimensional "robotic" experience in a physical body, with a higher-dimensional part of us retained from life to life? Just as the Cylons on Battlestar Galactica were evolving to become more human, is it possible that we too are evolving to become more and more like our true higher-dimensional Selves?

Or are we actually more like the humans on Battlestar Galactica? Will we focus only upon material things and wind up creating robots that serve and ultimately destroy us? It's actually happening, you know. We now have computer systems that can understand speech in limited contexts, translate language, recognize images, logically reason, and navigate terrain. We are also creating more and more complex virtual versions of ourselves. On the Internet we have avatars in online game worlds. On the battlefield we have remotely-controlled drones that strike our enemies.

So the question is—what is our next step? Will we focus only upon recreating ourselves as machines, and become more and more robotic and less and less who we are? Or will we try to evolve and become more like our true inner Selves—the higher dimensional passengers in the carriages of our being?

THE BIGGER PICTURE

At times like these, it can be useful to take a step back and see the bigger picture. What is the state of humanity as a whole? What are our collective stories? And what is the state of the Earth itself?

Some have proposed that Earth is really one big complex organism called "Gaia".[1] Originated by environmentalist James Lovelock, the Gaia hypothesis states that the biosphere and all physical components of the Earth work together to maintain a proper state of balance, just as a living organism would. And while it is unlikely that Gaia is going to disappear any time soon—barring a collision with a giant asteroid or some other cataclysmic event—it will be her tendency, just as it is our own body's tendency, to try and regain homeostasis or equilibrium after enduring a shock to her system.

That is just what seems to be happening right now. Over the past several hundred years—a very short period of time for a planet—human activity has disturbed Gaia's balance. We've added too many chemicals into the atmosphere, polluted the oceans and waterways too severely, wiped out too many species of plants and animals, and deforested on a grand scale. Gaia is now pushing back, because that's what an organism must do in order to survive.

Now, if you look at a chart of human population growth on Earth, you will quickly see that the rise of industrial civilization and the use of fossil fuels have coincided with a sharp exponential rise in human population. Two thousand years ago, all of Gaia held only 200 million people—much less than the current population of the United States. In 1800, the total world population was still only one billion. By 1900, it had grown to 1.6 billion, and in the past 100 years—in just three or four generations—the population has risen to nearly 7 billion. Projections now indicate that we will reach 10 billion by 2100.

In the short time span since the invention of the automobile, airplane, and the computer, human population seems to have grown beyond what Gaia can handle—and we are beginning to feel the effects. Fresh water and fish supplies are becoming scarcer and the oceans are at risk as we fill them with garbage, pollute them with oil, and acidify them with carbon dioxide falling out of the atmosphere. While some argue that technology will ultimately come to the rescue, chances are that Gaia will reassert herself much more powerfully than any technology can compensate for. And just as a population of deer can explode and die off, so too can humankind.

Look around you. The polar icecaps are melting and the seas are beginning to rise. Fairly large populated areas of the planet will likely disappear in the next hundred years. As temperatures rise, storms will intensify and pests and diseases will proliferate. As food and fresh water become scarcer, regional tensions will increase, creating more warfare and death. Is this our future? Perhaps—but not necessarily.

Remember, just because something is probable doesn't make it inevitable. There might be a different possible future for us, and to the extent that we can evolve and use the power of consciousness to guide humanity toward that future, more of us will survive the coming challenges for our planet and our civilization. In fact, it may be possible that this state of affairs will *help* us grow and evolve. The cultural, political, intellectual, and spiritual evolution of humanity has always been driven by crises like these.

As our numbers have grown upon the Earth, so have the concomitant pressures of survival. These have spurred us on to create new technologies, social structures, and ways of understanding our world—and they have also helped us to evolve our consciousness. As a result, the changes and pressures we are witnessing today may simply be the next critical juncture, the next opportunity for growth. *We may be standing at a collective choice point and it is now time for us to make our choice*—to move forward and successfully evolve, or to choose inaction and extinction. The stakes couldn't be higher.

Naturally, the possible futures that lie before us—ones of scarcity, warfare, and decimation, and ones of evolution and transcendence—are also reflected in our collective stories. The first type of future is echoed in post-apocalyptic movies like *Mad Max* and *Waterworld*. These are stories of a world engaged in a dog-eat-dog battle for survival. They make us fearful and send us running to our various tribal niches, preparing for battle and hoarding and gorging while we can.

Thankfully, many of us are becoming engaged in the other kind of story. It reflects a more hopeful future—one in which humanity comes together in fellowship and love. Self-development and mutual understanding enable enough of us to realize that we must voluntarily lower the burden of human population upon Gaia's back, before disease and disaster force it upon us. It is also a story of sustainability. Rather than hoarding and gorging, each person aims for only what he or she really needs to be happy. People come to understand that happiness is better derived from community, art, music, culture, nature, and love, than from material possessions. And when it comes to technology, the story of our brighter future focuses on collective betterment rather than on greed and power.

I know that this brighter future for humanity might seem downright improbable right now. But it is definitely *possible*. And as more of us decide that we want it and envision it as PURE GOAL, it will become more probable. So let's do it!

CHAPTER 36

✦

THE WAY FORWARD

Many books have been written and many workshops and lectures have been given about manifesting and creating one's dreams. This book might be considered to be one of them. But that's not why I wrote it. My goal isn't for you to make more money or to find love, though I certainly do wish that for you. Instead, my goal is to enable you to develop a deeper form of awareness. And once you do, you will find that your life *does* become happier and that you *do* achieve more of what you desire. More importantly, though, you will become a better world citizen—one who can join with others to make sure that our civilization survives on this, our only planetary home, Gaia.

The idea that a human being is merely a physical machine is failing us. It doesn't jibe with scientific results about paranormal phenomena, the wisdom of alternative medical systems like acupuncture and homeopathy, or even the implications of quantum physics. Indeed, conventional medical solutions to health have now become leading causes of death.[1,2]

The notion of "man as machine" certainly isn't making us happy either. People are increasingly experiencing a lack of meaning or purpose in their lives. Feelings of ennui, denial, and hopelessness have become more and more prevalent as Gaia manifests more symptoms of planetary ill health. So the idea that our bodies and our planet are big tinker toys that simply need more chemicals, gadgets, and gizmos is getting a bit thin. It is clear that we need a new and deeper perspective. A global shift in consciousness is required so that we can repair our bodies, our families, our societies, and Gaia herself.

While it is true that religious institutions have sometimes brewed hatred and strife in our world, it is also true that every religion has, at its core, a deep message of wisdom that can help us. This message stresses the unity of all things—a unity comprised of the collective interplay of energies out of which all creation springs forth. Call it God, Allah, Brahman, The Force, or the energy of Love—call it what you will. We are all part of it, and we are all one with it. *You* are part of it. *You* are one with it. And this innate piece of the infinite field of consciousness within you has creative potential. It is not in your head, nor is it in your heart. It extends far beyond the limits of your physical body into higher dimensions in space.

The Hindu masters described the realization of the Self as "I Am That." In the Bible, God provides the self-descriptive name "I Am That I Am," represented by the four Hebrew letters *yud, heh, vav, heh—YHVH.* The Hebrew root of this name, "HVH," implies a state of beingness. But the "Y" part of the divine name connotes the future tense. The implication is that the God force not only *is*, but is in an expansive and creative state of *becoming.*[3]

The same is true for us. Just as the universal field of God-ness is the root of all that is, was, and will be, so too are we all a part of this awesome and infinite creative process. Each one of us is an intrinsic part of a greater whole, acting as a co-creator in the greater field of consciousness. Do not fear this fullness of your being. Instead, seek it and embrace it. The fact is, you cannot escape it. Because even if you aren't aware of its existence, it is there.

Remember: You *do* have the potential to realize who you truly are. Decide now to take the reins of your carriage and take charge. Join with others to help create a new and better world and begin your journey toward active consciousness. And as you travel down its forked path—*CHOOSE JOY.*

NOTES

Preface
1. A.L. Lansky. "Consciousness As An Active Force." *The Noetic Journal*, Volume 2, Number 1 (January 2000). Also see: *www.renresearch.com/consciousness.html*.

PART I. A Fork in the Road

Chapter 1. Inner Space: The Ultimate Frontier
1. M.P. Georgeff and A.L. Lansky. "Reactive Reasoning and Planning." *Proceedings of the Sixth National Conference on Artificial Intelligence (AAAI-87)*, Seattle, Washington (July 1987).
2. A.L. Lansky. "Localized Planning with Action-Based Constraints." *Artificial Intelligence*, Volume 98, Number 1-2, pp. 49–136 (January 1998).
3. D. Dennett. *Consciousness Explained*. Boston: Little, Brown and Company (1991).
4. M. Kaku. *Hyperspace: A Scientific Odyssey Through Parallel Universes, Time Warps, and the 10th Dimension*. New York: Oxford University Press (1994).
5. L. Randall. *Warped Passages: Unraveling the Mysteries of the Universe's Hidden Dimensions*. New York: Harper Perennial (2006).
6. E.A. Rauscher and R. Targ. "Investigation of a Complex Space-Time Metric to Describe Precognition of the Future." *Frontiers of Time: Retrocausation— Experiment and Theory, AIP Conference Proceedings*, Volume 863, pp. 121–146 (2006).
7. R. Rucker. *The Fourth Dimension: A Guided Tour of Higher Universes*. Boston: Houghton Mifflin Company (1984).
8. J.K. Rowling. *Harry Potter and the Half-Blood Prince*. New York: Scholastic Paperbacks (2006).
9. M. Talbot. *The Holographic Universe*. New York: Harper Perennial, p. 200 (1992).

Chapter 2. A Glimpse at Four Dimensions
1. E.A. Abbott. *Flatland: A Romance of Many Dimensions*. New York: Penguin Books, Ltd. (1984).
2. D. Radin. *Entangled Minds: Extrasensory Experiences in a Quantum Reality*. New York: Paraview (2006).
3. D. Radin. *The Conscious Universe: The Scientific Truth of Psychic Phenomena*. San Francisco: Harper Edge (1997).
4. L. McTaggart. *The Field: The Quest for the Secret Force of the Universe*. New York: HarperCollins Publishers, Inc. (2002).
5. L. McTaggart. *The Intention Experiment: Using Your Thoughts to Change Your Life and the World*. New York: Free Press (2007).
6. M. Kaku. *Hyperspace: A Scientific Odyssey Through Parallel Universes, Time Warps, and the 10th Dimension*. New York: Oxford University Press (1994).

7. L. Randall. *Warped Passages: Unraveling the Mysteries of the Universe's Hidden Dimensions*. New York: Harper Perennial (2006).

8. D. Bohm. *Wholeness and the Implicate Order*. London: Routledge Classics (1980).

Chapter 3. A Miraculous Cure

1. J. Reichenberg-Ullman. "A Homeopathic Approach to Behavioral Problems." *Mothering*, Number 74, pp. 97–101 (Spring 1995).

2. A.L. Lansky. *Impossible Cure: The Promise of Homeopathy*. Portola Valley, California: R.L.Ranch Press (2003).

3. J. Winston. *The Faces of Homoeopathy*. New Zealand: Great Auk Publishing (1999).

4. M.L. Rao, et al. "The Defining Role of Structure (Including Epitaxy) in the Plausibility of Homeopathy." *Homeopathy*, 96, pp. 175–182 (2007).

5. R. Roy, et al. "The Structure of Liquid Water: Novel Insights from Materials Research and Potential Relevance to Homeopathy." *Materials Research Innovation*, 9 (4): pp. 557–608 (2005).

6. L. Montagnier, et al., "Electromagnetic Signals Are Produced by Aqueous Nanostructures Derived from Bacterial DNA Sequences." *Interdiscip Sci Comput Life Sci,* 1: 81–90 (2009).

7. A.L. Lansky. "Consciousness As An Active Force." *The Noetic Journal*, Volume 2, Number 1 (January 2000). Also see: *www.renresearch.com/consciousness.html*.

Chapter 4. Fertile Soil

1. D. Radin. *Entangled Minds: Extrasensory Experiences in a Quantum Reality*. New York: Paraview (2006).

2. D. Radin. *The Conscious Universe: The Scientific Truth of Psychic Phenomena*. San Francisco: Harper Edge (1997).

3. B.A. Brennan. *Hands of Light: A Guide to Healing Through the Human Energy Field*. New York: Bantam Books (1987).

4. S. Roman. *Living With Joy: Keys to Personal Power and Spiritual Transformation*. Tiburon, California: H.J. Kramer, Inc. (1986).

5. S. Roman. *Personal Power Through Awareness: A Guidebook for Sensitive People*. Tiburon, California: H.J. Kramer, Inc. (1986).

6. S. Roman. *Spiritual Growth: Being Your Higher Self.* Tiburon, California: H.J. Kramer, Inc. (1992).

7. S. Roman. *Soul Love: Awakening Your Heart Centers*. Tiburon, California: H.J. Kramer, Inc. (1997).

Chapter 5. What Is Consciousness?

1. S. Blackmore. *Conversations on Consciousness: What the Best Minds Think About the Brain, Free Will, and What It Means to Be Human*. New York: Oxford University Press, p. 82 (2006).

2. Ibid, p. 42.

3. P. van Lommel, et al. "Near-Death Experience in Survivors of Cardiac Arrest: A Prospective Study in the Netherlands." *Lancet*, 358(9298), pp. 2039–2045 (December 15, 2001).

4. T.C.Moody. "Conversations With Zombies." *Journal of Consciousness Studies*, 1 (2), pp. 196–200 (1994).

5. S. Blackmore. *Conversations on Consciousness: What the Best Minds Think About the Brain, Free Will, and What It Means to Be Human.* New York: Oxford University Press, p. 181 (2006).

Chapter 6. The Road to Active Consciousness

1. A. Turing. "Computing Machinery and Intelligence." *Mind*, Vol. 59, No. 236, pp. 433–460 (October 1950). Also see: *en.wikipedia.org/wiki/Turing_test*.

2. P.D. Ouspensky. *In Search of the Miraculous: The Teachings of G.I. Gurdjieff.* San Diego: Harcourt, Inc., pp. 19–20 (1949).

3. S.R. Maharshi, with editor D. Godman. *Be As You Are: The Teachings of Sri Ramana Maharshi.* New York: Penguin Books, Ltd. (1989).

4. P.D. Ouspensky. *In Search of the Miraculous: The Teachings of G.I. Gurdjieff.* San Diego: Harcourt, Inc. (1949).

5. Ibid., pp. 144–145.

6. E. Tolle, *The Power of Now: A Guide to Spiritual Enlightenment.* Novato, California: New World Library, p. 177 (1999). Reprinted with permission from New World Library. *www.NewWorldLibrary.com*.

7. P.D. Ouspensky. *In Search of the Miraculous: The Teachings of G.I. Gurdjieff.* San Diego: Harcourt, Inc., p. 104 (1949).

Chapter 7. A Path Emerges

1. A.L. Lansky. *Impossible Cure: The Promise of Homeopathy.* Portola Valley, California: R.L.Ranch Press (2003).

2. G. Craig. *The EFT Manual.* Energy Psychology Press (2008). Also see: *www.eftuniverse.com*.

Chapter 8. Start Evolving—Now

1. R. Moss. *The Mandala of Being: Discovering the Power of Awareness.* Novato, California: New World Library, pp. xvi–xvii (2007). Reprinted with permission from New World Library. *www.NewWorldLibrary.com*.

2. Ibid., p. xxi.

3. K. Wilber. *A Brief History of Everything.* Boston: Shambhala (2000).

4. D. Radin. *Entangled Minds: Extrasensory Experiences in a Quantum Reality.* New York: Paraview (2006).

5. P.D. Ouspensky. *In Search of the Miraculous: The Teachings of G.I. Gurdjieff.* San Diego: Harcourt, Inc., p. 309 (1949).

PART II. The Mystery that Surrounds You
1. R. Sheldrake. *Seven Experiments That Could Change the World: A Do-It-Yourself Guide to Revolutionary Science.* Rochester, Vermont: Park Street Press, p. xiii (1995).
2. L. McTaggart. *The Field: The Quest for the Secret Force of the Universe.* New York: HarperCollins Publishers, Inc. (2002).
3. L. McTaggart. *The Intention Experiment: Using Your Thoughts to Change Your Life and the World.* New York: Free Press (2007).
4. D. Radin. *Entangled Minds: Extrasensory Experiences in a Quantum Reality.* New York: Paraview (2006).
5. D. Radin. *The Conscious Universe: The Scientific Truth of Psychic Phenomena.* San Francisco: Harper Edge (1997).
6. R. Targ and J. Katra. *Miracles of Mind: Exploring Nonlocal Consciousness and Spiritual Healing.* Novato, California: New World Library (1998).
7. L. Dossey. *Healing Words: The Power of Prayer and the Practice of Medicine.* San Francisco: HarperSanFrancisco (1993).
8. P.D. Ouspensky. *In Search of the Miraculous: The Teachings of G.I. Gurdjieff.* San Diego: Harcourt, Inc. (1949).
9. R. Steiner. *Anthroposophy and the Inner Life: An Esoteric Introduction.* Bristol, England: Rudolf Steiner Press (1931).

Chapter 9. Silicon Valley Meets Diagon Alley
1. D. Radin. "Unconscious Perception of Future Emotions: An Experiment in Presentiment." Journal of Scientific Exploration. 11, pp. 163–180 (1997).
2. D. Radin. "Psychophysiological Evidence of Possible Retrocausal Effects in Humans." *Frontiers of Time: Retrocausation—Experiment and Theory.* American Institute of Physics (AIP) Conference Proceedings, Volume 863, pp. 193–213 (2006).
3. R. Targ and J. Katra. *Miracles of Mind: Exploring Nonlocal Consciousness and Spiritual Healing.* Novato, California: New World Library, p. 49 (1998).
4. M. Talbot. *The Holographic Universe.* New York: Harper Perennial, p. 230 (1992).
5. Ibid., p. 233.
6. R. Targ and H. Puthoff. "Information Transmission Under Conditions of Sensory Shielding." *Nature*, 251, pp. 602–607 (18 October 1974).
7. R.G. Jahn and B.J. Dunne. "On the Quantum Mechanics of Consciousness, with Application to Anomalous Phenomena." *Foundations of Physics.* 16(8), pp. 721–772 (1986).

Chapter 10. Entanglements

1. M. Arndt, et al. "Wave–Particle Duality of C60 Molecules." *Nature*; 401:680–682 (1999).

2. Ghosh, et al. "Coherent Spin Oscillations in a Disordered Magnet." *Science*, 296:2195–2198 (2002).

3. D. Radin. *Entangled Minds: Extrasensory Experiences in a Quantum Reality*. New York: Paraview (2006).

4. L. McTaggart. *The Intention Experiment: Using Your Thoughts to Change Your Life and the World*. New York: Free Press, pp. 56–61 (2007).

5. Ibid., p. 50.

6. Ibid., p. 61.

7. L. Dossey. *Healing Words: The Power of Prayer and the Practice of Medicine*. San Francisco: HarperSanFrancisco (1993).

8. L. McTaggart. *The Intention Experiment: Using Your Thoughts to Change Your Life and the World*. New York: Free Press, p. 93 (2007).

9. R. Sheldrake. *The Presence of the Past: Morphic Resonance and the Habits of Nature*. Rochester, Vermont: Park Street Press (1988).

10. R. Sheldrake. *Seven Experiments That Could Change the World: A Do-It-Yourself Guide to Revolutionary Science*. Rochester, Vermont: Park Street Press (1995).

11. Ibid., p. 141.

12. Ibid., p. 135.

13. P. Pearsall. *The Heart's Code: Tapping the Wisdom and Power of Our Heart Energy*. New York: Broadway Books (1998).

14. H. Bennett and S. Sparrow. "The Thinking Heart: An Interview with Paul Pearsall." See: *www.paulpearsall.com/info/press/4.html*.

Chapter 11. The Field

1. E. Laszlo. *Science and the Akashic Field: An Integral Theory of Everything*. Rochester, Vermont: Inner Traditions, p. 46 (2004).

2. R. Sheldrake. *The Presence of the Past: Morphic Resonance and the Habits of Nature*. Rochester, Vermont: Park Street Press (1988).

3. E. Laszlo. *Science and the Akashic Field: An Integral Theory of Everything*. Rochester, Vermont: Inner Traditions (2004).

4. Ibid., p. 69.

5. Ibid., p. 47.

6. Ibid., pp. 52–53.

7. W.A. Tiller and W.E. Dibble, Jr. "New Experimental Data Revealing an Unexpected Dimension to Materials Science and Engineering," *Materials Research Innovation*, 5, pp. 21–34 (2001).

8. L. McTaggart. *The Intention Experiment: Using Your Thoughts to Change Your Life and the World*. New York: Free Press, pp. 113–116 (2007).

9. W. Tiller. *Conscious Acts of Creation: The Emergence of a New Physics.* Walnut Creek, California: Pavior Publishing (2001).
10. L. McTaggart. *The Intention Experiment: Using Your Thoughts to Change Your Life and the World.* New York: Free Press, pp. 116–123 (2007).

Chapter 12. When You Have the Right Vibe, It's Not a Coincidence

1. M. Talbot. *The Holographic Universe.* New York: Harper Perennial (1992).
2. Ibid.
3. C. Jung. *The Archetypes and the Collective Unconscious.* Princeton: Princeton University Press (1981).
4. R. Sheldrake. *The Presence of the Past: Morphic Resonance and the Habits of Nature.* Rochester, Vermont: Park Street Press, p. 168 (1988).
5. R.D. Nelson, et al. "Field REG Anomalies in Group Situations." *Journal of Scientific Exploration,* 10(1), pp. 111–141 (1996).
6. R.D. Nelson, et al. "Field REG II: Consciousness Field Effects: Replications and Explorations." *Journal of Scientific Exploration,* 12(3), pp. 425–454 (1998).
7. R.D. Nelson, et al. "Correlations of Continuous Random Data with Major World Events." *Foundations of Physics Letters.* 15(6), pp. 537–550 (2002).
8. D.I. Radin. "Exploring Relationships Between Random Physical Events and Mass Human Attention: Asking For Whom the Bell Tolls." *Journal of Scientific Exploration.* 16(4), pp. 533–547 (2002).
9. L. McTaggart. *The Intention Experiment: Using Your Thoughts to Change Your Life and t he World.* New York: Free Press, pp. 180–181 (2007).
10. C. Jung. *Jung on Synchronicity and the Paranormal: Key Readings.* London: Routledge (1977).
11. R. Rucker. *The Fourth Dimension: A Guided Tour of Higher Universes.* Boston: Houghton Mifflin Company, p. 186 (1984).
12. C. Jung. *The Archetypes and the Collective Unconscious.* Princeton: Princeton University Press (1981).
13. S. Blackmore. *Conversations on Consciousness: What the Best Minds Think About the Brain, Free Will, and What It Means to Be Human.* New York: Oxford University Press, p. 118–119 (2006).

Chapter 13. A Meaningful Cure

1. S. Hahnemann. *Organon of the Medical Art (Sixth Edition).* Edited and annotated by Wenda Brewster O'Reilly, based on a translation by Stephen Decker, Redmond, Washington: Birdcage Books (1996).
2. M.L. Rao, R. Roy, I.R. Bell, and R. Hoover, "The Defining Role of Structure (Including Epitaxy) in the Plausibility of Homeopathy." *Homeopathy,* 96, pp. 175–182 (2007).

3. E. Davenas, et al. "Human Basophil Degranulation Triggered by Very Dilute Antiserum Against IgE." *Nature*, Volume 333, Number 6176, pp. 816–181 (June 1988).

4. H. Stevenson. "Quackbusters Are Busted!" (July 2010). See: *http://www.gaia-health.com/articles251/000277-quackbusters-are-busted.shtml*.

5. J. Aissa, et al. "Transatlantic Transfer of Digitized Antigen Signal by Telephone Link." *Journal of Allergy and Clinical Immunology*, 99: S175 (1997).

6. V. Brown and M. Ennis. "Flow-Cytometric Analysis of Basophil Activation: Inhibition by Histamine at Conventional and Homeopathic Concentrations." *Inflammation Research*, 50, Supplement (2), S47–S48 (2001).

7. P. Belon, et al. "Histamine Dilutions Modulate Basophil Activation." *Inflammation Research*, 53, pp. 181–188 (2004).

8. L. Montagnier, et al., "Electromagnetic Signals Are Produced by Aqueous Nanostructures Derived from Bacterial DNA Sequences." *Interdiscip Sci Comput Life Sci*, 1: 81–90 (2009).

9. M. Emoto. *The Hidden Messages in Water*. New York: Atria Books (2005).

10. E. C. Whitmont. *Psyche and Substance*. Berkeley, California: North Atlantic Books and Homeopathic Educational Services (1991).

11. Ibid., p. 86.

12. R. Vermeulen. *Synoptic Materia Medica 2*. Haarlem, The Netherlands: Merlijn Publishers (1996).

13. Lansky, Amy L. *Impossible Cure: The Promise of Homeopathy*. Portola Valley, California: R.L.Ranch Press, pp. 127–129 (2003).

Exercise 2. Being Present in Inner Sensation

1. G. Craig. *The EFT Manual*. Energy Psychology Press (2008). Also see: *www.eftuniverse.com*.

PART III. The Choice Point

CHAPTER 14. Forces and Fields

1. E. Laszlo. *Science and the Akashic Field: An Integral Theory of Everything*. Rochester, Vermont: Inner Traditions, p. 46 (2004).

2. M. Kaku. *Hyperspace: A Scientific Odyssey Through Parallel Universes, Time Warps, and the 10th Dimension*. New York: Oxford University Press (1994).

3. E. Laszlo. *Science and the Akashic Field: An Integral Theory of Everything*. Rochester, Vermont: Inner Traditions, p. 77 (2004).

4. J.S. Hagelin, et al. "Effects of Group Practice of the Transcendental Meditation Program on Preventing Violent Crime in Washington, DC: Results of the National Demonstration Project, June–July 1993." *Social Indicators Research*, 47: 153–201 (1999).

5. D.W. Orme-Johnson, et al. "Preventing Terrorism and International Conflict: Effects of Large Assemblies of Participants in the Transcendental Meditation and TM–Sidhi Programs." *Journal of Offender Rehabilitation*, 36: 283–302 (2003).
6. Bibliography of studies on Transcendental Meditation. See: *www.mum.edu/ tm_research*.
7. R. Sheldrake. *Seven Experiments That Could Change the World: A Do-It-Yourself Guide to Revolutionary Science*. Rochester, Vermont: Park Street Press, pp. 217–219 (1995).

Chapter 15. *A Radical Hypothesis—Consciousness in Higher Dimensions*

1. P.D. Ouspensky. "The Fourth Dimension." An essay originally appearing in 1908. In *A New Model of the Universe* (1931). Reprint, New York: Random House (1971).
2. E. Laszlo. *Science and the Akashic Field: An Integral Theory of Everything*. Rochester, Vermont: Inner Traditions, p. 172 (2004).
3. P. Feyerabend. *Against Method*. London: Verso (1975).
4. R. Rucker. *The Fourth Dimension: A Guided Tour of Higher Universes*. Boston: Houghton Mifflin Company (1984).
5. L. Randall. *Warped Passages: Unraveling the Mysteries of the Universe's Hidden Dimensions*. New York: Harper Perennial (2006).
6. R. Rucker. *The Fourth Dimension: A Guided Tour of Higher Universes*. Boston: Houghton Mifflin Company, p. 59 (1984).
7. Ibid., p. 3.
8. C. de B. Evans, *Meister Eckhart by Franz Pfeiffer*, 2 volumes, London: John M. Watkins, p. 209 (1924 and 1931).
9. H. Everett. " 'Relative State' Formulation of Quantum Mechanics." *Reviews of Modern Physics*, Volume 29, Number 3 (July 1957).

Chapter 16. *The Process of Active Consciousness*

1. E. Hicks and J. Hicks. *The Amazing Power of Deliberate Intent*. Carlsbad, California: Hay House, Inc., p. 2 (2006).

Chapter 17. *The Force Is Within You*

1. M. Talbot. *The Holographic Universe*. New York: Harper Perennial, p. 212 (1992).
2. R. Sheldrake. *Seven Experiments That Could Change the World: A Do-It-Yourself Guide to Revolutionary Science*. Rochester, Vermont: Park Street Press, p. 212 (1995).
3. K. Wilber. *A Brief History of Everything*. Boston: Shambhala, p. 313 (2000).
4. Ibid., p. 17.

5. R. Peoc'h. "Psychokinetic Action of Young Chicks on the Path of an Illuminated Source." *Journal of Scientific Exploration,* 9(2), p. 223 (1995).

6. L. McTaggart. *The Field: The Quest for the Secret Force of the Universe.* New York: HarperCollins Publishers, Inc., pp. 117–118 (2002).

Chapter 18. Four Steps of Active Consciousness

1. D. Pinchbeck. *2012: The Return of Quetzalcoatl.* New York: Jeremy Tarcher / Penguin, p. 368 (2004).

2. E. Hicks and J. Hicks. *The Amazing Power of Deliberate Intent.* Carlsbad, California: Hay House, Inc. (2006).

3. Ibid., p. 226.

4. J. Sams and R. Carson. *Medicine Cards: The Discovery of Power Through the Ways of Animals.* Rochester, Vermont: Bear & Company, p. 158 (1988).

5. E. Hicks and J. Hicks. *The Amazing Power of Deliberate Intent.* Carlsbad, California: Hay House, Inc. (2006).

6. P.D. Ouspensky. *In Search of the Miraculous: The Teachings of G.I. Gurdjieff.* San Diego: Harcourt, Inc., p. 52 (1949).

Chapter 19. How Does It Work?

1. D. Loye. *The Sphinx and the Rainbow: Brain, Mind, and Future Vision.* IUniverse, pp. 158–165 (1999).

2. F.D. Peat. *Synchronicity: The Bridge Between Matter and Mind.* New York: Bantam (1987).

3. L. McTaggart. *The Intention Experiment: Using Your Thoughts to Change Your Life and the World.* New York: Free Press, p. 165 (2007).

4. E.R. Gruber. "Conformance Behavior Involving Animal and Human Subjects." *European Journal of Parapsychology,* 3(1), pp. 36–50 (1979).

5. L. McTaggart. *The Intention Experiment: Using Your Thoughts to Change Your Life and the World.* New York: Free Press, p. 166 (2007).

6. Ibid., p. 170.

7. Ibid., p. 174.

8. R. Bandler and J. Grinder. *The Structure of Magic.* Science and Behavior Books (1975).

9. G. Craig. *The EFT Manual.* Energy Psychology Press (2008). Also see: *www. eftuniverse.com.*

Chapter 20. Demystifying the Mysterious

1. P. Yogananda. *Autobiography of a Yogi.* Los Angeles: Self-Realization Fellowship, p. 134 (1973).

2. T. Walker. *The Force Is With Us: The Conspiracy Against the Supernatural, Spiritual and Paranormal.* Gatlinburg, Tennessee: Roaring Fork Limited, p. 272 (2005).

PART IV. Take A Deeper Look
1. P.D. Ouspensky. *In Search of the Miraculous: The Teachings of G.I. Gurdjieff.* San Diego: Harcourt, Inc., p. 88 (1949).
2. N. Scully. *Alchemical Healing: A Guide to Spiritual, Physical, and Transformational Medicine.* Rochester: Bear & Company, p. 321 (2003).

Chapter 21. The Body Esoteric
1. R. Steiner. *Anthroposophy and the Inner Life: An Esoteric Introduction.* Bristol, England: Rudolf Steiner Press (1931).
2. B.A. Brennan. *Hands of Light: A Guide to Healing Through the Human Energy Field.* New York: Bantam Books (1987).
3. W.A. Tiller. *Science and Human Transformation: Subtle Energies, Intentionality and Consciousness.* Walnut Creek, California: Pavior (1997).
4. T. Walker. *The Force Is With Us: The Conspiracy Against the Supernatural, Spiritual and Paranormal.* Gatlinburg, Tennessee: Roaring Fork Limited, p. 284 (2005).
5. K. Heinemann and M. Ledwith. *The Orb Project.* New York: Atria Books; Hillsboro, Oregon: Beyond Words Publishing (2007).
6. M. Talbot. *The Holographic Universe.* New York: Harper Perennial, p. 258 (1992).
7. R. Steiner. *Anthroposophy and the Inner Life: An Esoteric Introduction.* Bristol, England: Rudolf Steiner Press, pp. 30–31 (1931).
8. S. Rinpoche. *The Tibetan Book of Living and Dying.* New York: HarperOne (1994).
9. R. Steiner. *Anthroposophy and the Inner Life: An Esoteric Introduction.* Bristol, England: Rudolf Steiner Press, pp. 92–94 (1931).

Chapter 22. The Higher Energy Bodies—From Here to Eternity
1. Z.b.S. Halevi. *Kabbalah and Psychology.* York Beach, Maine: Samuel Weiser, Inc. (1986).
2. J. Richman. "Astral Plane." *Modern Lovers,* Beserkley (1977).
3. P.D. Ouspensky. *In Search of the Miraculous: The Teachings of G.I. Gurdjieff.* San Diego: Harcourt, Inc., p. 41 (1949).
4. Music of the Spheres. See: *en.wikipedia.org/wiki/Music_of_the_spheres.*
5. R. Steiner. *Anthroposophy and the Inner Life: An Esoteric Introduction.* Bristol, England: Rudolf Steiner Press, pp. 65, 67–68 (1931).
6. Ibid., p. 35.
7. Ibid., p. 76.
8. S. LaBerge, Stephen. *Lucid Dreaming.* Louisville, Colorado: Sounds True, Inc. (2009).

9. T.W.R inpoche. *The Tibetan Yogas of Dream and Sleep.* Ithaca, New York: Snow Lion Publications (1998).

10. S. LaBerge, Stephen. *Lucid Dreaming.* Louisville, Colorado: Sounds True, Inc. (2009).

11. L. Levitan and S. LaBerge. "Other Worlds: Out-of-Body Experiences and Lucid Dreams." *Nightlight* (The Lucidity Institute), 3(2-3) (1991). Also see: *www.Lucidity.com/NL32.OBEandLD.html.*

12. R. Steiner. *Anthroposophy and the Inner Life: An Esoteric Introduction.* Bristol, England: Rudolf Steiner Press, p. 77 (1931).

13. K. Wilber. *A Brief History of Everything.* Boston: Shambhala (2000).

14. S. Grof. *When The Impossible Happens: Adventures in Non-ordinary Reality.* Boulder, Colorado: Sounds True, Inc. (2006).

15. Ibid., pp. 138–139.

16. *www.edgarcayce.org.*

17. K. Ring. *Heading Toward Omega: In Search of the Meaning of the Near-Death Experience.* New York: Harper Perennial (1985).

18. R. Steiner. *Anthroposophy and the Inner Life: An Esoteric Introduction.* Bristol, England: Rudolf Steiner Press, p. 129 (1931).

19. J. Roberts. *Seth Speaks: The Eternal Validity of the Soul.* San Rafael, California: Amber-Allen Publishing (1994). Also see: *en.wikipedia.org/wiki/Jane_Roberts.*

20. J. Roberts. *The Oversoul Seven Trilogy: The Education of Oversoul Seven, the Further Education of Oversoul Seven, Oversoul Seven and the Museum of Time.* San Rafael, California: Amber-Allen Publishing; Novato, California: New World Library (1995).

21. R. Steiner. *Anthroposophy and the Inner Life: An Esoteric Introduction.* Bristol, England: Rudolf Steiner Press, p. 130 (1931).

Chapter 23. Emanations from the Causal Realm

1. Tree of Life. See: *en.wikipedia.org/wiki/Sephirot.*

2. Z.b.S. Halevi. *Kabbalah and Psychology.* York Beach, Maine: Samuel Weiser, Inc. (1986).

3. C. Low. *www.digital-brilliance.com/kab.* An excellent web site with introductory material on Kabbalah.

4. Ibid.

5. B. Layton. *The Gnostic Scriptures: A New Translation with Annotations and Introductions (The Anchor Yale Bible Reference Library).* New Haven: Yale University Press (1995).

6. P.D. Ouspensky. *In Search of the Miraculous: The Teachings of G.I. Gurdjieff*. San Diego: Harcourt, Inc. (1949).

7. S. Aurobindo. *The Yoga and Its Objects*. Pondicherry, India: Sri Aurobindo Ashram (2002).

Chapter 24. Visits With Other Realms

1. R. Steiner. *An Outline of Esoteric Science*. Anthroposophic Press, p. 22 (1997).

2. H. Cumming and K. Leffler. *John of God: The Brazilian Healer Who's Touched the Lives of Millions*. New York: Atria Books; Hillsboro, Oregon: Beyond Words Publishing (2007).

3. Dadaji. See: *www.dadaji.info*.

4. M. Talbot. *The Holographic Universe*. New York: Harper Perennial, pp. 109–110 (1992).

5. M.P. Somé. *Of Water and Spirit: Ritual, Magic, and Initiation in the Life of an African Shaman*. New York: Penguin (1995). Also see: *www.malidoma.com*.

6. S. Grof. *When The Impossible Happens: Adventures in Non-ordinary Reality*. Boulder, Colorado: Sounds True, Inc., p. 211 (2006).

7. P. Hawken. *The Magic of Findhorn*. New York: Bantam Books (1976).

8. G. Hancock. *Supernatural: Meetings with the Ancient Teachers of Mankind*. The Disinformation Company (2007).

9. J. Moore and B. Lamb. *Crop Circles Revealed: Language of the Light Symbols*. Light Technology Publications (2001).

10. L. Kitei. *The Phoenix Lights: A Skeptic's Discovery that We Are Not Alone*. Newburyport, Massachusetts: Hampton Roads Publishing Company (2010). Also see: *www.thephoenixlights.net*.

11. D. Radin. "The Enduring Enigma of the UFO." *Shift*, No. 21, pp. 22–27 (Winter 2008-2009).

12. *www.disclosureproject.org*.

13. L. Kean. *UFOs: Pilots and Government Officials Go On the Record*. Crown (2010).

14. D. Radin. "The Enduring Enigma of the UFO." *Shift*, No. 21, pp. 22–27 (Winter 2008-2009).

PART V. Enter Within

Chapter 25. What You Are and What You Are Not

1. P.D. Ouspensky. *In Search of the Miraculous: The Teachings of G.I. Gurdjieff*. San Diego: Harcourt, Inc., p. 150 (1949).

2. Ibid., p. 239.

3. E. Tolle. *The Power of Now: A Guide to Spiritual Enlightenment*. Novato, California: New World Library (1999).

4. Ibid., pp. 30–31. Reprinted with permission from New World Library. *www. NewWorldLibrary.com*.

5. P.D. Ouspensky. *In Search of the Miraculous: The Teachings of G.I. Gurdjieff*. San Diego: Harcourt, Inc., p. 155 (1949).

6. Ibid., p. 153.

Chapter 26. Self-Remembering—the Path to Enlightenment

1. E. Hicks and J. Hicks. *The Amazing Power of Deliberate Intent*. Carlsbad, California: Hay House, Inc. (2006).

2. Tolle, Eckhart. *The Power of Now: A Guide to Spiritual Enlightenment*. Novato, California: New World Library, p. 102 (1999). Reprinted with permission from New World Library. *www.NewWorldLibrary.com*.

3. A. Newberg and M.R. Waldman. *How God Changes Your Brain*. Random House Publishing Group (2009).

Chapter 27. Methods and Tools for Accessing Non-Ordinary States of Awareness

1. D. Pinchbeck. *2012: The Return of Quetzalcoatl*. New York: Jeremy Tarcher / Penguin, p. 369 (2004).

2. L. McTaggart. *The Intention Experiment: Using Your Thoughts to Change Your Life and the World*. New York: Free Press, pp. 65–81 (2007).

3. A. Lutz, et al. "Long–Term Meditators Self-Induce High–Amplitude Gamma Synchrony During Mental Practice." *Proceedings of the National Academy of Sciences*, Vol. 101, No. 46, pp. 16369–16373 (November 16, 2004). Also see: *www. pnas.org/content/101/46/16369.full*.

4. R.J. Davidson, et al. "Alterations in Brain and Immune Function Produced by Mindfulness Meditation." *Psychosomatic Medicine*, 65, pp. 564–570 (2003).

5. M.P. Somé. *Of Water and Spirit: Ritual, Magic, and Initiation in the Life of an African Shaman*. New York: Penguin (1995). Also see: *www.malidoma.com*.

6. V.S tibal. *Theta Healing: Go Up and Seek God, Go Up and Work With God*. Rolling Thunder (2007).

7. L. McTaggart. *The Intention Experiment: Using Your Thoughts to Change Your Life and the World*. New York: Free Press, p. 134 (2007).

8. S. Wilde. *The Art of Meditation*. Carlsbad, California: Hay House Audio Books (1998).

9. P.D. Ouspensky. *In Search of the Miraculous: The Teachings of G.I. Gurdjieff.* San Diego: Harcourt, Inc., pp. 351–352 (1949).

10. Ibid., p. 353.

11. S. Grof and C. Grof. *Holotropic Breathwork: A New Approach to Self-Exploration and Therapy.* New York: Excelsior Editions / State University of New York (2010).

12. D. Radin. *Entangled Minds: Extrasensory Experiences in a Quantum Reality.* New York: Paraview (2006).

13. D. Radin. *The Conscious Universe: The Scientific Truth of Psychic Phenomena.* San Francisco: Harper Edge (1997).

14. S. Roman. *Personal Power Through Awareness: A Guidebook for Sensitive People.* Tiburon, California: H.J. Kramer, Inc., p. 106 (1986). Reprinted with permission from H.J. Kramer/ New World Library. *www.NewWorldLibrary.com.*

PART VI. Playground of the Spirit

1. G. Craig. *The EFT Manual.* Energy Psychology Press (2008). Also see: *www.eftuniverse.com.*

Chapter 28. Facing Your Stories: Releasing the Self from the Fiction of the Mind

1. P.D. Ouspensky. *In Search of the Miraculous: The Teachings of G.I. Gurdjieff.* San Diego: Harcourt, Inc., p. 267 (1949).

2. S. Roman. *Soul Love: Awakening Your Heart Centers.* Tiburon, California: H.J. Kramer, Inc. (1997).

3. Ibid., pp. 3–8.

Chapter 29. Where Do You Go When You're Not Here and Now?

1. R. Moss. *The Mandala of Being: Discovering the Power of Awareness.* Novato, California: New World Library, p. 158 (2007). Reprinted with permission from New World Library, Novato, CA, *www.NewWorldLibrary.com.*

2. Ibid., p. 162. Reprinted with permission from New World Library, Novato, CA, *www.NewWorldLibrary.com.*

3. P.D. Ouspensky. *In Search of the Miraculous: The Teachings of G.I. Gurdjieff.* San Diego: Harcourt, Inc., p. 181 (1949).

Chapter 31. Feeling Good in Spite of Yourself

1. G. Sherman, Perceptual Integration course study materials.

2. G. Craig. *The EFT Manual.* Energy Psychology Press (2008). Also see: *www.eftuniverse.com.*

3. P.D. Ouspensky. *In Search of the Miraculous: The Teachings of G.I. Gurdjieff.* San Diego: Harcourt, Inc., p. 196 (1949).

4. G. Craig. *The EFT Manual.* Energy Psychology Press (2008). Also see: *www.eftuniverse.com.*

5. E. Hicks and J. Hicks. *The Amazing Power of Deliberate Intent.* Carlsbad, California: Hay House, Inc. (2006).

Chapter 32. Gratitude

1. S. Roman. *Living With Joy: Keys to Personal Power and Spiritual Transformation.* Tiburon, California: H.J. Kramer, Inc., p. 101 (1986). Reprinted with permission from H J Kramer/ New World Library. *www.NewWorldLibrary.com.*

Chapter 33. Experiments in Active Consciousness

1. L. McTaggart. *The Intention Experiment: Using Your Thoughts to Change Your Life and the World.* New York: Free Press, pp. 199–219 (2007).

2. D.W. Orme-Johnson, et al. "Preventing Terrorism and International Conflict: Effects of Large Assemblies of Participants in the Transcendental Meditation and TM-Sidhi Programs." *Journal of Offender Rehabilitation,* 36: 283–302 (2003).

3. Transcendental Meditation studies. For a good bibliography, see: *www.mum.edu/tm_research.*

PART VII. Choose Joy

Chapter 34. Evolution Is Inherent

1. K. Wilber, Ken. *A Brief History of Everything.* Boston: Shambhala, pp. 20–21 (2000).

2. E. Laszlo. *Science and the Akashic Field: An Integral Theory of Everything.* Rochester, Vermont: Inner Traditions, p. 167 (2004).

3. D. Pinchbeck. *2012: The Return of Quetzalcoatl.* New York: Jeremy Tarcher / Penguin, p. 173 (2004).

4. Satprem. *Sri Aurobindo, or the Adventures of Consciousness.* New Delhi, India: Mira Aditi, Mysore, and the Mother's Institute of Research (1964).

Chapter 35. Technology and the Soul

1. J. Lovelock. *Gaia: A New Look at Life on Earth.* New York: Oxford University Press, USA (2000).

Chapter 36. The Way Forward

1. B. Starfield. "Is U.S. Health Really the Best in the World?" *Journal of the American Medical Association (JAMA),* 284(4), pp. 483–485 (July 2000).

2. G. Null and M. Feldman. *Death By Medicine.* Edinburg, Virginia: Praktikos Books (2010).

3. M. Lerner. *Jewish Renewal: A Path to Healing and Transformation.* New York: Grosset/Putnam (1994).

BIBLIOGRAPHY

Abbott, Edwin A. *Flatland: A Romance of Many Dimensions*. New York: Penguin Books, Ltd. (1984).

Aissa, J. et al. "Transatlantic Transfer of Digitized Antigen Signal by Telephone Link." *Journal of Allergy and Clinical Immunology*, 99: S175 (1997).

Arndt, M. et al. "Wave-Particle Duality of C60 Molecules." *Nature*; 401:680–682 (1999).

Aurobindo, Sri. *The Yoga and Its Objects*. Pondicherry, India: Sri Aurobindo Ashram (2002).

Bandler, Richard and John Grinder. *The Structure of Magic*. Science and Behavior Books (1975).

Belon, P. et al. "Histamine Dilutions Modulate Basophil Activation." *Inflammation Research*, 53, pp. 181–188 (2004).

Bennett, Hal and Susan Sparrow. "The Thinking Heart: An Interview with Paul Pearsall." See: *www.paulpearsall.com/info/press/4.html*.

Blackmore, Susan. *Conversations on Consciousness: What the Best Minds Think About the Brain, Free Will, and What It Means to Be Human*. New York: Oxford University Press (2006).

Bohm, David. *Wholeness and the Implicate Order*. London: Routledge Classics (1980).

Brennan, Barbara Ann. *Hands of Light: A Guide to Healing Through the Human Energy Field*. New York: Bantam Books (1987).

Brown, V. and M. Ennis. "Flow-Cytometric Analysis of Basophil Activation: Inhibition by Histamine at Conventional and Homeopathic Concentrations." *Inflammation Research*, 50, Supplement (2), S47–S48 (2001).

Craig, Gary. *The EFT Manual*. Energy Psychology Press (2008). Also see: *www.eftuniverse.com*.

Cumming, Heather and Karen Leffler. *John of God: The Brazilian Healer Who's Touched the Lives of Millions*. New York: Atria Books; Hillsboro, Oregon: Beyond Words Publishing (2007).

Davenas, E. et al. "Human Basophil Degranulation Triggered by Very Dilute Antiserum Against IgE." *Nature*, Volume 333, Number 6176, pp. 816–181 (June 1988).

Davidson, Richard J., et al. "Alterations in Brain and Immune Function Produced by Mindfulness Meditation." *Psychosomatic Medicine*, 65, pp. 564–570 (2003).

Dennett, Daniel. *Consciousness Explained*. Boston: Little, Brown and Company, (1991).

Dossey, Larry. *Healing Words: The Power of Prayer and the Practice of Medicine*. San Francisco: HarperSanFrancisco (1993).

Emoto, Masaru. *The Hidden Messages in Water*. New York: Atria Books (2005).

Evans, C. de B. *Meister Eckhart by Franz Pfeiffer*, 2 volumes, London: John M. Watkins (1924 and 1931).

Everett, Hugh. " 'Relative State' Formulation of Quantum Mechanics." *Reviews of Modern Physics*, Volume 29, Number 3 (July 1957).

Feyerabend, Paul. *Against Method*. London: Verso (1975).

Georgeff, M.P. and A. Lansky, "Reactive Reasoning and Planning." *Proceedings of the Sixth National Conference on Artificial Intelligence (AAAI-87)*, Seattle, Washington (July 1987).

Ghosh, et al. "Coherent Spin Oscillations in a Disordered Magnet." *Science*, 296:2195–2198 (2002).

Grof, Stanislav. *When The Impossible Happens: Adventures in Non-ordinary Reality*. Boulder, Colorado: Sounds True, Inc. (2006).

Grof, Stanislav and Christina Grof. *Holotropic Breathwork: A New Approach to Self-Exploration a nd Therapy*. New York: Excelsior Editions / State University of New York (2010).

Gruber, Elmar R. "Conformance Behavior Involving Animal and Human Subjects." *European Journal of Parapsychology*, 3(1), pp. 36–50 (1979).

Hagelin, J.S., et al. "Effects of Group Practice of the Transcendental Meditation Program on Preventing Violent Crime in Washington, DC: Results of the National Demonstration Project, June–July 1993." *Social Indicators Research*, 47:153–201 (1999).

Hahnemann, Samuel. *Organon of the Medical Art (Sixth Edition)*. Edited and annotated by Wenda Brewster O'Reilly, based on a translation by Stephen Decker, Redmond, Washington: Birdcage Books (1996).

Halevi, Z'ev ben Shimon. *Kabbalah and Psychology*. York Beach, Maine: Samuel Weiser, Inc. (1986).

Hancock, Graham. *Supernatural: Meetings with the Ancient Teachers of Mankind.* The Disinformation Company (2007).

Hawken, Paul. *The Magic of Findhorn.* New York: Bantam Books (1976).

Heinemann, Klaus and Miceal Ledwith. *The Orb Project.* New York: Atria Books; Hillsboro, Oregon: Beyond Words Publishing (2007).

Hicks, Esther and Jerry Hicks. *The Amazing Power of Deliberate Intent.* Carlsbad, California: Hay House, Inc. (2006).

Jahn, R.G., and B.J. Dunne. "On the Quantum Mechanics of Consciousness, with Application to Anomalous Phenomena." *Foundations of Physics.* 16(8), pp. 721–772 (1986).

Jung, Carl. *Jung on Synchronicity and the Paranormal: Key Readings.* London: Routledge (1977).

Jung, Carl. *The Archetypes and the Collective Unconscious.* Princeton: Princeton University Press (1981).

Kaku, Michio. *Hyperspace: A Scientific Odyssey Through Parallel Universes, Time Warps, and the 10th Dimension.* New York: Oxford University Press (1994).

Kean, Leslie. *UFOs: Pilots and Government Officials Go On the Record.* Crown (2010).

Kitei, Lynne. *The Phoenix Lights: A Skeptic's Discovery that We Are Not Alone.* Newburyport, Massachusetts: Hampton Roads Publishing Company (2010). Also see: *www.thephoenixlights.net.*

LaBerge, Stephen. *Lucid Dreaming.* Louisville, Colorado: Sounds True, Inc. (2009).

Lansky, Amy L. "Consciousness As An Active Force." *The Noetic Journal,* Volume 2, Number 1 (January 2000). Also see: *www.renresearch.com/consciousness.html.*

Lansky, Amy L. *Impossible Cure: The Promise of Homeopathy.* Portola Valley, California: R.L. Ranch Press (2003).

Lansky, Amy L. "Localized Planning with Action-Based Constraints." *Artificial Intelligence,* Volume 98, Number 1-2, pp. 49–136 (January 1998).

Laszlo, Ervin. *Science and the Akashic Field: An Integral Theory of Everything.* Rochester, Vermont: Inner Traditions (2004).

Layton, Bentley. *The Gnostic Scriptures: A New Translation with Annotations and Introductions (The Anchor Yale Bible Reference Library).* New Haven: Yale University Press (1995).

Lerner, Michael. *Jewish Renewal: A Path to Healing and Transformation.* New York: Grosset/Putnam (1994).

Levitan, Lynne and Stephen LaBerge. "Other Worlds: Out-of-Body Experiences and Lucid Dreams." *Nightlight* (The Lucidity Institute), 3(2–3) (1991). Also see: *www.Lucidity.com/NL32.OBEandLD.html.*

Lovelock, James. *Gaia: A New Look at Life on Earth.* New York: Oxford University Press, USA (2000).

Loye, David. *The Sphinx and the Rainbow: Brain, Mind, and Future Vision.* IUniverse (1999).

Lutz, Antoine, et al. "Long-Term Meditators Self-Induce High-Amplitude Gamma Synchrony During Mental Practice." *Proceedings of the National Academy of Sciences,* Vol. 101, No. 46, pp. 16369–16373 (November 16, 2004). Also see: *www.pnas.org/content/101/46/16369.full.*

Maharshi, Sri Ramana, with editor David Godman. *Be As You Are: The Teachings of Sri Ramana Maharshi.* New York: Penguin Books, Ltd. (1989).

McTaggart, Lynne. *The Field: The Quest for the Secret Force of the Universe.* New York: HarperCollins Publishers, Inc. (2002).

McTaggart, Lynne. *The Intention Experiment: Using Your Thoughts to Change Your Life and the World.* New York: Free Press (2007).

Miller, Ellen and Gary Sherman. *Silence and the Soul: Awakening Inner Wisdom.* Inner Harmonics Press (2002).

Montagnier, Luc, et al., "Electromagnetic Signals Are Produced by Aqueous Nanostructures Derived from Bacterial DNA Sequences." *Interdiscip Sci Comput Life Sci,* 1: 81–90 (2009).

Moss, Richard. *The Mandala of Being: Discovering the Power of Awareness.* Novato, California: New World Library (2007).

Moody, Todd C. "Conversations With Zombies." *Journal of Consciousness Studies,* 1 (2), pp. 196–200 (1994).

Nelson, Roger D., et al. "Correlations of Continuous Random Data with Major World Events." *Foundations of Physics Letters.* 15(6), pp. 537–550 (2002).

Nelson, Roger D., et al. "Field REG Anomalies in Group Situations." *Journal of Scientific Exploration,* 10(1), pp. 111–141 (1996).

Nelson, Roger, D., et al. "Field REG II: Consciousness Field Effects: Replications and Explorations." *Journal of Scientific Exploration*, 12(3), pp. 425–454 (1998).

Moore, Judith and Barbara Lamb. *Crop Circles Revealed: Language of the Light Symbols*. Light Technology Publications (2001).

Newberg, Andrew and Mark Robert Waldman. *How God Changes Your Brain*. Random House Publishing Group (2009).

Null, Gary and Martin Feldman. *Death By Medicine*. Edinburg, Virginia: Praktikos Books (2010).

Orme-Johnson, D.W., et al. "Preventing Terrorism and International Conflict: Effects of Large Assemblies of Participants in the Transcendental Meditation and TM-Sidhi Programs." *Journal of Offender Rehabilitation*, 36: 283–302 (2003).

Ouspensky, P.D. *In Search of the Miraculous: The Teachings of G.I. Gurdjieff*. San Diego: Harcourt, Inc. (1949).

Pearsall, Paul. *The Heart's Code: Tapping the Wisdom and Power of Our Heart Energy*. New York: Broadway Books (1998).

Peat, F. David. *Synchronicity: The Bridge Between Matter and Mind*. New York: Bantam (1987).

Peoc h, René. Psychokinetic Action of Young Chicks on the Path of an Illuminated Source." *Journal of Scientific Exploration*, 9(2), p. 223 (1995).

Pinchbeck, Daniel. *2012: The Return of Quetzalcoatl*. New York: Jeremy Tarcher / Penguin (2004).

Radin, Dean. *Entangled Minds: Extrasensory Experiences in a Quantum Reality*. New York: Paraview (2006).

Radin, Dean. "Exploring Relationships Between Random Physical Events and Mass Human Attention: Asking For Whom the Bell Tolls." *Journal of Scientific Exploration*. 16(4), pp. 533–547 (2002).

Radin, Dean. "Psychophysiological Evidence of Possible Retrocausal Effects in Humans." *Frontiers of Time: Retrocausation—Experiment and Theory*. American Institute of Physics (AIP) Conference Proceedings, Volume 863, pp. 193–213 (2006).

Radin, Dean. *The Conscious Universe: The Scientific Truth of Psychic Phenomena*. San Francisco: Harper Edge (1997).

Radin, Dean. "The Enduring Enigma of the UFO." *Shift*, No. 21, pp. 22–27 (Winter 2008-2009).

Radin, Dean. "Unconscious Perception of Future Emotions: An Experiment in Presentiment." *Journal of Scientific Exploration*. 11, pp. 163–180 (1997).

Randall, Lisa. *Warped Passages: Unraveling the Mysteries of the Universe's Hidden Dimensions*. New York: Harper Perennial (2006).

Rao, Manju Lata, Rustom Roy, Iris R. Bell, and Richard Hoover, "The Defining Role of Structure (Including Epitaxy) in the Plausibility of Homeopathy." *Homeopathy*, 96, pp. 175–182 (2007).

Rauscher, Elizabeth A. and Russell Targ, "Investigation of a Complex Space-Time Metric to Describe Precognition of the Future." *Frontiers of Time: Retrocausation—Experiment and Theory, AIP Conference Proceedings*, Volume 863, pp. 121–146 (2006).

Reichenberg-Ullman, Judyth. "A Homeopathic Approach to Behavioral Problems." *Mothering*, Number 74, pp. 97–101 (Spring 1995).

Ring, Kenneth. *Heading Toward Omega: In Search of the Meaning of the Near-Death Experience*. New York: Harper Perennial (1985).

Rinpoche, Sogyal. *The Tibetan Book of Living and Dying*. New York: HarperOne (1994).

Rinpoche, Tenzin Wangyal. *The Tibetan Yogas of Dream and Sleep*. Ithaca, New York: Snow Lion Publications (1998).

Roberts, Jane. *Seth Speaks: The Eternal Validity of the Soul*. San Rafael, California: Amber-Allen Publishing (1994). Also see: *en.wikipedia.org/wiki/Jane_Roberts*.

Roberts, Jane. *The Oversoul Seven Trilogy: The Education of Oversoul Seven, the Further Education of Oversoul Seven, Oversoul Seven and the Museum of Time*. San Rafael, California: Amber-Allen Publishing; Novato, California: New World Library (1995).

Roman, Sanaya. *Living With Joy: Keys to Personal Power and Spiritual Transformation*. Tiburon, California: H.J. Kramer, Inc. (1986).

Roman, Sanaya. *Personal Power Through Awareness: A Guidebook for Sensitive People*. Tiburon, California: H.J. Kramer, Inc. (1986).

Roman, Sanaya. *Soul Love: Awakening Your Heart Centers*. Tiburon, California: H.J. Kramer, Inc. (1997).

Roman, Sanaya. *Spiritual Growth: Being Your Higher Self*. Tiburon, California: H.J. Kramer, Inc. (1992).

Rowling, J.K. *Harry Potter and the Half-Blood Prince*. New York: Scholastic Paperbacks (2006).

Roy, Rustom, William Tiller, Iris R. Bell, et al. "The Structure of Liquid Water: Novel Insights from Materials Research and Potential Relevance to Homeopathy." *Materials Research Innovation*, 9 (4): 557–608 (2005).

Rucker, Rudy. *The Fourth Dimension: A Guided Tour of Higher Universes*. Boston: Houghton Mifflin Company (1984).

Sams, Jamie and Richard Carson. *Medicine Cards: The Discovery of Power Through the Ways of Animals*. Rochester, Vermont: Bear & Company (1988).

Satprem. *Sri Aurobindo, or the Adventures of Consciousness*. New Delhi, India: Mira Aditi, Mysore, and the Mother's Institute of Research (1964).

Scully, Nicki. *Alchemical Healing: A Guide to Spiritual, Physical, and Transformational Medicine*. Rochester: Bear & Company (2003).

Sheldrake, Rupert. *Seven Experiments That Could Change the World: A Do-It-Yourself Guide to Revolutionary Science*. Rochester, Vermont: Park Street Press (1995).

Sheldrake, Rupert. *The Presence of the Past: Morphic Resonance and the Habits of Nature*. Rochester, Vermont: Park Street Press (1988).

Somé, Malidoma Patrice. *Of Water and Spirit: Ritual, Magic, and Initiation in the Life of an African Shaman*. New York: Penguin (1995). Also see: *www.malidoma.com*.

Starfield, Barbara. "Is U.S. Health Really the Best in the World?" *Journal of the American Medical Association (JAMA)*, 284(4), pp. 483–485 (July 2000).

Steiner, Rudolf. *An Outline of Esoteric Science*. Hudson, New York: Anthroposophic Press, p. 22 (1997).

Steiner, Rudolf. *Anthroposophy and the Inner Life: An Esoteric Introduction*. Bristol, England: Rudolf Steiner Press (1931).

Steiner, Rudolf. *The Spiritual Hierarchies and the Physical World: Reality and Illusion*. Hudson, New York: Anthroposophic Press (1996).

Stevenson, Heidi. "Quackbusters Are Busted!" (July 2010). See: *http://www.gaia-health.com/articles251/000277-quackbusters-are-busted.shtml*.

Stibal, Vianna. *Theta Healing: Go Up and Seek God, Go Up and Work With God*. Rolling Thunder (2007).

Talbot, Michael. *The Holographic Universe*. New York: Harper Perennial (1992).

Targ, Russell and Jane Katra. *Miracles of Mind: Exploring Nonlocal Consciousness and Spiritual Healing*. Novato, California: New World Library (1998).

Targ, Russell and Harold Puthoff. "Information Transmission Under Conditions of Sensory Shielding." *Nature*, 251, pp. 602–607 (18 October 1974).

Tiller, William A. *Conscious Acts of Creation: The Emergence of a New Physics.* Walnut Creek, California: Pavior Publishing (2001).

Tiller, William A. *Science and Human Transformation: Subtle Energies, Intentionality and Consciousness.* Walnut Creek, California: Pavior (1997).

Tiller, William A. and Walter E. Dibble, Jr. "New Experimental Data Revealing an Unexpected Dimension to Materials Science and Engineering." *Materials Research Innovation*, 5, pp. 21–34 (2001).

Tolle, Eckhart. *The Power of Now: A Guide to Spiritual Enlightenment.* Novato, California: New World Library (1999).

Turing, Alan. "Computing Machinery and Intelligence." *Mind*, Vol. 59, No. 236, pp. 433–460 (October 1950). Also see: *en.wikipedia.org/wiki/Turing_test*.

Van Lommel, P., R. van Wees, V. Meyers, and I. Elfferich. "Near-Death Experience in Survivors of Cardiac Arrest: A Prospective Study in the Netherlands." *Lancet*, 358(9298), pp. 2039–2045 (December 15, 2001).

Vermeulen, F rans. *Synoptic Materia Medica 2.* Haarlem, The Netherlands: Merlijn Publishers (1996).

Walker, Thomas. *The Force Is With Us: The Conspiracy Against the Supernatural, Spiritual and Paranormal.* Gatlinburg, Tennessee: Roaring Fork Limited (2005).

Whitmont, Edward C. *Psyche and Substance.* Berkeley, California: North Atlantic Books and Homeopathic Educational Services (1991).

Wilber, Ken. *A Brief History of Everything.* Boston: Shambhala (2000).

Winston, Julian. *The Faces of Homoeopathy.* New Zealand: Great Auk Publishing (1999).

Wilde, Stuart. *The Art of Meditation.* Carlsbad, California: Hay House Audio Books (1998).

Yogananda, Paramahansa. *Autobiography of a Yogi.* Los Angeles: Self-Realization Fellowship (1973).

INDEX

Crop circles 179
Crystal experiment 66

D

Dadaji 176
Dalai Lama 37, 236
Death 155–156, 166–168
Defense mechanisms 192
Dennett, Daniel 23–25
Dimensions (spatial)
　four 3, 11–15, 72, 96–104
　higher 6, 95–104
　two 11–15, 98
Divination 209
Dreamtime, aboriginal 178
Drifts, into altered states 229–230
Drugs 205

E

Easy problem (vs. hard problem) 24
Emanation 169–174
Emerald tablet of Hermes
　Trismegistus 142
Emotion 134–137
　as body sensation 88
　as touch 241–242
Emotional Freedom Technique
　(EFT) 38, 87, 129–130
Emotional guidance system 121,
　201
Emotional link (enhancing psi) 20,
　61
Emoto, Masaru 81
Energetic signatures in water 17
Entanglement 60
Environmental conditions
　(enhancing psi) 256
Essence 190, 194–195

Etheric body 65, 132, 143–144,
　144–156
Eurythmy 153
Everett, Hugh 103
Evolution 42–47, 265–268
　collective 42
　external 42
　individual 42
　internal 42
　resistance to 43
　stages of 43–47
　world-centric stage 44–45
Exercise format 220
Exercises 48, 86, 134, 182, 213, 228–
　230, 232, 234, 237, 240, 246–
　247, 249
　day-to-day 137, 224, 238, 241–
　243
　two-person 222, 248
Experiments 251–261, 259–260
　guidelines 252–253
Explicate order 15

F

Facebook 44
Feeling good 236–244
Feet. Seat. Back. 49
Felix Felicis 6, 28
Field 91
　Akashic 67, 91
　consciousness 92
　meaning, of 74–76, 125
　morphic 72, 91
　odic 132
　psi 91
　unified 67, 92
　zero-point 67–69, 91
Flatland 11–15
Force man 160

ABOUT THE AUTHOR

Even as a child growing up outside Buffalo, New York, Amy Lansky sensed that the world was a bit more mysterious than it appeared on the surface. After many years working as a computer scientist, she now pursues her life passion—to uncover deeper truths hidden behind the veil of our consensual reality.

Lansky's first book, *Impossible Cure: The Promise of Homeopathy (www.impossiblecure.com)*, explored an unconventional form of healing—*homeopathy*. It quickly became one of the best-selling introductory books on homeopathic medicine and is now used as a patient education book and textbook all over the world. In this, her second book, Lansky explores the mysterious realm of human consciousness. *Active Consciousness: Awakening the Power Within* draws on her interest in paranormal phenomena, her expertise in alternative medicine, her meditation studies, and even her research experience in artificial intelligence.

Lansky graduated from the University of Rochester in 1977 with degrees in mathematics and computer science, and she received her doctorate in computer science from Stanford University in 1983. She did research work in artificial intelligence at several Silicon Valley institutions, including SRI International and NASA Ames Research Center, until she left the field in 1998 to pursue her interest in homeopathic medicine. This unusual move was prompted by the miraculous cure of her son's autism with homeopathy. Since 2005, Lansky has been a student of Gary Sherman and Ellen Miller, the creators of a system of self-development and inquiry called *perceptual integration (www.deepening.com)*.

Amy Lansky is widely regarded as an expert writer and speaker on homeopathy. She has been featured at several conferences, her articles have appeared in leading magazines and online forums, and she hosted a radio show on homeopathic treatment of autism on Autism One Radio from 2006–2009. Lansky also served on the board of the National Center for Homeopathy from 2004–2011. She currently lives in the San Francisco Bay Area with her husband Steve Rubin, and is an avid pianist, vocalist, and painter. She also enjoys needlework, swimming, and canoeing the lakes of Canada.

CPSIA information can be obtained at www.ICGtesting.com
Printed in the USA
LVOW041715160212

269024LV00004B/101/P

THE ILIAD AND THE ODYSSEY

STORIES FROM HOMER'S EPICS

TABLE OF CONTENTS

STORIES FROM THE ODYSSEY

HOMER: THE POET FOR ALL AGES

"With the Bible and Shakespeare, the Homeric poems are the best training for life. There is no good quality that they lack: manliness, courage, reverence for old age and for the hospitable hearth; justice, piety, pity, a brave attitude toward life and death, are all conspicuous in Homer. Homer is a poet for all ages."
—*Andrew Lang*

More than twenty-five hundred years ago, the people of a little Greek city somewhere on the shore of the Aegean Sea were gathered to celebrate the gods of their native land.

They met in the open air. The sun shone full on rocky cliffs, on the blue water of the bay, and on the glistening marble of temple and palace. The king and queen sat on thrones before the portico of the temple, surrounded by the elders and priests.

The crowd below was clothed in bright colors. Some of the youths wore the laurel wreaths they had won in the games and races of the morning. Now, in the quiet of the afternoon, all were waiting eagerly to hear a poet tell stories of the great deeds of their ancestors.

---

reverence: great respect; honor
hospitable: friendly and welcoming to guests
hearth: the place in front of a fireplace, used to stand for the idea of home
piety: devotion (usually, religious devotion)
conspicuous: easily seen
Andrew Lang: a nineteenth-century scholar and writer, whose works
    include a translation of the *Iliad* and the *Odyssey*
laurel: The ancient Greeks used the foliage of the laurel tree to
    crown victors.

Imagine: a man of many years, serious and noble in bearing, comes forth from the temple, bearing a lyre in his hand. He kneels before the king, then rises and touches the strings of his lyre:

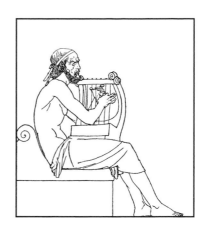

Sing, goddess, the wrath of Achilles, Peleus's son.

His words rise over the marketplace, and a deeper silence falls over the people as the great story sweeps forth in the beautiful verses. The morning's races, the festival, the beauties of the city—all are forgotten as the listeners journey with the poet across the shining sea to fight with mighty Achilles on the windswept plains before the great city of Troy. The present grows dim, while the deeds and glories of the past grow bright, brought to life by the ringing verses of Homer's *Iliad* and *Odyssey*.

We do not know who Homer was, or when and where he lived. One legend says that long ago in Greece, a blind poet, Homer, wandered from city to city and earned his living by reciting poems, including the *Iliad* and the *Odyssey*, two great epics—which is the name for long poems that set forth in a grand manner the deeds of great heroes.

Some people believe that such a poet really lived, and that he composed the *Iliad* and the *Odyssey* himself and recited them in the cities where he stayed. Others believe that he had

---

lyre: a musical instrument like a small harp

much less to do with the making of the poems. They say that the *Iliad* and the *Odyssey* belong to the time long before written history, when the stories of heroes' deeds were sung and recited, and so passed down by word of mouth from one generation to another. In this way, they believe, these great poems grew, being added to and gradually shaped through many years.

Whatever the source of the poems, however, they must have been recited for a good many years before they were finally written down. For writing was not known in Greece until the middle of the seventh century B.C., and the *Iliad* and the *Odyssey* go far back of that.

Probably we shall never really know the facts. But it is pleasing to think that the blind wandering poet had at least a hand in shaping these great poems. And it is wonderful that through all these hundreds of years, the fame of a man of whom so little is known has persisted so strongly. His fame seems to grow with the years, for as we learn more about the long-ago times, we appreciate more and more how great the *Iliad* and the *Odyssey* really are.

The *Iliad* tells of Achilles, the bravest of the Greeks, who besieged the city of Troy; and, of Hector, the bravest of Troy's defenders, who fell at last by the hand of his heroic foe. (The title, *Iliad*, comes from the word *Ilium*, which is the Greek name for Troy.)

The *Odyssey* tells of Odysseus (also known as Ulysses), one of the Greek chieftains at Troy. After the fighting ended, Odysseus wandered for many years and met many adventures before he finally reached his home and his faithful wife, Penelope.

---

persisted: lasted; endured
besieged: attacked and surrounded

These great epics were first recited on some such occasion as we have imagined, and since then they have never been forgotten. They tell of a past so distant that it is scarcely known except through their verses, and of gods who have long since ceased to be worshiped. Yet these epics are as fresh and alive today as when they were first chanted to the youths and maidens of that forgotten Grecian city.

THE GREEK GODS

If you have read Greek myths before, then you know that the actors in these stories include not only humans but also many gods.

The Greeks believed in many gods, male and female, all under the rule of the king of the gods, Zeus. They lived on a snow-capped peak called Mount Olympus, where they gathered from time to time in Zeus's banquet hall to discuss the affairs of men. The gods were thought to be immortal, and to have extraordinary powers, such as the ability to change into the shapes of different animals, or to fly, or to hurl thunderbolts from the sky.

And yet, despite their immortality and extraordinary powers, the Greeks imagined their gods living much as people do: eating, drinking, working, playing, and sleeping. Though the gods were supposed to reward good people and punish the bad, the Greeks told many stories in which the gods were cruel, jealous, selfish, vengeful, and in general displayed some of the worst human failings.

In the *Iliad*, which tells the story of a great war between the Greeks and the Trojans, the gods take sides, some favoring

---

vengeful: seeking revenge; eager to get even with someone
Trojans: the people of the city of Troy

the Greeks, and others the Trojans. In the *Odyssey*, it is the wrath of the sea god, Poseidon, that throws Odysseus off his course and keeps him from reaching home for many years.

After the Greeks, another great people rose to power, the Romans, in the land now called Italy. The Romans borrowed many ideas and customs from the Greeks, including their religion. The Romans worshiped the same gods as the Greeks, but called them by different names, as shown in the following table. This book refers to the gods by their Greek names, but in other books of myths, you will sometimes see the Greek names, and sometimes the Roman.

Greek name	Roman name	
Zeus	Jupiter	king of the gods
Hera	Juno	wife of Zeus, queen of the gods
Athena	Minerva	goddess of wisdom
Aphrodite	Venus	goddess of love and beauty
Eros	Cupid	god of love, son of Aphrodite
Ares	Mars	god of war
Artemis	Diana	goddess of the moon and hunting
Hephaestus	Vulcan	god of fire and the forge
Hermes	Mercury	the messenger god
Demeter	Ceres	goddess of corn and growing things
Persephone	Proserpina	daughter of Demeter
Phoebus Apollo	Apollo	god of the sun, music, and poetry
Poseidon	Neptune	god of the sea
Hades	Pluto	god of the underworld

WHAT HAPPENED
BEFORE THE *ILIAD*

What Happened Before the *Iliad*

When Homer's Iliad *opens, the war between the Trojans and Greeks, known as the Trojan War, is already underway. But how did the war begin? Who are the major characters on each side? Most of Homer's listeners would have known the answers to these questions from other stories already familiar to them. Here are some of those stories to help prepare you for the story of the* Iliad.

The Judgment of Paris

Far across the Aegean Sea that lies to the east of Greece, there once flourished a great city. This city was called Ilium by its own people, but in story and song it is known as Troy. It stood on a sloping plain some distance back from the shore, and was surrounded by high, strong walls that no enemy could scale or batter down. When the Trojans looked at the solid walls and noble buildings of their city, they boasted, "Ilium will stand forever."

King Priam, the ruler of this great city, seemed favored by the gods, for he had great wealth, the swiftest horses, and many strong and brave sons. The strongest and bravest was named Hector, while the youngest and most beautiful was Paris.

---

flourished: thrived; prospered
scale: climb
favored: treated with special regard or kindness

Just before Paris was born, the oracle had prophesied that Priam's wife, Queen Hecuba, would give birth to a burning torch that would one day burn to the ground the strong walls and high towers of Troy. When the king and queen saw the beautiful face and noble features of the newborn babe, they could hardly believe that he was destined to be the ruin of his people.

But they also knew that to ignore the prophecies of the oracle would be unwise indeed. And so they faced a terrible choice: to await the certain destruction of their city, or to destroy the lovely child.

King Priam feared for the safety of his people. And so, with great sadness, he commanded that a shepherd should carry the babe to Mount Ida, and leave him there to die.

The shepherd obeyed the king unwillingly, and then returned to his home, heavy at heart, thinking of the helpless baby he had left alone on the mountain. At last he could bear the thought no longer and he hastened back. To his joy, he found the little prince still alive, so he carried him home in secret and kept him there as his own child.

Paris, as the boy was named, grew up with the shepherd lads, never suspecting that he was a king's son. He grew tall and straight, and so beautiful that his fame spread abroad. So he tended sheep on the mountainside while the time drew near when the prophecy was to be fulfilled.

---

oracle: in mythology, a being who was believed to have knowledge from the gods
prophesied: predicted
hastened: hurried

Now it happened at this time in Greece that a great wedding was to be held between the king of a far-off country and a fair sea-nymph, Thetis. Kings and queens, and princes and princesses were invited to the wedding feast, and even the great gods came to do honor to Thetis.

Upon a high throne at the head of the hall sat mighty Zeus, and near him was proud Hera, his wife. There also were the shining sun god and his sister, the silver-footed moon goddess. Athena, the goddess of wisdom, came too, and Aphrodite, the goddess of beauty, and many others.

In the midst of the festivities, there entered suddenly Eris, the goddess of discord. She alone among the gods had not been invited, but this did not prevent her from making an unwelcome appearance. Before anyone had time to cry, "Beware!" she had cast a golden apple upon the table and then disappeared. Swift-footed Hermes seized the apple and read aloud the message inscribed upon it: *For the fairest*.

Not even Eris herself could have wished for greater results from her clever plan. At once strife arose in the hall of feasting, for each goddess thought that she deserved the apple. Most eager of all were Hera, Athena, and Aphrodite; before them, mortal maidens and lesser goddesses wisely became silent.

Among these three, the quarrel rose higher and higher, until Zeus commanded that a judge should decide the question once and for all, and let them have peace. He was unwilling to make the decision himself, for he knew that to choose one would be to risk the wrath of the other two. So he

---

nymph: in mythology, a beautiful maiden that lived in the forest, trees, or water
discord: disagreement; conflict
strife: bitter disagreement

announced that he would appoint a judge who should declare which goddess was the fairest.

To Hera, Athena, and Aphrodite, he said, "Take yourselves with all due haste to Mount Ida. There you will find a fair young shepherd tending the flocks. Indeed, it is said that there is no man fairer. He shall decide to whom the apple belongs."

The three goddesses soon came to the mountainside where Paris tended his sheep, and handing him the golden apple, they asked to whom he would award it. The youth gazed upon them in wonder, quite unable to say which one was the most beautiful.

Each goddess in turn tried to win his favor by offering gifts. First Hera spoke, tempting him with the promise of a mighty empire and great wealth. Athena offered him glory and victory in war, and wisdom which would make him worthy of all honor. But then Aphrodite smiled upon him, and whispered close into his ear, "Choose me, fair youth, and I will give you the fairest woman in the world for your wife."

At her words, Paris forgot the longing for wealth and power that Hera's offer had sparked in him. He forgot his desire for victory and wisdom. To Aphrodite he gave the golden apple. This judgment of Paris was the beginning of many troubles. Little did he know that his choice meant ruin for his country, and for thousands of happy men and women.

Hera and Athena departed with hearts full of wrath. But Aphrodite smiled upon Paris and told him to bide his time until her promise should be fulfilled.

From that day Paris was restless and discontented. He no longer cared to tend his flocks upon the mountain, or to strive with the other young shepherds in the footrace and wrestling match.

bide his time: wait

One morning, he left his mountain home and went down to the city of Troy. On that day it chanced that great games were being held there, and Paris, taking part in the sports, put to shame all the other young men, for Aphrodite had given him godlike strength and swiftness.

King Priam, seeing Paris in action, asked, "Who is this noble youth? Of what family, and what place? I know him not, yet he seems to me almost as familiar as one of my own sons." No one knew, so they began to ask about. And at length the old shepherd stepped forth from among the spectators and told the king that Paris was really the prince who had been left on the mountainside to die. Upon hearing this, Priam and Hecuba received their lost son joyfully, giving no thought to the prophecy that he should be the ruin of their city.

Paris came to dwell in the king's palace and returned no more to the shepherd's home. Honors were heaped upon him, and riches and power were at his command. Yet he never forgot the promise of Aphrodite nor ceased to long for its fulfillment.

THE BEAUTIFUL HELEN

At this time, one lady was by far the fairest in the world— Helen, the daughter of King Tyndarus. Every young prince heard of her beauty, and all desired to marry her.

Helen's father, King Tyndarus, was a wise man. When he saw kings and princes coming from afar to seek his daughter in marriage, he knew that only one of them could be made happy, and he did not wish the others to become his enemies. Therefore, before he chose a husband for Helen, as was the custom of the time, he gathered the suitors before him and spoke thus:

"You do me great honor, my lords, but there is something which troubles me. You are many, and my daughter can have but one husband. How will it be when she makes her choice? Will I have only one friend and a score of enemies? My daughter would rather die unmarried than bring trouble upon me and my people. Therefore her resolve is this: you must swear a great oath that you will defend her and her husband, whomever she may choose, and that if he or she suffers any wrong, you will avenge it."

These words pleased the suitors, and they all pledged that they would defend Helen and her husband against all injury that might be done to them.

So Helen was wed to Menelaus, king of that part of Greece called Laconia, famed for the strength of its warriors. He took her to his palace in the capital city of Sparta. As for the disappointed suitors, they were men of honor, so they went home in peace, vowing to come to Helen's defense if ever they should be called.

Years went by, and at length Paris was sent by his father, King Priam of Troy, on a mission to Greece. He came to Sparta and was received with the hospitality befitting a prince from a faraway land. King Menelaus ordered a great feast, at which Paris was the guest of honor. That night, amidst the fine wine and pleasing conversation, Paris first looked upon the face of Helen, and Aphrodite whispered to him that this was the woman she had promised him for a wife.

---

suitors: men who court a woman with the hope of marrying her
resolve: firm decision
avenge: to get revenge for; to get even for
befitting: worthy of; fit for

Paris knew that he had never seen, and never could see, a lady so lovely and gracious as Helen. And so while Menelaus was away, and with Aphrodite's aid, he stole the beautiful Helen and departed in his ships for Troy.

When Menelaus returned and learned what had happened, he was filled with grief and rage. He vowed to make war upon Troy and bring it to the dust. He called upon the kings and princes of Greece to remember their pledge and come to his aid.

This call was not to their liking, and some were reluctant to obey, but at last a great army was gathered together. One hundred thousand men and twelve hundred ships made ready to cross the sea to Troy to punish Paris and to restore Helen to Menelaus. Even the gods took sides. Hera and Athena had never forgiven Paris; therefore they favored the Greeks. But Aphrodite used her power to help the Trojans. Apollo, god of the sun, and Ares, god of war, also were on the side of the Trojans.

And so it was that a great army prepared for war. Determined to defend the honor of Greece, all rallied to the cause—all but two: Odysseus and Achilles.

ODYSSEUS

One of the greatest of the suitors who had pledged themselves to Helen's defense was Odysseus. This noble king was famed alike for his brave deeds and for his sharp and active mind, always ready for any turn of events. For many years now, he had ruled his island home in peace. He had a

---

reluctant: hesitant; unwilling
rallied: joined for a common purpose

fair young wife, Penelope, and a little son, Telemachus, whom he loved dearly. When the message came from Menelaus, asking his help in the rescue of Helen, he was at first unwilling to go.

It seemed to him a wild and foolish undertaking. It had been prophesied that if he went on this journey he should not return to his home for twenty years. He thought of the pain and trouble and warlike work of those twenty years, and looked on the loving faces of his wife and son, and chose to return no answer to Menelaus.

But the leaders of the Greeks were not willing to lose so good a warrior. When they received no reply to their message, Menelaus and some of his companions set out to journey to the land of Odysseus and find out the reason.

Odysseus, hearing that they had come, determined to trick them by pretending that he was out of his mind. He put on his richest garments, yoked an ox and a mule to his plow, and went out into his fields. As he plowed, he scattered salt into the furrows, pretending that he thought it was seed.

But for once there was someone more clever than he. One of the followers of Menelaus suspected that Odysseus was playing a trick upon them, and decided to find out whether he was really mad or not. Just as the plow came opposite to him, the man suddenly took the baby son of Odysseus from the arms of the nurse and placed him on the ground directly in front of the ox. The sight of his son's danger made Odysseus forget his acting. He turned the plow aside and sprang forward to save his child. So Menelaus and his companions knew that the madness of Odysseus was a trick.

---

yoked: to attach to a frame for pulling
furrows: shallow trenches left in a field after plowing

He turned the plow aside to save his child.

After this, Odysseus could no longer find any excuse for remaining at home. But though he had been unwilling to set out upon this war, he proved one of the greatest of its heroes. Indeed, it was not very long after this that he was able to do the Greeks a great service.

THE GODLIKE ACHILLES

One of the fairest of the Greek youths was Achilles. He was the son of King Peleus and the sea-nymph Thetis, at whose wedding the apple of discord had fallen. His godlike beauty was like that of Thetis, his mother, and he had the warlike strength of his kingly father. He was trained with the greatest care in all manly exercises, and showed greater strength and valor than any other youths of the land.

When Helen was stolen away and all Greece rose in arms to rescue her, Thetis was sad at heart. Zeus himself had told her that if Achilles went to this war, he would never return alive. Thetis knew well that this was true. She herself was immortal because she was a sea-nymph and belonged to the race of the gods; but Achilles was in part mortal.

When he was a baby, his mother had desired to make him immortal. So she had carried him to the dark realm of the underworld, and had bathed him there in the waters of the river Styx. The water of this river had such power that whatever it touched was safe from any mortal harm forever.

But there was one tiny spot upon his heel that had not been touched by the water. It was the place where Thetis had held him when she dipped him into the stream. She had forgotten to bathe it until she had returned to the earth once more, and it was then too late. This one spot upon his heel, she knew, would cause his death.

Before the first clash of arms sounded throughout Greece, Thetis had hurried Achilles away to an island across the sea. There she hid him, dressed as a girl, among the daughters of the king of that island.

valor: strength of will and great courage
realm: kingdom
mortal: fatal; causing death

The Greek leaders had been told by a trusted wise man that their war would not be successful unless the youthful Achilles accompanied them to Troy. The leaders, therefore, sought Achilles at his father's court; but he was not to be found. Odysseus then set out to discover where the youth was hidden.

At length he found out what Thetis had done, and he set out at once for the island. The boy was so well disguised that no one could have guessed that he was not a girl, but Odysseus devised a plan to discover him.

Dressing himself as a traveling merchant, he gained entrance to the king's garden, where the maidens were playing. From a large pack he carried, he brought forth golden rings, shining jewelry, and brightly colored scarves, which the maidens all examined eagerly—all except one tall maiden who stood aside and seemed to care little for them. Odysseus noted her keenly and determined to test her further. He drew from his pack a splendid sword, its blade sharp, strong, and gleaming in the sun. At once the tall maiden stepped forth and grasped the hilt and swung the sword with ease and delight.

Odysseus was now certain that this was the youth whom he sought. He announced his errand and called upon Achilles to join the Greeks in their war against the Trojans. The boy, weary of his soft and easy life, readily agreed to accompany them.

He returned at once to his father's court to make ready. His mother, telling him of Zeus's prophecy, tearfully begged him to remain at home, but Achilles could not be moved. He girded on his shining armor and prepared himself for battle.

keenly: with sharp interest and insight
girded: fastened

At once the tall maiden stepped forth and grasped the hilt.

Gathering his father's trusted warriors, he bade them make ready to go with him. They answered his summons with glad hearts, for they were proud to accompany this youth who was destined to perform mighty deeds.

But Thetis watched them depart in their great ships with a heavy heart. She feared that never again should she behold her godlike son.

---

bade: commanded
summons: call to action

STORIES FROM THE *ILIAD*

Stories from the *Iliad*

adapted from the retelling by Alfred J. Church

Prologue: The Long Siege

Across the sea came a host of Greeks, armed for war and bent upon the conquest of Troy. They came because one of the princes of Troy, Paris, had done a great wrong to Greece when he had carried away the beautiful Helen, wife of Menelaus of Sparta. Crying out for vengeance, they came in a thousand ships, with sails and oars, and landed on the beach at the foot of the plain. They challenged the warriors of Troy to come out on the plain and meet them in battle.

Thus the siege was begun. For more than nine years the city of Troy was surrounded by determined foes. But the walls were strong, and the men who defended them were brave. Many fierce battles were fought outside the gates. Sometimes the victory seemed to be with the Greeks, sometimes with the Trojans—but neither could gain any great advantage over the other. The Trojans could not drive the invaders from their shores; the Greeks could not force their way past the strong walls into the city.

One hero after another was slain, now on this side, now on that. Many were the losses on both sides, and great the suffering and grief. But still the struggle went on.

During the long siege, the Greeks sometimes took the battle beyond Troy to neighboring kingdoms friendly to the Trojans.

---

siege: the act of surrounding a city or fortress for a long time, cutting it off
 from supplies, to force it to surrender
host: a great many
bent: strongly determined
conquest: the act of conquering, or overcoming, by military force
vengeance: revenge; getting back at or getting even with someone

*Leaving part of their army to watch Troy, the rest the Greeks went
to plunder other cities, taking food, cattle, wine, and sometimes
women, whom they forced to work as slaves. All of these spoils
were divided among the Greek chieftains, with the first choice
going to the leader of all the Greek army, Agamemnon, the brother
of Menelaus.*

*After one of these raids, Agamemnon took for himself as a prize
of war a girl named Chryseis. She was the daughter of Chryses, a
priest of Apollo, the god who was worshiped in the plundered city.*

*It is at this point in the course of events of the Trojan War that
Homer begins the* Iliad.

THE QUARREL

This is the story of the anger of Achilles, that brought
countless ills upon the Achaeans, from the day on which
King Agamemnon and great Achilles first fell out with
one another.

It happened that Chryses, priest of Apollo, came to
Agamemnon and the other Greek chiefs. He had come to
offer much gold to ransom his daughter, Chryseis. On his
knees he begged them to take the gold and give him back the
girl. "If you will do this," he said, "may the gods help you to
take the city of Troy, and bring you back safe to your homes."

---

plunder: to use force to steal goods
spoils: stolen items; loot or goods taken from an enemy, particularly
 during war
chieftains: leaders of different groups
Achaeans: another name for the ancient Greeks
fell out with: quarreled; refused to have any dealings with
ransom: to pay to release a captured person

All the other chiefs were willing, but Agamemnon cried, "Away with you, old man. Do not linger here now and do not come again, or it will go hard on you, though you are a priest. As for your daughter, I will carry her back with me when I have taken Troy."

The old man left in great fear and sadness. He prayed to Apollo, and Apollo was angry that his priest should suffer such treatment. He came down from his palace atop Mount Olympus, shooting arrows among the Greeks, and each arrow carried deadly plague. For nine days the people died, and on the tenth day Achilles, the most valiant of the Greeks, called an assembly.

"Let us ask the soothsayers why Apollo is angry with us," said Achilles.

Then Calchas the soothsayer stood up. "You wish to know why Apollo is angry. I will tell you, but first you must promise to stand by me, for King Agamemnon will be angry when he hears what I have to say."

"Speak," said Achilles. "No man shall harm you while I live—nay, not Agamemnon himself."

Then Calchas said, "Apollo is angry because, when his priest came to ransom his daughter, Agamemnon refused him. Now, you must send back the girl, and take no money for her."

Then Agamemnon stood up and cried, "You are always the bearer of evil tidings! But so be it—I will give her up if I must, for I would not have the people die. But I will have some other share of the spoils. You must find me another prize instead, for I shall not be without one."

valiant: brave and noble
assembly: gathering; meeting
soothsayers: persons who, the ancient Greeks believed, could predict
    the future
tidings: news

And Achilles answered, "How shall we find you another prize? Those we took from the cities have been awarded; we cannot take back prizes that have already been given. Therefore, give back this girl, and if ever Zeus grants us to sack the city of Troy, we will make it up to you three and four times over."

Then Agamemnon said, "Achilles, valiant though you be, you shall not thus outwit me. Are you to keep your own prize, while I sit tamely under my loss and give up the girl at your bidding? No—Achilles, I will come to your tent and take your own prize, the maiden Briseis."

The face of Achilles grew red with anger as he cried, "Never was there a king so shameless and greedy! I have no quarrel with the Trojans; I have been fighting in your cause and that of your brother, Menelaus. You leave me to fight while you sit in your tent at ease. But when the spoil is divided, you take the lion's share. And now you will take the little that was given to me. I will not stay here to be shamed and robbed. I will return home with my ships, for I will not stay here dishonored to gather gold and goods for you."

"Go," said Agamemnon, "and take your men with you. I have other chieftains as brave, who know that I am master here."

Then Achilles was mad with rage. He had half drawn his sword when the goddess Athena appeared beside him, though no one else in the assembly could see her. She caught Achilles by the hand and said, "I have come to stay your rage. Use bitter words if you will, but do not draw your sword."

---

sack: plunder; loot; in wartime, to take the valuables from a captured town
stay: to stop; to halt

"I have come to stay your rage."

Achilles answered, "No matter how angry a man may be, he must do as you command." Then he thrust the heavy sword back into the scabbard and turned to Agamemnon.

"Drunkard, with the eyes of a dog and the heart of a deer! Never fighting in the front of the battle! You would rather go round and rob the prizes from any man who stands up to you. I swear to you, that from this time forth, you may look for Achilles but you shall not find him. When your men fall dying by the murderous hand of Hector, you shall not know

---

scabbard: a sheath or cover for a sword

Hector: son of King Priam of Troy, and Troy's greatest warrior

how to help them, and you shall tear your heart with rage for the hour when you wronged the best of the Achaeans."

And Achilles went apart from his comrades and sat down upon the seashore, full of bitter anger.

Then Agamemnon went forth and took counsel with the chiefs, and soon the shrill-voiced heralds called the Greek host to battle. Many nations and many chiefs were there, but none that could compare with valiant Achilles—Achilles, whose very being ached for the clang of sword upon sword in battle, but who now sat apart and would not fight.

Hector and Andromache

Now the sons of Troy and their allies came forth from the gates of the city and set themselves in battle array. The most famous of their chiefs were Hector, son of Priam, bravest and best of all, and Aeneas, son of the goddess Aphrodite.

Across the wide plain that separated the shore from the high walls of Troy, the Greeks went forward to the battle silently and in order after their chiefs. But from the Trojan army came loud shouts and cries. On both sides the gods urged them on.

With Ares, the god of war, at his side, Hector dealt death and destruction through the ranks of the Greeks. Hera and Athena saw this and were angered. They passed down to earth and urged on the Greeks. With renewed strength, the Greeks fought so fiercely that, even without Achilles, they forced the Trojans to flee behind the walls of the city for safety.

comrades: fellow soldiers; companions
heralds: messengers; announcers
array: arrangement; formation

When Hector passed through the gates into the city, he bid the mothers of Troy assemble in the temple of Athena to see if their prayers might calm the anger of the goddess. Andromache, the wife of Hector, saw him and hastened to meet him. With her was a nurse bearing Hector's only child, with a head like a star, so bright was his golden hair. Hector smiled when he saw the child, but Andromache clasped Hector's hand and wept, saying:

"Oh, Hector, your courage will be your death. Some day all the Greeks will join together and rush upon you and slay you. It were better for me to die than to lose you, for I have no comfort but you. My father is dead, for the great Achilles killed him when he took our city. He killed him, but he did him great honor, for he would not take his arms for spoil, but burned them with him on the funeral pyre. And my seven brothers, they too are dead, for the great Achilles killed them all in one day. My dear mother, too, is dead. You are father to me, and mother, and brother, and husband also. Have pity, then, and stay there upon the city wall, lest you leave me a widow, and your child an orphan."

Hector answered her, "Dear wife, leave these things to me. I am not willing that any son or daughter of Troy should see me keeping away from battle. I hate the very thought of it; I must always be in the front."

Then Hector stretched out his arms to take the child. But the child drew back in the arms of his nurse with a loud cry, for he was frightened by his father's bronze helmet, which shone so brightly, and by the horsehair plume, which nodded so

bid: told; requested
pyre: a pile of materials, such as wood, used for burning a body as part
  of a funeral ritual
lest: for fear that
plume: a showy feather used for decoration

awfully. Then father and mother laughed aloud. And Hector
took the helmet from his head and laid it on the ground, and
caught the child in his hands and kissed him, praying aloud:

"Grant, Father Zeus and all ye gods, that this child may be
great among the sons of Troy; and may they say some day,
when they see him carrying home the bloody spoils of war,
'He is an even greater man than his father!' And his mother
shall be glad."

Then he gave the child to its mother; she clasped him to her and smiled a tearful smile. Her husband had pity on her and stroked her with his hand and said:

"Do not let these things trouble you. No man will kill me unless fate orders it; but no man may escape fate, be he cowardly or brave. Go, carry on your tasks at the shuttle and the loom, and give your maids their tasks. Let me take thought for the battle."

Then Hector took up his helmet from the ground, and white-armed Andromache went to her home, often turning back her eyes. And when she came to her home, she called all her maids together, and they wept and wailed for Hector as though he were already dead. And indeed, she thought in her heart that she should never see him coming home again safe from the battle.

But Hector went into battle with renewed fury, and everywhere the Greeks gave way before him.

AGAMEMNON'S APPEAL TO ACHILLES

On the windswept plains before the high walls of Troy, the Greeks and Trojans clashed in battle. Many a brave warrior fell, leaving their bodies in bloody pools as food for dogs and vultures, while their souls fled groaning to the dark realm of the dead.

Without Achilles, the Greeks could not stand against the strength and fury of Hector, who slew many and stripped

---

fate: destiny; to the ancient Greeks, the cause or will by which
    things happen
shuttle: a part of a loom
loom: a frame used to weave threads into cloth
slew: killed

them of their armor. The Greeks were pushed back to the shore, where the fighting raged by their ships.

And now the sun sank into the sea, and the night fell. The Trojans were angry that darkness had come and that they could not see any longer. But the Greeks were glad, for the night was a shelter to them, and gave them time to breathe.

Then Hector called the Trojans to gather at a place near the river, where the ground was clear of dead bodies. He stood in the middle of the people, holding in his hand a spear of some sixteen feet in length, with a shining head of bronze and a band of gold fastening the head to the shaft. When all were assembled, he spoke:

"Hearken, men of Troy, and ye, our allies who fight with us. I thought that today we should destroy the army of the Greeks and burn their ships, and go back to Troy and live in peace. But night has come and hindered us from finishing our work. Let us sit down, therefore, and rest and take a meal. Loose your horses from their chariots, and give them their food. Go, some of you, to the city, and fetch cattle and sheep and wine and bread, that we may have plenty to eat and drink. I will say no more, but know this: tomorrow we will arm ourselves and drive these Greeks to their ships, and, if the gods are willing, burn their ships with fire. Tomorrow we shall surely bring ruin on the Greeks!"

So Hector spoke, and all the Trojans shouted with joy.

While the Trojans feasted, full of hope that they would soon be rid of their enemies, the Greeks were full of trouble and fear. No one among them was more sad at heart than King Agamemnon. He called his chiefs together. When they

---

hearken: to listen
hindered: stood in the way of

had gathered, not a word did they say, but looked sadly upon the ground. At last Agamemnon stood and spoke:

"Lords and rulers of the Achaeans, truly the great Zeus seems to hate me. Once he promised that I should take this city of Troy and return home in safety, but this promise he has not kept. I must go back to the place from which I came, without honor, and without many of the friends who came with me. Now, before we all perish, let us flee in our ships to our own land, for Troy is not ours to take."

And when the king finished this speech, the chiefs still sat saying not a word. Then old Nestor, wisest of all the Greeks, stood up in his place and said, "O king, Zeus has made you lord over many nations, and put many things into your hand. Therefore you are the more bound to listen to wise words, even though they may not please you. It was an evil day, O king, when you took the maiden Briseis from Achilles. The other chiefs did not consent to your deed, and I myself advised you not to do it. But you would not listen. Rather, you followed your own pride and pleasure, and shamed the bravest of your followers, taking from him the prize he had won with his own valor. Undo this evil deed, and make peace with this man you have wronged. Speak pleasant words to him, and give him noble gifts."

Agamemnon stood and said, "You have spoken truly, old sir. I acted as a fool that day—I do not deny it. For not only is Achilles a great warrior, but he is also dear to Zeus—and he who is dear to Zeus is worth armies of men. See how we are put to flight when he stands aside from the battle! This, surely, is the doing of Zeus. And now, as I did him wrong, so

---

perish: to die
consent: to agree

I will make amends. I will send back the maiden Briseis, and give him much more besides."

Three chiefs—Odysseus, Ajax, and Phoenix—were sent to take this message to Achilles. They went along the shore of the sea and to the camp of the Myrmidons, as the men of Achilles were called. There they found him playing on the harp, and as he played he sang a song about the valiant deeds done by heroes of old. By him sat his dear friend, Patroclus.

So the three chiefs came forward, led by Odysseus. When Achilles saw them, he jumped from his seat in astonishment. And Patroclus also rose, to do them honor.

"You are welcome, my friends," cried Achilles, "for though I am angry with the king, you are not the less my friends."

He bade them sit, and had wine and food brought to them. Patroclus poured the wine, strong and sweet, and gave each man his cup, and then prepared the feast. When they had had enough, Odysseus spoke:

"Hail, Achilles! Truly we have had no lack of feasting. But this is not a day to think of feasting, for destruction is close at hand. This very day the Trojans came near to burning our ships. Therefore have we come to ask that you no longer stand aside from the battle, but come and help us as of old. For truly our need is great. Hector rages furiously, saying that Zeus is with him. He vows that he will burn our ships with fire and destroy us all while we are choked with the smoke of the burning. Now, therefore, stir yourself, before it is too late. The king has sent us to offer you gifts, great and many, for the wrong that he did to you. So great and so many are they that no one can say that these are not worthy."

Odysseus described all the things Agamemnon had promised to give. And when he had finished, he said, "Be content: take these gifts. And if you have no thought for

Agamemnon, yet have thought for the people who perish because you stand aside from the battle. Take the gifts, therefore, for by so doing you will have wealth and honor and love from the Greeks, and great glory also, for you will slay Hector. He is ready to meet you in battle, for he is proud and thinks there is none among the Greeks who can stand against him."

Achilles answered, "I will speak plainly, Odysseus, and say what is in my heart—for, as for that man who thinks one

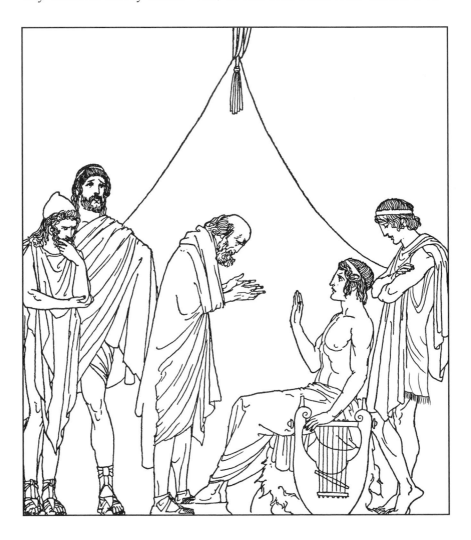

thing in his heart but says another thing with his tongue, he is hateful to me as death itself. Tell me now, what does it profit a man to be always fighting day after day? Even as a bird carries food to its nestlings till they are fledged, and never ceases to work for them, while she is herself but ill fed, so has it been with me. I took twelve cities to which I traveled in ships, and eleven to which I went by land, and from all I carried away much spoil. All this I brought to King Agamemnon, and he, who all the time stayed safe in his tent, gave a few things to me and others, but kept the greater part for himself. And then what did he do? He left to the other chiefs that which he had given them, but what he had given me, he took away. So, let him not ask me any more to fight against the Trojans. There are other chiefs whom he has not wronged and shamed; let him go to them to keep away the devouring fire from the ships. As for me, neither with Hector nor with any of the sons of Troy will I fight again. Tomorrow I will store my ships with food and water and launch them on the sea."

So vehement was Achilles that his listeners sat silent. Then Achilles continued, speaking quietly:

"Often in time past I have thought to marry a wife, to settle down in peace. For long ago, my mother, Thetis of the sea, said to me, 'My son, two destinies lie before you, and you may choose only one. If you stay in this land and fight against Troy, then you will never go back to your own land but will die in your youth. Only your name will live forever. But if you will leave this land and go back to your home, then you shall live long, even to old age, but your name will

---

nestlings: baby birds
fledged: grown up and ready to fly
vehement: forceful; intense

be forgotten.' Once I thought that fame was a better thing than life; but now my mind is changed, for indeed my fame is taken from me, since Agamemnon has put me to shame before all my people."

When Ajax heard this, he rose and said, "Let us go. We shall do no good here today. Achilles cherishes his anger and cares nothing for his comrades or his people. One man will take the price of blood from another, even though he has slain a brother or a son. He takes the gold and puts away his anger. But this man keeps his anger, and all for the sake of a girl. What he desires, I do not know. Surely he seems to lack reason."

Achilles answered, "You speak well, great Ajax. Nevertheless, the anger is yet hot in my heart, because Agamemnon put me to shame before all the people. But go, and take this message: I will not arise to do battle with the Trojans till Hector shall come to these tents and seek to set fire to my ships. But if he shall do this, then I will arise, and I will stop him, however eager he may be for the battle."

So the messengers departed to carry the words of Achilles to King Agamemnon.

The Arming of Patroclus

Patroclus, of all men the dearest friend to Achilles, had been moved by the words of Odysseus and Ajax. He knew that the Greeks were in sore need of Achilles and his troops, and that the very sight of Achilles in his shining armor would strike terror into the hearts of the Trojans. So he went to his friend and said:

---

cherishes: cares for deeply; nurtures
in sore need of: greatly needed

"Be not angry with me, great Achilles, for the Greeks are in great trouble. Many of the bravest are wounded, while you stand apart with your anger. If you will not go to battle, let me go, and your men with me. Let me put on your armor; so shall the Trojans be frightened, thinking that Achilles is in the battle, and the Greeks shall have a breathing space."

Achilles answered, "I said that I should not fight again till the Trojans should bring the fire near to my own ships. But now, as I see the people are in great need, it is time to give help—for I see the Trojans are gathered about the ships, while the Greeks scarcely have room to stand between their enemies and the sea. Go you, then, and put on my armor, and lead my people to the fight. Go and keep the fire from the ships. But when you have done this, come back and fight no more with the Trojans. Mind me: when you feel the joy of battle in your heart, do not be over-bold. When you have driven the Trojans from our ships, do not pursue them. Do not go near the wall of Troy, lest a god meet and harm you."

As they talked, the men of Troy set torches to the ships, and a great flame shot up to the sky. When Achilles saw it, he cried, "Hasten, Patroclus, for I see the fire rising from the ships. Put on my armor, and I will call my people to the war."

So Patroclus put on the armor—breastplate and shield and helmet—and bound upon his shoulder the silver-studded sword, and took a mighty spear in his hand—though not the great Pelian spear, which no man could wield but Achilles. Then he mounted the chariot of Achilles, drawn by the mighty horses that were a gift from Zeus himself.

While he did this, Achilles called his Myrmidons to battle. Fifty ships had he brought to Troy, and in each there were fifty men. To them he said, "Forget not the bold words

wield: to handle with skill

The men of Troy set torches to the ships.

that you spoke against the men of Troy, complaining that I
kept you from the battle against your will. Now you have
your wish."

So the warriors went to battle in close array, helmet to
helmet and shield to shield, close as the stones with which a
builder makes a wall. And Patroclus, in the armor of Achilles,
went in front.

Then Achilles went to his tent and took from his chest a great cup which Thetis, his mother, had given him. No man except Achilles drank from that cup, and he poured out of it offerings to no god but Zeus. First he cleansed it; then he washed his hands, and, standing before his tent, poured out wine to Zeus, saying, "O Zeus, I send my comrade to this battle. Make him strong and bold, and give him glory, and bring him home safe to the ships, and my people with him."

So he prayed, and Zeus heard his prayer: part he granted, but part he would deny.

When Patroclus came to the battle and the men of Troy beheld him, they thought that Achilles had forgotten his anger and come forth. Then the men of Troy turned to flee, and many chiefs fell by the spears of the Greeks.

But there were some among the Trojans and their allies who would not flee. Among these was Sarpedon, who came from a city far beyond Troy. When he saw his comrades flying before Patroclus, he cried aloud, "Stand now and be of good courage! I myself will try this great warrior and see what he can do." Then he flung his spear at Patroclus. The spear flew wide of the mark. Then Patroclus flung his spear and it struck Sarpedon even through the heart. From his chariot, he fell, as a pine or a poplar falls on the hills before the woodsman's ax. And as he fell, he cried out, "Suffer not the Greeks to spoil me of my arms." And so saying, he died.

Hector and the men of Troy were much troubled, for among the allies there was none braver than Sarpedon. So they charged and drove back the Greeks from the body. The Greeks charged again in their turn. No one would have known the great Sarpedon as he lay in the middle of the

---

suffer not: do not allow

It struck Sarpedon even through the heart.

tumult, so covered was he with dust and blood. At last the
Greeks drove back the Trojans from the body and stripped it
of its arms; but the body itself they did not harm, for at the
bidding of Zeus, Apollo came down and carried it from the
fray, and gave it to Sleep and Death that they should carry it
to the homeland of the fallen warrior.

Then Patroclus, forgetting the command of Achilles that
he return at once after driving the Trojans from the ships,
thought in his heart, "Now shall I take the city of Troy." He
rushed ahead across the plain until he came to the very gates
of the city. Three times he scaled the wall, and three times did
Apollo push him back. When Patroclus climbed for the

tumult: commotion; confused uproar
fray: fighting

fourth time, Apollo cried to him in a dreadful voice, "Go back, Patroclus! It is not for you to take the great city of Troy, no, nor even for Achilles, who is a far better warrior than you." Patroclus went back, for he feared the anger of the god. But though he thought no more of taking the city, he raged no less against the Trojans.

Then Apollo stirred up the spirit of Hector. Leaping into his chariot, Hector urged the Trojans on. "We will see whether we can drive back this Patroclus," he said, "for it must be he—Achilles he is not, though he wears his armor."

When Patroclus saw them coming, he took a great stone from the ground and cast it into the air. The stone struck the charioteer full on the helmet. As the man fell head first from the chariot, Patroclus laughed aloud and cried, "Who would have thought that there would be such skillful divers in the city of Troy?"

Three times did Patroclus charge into the ranks of the Trojans, and each time he slew nine warriors. But when he charged for the fourth time, Apollo stood behind him and struck him such a great blow on the neck that his eyes grew dim. The helmet fell to the ground, and the horsehair plume was soiled with dust. Never before had that headpiece, the helmet of Achilles, touched the earth. The spear also that he carried in his hand was broken, and the shield fell from his arm, and the breastplate on his body was loosened. Then, as he stood confused and without defense, one of the Trojans wounded him in the back with his spear. Patroclus turned to flee, but Hector thrust with his spear and hit him above the hip.

Patroclus fell to the ground, and Hector stood over him and cried, "Did you think to spoil our city, Patroclus? Instead, you are slain, and the great Achilles cannot help you."

dreadful: causing great fear

Leaping into his chariot, Hector urged the Trojans on.

But Patroclus answered, "You boast too much, Hector. It was not you that slew me, but Apollo. And mark you, death is close to you by the hand of the great Achilles."

Hector replied, "Why do you prophesy my death? It may be that, as I have slain you, so shall I slay the great Achilles." So Hector spoke, but his words went unheard by Patroclus, who lay dead.

Fierce was the fight about the body of Patroclus, and many heroes on both sides fell. First to fall was the man who had wounded Patroclus in the back, for when he came near to strip the dead man of his arms, Menelaus rushed at him with his spear and slew him. Then Hector came and stood over the body,

and Menelaus did not dare to go against him, for he knew he was no match for him in fighting. So Hector stripped off the arms of Patroclus, the arms which Achilles had given him to wear, and put them on himself. When Zeus saw him do this, he was angry, and said, "These arms will cost Hector dear."

The battle for the body of Patroclus grew fiercer and fiercer. For the Greeks said, "It were better that the earth should open and swallow us alive than that we should let the Trojans carry off the body of Patroclus." And the Trojans said, "Now if we must be slain fighting for the body of this man, be it so, but we will not yield."

As they fought, the horses that pulled the chariot of Achilles, which Patroclus had driven into battle, stood apart and would not move. The tears rushed from their eyes, for

---

roused: moved to action
dear: at a high price

they loved Patroclus, and they knew that he was dead. Still they stood, and they would neither enter the battle nor turn back to the ships. And the Greeks could not move them with the lash or with threat or with gentle words. They stood, their heads drooped to the ground, the tears trickling from their eyes, their long manes trailing in the dust.

When Zeus saw them, he pitied them. And he said, "It was not wise that I gave you, immortal creatures as you are, to a mortal man, for of all things that live and move upon the earth, surely man is the most miserable. But Hector shall not have you. It is enough for him—yea, it is too much—that he should have the arms of Achilles."

Then the horses moved from their places and obeyed their driver as before. And Hector could not take them, though he longed to do so.

All this time, as the battle raged around the body of Patroclus, a messenger made his way to Achilles. He found the great warrior by the door of his tent. Then he said, weeping as he spoke, "I bring bad news for you. Patroclus is dead, and Hector has his arms, but even now the Greeks and Trojans are fighting for his body."

Achilles threw himself upon the ground and took the dust of the plain in his hands and poured it on his head. He wept and tore his hair. But his mother, Thetis, heard his cry, and from the depths of the sea she came and laid her hand on his head and asked, "Why do you weep, my son?"

Achilles answered, "My friend Patroclus is dead, and Hector has the arms which I gave him to wear. I care not to live, except to avenge his death."

Then Thetis said, "My son, do not speak so. You know that when Hector dies, then is the hour near when you also must die."

Then Achilles cried in great anger, "I would that I could die this hour, for I sent my friend to his death—and I, who am greater in battle than all the Achaeans, could not help him. Cursed be the anger that sets men to strive against one another, as it made me strive with Agamemnon. As for my fate—what does it matter? Let it come when it may, as long as first I have my vengeance upon Hector. Therefore, mother, do not seek to keep me back from the battle."

Thetis answered, "Be it so, my son. But you cannot go into battle without arms. Tomorrow I will go to Hephaestus and have him make new arms for you."

While they talked the men of Troy drove the Greeks back more and more. Then the body of Patroclus would have fallen to the Trojans, had not Zeus sent a messenger to Achilles.

"Rouse thee, Achilles," said the messenger, "or the body of Patroclus will be a prey for the dogs of Troy."

Achilles answered, "How shall I go?—for arms have I none, nor do I know of any man's I might wear."

The messenger replied, "Go only to the trench and show yourself; then the Trojans will draw back, and the Greeks will have a breathing space."

So Achilles ran to the trench. And Athena put her great shield about his shoulders, and set a circle of gold above his head that shone like a flame of fire. Then he cried out, and his voice was as the sound of a trumpet. It was a sound terrible to hear, and the hearts of the men of Troy were filled with fear. They stood in dumb amaze when they saw above his head the flaming fire that Athena had kindled. The very horses were frightened and started so that the chariots clashed together.

---

kindled: lit; set ablaze

Three times Achilles shouted across the trench, and three times the Trojans fell back. Then the Greeks took up the body of Patroclus and put it on a bier and carried it to the tent of Achilles, as Achilles himself, weeping, walked by the side of the body.

They washed the body of Patroclus, and put ointment into the wounds, and laid it on a bed, and covered it with linen from head to foot, and over this draped a white robe. And all through the night there was great mourning for Patroclus in the camp of the Greeks.

THE MAKING OF THE ARMS

Thetis, immortal mother of Achilles, went to the house of Hephaestus, the god of all those who worked in gold and silver and iron. She found him busy at his work, making cauldrons for the palace of the gods on Mount Olympus. These cauldrons had golden wheels beneath them with which they could move on their own power into the chambers of the palace and back out again, as the gods willed.

When Hephaestus heard that Thetis wished to see him, he smiled and said, "Truly, there could be no guest more welcome than Thetis. When my mother cast me out from her because I was lame, it was Thetis and her sister who received me in their house under the sea. Nine years I dwelt with them, and hammered many a pretty trinket for them in a cave close by. Truly, I would give my life to serve Thetis."

Then he put away his tools, washed himself, and came into the house. To Thetis he said, "Tell me all that is in your mind, for I will do all that you desire if only it can be done."

---

bier: a frame on which to carry a dead body
cauldrons: large kettles

Then Thetis told of how her son Achilles had been shamed by Agamemnon, and of his great anger, and all that came to pass afterwards, and how Patroclus had been slain in battle, and how the arms were lost. Having told this, she said, "Hephaestus, make for my son, Achilles, I pray you, a shield and a helmet, and greaves for his legs, and a strong breastplate."

Hephaestus answered, "I will make for him such arms as men will wonder at when they see them." So he went to his forge and turned the bellows to the fire and bade them work, for they needed no hand to work them. And he put copper and tin and gold and silver into the fire to make them soft, and took the hammer in one hand and the tongs in the other.

First he made a shield, great and strong. On it he made an image of the earth and the sky and the sea, with the sun and the moon and all the stars. Also, he made images of two cities: in one city there was peace, and in the other city there was war. In the city of peace they led a bride to the house of her husband with music and dancing. But round about the city of war there was an army of besiegers, and on the wall stood men defending it. Also, the men of this same city had set an ambush by a river at a place where the cattle came down to drink. And when the cattle came down, the men that lay in ambush rose up quickly and took them, and slew the herdsmen. And the army of the besiegers heard the cry, and rode on horses, and came quickly to the river, and fought with the men who had taken the cattle.

---

greaves: protective armor for the shins
forge: a furnace where metal is melted and shaped
bellows: a tool that pumps air, used by a blacksmith to feed a fire
ambush: a trap for an enemy; a sudden surprise attack

Also, he made the image of one field in which men were plowing, and of another in which reapers reaped the corn; and behind the reapers came boys who gathered the corn in their arms and bound it in sheaves. At the top of the field stood the master, glad at heart because the harvest was good.

He made, too, the image of a vineyard, and through the vineyard there was a path, and along the path went young men and maids bearing baskets of grapes, and in the midst stood a boy holding a harp of gold, who sang a pleasant song. Also he made a herd of oxen going from the stalls to the pasture; and close by, two lions had laid hold of a great bull and were devouring it, while the dogs stood far off and barked.

He made as well the image of a dance of men and maids. The men wore daggers of gold hanging from silver belts, and the maids wore gold crowns round their heads. And round about the shield, he made the ocean, like a great river.

Also he made a strong breastplate, and a great helmet with a ridge of gold in which the plumes should be set, and greaves of tin for the legs. When he had finished all this work, he gave the armor to Thetis. She flew swift as a hawk to her son, and found him lying on the ground, weeping aloud, holding in his arms the body of Patroclus.

Catching her son by the hand, the goddess said, "Come now, let us leave. It was the will of the gods that he should die. But you must think about other things. Come, and take this gift from Hephaestus—armor of exceeding strength and beauty, such as no man has ever yet worn."

As she spoke, she placed the armor at the feet of Achilles. It shone so brightly that it dazzled the eyes of the Myrmidons. Achilles took up the arms, and his eyes blazed with fire, and he rejoiced in his heart. "Mother," he said, "these indeed are such arms as only the gods could make. Gladly will I put them on for the battle."

THE VENGEANCE OF ACHILLES

So Achilles gathered the Greeks for the battle, and his armor flashed like fire. On the wide plain between the shore and the high-walled city, the two armies gathered.

Then Apollo spoke to Aeneas, the son of Aphrodite and a Trojan nobleman, and among the Trojans second only to Hector in fame and valor. "Stand up against Achilles," said the god to the Trojan prince. "Drive straight at him with your spear, and do not fear his fierce words and looks."

So Aeneas came forth to meet Achilles. And Achilles said to him, "What do you mean by this, Aeneas? Do you think to slay me? Have the Trojans promised to make you their king if you prevail over me? You will not find it an easy task."

Aeneas said, "Son of Peleus, you will not frighten me with your words, for I also am the son of a goddess. Come, let us try who is the better of us two."

So he cast his spear, and it struck full on the shield of Achilles, and made so dreadful a sound that Achilles himself was shaken. But a shield made by a god could not be shattered by the spear of a mortal man. Indeed, it pierced the first and second layers, which were of bronze, but was stopped by the third, which was of gold, and touched not the last two layers, made of tin.

Now Achilles threw his spear. Easily it pierced the shield of the Trojan, and, though it did not wound him, it came so close that he was deadly frightened. Yet he did not flee, for when Achilles drew his sword and rushed at

prevail: to triumph

him, he took up a great stone from the ground to throw at him. Nevertheless he would certainly have been slain were it not for the help of the gods. For it was decreed that Aeneas and his children after him should reign over Troy in the years to come. Therefore Poseidon, upon the order of Zeus, hid Aeneas in a cloud of fog, then caught him up and carried him away from the battle. But first he took Achilles's spear from the shield and laid it at the hero's feet. As the fog cleared, Achilles saw his spear and cried, "Here is a great wonder. My spear that I threw I see lying at my feet, but the man at whom I threw it, I see not. Truly this Aeneas must be dear to the gods."

Then he rushed into the battle, slaying right and left. As the Trojans fled before Achilles, they came to the river Xanthus, and they leaped into it till it was full of horses and men. Achilles left his spear upon the bank and rushed into the water with only his sword. And the Trojans were like fishes in the sea when they flee from a dolphin: in rocks and shallows they hide themselves, but the great beast devours them apace.

Back and yet further back Achilles drove the men of Troy before him, closer and closer to the city walls. That hour the Greeks would have taken Troy, but Apollo saved it by drawing Achilles away from the city. And the way in which he saved the city was this. He put courage into the heart of Agenor, a Trojan chief, who stood by the gate waiting for Achilles. And when Achilles came near, Agenor threw his spear and struck his leg beneath the knee. But the strong greave turned aside the spear. Enraged, Achilles rushed to slay his attacker. But Apollo lifted Agenor from the ground and set him safely within the city walls.

apace: swiftly; rapidly

Then Apollo took the form of Agenor, and fled before Achilles, and Achilles pursued him far from the walls of Troy. At last the god turned and spoke to him: "Why do you pursue me, swift-footed Achilles? Have you not yet discovered that I am a god, and all your fury is in vain? And now all the Trojans are safe within the city, and you are here, far out of the way, seeking to kill one who cannot die."

In great wrath Achilles answered him, "You have done me wrong in drawing me away from the city, Great Archer. Had I the power, you would pay dearly for this cheat."

The Trojans were now safe in the city, refreshing themselves after all their toil. Hector alone remained outside the walls, standing in front of the gates of the city.

From the high wall, King Priam spied Achilles rushing toward the city. He cried to Hector, "Oh my son, come within the walls, for you are the hope of the city."

Then Queen Hecuba cried to him, "O Hector, my son, have pity. Come, I beseech you, inside the walls, and do not stand in battle against him."

But Hector was resolved to await the coming of Achilles and meet him in battle. And as he waited, he thought, "It is better to meet in arms and see whether Zeus will give the victory to him or to me."

Achilles approached, brandishing his great spear, and the flashing of his arms was like fire or the sun when it rises. When he saw this, Hector trembled. His nerve failed him, and he turned to run. Fast he fled from the gates, and fast Achilles pursued him. Past the watchtower they ran, past the wild fig

---

in vain: useless
toil: hard labor
beseech: to beg
brandishing: waving in a threatening manner

tree, along the wagon road which went about the walls. On they ran, one fleeing, the other pursuing. Thrice they ran around the city, but Apollo helped Hector, or he could not have held out against Achilles, who was swiftest of foot among the sons of men.

As they sat in their place on the top of Mount Olympus, the gods looked on. And Zeus said, "This is a piteous thing I see. My heart is grieved for Hector. See how the great Achilles is pursuing him! Come, let us discuss the matter. Shall we save him from death, or shall we let him fall by the spear of Achilles?"

Athena replied, "What is this that you propose? Will you save a man that the fates appoint to die?"

Then Zeus said, "So it must be, but it is a thing I hate."

All this time, Hector still fled, and Achilles still pursued. Then Athena flew down to Achilles and said, "This is your day of glory. Stand here and take breath, and I will make Hector meet you." So Achilles stood, leaning on his spear.

Then Athena took the shape of one of Hector's brothers, Deiphobus, and came near to him, and said, "My brother, Achilles presses you hard; but come, we two will stand against him."

Hector answered, "O Deiphobus, I have always loved you, and now I love you still more, for you alone have come to my help, while the rest remain within the walls."

Then Hector turned to Achilles and cried out, "Three times have you pursued me round the walls and I dared not stand against you, but now I fear you no more. Only let us make this covenant: if Zeus gives the victory to me today, I will take your arms but return your body to the Greeks. Promise, therefore, to do the same with me."

---

thrice: three times
piteous: worthy of pity; pitiful
covenant: a formal agreement; a solemn promise

Achilles frowned and said, "Hector, do not speak to me of covenants. Men and lions make no promises to each other, neither is there any agreement between wolves and sheep. Come, let us fight, that I may have vengeance for the blood of all my comrades whom you have slain, and especially for Patroclus."

Then he threw his great spear, but Hector saw it coming and avoided it, crouching on the ground, so that it flew above his head and fixed itself in the earth. But Athena snatched it up and gave it back to Achilles, though Hector did not see this.

"You have missed your aim, great Achilles," said Hector. "You shall not drive your steel into my back, but here into my breast, if the gods will it so. But now look out for my spear."

Then Hector threw his long-shafted spear. True aim he took, for the spear struck the very middle of Achilles's shield. It struck, but it did not pierce it, and bounded far away, for the shield was not made by the hand of man. Then Hector cried, "Deiphobus, give me your spear!"

But Deiphobus was nowhere to be seen. Hector stood dismayed: he knew that his end was near. Then he said to himself, "The gods have brought my doom upon me. But if I must die, let me at least die doing such a deed as men will remember in the years to come."

He drew his mighty sword and rushed at Achilles. But Achilles charged to meet him, his shield before his breast, his helmet bent forward as he ran. The gleam of his spear-point was as the gleam of the evening star. Achilles well knew the one unprotected spot in the armor that Hector had taken from Patroclus. Into the spot where the neck joins the shoulder he drove his spear, and Hector fell in the dust.

Achilles drew his spear out of the body, and stripped off the bloody armor. All the Greeks came about the dead man, marveling at his strength and beauty. Looking at one another they said, "Surely this Hector is less dreadful now than in the day when he burned our ships with fire."

PRIAM'S APPEAL TO ACHILLES

Andromache did not yet know what had happened. She sat in her dwelling, weaving a purple mantle embroidered with flowers. But when the sound of wailing came to her from the town, she rose hastily in great fear and called to her maidens, "Come to me, O maidens, that I may see what has happened, for I heard the voice of the queen, and I fear that some evil has come to the Trojans."

She hastened through the city, with terror in her heart. When she came to the wall, she stood and looked; and lo, she saw Achilles dragging the body of Hector to the ships. Then her eyes grew dim, and she fell fainting.

When Priam saw Achilles take Hector's body, he determined to go forth and beg Achilles to give him the body of his dear son. He took a great cup and poured out wine to Zeus, and prayed: "Hear me, Father Zeus, and grant that Achilles may pity me. Send me a sign, in order that I may go with a good heart to the Greeks."

And Zeus heard him and sent an eagle, his favorite bird, as a sure sign. Then the old man mounted his chariot in haste, and with a herald drove forth from the palace.

---

mantle: a loose sleeveless garment, worn over other clothing
herald: an officer who acts as a messenger between leaders, especially
    in wartime

When Priam came to the tent of Achilles, he leaped down from the chariot and went to the tent. The king fell on the ground before Achilles, clasped his knees, and spoke: "Have pity on me, O Achilles. Think of your father: he is as old as I am, yet all is well for him so long as he knows you are alive, for he hopes to see you return from the land of Troy. But as for me, many valiant sons I have lost at your hands, and now the best of them all lies dead. Have pity, Achilles; I kiss the hands of the man who has killed my children."

Then the heart of Achilles was moved with pity, and he wept, thinking of his old father, and then of the dead Patroclus. He stood up before King Priam, and spoke: "How did you dare to come? You cannot raise your son from the dead."

But Priam answered, "Take the gifts which I have brought to ransom Hector, my son. Let me look upon him with my eyes. Then may the gods grant you safe return to your fatherland. If you are willing to let me bury Hector, let there be a truce between my people and the Greeks. For nine days let us mourn, and on the tenth we will bury him, on the eleventh raise a great tomb above him, and on the twelfth we will fight again, if fight we must."

And Achilles answered, "Be it so."

Wailing and weeping, Priam and the herald took the body to the city. A daughter of Priam was the first to see her father and the herald with the body, and she cried, "Sons and daughters of Troy, go to meet Hector, if ever you met him with joy as he came back in triumph from battle."

At once there was not a man or woman left in the city. Andromache led the way, and the queen and all the multitude followed. They took Hector to his home, and the minstrels mourned while the women wept aloud. Last of all came Helen, who cried out, "Many a year has passed since I came to Troy— would that I had died before! Never have I heard from your lips, O Hector, one bitter word. Therefore, I weep for you; no one is left in Troy to be my friend. All shun and hate me now."

For nine days the people of Troy gathered wood, and on the tenth they laid Hector upon the pile and lighted a

----

truce: a temporary stop in the fighting, agreed to by the opposing sides
minstrels: in ancient times, singers of verses, often about heroes and
    their deeds

fire beneath it. When the body was burned, his comrades gathered the bones and laid them in a chest of gold. This they covered with purple robes and put in a great coffin, and upon it they laid many great stones. Over all they raised a mighty mound. Thus they buried Hector, defender of Troy.

* * * * *

The Iliad *ends with the funeral of Hector. Other myths tell us of the fate of Achilles and of the fall of Troy.*

THE DEATH OF ACHILLES

As for Achilles, after the death of Hector, his day of doom was not far off.

When the funeral rites for Hector were ended, and the fighting was renewed, the Trojans did not go out onto the plain to meet the Greeks in battle. Instead, they fought from behind their high walls, shooting arrows at the Greeks.

More than all others, Achilles was determined to break through the gates of Troy. The arrows of the Trojans could not pierce the armor Hephaestus had made. Even without that armor, Achilles was protected from harm, because his mother had dipped him, when he was a babe, in the magical waters of the river Styx—all of him, that is, but his heel, by which she had held him when she immersed him in the dark waters.

On this occasion, as Achilles directed his unquenchable fury against the city gates, he was spied from above by a watcher from one of the high towers atop the walls of Troy. This was Paris, whose rash act had caused the war, and who

---

immersed: dipped into a liquid until covered
unquenchable: unable to be satisfied

now stood carefully aiming an arrow that he had dipped in a deadly poison. He let the arrow fly, and with Apollo's help, it hit its mark, piercing Achilles's vulnerable heel.

Achilles wheeled about, his face a mask of pain. Then, mastering himself, he stood straight and tall, and shouted defiantly to the towers above, "What coward sends death from afar rather than meet me in single combat? Come forth with sword and spear, and meet your doom!" Then he fell, lifeless, on the dusty plain of Troy.

Both Trojans and Greeks stood a moment in awed silence. Then the Trojans emerged from behind their gates, hoping to seize the body of Achilles. But the Greeks rushed forth with a fury increased by grief. And in the midst of a great battle, Ajax managed to lift the body and carry it back to the Greek camp as Odysseus held off the Trojans.

So the greatest of the Greeks was slain on the very spot where he had killed Hector. For seventeen days the Greeks mourned over his body, and on the eighteenth day they gave it burial by the side of his friend Patroclus. Over them both the Greeks raised a great mound that was the wonder of men in after times.

vulnerable: unprotected; subject to being wounded
defiantly: with bold challenge
single combat: fighting between two persons

THE TROJAN HORSE

Besides Hector and Achilles, many other heroes met their doom on the plains before the gates of Troy during the long years that the city was besieged. For the gods gave victory now to one army and now to the other.

At length it seemed as if the Greeks would have to sail away without recovering Helen and restoring her to Menelaus. Indeed, they might have failed, but at last Athena, always favoring the Greeks, put a thought into the mind of the crafty Odysseus.

At his orders, a great number of planks and boards were brought together on the plain outside the city. For many days, the noise of chopping and hammering and pounding was heard rising from the Greek camp.

Then one morning, the noise stopped. An eerie silence hung over the plains before Troy. The silence, however, was broken by the cries of the sentinels in the lofty towers atop the high walls of Troy.

"What is it?" cried the people of Troy as they hurried into the streets. "Are the Greeks attacking?"

"They are gone," said one of the sentinels.

"Who are gone?"

"The Greeks!" cried the sentinel. "No sign of them can be seen—no ships, nor tents, nor smoking fires."

"Our enemies have departed!" cried the people. "Peace and safety are ours again at last!"

Then the gates of the city were opened and the people poured out in throngs. Upon the wide plain of Troy, nothing

---

crafty: clever; tricky
eerie: strange; weird; causing great uneasiness
sentinels: watchmen; guards
lofty: rising to a great height
throngs: large crowds

was to be seen of the Greeks—nothing, that is, except a giant wooden horse.

When the people of Troy came upon the great horse, they looked with curiosity and suspicion. Why, they wondered, had the Greeks left this strange thing? And what should be done with it?

"Throw it into the sea!" said one man.

"Chop it open to see if there's anything inside," advised another.

"Burn it!" cried another. "Let us leave no trace of the Greeks to stain our soil."

But the loudest cries were the shouts of those who wished to drag the horse into the city and keep it as a token of their victory.

In the midst of this tumult, an even greater shouting was heard. "A Greek! A Greek!" came the cry. A group of men came forth, dragging a prisoner, led by a cord of oxhide twisted around his neck. As he stumbled along, the crowd jeered at him and pelted him with sticks and sand. His left ear was mangled, and his right arm seemed to hang useless at his side.

All at once, the uproar ceased, as a chariot approached, carrying an officer of the king.

"What prisoner is this?" he asked.

"He is a Greek!" answered his captors. "We found him in the tall grass by the marshes. He was already wounded so it was easy for us to take him."

"Already wounded!" said the officer. "That is strange indeed." Then turning to the prisoner, he said, "Tell me whether you are a Greek or whether you are a friend of Troy. What is your name, and what is your country?"

"My name," said the prisoner, "is Sinon, and though I am by birth a Greek, yet I have no country. Until ten days ago I counted myself a friend of Greece and fought among her heroes. But see these wounds—this bleeding ear, this shattered arm. Can I remain friendly to those who maimed me and would have taken my life?"

"Tell us what happened," said the officer, "and tell us, too, whether the Greeks have truly sailed away for good."

"Yes, I will tell you," said Sinon. "After so many long years of battle, the Greeks began to lose hope of ever taking Troy. At last it was decided to give up the siege and sail for home. But no sooner had this decision been made than great storms arose. It was impossible for any ship to put to sea. Then the Greek chieftains called the soothsayers and bade them tell what was the cause of these things, and by what means we might return home. Calchas was the first soothsayer to speak.

"'Athena is angry,' he said, 'and that is why the storms rage so fiercely on the sea. Never will Greek ships leave this shore until we build, in tribute to the goddess, a great statue of a horse, greater than any seen before.'

"Then another soothsayer stepped forth and said, 'The ships of Greece can never sail until a hero shall be sacrificed to Apollo.'

"Then Odysseus asked, 'Who is this hero that must be sacrificed?'

"And the soothsayer pointed to me, Sinon. At once, Odysseus, craftiest of men, bound me with cords and pronounced that I should die at sunrise the next day. But in the thick darkness of the night, I managed to steal away, and would have escaped unhurt had I not been discovered by Odysseus. Fiercely he attacked me and gave me the wounds you see upon my body. Yet in the darkness I eluded him and found shelter in the marshes by the shore. There I lay till I was dragged to this place. As to whether I am a friend of the Greeks, now you know."

"But what about the horse?" cried the crowd. "Tell us more of the wooden horse!"

eluded: escaped; got away from

"The horse," said Sinon, "was built as the soothsayer, Calchas, directed. He declared that it would bring peace and prosperity wherever it should go. But the Greeks were unwilling that it should ever be a benefit to Troy. Therefore they built it so wide and high that it cannot be taken through the gates of your city."

"Ah, that is their plan, is it?" cried the excited Trojans. "Well, we shall show them. Bring the horse into the city! Bring the wooden horse to the temple!"

But Laocoön, a priest of Troy, pressed forth through the crowd. "Beware, my countrymen, beware!" cried the old priest. "Have you not already seen enough of the deceit of the Greeks? This horse will not bring you happiness and prosperity but misery and ruin. Burn it to ashes, or cast it into the sea, but touch it not, for I fear the Greeks even though they offer gifts."

Saying this, he seized a spear and hurled it at the side of the great horse. It pierced the wood and, as if in answer, there arose from within a sound like the murmur of voices and the clash of arms.

Then suddenly, as the Trojans looked on in amazement, two great serpents rose from the sea. They had been sent by Poseidon, the god of the sea, and at this time a bitter enemy of Troy. With terrible silent swiftness, the serpents glided over the land and fell upon Laocoön and his two sons, who stood beside him. Wrapping the man and boys in their scaly coils, the serpents crushed the life from them.

This horrible sight was enough to convince the Trojans that the gods were displeased at the words of Laocoön. They

---

prosperity: success; wealth
deceit: trickiness; false and misleading practices

cried out that surely the horse was sacred to the gods and must be taken to their temple and treated with all honor.

With a rush, the Trojans opened the main gates, and pulled down part of the adjoining walls. They tied ropes about the wooden animal's legs and fixed rollers to its feet. With songs of joy, they dragged it into the city.

All this while, Sinon looked on with scorn hidden in his heart. He saw the great hole in the walls of Troy and smiled. The Greek plan was working even better than he had hoped. The craft of Odysseus was doing what ten years of war had failed to do.

Throughout the city there was feasting and rejoicing, until in the late hours of night the Trojan warriors fell into deep sleep. The city was wrapped in darkness, and the streets were silent and empty—except for one figure that crept quietly along, staying close to the walls.

The figure hurried down to the spot where the great horse was standing silent in the moonlight. Then he knocked three times on the horse's front leg. From within, there came an answering knock, and then a secret panel slid open in the horse's breast.

"Is all well, Sinon?" asked a deep voice.

"All is well, Odysseus. The foolish Trojans lie sleeping in their homes, little dreaming of what awaits them."

A rope ladder was let down, and Odysseus descended, followed by fifty other warriors.

"But Sinon," said Odysseus, "what are those scars upon your face? And that mangled ear? And is your arm also wounded? Did the Trojans injure you?"

---

adjoining: attached
scorn: strong dislike and disrespect; contempt

"The Trojans did not make these wounds," said Sinon. "I made them myself, to better persuade them to fall into our trap."

Odysseus smiled. "Good Sinon," he said, "people call me the man of wiles, but I say that title should belong to you. But come, now to end this business."

All this while, under cover of darkness, the Greek ships had slipped back from behind a nearby island where they had been hidden. Thousands of warriors poured forth on the shore. In answer to a signal fire from their countrymen within the city, the whole Greek army came charging in through the hole in the walls and through the gates.

The Trojans awoke from their dreams of peace to see their homes in flames. They fought bravely, but it was in vain. Fires were soon blazing in every direction. The Greeks swept through the streets, dealing death and destruction on all sides. They took Troy with all its rich treasures. And Aphrodite restored to Menelaus his wife, the beautiful Helen.

So ended the great Trojan War that began with an apple of discord and left a great city in fiery ruins.

wiles: clever and tricky plans

STORIES FROM THE ODYSSEY

STORIES FROM THE *ODYSSEY*

adapted from the retelling by Padraic Colum

PART 1:
A SON'S ADVENTURES

THE VISITOR TO TELEMACHUS

This is the story of Odysseus, the most renowned of all the heroes the Greek poets have told us of—of Odysseus, and his long wanderings after the fall of the high walls of Troy. And this story of Odysseus begins with his son, the youth who was called Telemachus.

It was when Telemachus was a child of a month old that a messenger came from Agamemnon, the great king, bidding Odysseus betake himself to the war against Troy. Odysseus reluctantly bade good-bye to his infant son, and to his young wife, Penelope, and to his father, old Laertes. He bade good-bye to his house and his lands and to the island of Ithaca where he was king, and thereafter he took his sailors and his fighting men with him and he sailed away.

The years went by and Odysseus did not return from Troy. After ten years the city was taken by the kings and princes of Greece, and the thread of war was wound up. But still

---

renowned: celebrated; well-known; famous
bade: said; told

Odysseus did not return. And now minstrels came to Ithaca with word of the deaths or the homecomings of the heroes who had fought in the war against Troy. But no minstrel brought any word of Odysseus. Ten years more went by. And now that infant son whom he had left behind, Telemachus, had grown up and was a young man of strength and purpose.

One day, as he sat sad and disconsolate in the house of his father, Telemachus saw a stranger come to the outer gate. There were many in the court outside, but no one went to receive the newcomer. Then, because he would never let a stranger stand at the gate without hurrying out to welcome him, and because, too, he had hopes that some day such a one would bring him tidings of his father, Telemachus rose up from where he was sitting and went to the gate at which the stranger stood.

"Welcome to the house of Odysseus," said Telemachus giving him his hand.

The stranger clasped it with a friendly clasp. "I thank you, Telemachus," he said, "for your welcome, and glad I am to enter the house of your father, the renowned Odysseus."

The stranger looked like one who would be a captain among soldiers. His eyes were gray and clear and shone wonderfully. In his hand he carried a great bronze spear. He and Telemachus went together through the court and into the hall. And when the stranger left his spear within the spearstand, Telemachus took him to a high chair and put a footstool under his feet.

---

minstrels: in ancient times, singers of verses, often about heroes and
    their deeds
disconsolate: unhappy; gloomy; dejected
court: courtyard; open space enclosed by walls or buildings
tidings: news

He had brought him to a place in the hall where the crowd would not come. There were many in the court outside and Telemachus would not have his guest disturbed by questions or clamors. A handmaid brought water for the washing of his hands, and poured it over them from a golden ewer into a silver basin. A polished table was left at his side. Then other servants set down bread and dishes of meat with golden cups, and afterwards the maids came into the hall and filled up the cups with wine.

But the servants who waited on Telemachus and his guest were disturbed by the crowd of men who now came into the hall. They seated themselves at tables and shouted out their orders. Great dishes of meat were brought to them and bowls of wine, and the men ate and drank and talked loudly to each other and did not refrain even from staring at the stranger who sat with Telemachus.

"Is there a wedding-feast in the house?" the stranger asked, "or do the men of your clan meet here to drink with each other?"

A flush of shame came to the face of Telemachus. "There is no wedding-feast here," he said, "nor do the men of our clan meet here to drink with each other. My guest, because you seem so friendly to my father's name, I will tell you who these men are and why they trouble this house."

Telemachus told the stranger how his father had not returned from the war of Troy although it was now ten years since the city was taken by those with whom he went. "Alas," Telemachus said, "he must have died on his way back to us,

---

clamors: loud noises
ewer: a pitcher or jug
refrain: to stop oneself from doing something
clan: families descended from the same ancestor

and I must think that his bones lie under some nameless channel of the ocean. Had he died in the fight at Troy, then the kings and princes would have made him a burial-mound worthy of his name and his deeds, and I, his son, would not be imposed upon by such men as you see here—men who are feasting and giving orders in my father's house and wasting the substance that he gathered."

"How come they to be here?" asked the stranger.

Telemachus told him about this also. When seven years had gone by from the fall of Troy and still Odysseus did not return, there were those who thought he was dead and would never be seen more in the land of Ithaca. Then many of the young lords of the land wanted Penelope, Telemachus's mother, to marry one of them. They came to the house to woo her for marriage. But she, ever hoping that he would return, would give no answer to them.

When he had told him all this Telemachus raised his head and looked at the stranger: "O my guest," he said, "wisdom and power shine out of your eyes. Speak now and tell me what I should do to save the house of Odysseus from ruin. And tell me too if you think it possible that my father should still be in life."

The stranger looked at him with his gray, clear, wonderfully-shining eyes. "As I look at you," said the stranger, "I mark your head and eyes, and I know they are such a head and such eyes as Odysseus had. Well, being the son of such a man, and of such a woman as the lady Penelope, your spirit surely shall find a way of destroying those suitors who would destroy your house."

---

imposed upon: taken advantage of
substance: goods; property
woo: to court; to seek the affection of
mark: take notice of
suitors: men who court a woman with the hope of marrying her

"Already," said Telemachus, "your gaze and your speech make me feel equal to the task of dealing with them."

"I think," said the stranger, "that Odysseus, your father, has not perished from the earth. He may yet win home through labors and perils. But you should seek for tidings of him. Hearken to me now and I shall tell you what to do.

"Tomorrow summon a council of all the chief men of the land of Ithaca, and stand up in that council and declare that the time has come for the suitors who waste your substance to scatter, each man to his own home. And after the council has been held, voyage to find out tidings of your father, whether he still lives and where he might be. Go to Sparta, to the home of Menelaus and Helen, and beg tidings of your father from them. And if you get news of his being alive, return. But if you learn that your father, the renowned Odysseus, is indeed dead and gone, then come back, and in your own country raise a great funeral mound to his memory. Then let your mother choose a good man to be her husband and let her marry him, knowing for a certainty that Odysseus will never come back to his own house. After that, you will have to punish those suitors who destroy the goods your father gathered and who insult his house by their presence. And when all these things have been done, you, Telemachus, will be free to seek out your own fortune: you will rise to fame, for I mark that you are handsome and strong and most likely to be a wise and valiant man. But now I must fare on my journey."

---

perished: died
perils: dangers
hearken: to listen
valiant: brave and noble
fare: to go; to travel

The stranger rose up from where he sat and went with Telemachus to the outer gate. Telemachus said, "What you have told me I shall not forget. I know you have spoken out of a wise and a friendly heart."

The stranger clasped his hands and went through the gate. And then, as he looked after him Telemachus saw the stranger change in his form. He became first as a woman, tall, with fair hair and a spear of bronze in her hand. And then the form of a woman changed too. It changed into a great sea-eagle that on wide wings rose up and flew high through the air. Telemachus knew then that his visitor was an immortal and no other than the goddess Athena, who had been his father's friend.

TELEMACHUS SPEAKS

When Telemachus went back to the hall, those who were feasting there had put the wine-cups from them and were calling out for the minstrel to come and sing some tale to delight them. As Telemachus went amongst them, one of the suitors said to another, "The guest who was with him has told Telemachus something that has changed his bearing. Never before did I see him hold himself so proudly."

The minstrel came and the suitors called upon him to sing them a tale. And he sang of the return of the kings and princes from Troy, and of how some god or goddess put a trouble upon them as they left the city they had taken. And as the minstrel began the tale, Penelope, Telemachus's lady-mother, was coming down the stairs with two handmaids behind her. She heard the words he sang, and she stood still

---

bearing: manner; the way one carries oneself

in her grief and drew her veil across her face. "Oh," she cried, "cease from that story that ever wastes my heart—the story that has brought me sorrow and that leaves me comfortless all my days!"

The minstrel would have ceased when Penelope spoke thus to him, but Telemachus went to the stairway where his lady-mother stood, and addressed her.

"My lady-mother," said he, "why should you not let the minstrel delight the company with such songs as the spirit moves him to give us? It is no blame to him if he sings of that which is sorrowful to us. As for you, my mother, you must learn to endure that story, for long will it be sung far and

---

wastes: weakens; seriously injures

wide. And you are not the only one who is bereaved—many another man besides Odysseus lost the happy day of his homecoming in the war of Troy."

Penelope, his lady-mother, looked in surprise at the youth who spoke to her so wisely. Was this indeed Telemachus who before had hardly lifted his head? And as she looked at him again she saw that he carried his head—that head of his that was so like Odysseus's—high and proudly. She saw that her son was now indeed a man.

Penelope spoke no word to him, for a new thought had come into her mind. She turned round and went back with her handmaids to the chamber where her loom and her distaff were. And as she went up the stairway and away from them, her suitors muttered one to the other that she would soon have to choose one of them for her husband.

Telemachus turned to those who were standing at the tables and addressed them: "Suitors of my mother," he said, "I have a word to say to you. Let us feast now in peace, without any brawling amongst us, and listen to the tale that the minstrel sings to us. But tomorrow let us have a council made up of the chief men of this land of Ithaca. I shall go to the council and speak there. I shall ask that you leave this house and feast on goods that you yourselves have gathered. Let the chief men judge whether I speak in fairness to you or not. If you do not heed what I will say openly at the council, before all the chief men of our land, then let it be on your own heads what will befall you."

bereaved: sorrowful due to the loss of a loved one
distaff: a tool used for holding flax or wool when spinning thread
brawling: fighting
council: a group of people who discuss issues and make decisions
heed: to pay attention to
befall: happen to

All the suitors marveled that Telemachus spoke so boldly. And one said, "Because his father, Odysseus, was king, this youth thinks he should be king by inheritance. But may Zeus never grant that he be king."

Then said Telemachus, "If Zeus should grant that I be king, I am ready to take up the kingship of the land of Ithaca with all its toils and all its dangers." And when Telemachus said that he looked like a young king indeed.

THE COUNCIL MEETING

As soon as it was dawn, Telemachus rose from his bed. He put on his raiment, bound his sandals on his feet, hung his sharp sword across his shoulder, and took in his hand a spear of bronze. Then he went forth to where the council was being held in the open air, and two swift hounds went beside him.

The chief men of the land of Ithaca were gathered for the council. When all were there, the man who was oldest among them, the lord Aegyptus, rose up and spoke. "Never since Odysseus summoned us together before he took ship for the war of Troy have we met in council," said he. "Why have we been brought together now? Has someone heard tidings of the return of Odysseus?"

Telemachus rose up to speak and the herald put a staff into his hands as a sign that he was to be listened to with reverence. Telemachus then spoke, addressing the old lord Aegyptus.

---

toils: hard labors
raiment: clothing
summoned: called; sent for
reverence: great respect; honor

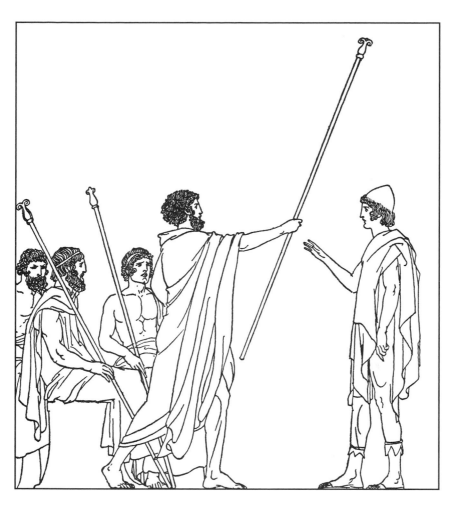

"I will tell you who it is," he said, "who has called the
men of Ithaca together in council, and for what purpose. I
have called you together, but not because I have had tidings
of the return of my father, the renowned Odysseus, nor
because I would speak to you about some affair of our
country. No. I would speak to you all because I suffer and
because I am at a loss. You have lost your king, but you can
put another king to rule over you. I have lost my father, and I
can have no other father in all my days. And that is not all
my loss, as I will show you now, men of Ithaca.

"For three years now my mother has been beset by men who come to woo her to be wife for one of them. Day after day they come to our house and kill and devour our beasts and waste the wine that was laid up against my father's return. They waste our goods and our wealth. If I were nearer manhood I would defend my house against them. But as yet I am not able to do it, and so I have to stand by and see our house and substance being destroyed."

So Telemachus spoke, and when his speech was ended Antinous, who was one of the suitors, rose up.

"Telemachus," said he, "why do you try to put us to shame in this way? It is not we but your mother who is to blame. We, knowing her husband Odysseus is no longer in life, have asked her to become the wife of one of us. She gives us no honest answer. Instead she has given her mind to a device to keep us still waiting. I will tell you of the council what this device is. The lady Penelope set up a great loom in her house and began to weave a wide web of cloth. To each of us she sent a message saying that when the web was woven, she would choose a husband from amongst us. 'Laertes, the father of Odysseus, is alone with none to care for him living or dead,' said she to us. 'I must weave a shroud for him against the time which cannot now be far off when old Laertes dies. Trouble me not while I do this. For if he should die and there be no winding-sheet to wrap him round, all the women of the land would blame me greatly.'

"We left the lady Penelope to weave the web, and the months have gone by and still the web is not woven. But

beset: troubled
device: a trick or scheme
shroud: a burial garment
against the time: to prepare for the time
winding-sheet: a cloth in which a dead body is wrapped

even now we have heard from one of her maids how Penelope tries to finish her task. What she weaves in the daytime she unravels at night. Never, then, can the web be finished and so does she try to cheat us.

"She has gained praise from the people for doing this. Let her be satisfied with their praise, then. We will live at her house and eat and drink there and give orders to her servants, and we shall see which will satisfy her best—to give an answer or to let the wealth of her house be wasted.

"As for you, Telemachus, I have these words to say to you. Lead your mother from your father's house and to the house of her father, Icarius. Tell Icarius to give her in marriage to the one she chooses from amongst us. Do this and no more goods will be wasted in the house that will be yours."

Then Telemachus rose and said, "Never will I lead my mother out of a house that my father brought her into. Quit my father's house, or, as I tell you now, the day may come when a doom will fall upon you there for your insolence in it."

And even as Telemachus spoke, two eagles from a mountain crest flew over the place where the council was being held. They wheeled above and flapped their wings and looked down upon the crowd with destruction in their gaze. They tore each other with their talons, and then flew away across the city.

An old man who was there, and skilled in the signs made by birds, told what was foreshown by the combat of the eagles in the air. "Odysseus," he said, "is not far from his friends. He will return, and his return will mean affliction for

---

quit: to leave
insolence: scornful disrespect
foreshown: foreshadowed; predicted
combat: fighting
affliction: suffering; great hardship

those who insult his house. Now let them make an end of their mischief." But the suitors only laughed at the old man, telling him he should go home and prophesy to his children.

Preparing to Embark

Telemachus went apart, and, going by himself, came to the shore of the sea. He dipped his hands into the seawater and prayed, saying, "O goddess Athena, who did come to my father's hall yesterday, I have tried to do as you bade me. But still the suitors of my mother hinder me from taking ship to seek tidings of my father."

Then he saw one who had the likeness of the wise old man, Mentor, coming towards him. But by the gray, clear, wonderfully-shining eyes, he knew that the figure was none other than the goddess Athena.

"Telemachus," said she, "I have seen in you something of the wisdom and the courage of Odysseus. Hear my counsel then, and do as I direct you. Go back to your father's house and be with the suitors for a time. And get together corn and barley-flour and wine in jars. And while you are doing all this I will gather together a crew for your ship. There are many ships in sea-girt Ithaca and I shall choose the best for you and we will rig her quickly and launch her on the wide deep."

When Telemachus heard her counsel he tarried no more but went back to the house and down into the treasure-vault.

---

prophesy: to predict something to come in the future
embark: to set out on a voyage; to board a ship
bade: commanded
hinder: to hold back; to get in the way of
counsel: advice
sea-girt: surrounded by the sea
tarried: waited; delayed

It was a spacious room filled with gold and bronze and chests of raiment and casks of wine. The doors of that vault were closed night and day. Eurycleia, who had been the nurse of Telemachus when he was little, guarded the place. She came to him, and he spoke to her:

"My nurse," said he, "none but yourself must know what I would do now, and you must swear not to speak of it to my lady-mother until twelve days from this. Fill twelve jars with wine for me now, and pour twelve measures of barley-meal into well-sewn skins. Leave them all together for me, and when my mother goes into the upper chamber, I shall have them carried away. Lo, nurse, I go to Sparta to seek tidings from Menelaus of Odysseus, my father."

When she heard him say this, the nurse Eurycleia lamented. "Ah, dear child," she cried, "how could you fare over wide seas and through strange lands, you who were

lamented: wailed; expressed great sorrow

never from your home? Stay here where you are well beloved. As for your father, he has long since perished among strangers—why should you put yourself in danger to find out that he is no more? Nay, do not go, Telemachus, but stay in your own house and in your own well-beloved country."

Telemachus said, "Dear nurse, it has been shown to me that I should go by a goddess. Is not that enough for you and for me? Now make all ready for me as I have asked you, and swear to me that you will say nothing of it to my mother until twelve days from this, or until she shall miss me herself."

Having sworn as he asked her, the nurse Eurycleia drew the wine into jars and put the barley-meal into the well-sewn skins. Telemachus left the vault and went back again into the hall. He sat with the suitors and listened to the minstrel sing about the going forth of Odysseus to the wars of Troy.

And while these things were happening the goddess Athena went through the town in the likeness of Telemachus. She went to this youth and that youth and told them of the voyage and asked them to make ready and go down to the beach where the boat would be. And then she went to a man called Noëmon, and begged him for a swift ship, and Noëmon gave it her.

When the sun sank and when the ways were darkened, Athena dragged the ship to where it should be launched and brought the tackling to it. The youths whom Athena had summoned—they were all of the age of Telemachus—came, and Athena roused them with talk of the voyage. And when the ship was ready she went to the house of Odysseus. Upon the suitors who were still in the hall she caused sleep to fall. They laid their heads upon the tables and slumbered beside

tackling: equipment

the wine cups. But Athena sent a whisper through the hall
and Telemachus heard and he rose up and came to where she
stood. Now she had on the likeness of old Mentor, the friend
of his father, Odysseus.

"Come," said she, "your friends are already at the oars.
We must not delay them."

They came to the ship, and Telemachus with a cheer
climbed into it. Then the youths loosed the ropes and sat

down at the benches to pull the oars. They set up the mast of pine, and they hauled up the sails, and a wind came and filled out the sails, and the ship dashed away. All night long Telemachus and his friends sat at the oars and under the sails, and felt the ship bearing them swiftly onward through the dark water.

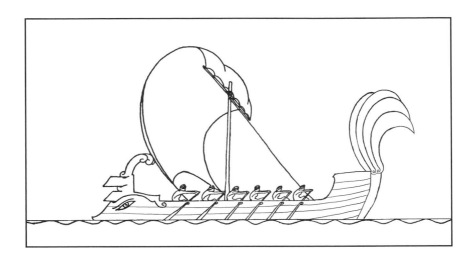

IN THE HALL OF MENELAUS

By sea and then by chariot Telemachus came to Sparta, to a country lying low amongst the hills. Telemachus stayed the chariot outside the gate of the king's dwelling.

To the king in his high hall came the steward. "Renowned Menelaus," said the steward, "there is a stranger outside, who has the look of a hero. What would you have me do with him? Shall I have his horses unyoked, bidding him enter the palace, or shall I let him fare on to another dwelling?"

---

stayed: stopped; halted
steward: person who manages a household
unyoked: freed from harnesses

"Why do you ask such a question?" said Menelaus in anger. "Have we not eaten the bread of other men on our wanderings, and have we not rested ourselves in other men's houses? Knowing this, you have no right to ask whether you should bid strangers enter or let them go past the gate of my dwelling. Go now and bid him enter and feast with us."

Then the steward went from the hall, and while he had servants unyoke the horses from the chariot, he led Telemachus into the palace. First he was brought to the bath, and when he had come from the bath refreshed, he was given a new cloak and mantle. When he had dressed he was led into the king's high hall. A maid brought water in a golden ewer and poured it over his hands into a silver basin. Then on a polished table the housedame placed bread and meat and wine upon it so that he might eat.

Menelaus came and said to Telemachus, "By your looks I know you to be of the line of kings. Eat now, and when you have refreshed yourself I will ask who you are and from what place you come."

But before the meal was finished, the lady Helen came into the high hall—Helen, for whom the kings and princes of Greece had gone to war. She watched Telemachus, and then the lady Helen said, "Menelaus, I am minded to tell you who this stranger is. No one was ever more like another than this youth is like great-hearted Odysseus. I know that he is no other than Telemachus, whom Odysseus left as a child, when, for my sake, the Greeks began their war against Troy."

Then Menelaus rose up and clasped the hand of Telemachus. "Never did there come to my house," said he, "a youth more welcome. For my sake did Odysseus endure

---

mantle: a loose sleeveless garment, worn over other clothing

much toil and many adventures. But Odysseus, I know, has not returned to his own land of Ithaca."

For many days Telemachus stayed in the house of King Menelaus. On the evening before he departed, Menelaus spoke to him of the famous deeds of his father, Odysseus.

"After we had taken and sacked King Priam's city," Menelaus concluded, "great troubles came upon us. Some of us sailed away, and some of us remained on the shore at the bidding of King Agamemnon, to make sacrifice to the gods. We separated, and the doom of death came to many of us.

"Of thy father, Telemachus, I have told thee what I myself have heard—how he stays on an island where the nymph Calypso holds him against his will: but where that island lies, I do not know. Odysseus is there, and he cannot return to his own country, seeing that he has no ship and no companions to help him make his way across the sea. But Odysseus was ever master of devices. And also he is favored greatly by the goddess, Pallas Athena. For these reasons, Telemachus, be hopeful that your father will yet reach his own home and country."

Later, Pallas Athena came to Menelaus where he lay in the vestibule of Menelaus's house. Telemachus was wakeful, thinking upon his father.

Athena stood before his bed and said to him, "Telemachus, no longer should you wander abroad, for the time has come

---

sacked: plundered; looted; took the valuables from a captured town in wartime

nymph: in mythology, a beautiful maiden that lived in the forest, trees, or water

Pallas Athena: another name used by the ancient Greeks for the goddess Athena

vestibule: the lobby or front hall of a building

when you should return. Come. Rouse Menelaus, and let him send you upon your way."

When Menelaus heard that his guest would depart, he told the lady Helen to bid the maids prepare a meal. He himself, with Helen his wife, went down into his treasure-chamber and brought forth gifts to Telemachus: a two-handled cup and a great mixing bowl of silver. And Helen took out of a chest a beautiful robe that she herself had made and embroidered. They came to Telemachus where he stood ready to depart. Then Menelaus gave him the beautiful cup and the great bowl of silver, and beautiful Helen came to him holding the embroidered robe.

"I too have a gift, dear child, for you," she said. "Bring this robe home and leave it in your mother's keeping. I want you to have it to give to your bride when you bring her into your father's halls."

Then were the horses yoked to the chariot and Telemachus bade farewell to Menelaus and Helen who had treated him so kindly. As Menelaus poured wine out of a golden cup as an offering to the gods, Telemachus prayed that he might find Odysseus, his father, in his home.

The son of Odysseus turned the horses towards the sea and drove the chariot to where his ship was anchored. Then Telemachus gathered his followers, and he bade them take on board the presents that Menelaus and Helen had given him.

They did this, and they raised the mast and the sails, and the rowers took their seats on the benches. A breeze came and the sails took it, and Telemachus and his companions sailed towards home. And all unknown to the youth, his father, Odysseus, was even then nearing his home.

PART 2:
A HERO'S RETURN

THE COMMAND TO CALYPSO

Ever mindful was Pallas Athena of Odysseus, although she might not help him openly because of a wrong he had done Poseidon, the god of the sea. But she spoke at the council of the gods, and she won from Zeus a pledge that Odysseus would now be permitted to return to his own land. On the day she went to Ithaca, and, as has been told, moved Telemachus to go on the voyage in search of his father—on that same day, Hermes, by the will of Zeus, went to the island where Odysseus was held by the nymph Calypso.

Beautiful indeed was that island. All round the cave where Calypso lived was a blossoming wood—alder, poplar and cypress trees were there, and on their branches roosted long-winged birds—falcons and owls and chattering sea-crows. Before the cave was a soft meadow in which thousands of violets bloomed. Four fountains gushed out of the ground and made clear streams through the grass. Across the cave grew a straggling vine, heavy with clusters of grapes. Calypso was within the cave, and as Hermes came near, he heard her singing one of her magic songs.

She was before a loom, weaving the threads with a golden shuttle. Now she knew Hermes and was pleased to see him on her island. But as soon as he spoke of Odysseus and how it was the will of Zeus that he should be permitted to leave the island, her song ceased.

---

mindful: aware of; thinking about
straggling: wandering

"Woe to me," she said, "and woe to any immortal who loves a mortal. I do not hold him here because I hate Odysseus, but because I love him greatly, and would have him dwell with me here. More than this, Hermes, I would make him an immortal so that he would know neither old age nor death."

"He does not desire to be freed from old age and death," said Hermes. "He desires to return to his own land and to live with his dear wife, Penelope, and his son, Telemachus. And Zeus, the greatest of the gods, commands that you let him go upon his way."

"I have no ship to give him," said Calypso, "and I have no company of men to help him to cross the sea."

"He must leave the island and cross the sea—Zeus commands it," Hermes said.

"I must help him to make his way across the sea if it must be so," Calypso said. Then she bowed her head and Hermes went from her.

Straightway Calypso left her cave and went down to the sea. By the shore Odysseus stayed, looking across the wide sea with tears in his eyes.

She came to him and she said, "Be not sorrowful any more, Odysseus. The time has come when you may depart from my island. Come now, I will show how I can help you on your way."

She brought him to the side of the island where great trees grew and she put in his hands a double-edged axe and an adze. Then Odysseus started to hew down the timber. Twenty trees he felled with his axe of bronze, and he smoothed them and made straight the line. Calypso came to him at the dawn of the next day. She brought augers for boring and he made the beams fast. He built a raft, making it very broad, and set a mast upon it and fixed a rudder to guide it. Calypso wove him a web of cloth for sails.

On the fifth day Calypso gave him garments for the journey and brought provision to the raft—two skins of wine, a great skin of water, corn, and many dainties. She showed Odysseus how to guide his course by the star that some call

straightway: right away; immediately
adze: a tool used for cutting, similar to an ax
hew: to cut
augers: tools used to bore holes
fast: tightly attached
dainties: delicacies; fine and pleasing foods

the Bear, and she bade farewell to him. He took his place on the raft and sailed away from the island where Calypso had held him for so long.

But not easily or safely did he make his way across the sea. The winds blew upon his raft and the waves dashed against it. A fierce blast came and broke the mast in the middle. The sail fell into the deep. Then Odysseus was flung down on the bottom of the raft. For a long time he lay there overwhelmed by the water that broke over him. The winds drove the raft to and fro—the South wind tossed it to the North to bear along, and the East wind tossed it to the West to chase.

Then a great wave came and shattered the raft. He held himself on a single beam as one holds himself on a horse, and then he threw himself into the waves. For two nights and

two days he was tossed about on the waters. When on the third day the dawn came and the winds fell, he saw land very near. A great wave took hold of him and flung him towards the shore.

At last he saw the mouth of a river. He swam towards it until he felt its stream flowing through the water of the sea. The river water was smooth for his swimming, and he came safely to a place where he might land, but with his flesh swollen and streams of salt water gushing from his mouth and nostrils. He lay on the ground without breath or speech, swooning with the terrible weariness that was upon him. But in a while his breath came back to him and his courage rose.

He went from the cold of the river up to the woods, and he found two olive trees growing side by side, twining together so that they made a shelter against the winds. He went and lay between them upon a bed of leaves, and with leaves he covered himself over. Sleep came on him, and at last he rested from perils and toils.

Nausicaa

And while he rested, Pallas Athena went to the city of the Phaeacians, to whose land Odysseus had now come. She came to the palace of the king, and, passing through all the doors, came to the chamber where the king's daughter, Nausicaa, slept. She entered into Nausicaa's dream, appearing as one of her girl-comrades. And in the dream she spoke to the princess:

"Nausicaa," she said, "the garments of your household are all uncared for, and the time is near when, more than ever,

swooning: fainting
twining: twisting

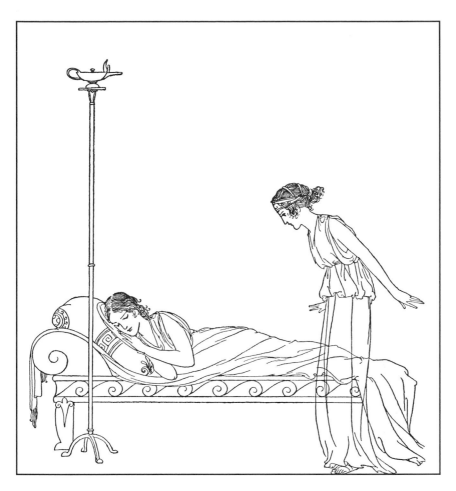

you have need to have much and beautiful raiment. Your marriage day will be soon. You will have to have many garments ready by that time—garments to bring with you to your husband's house, and garments to give to those who will attend you at your wedding. There is much to be done, Nausicaa. Be ready at the break of day, and take your maidens with you, and bring the garments of your household to the river to be washed. Beg your father to give you a wagon with mules to carry all the garments to be washed."

Nausicaa, when she rose, thought upon her dream, and she went through the palace and found her father. He was going to the assembly of the Phaeacians. She came to him, but she was shy about speaking of that which had been in her dream—her marriage day—since her parents had not spoken to her about such a thing. Saying that she was going to the river to wash the garments of the household, she asked for a wagon and for mules.

Her father smiled on her and said, "The mules and wagon you may have, Nausicaa, and the servants shall get them ready now."

Then Nausicaa gathered her maids together and they brought the soiled garments of the household to the wagon. And her mother, so that Nausicaa and her maids might eat while they were from home, put in a basket filled with dainties and a skin of wine. Also she gave them a jar of olive oil so that they might rub themselves with oil when bathing in the river.

Young Nausicaa herself drove the wagon. She mounted it and took the whip in her hands and started the mules, and they went through fields and by farms and came to the riverbank.

The girls brought the garments to the stream, and leaving them in the shallow parts trod them with their bare feet. When they had washed the garments they took them to the seashore and left them on the clean pebbles to dry in the sun. Then Nausicaa and her companions went into the river and bathed and sported in the water.

When they had bathed they sat down and ate the meal that had been put on the wagon for them. The garments were not yet dried and Nausicaa called on her companions to play.

assembly: gathering; meeting

They took a ball and threw it from one to the other, each singing a song that went with the game. Nausicaa threw the ball, and the girl whose turn it was to catch missed it. The ball went into the river and was carried down the stream. At that they all raised a cry. It was this cry that woke up Odysseus who, covered over with leaves, was then sleeping in the shelter of the two olive trees.

He crept out from under the thicket, and when he saw the girls in the meadow he wanted to go to them to beg for their help. But when they looked on him they were terribly frightened and they ran this way and that way and hid themselves. Only Nausicaa stood still, for Pallas Athena had taken fear from her mind.

Odysseus stood a little way from her and spoke to her in a beseeching voice. "I beg you, lady, to help me in my bitter need. I would kneel and clasp your knees, only I fear your anger. Have pity upon me. Yesterday was the twentieth day that I was upon the sea, driven hither and thither by the waves and the winds."

And still Nausicaa stood, and Odysseus looking upon her was filled with reverence, so noble she seemed. "I know not as I look upon you," he said, "whether you are a goddess or a mortal maiden. O lady, I know that you will be gracious to me. Show me the way to the town. Give me an old garment to cast about me. And may the gods grant your wish and heart's desire—a noble husband who will cherish you."

She spoke to him as a princess should, seeing that in spite of the sore plight he was in, he was a man of worth.

beseeching: begging; pleading
gracious: kind; merciful
cast: to throw
sore: causing pain; full of difficulty
plight: a difficult situation

"Stranger," she said, "since you have come to our land, you shall not lack for raiment nor aught else that is given to a suppliant. I will show you the way to the town also."

He asked what land he was in. "This, stranger," she said, "is the land of the Phaeacians, and Alcinous is king over them. And I am the king's daughter, Nausicaa."

Then she called to her companions. "Do not hide yourselves," she said. "This is not an enemy, but a helpless and an unfriended man."

The girls came back and they brought Odysseus to a sheltered place and they made him sit down and laid a garment beside him. One brought the jar of olive oil that he might clean himself when he bathed in the river. And Odysseus was very glad to get this oil, for his back and shoulders were all crusted over with flakes of brine. He went into the river and bathed and rubbed himself with the oil. Then he put on the garment that had been brought him. So well he looked that when he came towards them again the princess said to the maids, "Look now on the man who a while ago seemed so terrifying! He is most handsome and stately. Now, my maidens, bring the stranger meat and drink."

They served him with meat and drink and he ate and drank eagerly, for it was long since he had tasted food. And while he ate, Nausicaa and her companions went down to the seashore and gathered the garments that were now dried, singing songs the while.

When they were ready to go, Nausicaa went to Odysseus and said to him, "Stranger, if you would make your way into the city, come with us now, so that we may guide you. But

aught: anything
suppliant: a person in need who humbly asks for help or charity
brine: salty water

first listen to what I would say. While we are going through the fields and by the farms, walk you behind, keeping near the wagon. But when we enter the ways of the city, go no further with us. People might speak unkindly of me if they saw me with a stranger such as you. They might say, 'Who does Nausicaa bring to her father's house? Someone she would like to make her husband, most likely.' So that we may not meet with such rudeness I would have you come alone to my father's house."

So Nausicaa bade him. Then she touched the mules with the whip and the wagon went on, as Odysseus walked with the maids behind.

In the Hall of Alcinous

In the city, Odysseus met one who showed him the way to the palace of King Alcinous. Odysseus stood before the threshold of bronze and many thoughts were in his mind. But at last with a prayer to Zeus he crossed the threshold and went through the great hall.

Now on that evening the captains and the councilors of the Phaeacians sat with the king. Odysseus passed by them, and went where Arete, the queen, sat. And he knelt before her and clasped her knees with his hands and spoke to her in supplication: "Arete, Queen! May the gods give all who are here a happy life. I have come to beg that you would put me on my way to my own land, for long have I suffered sore affliction far from my friends."

Then, having spoken, Odysseus went and sat down in the ashes of the hearth with his head bowed. No one spoke for

threshold: entry point to a room; doorsill; plank or slab under a door
supplication: the act of humbly asking for help or charity

long. Then an aged councilor who was there spoke to the king. "O Alcinous," he said, "it is not right that a stranger should sit in the ashes by thy hearth. Bid the stranger rise, and let a chair be given him and supper set before him."

Then Alcinous took Odysseus by the hand, and raised him from where he sat, and bade his son give place to him. He sat on a chair inlaid with silver and the housedame brought him bread and wine and dainties. He ate, and King Alcinous spoke to the company and said, "Tomorrow I shall call you together and we will entertain this stranger with a feast in our halls, and we shall take counsel to see in what way we can convey him to his own land."

On the morrow, a bath was prepared for Odysseus, and he entered it and was glad of the warm water, for not since he had left the island of Calypso had he had a warm bath. He came from the bath and put on the beautiful raiment that had been given him and he walked through the hall, looking a king among men.

Now the maiden, Nausicaa, stood by a pillar as he passed, and she knew that she had never looked upon a man who was more splendid. She had thought that the stranger whom she had saved would have stayed in her father's house, and that one day he would be her husband. But now she knew that by no means would he abide in the land of the Phaeacians.

As he passed by, she spoke to him and said, "Farewell, O stranger! And when you are in your own country, think sometimes of me, Nausicaa, who helped you."

Odysseus took her hand and said to her, "Farewell, daughter of King Alcinous! May Zeus grant that I may return

---

on the morrow: the next day
abide: to stay in a place

to my own land. There every day shall I pay homage to my
memory of you, to whom I owe my life."

He passed on and he came to where the princes and
captains and councilors of the Phaeacians sat. His seat was
beside the king's. Then the minstrel, blind Demodocus, was
led in, and placed on a seat by a pillar. To him the gods had
given a good and an evil fortune—the gift of song with the
lack of sight. And when supper was served, Odysseus sent to
Demodocus a portion of his own meat. He spoke to the
minstrel, saying, "I would ask if you can sing of the Wooden
Horse that brought destruction to the Trojans. If you can, I

pay homage: express great respect and honor
fortune: fate; destiny

shall be a witness amongst all men how the gods have surely given you the gift of song."

Demodocus took down the lyre and sang. His song told how one part of the Greeks sailed away in their ships, while others with Odysseus were now in the center of Priam's city, all hidden in the great Wooden Horse which the Trojans themselves had dragged across their broken wall. Then the minstrel sang of how Odysseus and his comrades poured forth from the hollow of the horse and took the city.

As the minstrel sang, the heart of Odysseus melted within him and tears fell down his cheeks. None of the company saw him weeping except Alcinous the king. But the king cried out, "Let the minstrel cease, for there is one amongst us to whom his song is not pleasing. Ever since it began the stranger here has wept with tears flowing down his cheeks."

The minstrel ceased, and all the company looked in surprise at Odysseus, who sat with his head bowed and his mantle wrapped around his head. Why did he weep? No one had asked of him his name, for each knew it was more noble to serve a stranger without knowing his name.

Said the king, speaking again, "You are as a brother to us, O unknown guest. But will you not be brotherly to us? Tell us by what name they call you in your own land. Tell us, too, of your land and your city. And tell us where you were borne on your wanderings, and to what lands and peoples you came. As a brother tell us why you weep and mourn in spirit over the tale of the going forth of the Greeks to the war of Troy. Did you have a kinsman who fell before Priam's city? Or did you have a loving friend who fell there?"

---

lyre: a musical instrument like a small harp
borne: carried; directed

ODYSSEUS TELLS HIS TALE

Then Odysseus spoke before the company and said, "O Alcinous, famous king, it is good to listen to a minstrel such as Demodocus. And as for me, I know of no greater delight than when men feast together with open hearts, and when a minstrel sings them noble songs. This seems to me to be happiness indeed. But you have asked me to speak of my wanderings and my toils. Ah, where can I begin that tale? For the gods have given me more woes than a man can speak of!

"But first of all I will declare to you my name and my country. I am Odysseus, son of Laertes, and my land is Ithaca. And now I will tell you, king, and tell the princes and captains and councilors of the Phaeacians, the tale of my wanderings.

"The wind bore my ships from the coast of Troy, with our white sails hoisted. We should soon have come to our own country, all unhurt, but the north wind came and swept us from our course and drove us wandering.

"Then for nine days we were borne onward by terrible winds, and away from all known lands. On the tenth day we came to a strange country. Many of my men landed there. The people of that land were harmless and friendly, but the land itself was most dangerous. For there grew there the honey-sweet fruit of the lotus that makes all men forgetful of their past and neglectful of their future. And those of my men who ate the lotus that the dwellers of that land offered them became forgetful of their country and of the way before them. They wanted to abide forever in the land of the lotus. They wept when they thought of all the toils before them and

hoisted: raised
neglectful: not paying attention

103

of all they had endured. I led them back to the ships, and I had to place them beneath the benches and leave them in bonds. Then, when I had got all my men upon the ships, we made haste to sail away.

"Later we came to the land of the Cyclopes, a giant people. There is an empty island outside the harbor of their land, and on it there is a well of bright water that has poplars

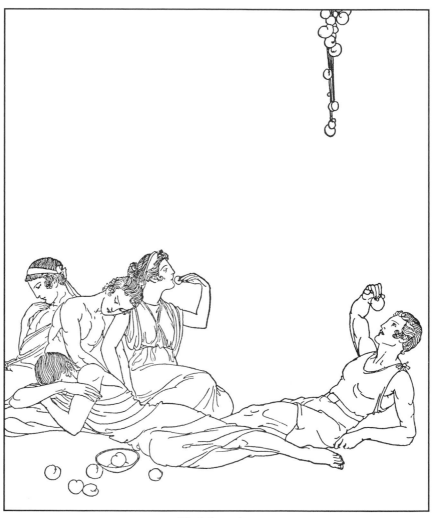

The lotus-eaters

growing round it. We came to that empty island, and we beached our ships and took down our sails.

"As soon as the dawn came we went through the island, starting the wild goats that were there in flocks, and shooting them with our arrows. We killed so many wild goats there that we had nine for each ship. Afterwards we looked across to the land of the Cyclopes, and we heard the sound of voices and saw the smoke of fires and heard the bleating of flocks of sheep and goats.

"I called my companions together and I said, 'It would be well for some of us to go to that other island. With my own ship and the men on it, I shall go there. The rest of you abide here. I will find out what manner of men live there, and whether they will treat us kindly and give us gifts that are due to strangers—gifts of provisions for our voyage.'

"We embarked and we came to the land. There was a cave near the sea, and round the cave there were mighty flocks of sheep and goats. I took twelve men with me and I left the rest to guard the ship. We went into the cave and found no man there. There were baskets filled with cheeses, and vessels of whey, and pails and bowls of milk. My men wanted me to take some of the cheeses and drive off some of the lambs and kids and come away. But this I would not do, for I would rather that he who owned the stores would give us of his own free will the offerings due to strangers.

"While we were in the cave, he whose dwelling it was returned to it. He carried on his shoulder a great pile of wood for his fire. Never in our lives did we see a creature so frightful as this Cyclops was. He was a giant, and, what made him terrible to behold, he had but one eye, and that single eye was in his forehead. He cast down on the ground

---

provisions: necessary supplies, such as food and water

the pile of wood that he carried, making such a din that we fled in terror into the corners and recesses of the cave. Next he drove his flocks into the cave and began to milk his ewes and goats. And when he had the flocks within, he took up a stone that not all our strengths could move, and set it as a door to the mouth of the cave.

"The Cyclops kindled his fire, and when it blazed up he saw us in the corners and recesses. He spoke to us. Our hearts were shaken with terror at the sound of his deep voice.

"I spoke to him saying that we were Agamemnon's men on our way home from the taking of Priam's city, and I begged him to deal with us kindly, for the sake of Zeus who is ever in the company of strangers and suppliants. But he answered me saying, 'We Cyclopes pay no heed to Zeus, nor to any of the gods. In our strength and our power we deem that we are mightier than they. I will not spare you, neither will I give you aught for the sake of Zeus, but only as my own spirit bids me. And first I would have you tell me how you came to our land.'

"I knew it would be better not to let the Cyclops know that my ship and my companions were at the harbor of the island. Therefore I spoke to him guilefully, telling him that my ship had been broken on the rocks, and that I and the men with me were the only ones who had escaped utter doom.

"I begged again that he would deal with us as just men deal with strangers and suppliants, but he, without saying a word, laid hands upon two of my men, and swinging them by the legs, dashed their brains out on the earth. He cut them to pieces and ate them before our very eyes. We wept and we prayed to Zeus as we witnessed a deed so terrible.

---

din: a loud ongoing noise; a clamor
recesses: hidden parts
guilefully: with cunning or trickery

"Next the Cyclops stretched himself among his sheep and went to sleep beside the fire. Then I debated whether I should take my sharp sword in my hand, and feeling where his heart was, stab him there. But second thoughts held me back from doing this. I might be able to kill him as he slept, but not even with my companions could I roll away the great stone that closed the mouth of the cave.

"Dawn came, and the Cyclops awakened, kindled his fire, and milked his flocks. Then he seized two others of my men and made ready for his mid-day meal. And now he rolled away the great stone and drove his flocks out of the cave.

"I had pondered on a way of escape, and I had thought of something that might be done to baffle the Cyclops. I had with me a great skin of sweet wine, and I thought that if I could make him drunk with wine, I and my companions might overcome him. But there were other preparations to be made first. On the floor of the cave there was a great beam of olive wood which the Cyclops had cut to make a club. It was yet green. I and my companions went and cut off a fathom's length of the wood, and sharpened it to a point and took it to the fire and hardened it in the glow. Then I hid the beam in a recess of the cave.

"The Cyclops came back in the evening, and opening up the cave drove in his flocks. Then he closed the cave again with the stone and went and milked his ewes and his goats. Again he seized two of my companions. I went to the terrible creature with a bowl of wine in my hands. He took it and drank it and cried out, 'Give me another bowl of this, and tell me your name that I may give you gifts for bringing me this honey-tasting drink.'

"Again I spoke to him guilefully and said, 'Noman is my name. Noman my father and my mother call me.'

"'Give me more of the drink, Noman,' he shouted. 'And the gift that I shall give is that I shall make you the last of your fellows to be eaten.'

"I gave him wine again, and when he had taken the third bowl he sank backwards with his face upturned, and sleep came upon him. Then I, with four companions, took that beam of olive wood, now made into a hard and pointed

pondered: thought deeply
fathom: a unit of six feet, usually used to measure the depth of water

108

stake, and thrust it into the ashes of the fire. When the pointed end began to glow we drew it out of the flame. Then I and my companions laid hold on the great stake and, dashing at the Cyclops, thrust it into his eye. He raised a terrible cry that made the rocks ring and we dashed away into the recesses of the cave.

"His cries brought other Cyclopes to the mouth of the cave, and they, naming him as Polyphemus, called out and asked him what ailed him. 'Noman,' he shrieked out, 'Noman is slaying me by guile.' They answered him saying, 'If no man is slaying you, there is nothing we can do for you, Polyphemus.' Saying this, they went away from the mouth of the cave without attempting to move away the stone.

"Polyphemus then, groaning with pain, rolled away the stone and sat before the mouth of the cave with his hands outstretched, thinking that he would catch us as we dashed out. I showed my companions how we might pass by him. I laid hands on certain rams of the flock and I lashed three of them together. Then on the middle ram I put a man of my company. Thus every three rams carried a man. As soon as the dawn had come the rams hastened out to the pasture, and, as they passed, Polyphemus laid hands on the first and the third of each three that went by. They passed out and Polyphemus did not guess that the ram he did not touch carried out a man.

"For myself, I took a ram that was the strongest and fleeciest of the whole flock and I placed myself under him, clinging to the wool of his belly. As this ram, the best of all his flock, went by, Polyphemus, laying his hands upon him, said, 'Would that you, the best of my flock, were endowed

lashed: tied together with some kind of cord
endowed: naturally provided

with speech, so that you might tell me where Noman, who has blinded me, has hidden himself.' The ram went by him, and when he had gone a little way from the cave I loosed myself from him and went and set my companions free.

"We gathered together many of Polyphemus's sheep and we drove them down to our ship. The men we had left behind would have wept when they heard what had happened to six of their companions. But I bade them take on board the sheep we had brought and pull the ship away from that land. Then when we had drawn a certain distance from

the shore I could not forbear to shout my taunts into the cave of Polyphemus. 'Cyclops,' I cried, "you thought that you had the company of a fool and a weakling to eat. But your evil deeds have been punished.'

"So I shouted, and Polyphemus came to the mouth of the cave with great anger in his heart. He took up rocks and cast them at the ship and they fell before the prow. The men bent to the oars and pulled the ship away or it would have been broken by the rocks he cast. And when we were farther away I shouted to him, 'Cyclops, if any man should ask who it was set his mark upon you, say that he was Odysseus, the son of Laertes.'

"Then I heard Polyphemus cry out, 'I call upon Poseidon, the god of the sea, whose son I am, to avenge me upon you, Odysseus. I call upon Poseidon to grant that you, Odysseus, may never come to your home, or if the gods have ordained your return, that you come to it after much toil and suffering, in an evil plight and in a stranger's ship, to find sorrow in your home.'

"So Polyphemus prayed, and, to my evil fortune, Poseidon heard his prayer. But we went on in our ship rejoicing at our escape. We came to the island where my other ships were. All the company rejoiced to see us, although they had to mourn for their six companions slain by Polyphemus. We divided among the ships the sheep we had taken from Polyphemus's flock and we sacrificed to the gods. At the dawn of the next day we raised the sails on each ship and we sailed away."

---

forbear: to hold back from doing something
taunts: insults; sarcastic challenges
avenge: to get revenge for; to get even for
ordained: decreed or ordered beforehand

Odysseus Tells of Aeolus and Circe

"We came to the island where Aeolus, the Lord of the Winds, he who can give mariners a good or a bad wind, has his dwelling. The Lord of the Winds treated us kindly and kept us at his dwelling for a month. When the time came for us to leave, Aeolus gave a bag made from the hide of an ox, and in that bag were all the winds that blow. He made the mouth of the bag fast with a silver cord, so that no wind that might drive us from our course could escape. Then he sent the West Wind to blow on our sails that we might reach our own land as quickly as a ship might go.

"For nine days we sailed with the West Wind driving us, and on the tenth day we came in sight of Ithaca, our own land. We saw its coast and the beacon fires upon the coast and the people tending the fires. Then I thought that the curse of the Cyclops was vain and could bring no harm to us. Sleep, which I had kept from me for long, I let weigh me down, and I no longer kept watch.

"Then even as I slept, the misfortune that I had watched against fell upon me. For now my men spoke together and said, 'There is our native land, and we come back to it after ten years' struggles and toils, with empty hands. But our lord Odysseus brings gold and silver from Priam's treasure-chamber in Troy. And Aeolus too has given him a treasure in an ox-hide bag. Let us take something out of that bag while he sleeps.'

"So they spoke, and they unloosed the mouth of the bag, and behold! all the winds that were tied in it burst out. Then the winds drove our ship towards the high seas and away

---

mariners: sailors; sea travelers
fast: closed tightly
vain: useless

from our land. What became of the other ships I know not. I awoke and I found that we were being driven here and there by the winds.

"The winds brought us back again to the floating island of Aeolus. We landed and I went to the dwelling of the Lord of the Winds. 'How now, Odysseus?' said he. 'How is it you have returned so soon? Did I not give you a fair wind to take you to your own country, and did I not tie up all the winds that might be contrary to you?'

"'My evil companions,' I said, 'have undone all the good that you did for me, O King of the Winds. They opened the bag and let all the winds fly out. And now help me, Aeolus, once again.'

"But Aeolus said to me, 'Far be it from me to help such a man as you—a man surely accursed by the gods. Go from my island, for nothing will I do for you.' Then I went from his dwelling and took my way down to the ship.

"We sailed away with heavy hearts. Next we came to the island where we met with Circe, the Enchantress. For two days and two nights we were on that island without seeing any sign of a habitation. On the third day I saw smoke rising up from some hearth. I spoke of it to my men, and it seemed good to us that part of our company should go to see if there were people there who might help us. We drew lots to find out who should go, and it fell to the lot of Eurylochus to go with part of the company, while I remained with the other part.

"So Eurylochus went with two and twenty men. In the forest glades they came upon a house built of polished stones. All round that house wild beasts roamed—wolves

habitation: a dwelling; a home
glades: open spaces in the woods

and lions. But these beasts were not fierce. As Eurylochus and his men went towards the house, the lions and wolves fawned upon them like house dogs.

"But the men were frightened and stood round the outer gate of the court. They heard a voice within the house singing, and it seemed to them to be the voice of a woman, singing as she went to and fro before a web she was weaving on a loom. The men shouted, and she who had been singing opened the polished doors and came out of the dwelling. She was very fair to see. As she opened the doors of the house she asked the men to come within and they went into her halls.

"But Eurylochus tarried behind. He watched the woman and he saw her give food to the men. But he saw that she mixed a potion with what she gave them to eat and with the wine she gave them to drink. No sooner had they eaten the food and drunk the wine than she struck them with a wand, and behold! the men turned into swine. Then the woman drove them out of the house and put them in the swine-pens and gave them acorns to eat.

"When he saw these happenings, Eurylochus ran back through the forest and told me all. Then I cast about my shoulder my good sword of bronze, and, bidding Eurylochus stay by the ships, I went through the forest and came to the house of the enchantress. I stood at the outer court and called out. Then Circe the Enchantress flung wide the shining doors, and called to me to come within. I entered her dwelling and she brought me to a chair and put a footstool under my feet. Then she brought me in a golden cup the wine into which she had cast a harmful potion.

---

fawned upon: showed affection in an eager, obedient way
swine: pigs; hogs; boars

"As she handed me the cup I drew my sword and sprang at her as one eager to slay her. She shrank back from me and cried out, 'Who are you who are able to guess at my enchantments? Verily, you must be Odysseus, of whom Hermes told me. Nay, put up your sword and let us two be friendly to each other. In all things I will treat you kindly.'

"But I said to her, 'Nay, Circe, you must swear to me first that you will not treat me guilefully.'

enchantments: magic spells
verily: truly

"She swore by the gods that she would not treat me guilefully, and I put up my sword. Then the handmaidens of Circe prepared a bath, and I bathed and rubbed myself with olive oil, and Circe gave me a new mantle and doublet. The handmaidens brought out silver tables, and on them set golden baskets with bread and meat in them, and others brought cups of honey-tasting wine. I sat before a silver table but I had no pleasure in the food before me.

"When Circe saw me sitting silent and troubled she said, 'Why, Odysseus, do you sit like a speechless man? Do you think there is a drug in this food? But I have sworn that I will not treat you guilefully, and that oath I shall keep.'

"And I said to her, 'O Circe, Enchantress, what man of good heart could take meat and drink while his companions are as swine in swine-pens? If you would have me eat and drink, first let me see my companions in their own forms.'

"Circe, when she heard me say this, went to the swine-pen and anointed each of the swine with a charm. As she did, the bristles dropped away and my companions became men again, and were even taller and handsomer than they had been before.

"After that we lived on Circe's island in friendship with the enchantress. She did not treat us guilefully again and we feasted in her house for a year.

"But in all of us there was a longing to return to our own land. And my men came to me and craved that I should ask Circe to let us go on our homeward way. She gave us leave to go and she told us of the many dangers we should meet on our voyage."

doublet: jacket
anointed: put an oil or ointment on

"**W**hen the sun sank and darkness came on, my men went to lie by the hawsers of the ship. Then Circe the Enchantress took my hand, and told me of the voyage that was before us.

"'To the Sirens first you shall come,' said she, 'to the Sirens, who sit in their field of flowers and bewitch all men who come near them. He who comes near the Sirens without knowing their ways and hears the sound of their voices— never again shall that man see wife or child, or have joy of his homecoming. All round where the Sirens sit are great heaps of the bones of men. But I will tell you, Odysseus, how you may pass them.

"'When you come near put wax over the ears of your company lest any of them hear the Sirens' song. But if you yourself would hear them, have your men bind you hand and foot to the mast. And if you beseech them to loose you, then must they bind you with tighter bonds. When your companions have driven the ship past where the Sirens sing, then you can be unbound.

"'Past where the Sirens sit there is a dangerous place indeed. On one side there are great rocks which the gods call the Wandering Rocks. No ship ever escapes that goes that way. And round these rocks the planks of ships and the bodies of men are tossed by waves of the sea and storms of fire. One ship only ever passed that way, Jason's ship, the *Argo*, and that ship would have been broken on the rocks if Hera the goddess had not helped it to pass, because of her love for the hero Jason.

---

hawsers: large ropes for towing or tying a ship
lest: for fear that
Jason: hero of Greek mythology who went in search of the Golden Fleece

"'On the other side of the Wandering Rocks are two peaks through which you will have to take your ship. In the middle of one peak there is a cave, and that cave is the den of a monster named Scylla. This monster has six necks and on each neck there is a hideous head. She holds her heads over the gulf, seeking for prey and yelping horribly. No ship has ever passed that way without Scylla seizing and carrying off the body of a man in each mouth of her six heads.

"'Out of the other peak a fig tree grows, and below that fig tree Charybdis has her den. She sits there sucking down the water and spouting it forth. May you not be near when she sucks the water down, for then nothing could save you. Keep nearer to Scylla's than to Charybdis's rock. It is better to lose six of your company than to lose your ship and all your men. Keep near Scylla's rock and drive right on.

"'If you should pass the deadly rocks guarded by Scylla and Charybdis, you will come to the island where the Cattle of the Sun graze. Do no hurt to those herds. If you hurt them, I foresee ruin for your ship and your men, even though you yourself should escape.'

"So Circe spoke to me, and having told me such things, she took her way up the island. Then I went to the ship and roused my men. Speedily they went aboard and struck the water with their oars. Then the sails were hoisted and a breeze came and we sailed away from the Isle of Circe, the Enchantress.

"I told my companions what Circe had told me about the Sirens. I took a great piece of wax and broke it and kneaded it until it was soft. Then I covered the ears of my men, and they bound me upright to the mast of the ship. The wind dropped and the sea became calm as though a god had stilled the waters. My company took their oars and pulled

kneaded: pressed and squeezed with the hands

away. When the ship was within a man's shout from the land, the Sirens spied us and raised their song.

"'Come hither, come hither, O Odysseus,' the Sirens sang. 'We know all things—all the travail the Greeks had in the war of Troy, and we know all that hereafter shall be upon the earth. Odysseus, Odysseus, come to our field of flowers, and hear the song that we shall sing to you.'

"My heart was mad to listen to the Sirens. I nodded my head to the company commanding them to unloose me, but they bound me the tighter, and bent to their oars and rowed on. When we had gone past the place of the Sirens, the men took the wax from their ears and loosed me from the mast.

"But no sooner had we passed than I saw smoke rising and heard the roaring of the sea. My company threw down their oars in terror. I went among them to hearten them. I told them nothing of the monster Scylla, lest the fear of her should break their hearts. And now we began to drive through that narrow strait. On one side was Scylla and on the other Charybdis. Fear gripped the men when they saw Charybdis gulping down the sea. But as we drove by, the monster Scylla seized six of my company—the hardiest of the men who were with me. As they were lifted up in the mouths of her six heads, they called to me in their agony. But I could do nothing to aid them. They were carried up to be devoured in the monster's den. Of all the sights I have seen on the ways of the water, that sight was the most pitiful.

"Having passed the rocks of Scylla and Charybdis, we came to the island of the Cattle of the Sun. I spoke to my company and told them that we should drive past that island and not venture to go upon it.

---

travail: hard, painful work
venture: to undertake or proceed in something risky

"The hearts of my men were broken at that sentence, and Eurylochus answered me, speaking sadly: 'It is easy for you, O Odysseus, to speak like that, for you are never weary, and you have strength beyond measure. But is your heart of iron that you will not allow your companions to set foot upon shore where they may rest themselves from the sea and prepare their supper at their ease?'

"So Eurylochus spoke and the rest of the company joined in what he said. Their force was greater than mine. Then said I, 'Swear to me a mighty oath, one and all of you, that if we go upon this island none of you will slay the cattle out of any herd.'

"They swore the oath that I gave them. We landed near a spring of fresh water, and the men got their supper ready. Having eaten their supper they fell to weeping, for they thought upon their comrades that Scylla had devoured. Then they slept.

"The dawn came, but we found that we could not take our ship out of the harbor, for the North Wind and the East Wind blew a hurricane. So we stayed upon the island and the days and the weeks went by. When the corn we had brought in the ship was all eaten the men went through the island, fishing and hunting, but they got little to stay their hunger.

"One day while I slept, Eurylochus gave the men a most evil counsel. 'Every death,' he said, 'is hateful to man, but death by hunger is by far the worst. Rather than die of hunger let us drive off the best cattle from the herds of the Sun. Then, if the gods would wreck us on the sea for the deed, let them do it. I would rather perish on the waves than die in the pangs of hunger.'

"So he spoke, and the rest of the men approved of what he said. They slaughtered the Cattle of the Sun and roasted their flesh. It was then that I awakened from my sleep. As I came down to the ship the smell of the roasting flesh came to me. Then I knew that a terrible deed had been committed and that a dreadful thing would befall all of us.

"For six days my company feasted on the best of the cattle. On the seventh day the winds ceased to blow. Then we went to the ship and set up the mast and the sails and fared out again on the deep.

"But, having left that island, no other land appeared, and only sky and sea were to be seen. A cloud stayed always above our ship and beneath that cloud the sea was darkened. The West Wind came in a rush, and the mast broke, and, in breaking, struck off the head of the pilot, and he fell straight down into the sea. A thunderbolt struck the ship and the men were swept from the deck. Never a man of my company did I see again.

"The South Wind came and it drove the ship back toward the terrible rocks of Scylla and Charybdis. All night long I was borne on, and, at the rising of the sun, I found myself near Charybdis. My ship was sucked down. But I caught the branches of the fig tree that grew out of the rock and hung to it like a bat. There I stayed until the timbers of my ship were cast up again by Charybdis. I dropped down on them. Sitting on the boards I rowed with my hands and passed the rock of Scylla without the monster seeing me.

"Then for nine days I was borne along by the waves, and on the tenth day I came to the island where the nymph Calypso dwells. She took me to her dwelling and treated me kindly. But why tell the remainder of my toils? To you, O king, and to thy noble wife, I told how I came from Calypso's Island, and I am not one to repeat a plain-told tale."

"I caught the branches of the fig tree that grew out of the rock."

THE RETURN TO ITHACA

Odysseus finished, and the company in the hall sat silent, like men enchanted. Then King Alcinous spoke and said, "Tomorrow we will give you a ship and an escort, and we will land you in Ithaca, your own country." The princes, captains, and councilors, marveling that they had met the renowned Odysseus, went each to his own home. When the dawn came, each carried gifts for Odysseus down to the ship on which he was to sail.

When the sun was near its setting, Odysseus said, "Farewell to you, O queen! May you long rejoice in your house and your children, and in your husband, Alcinous, the renowned king."

He went aboard the ship, and straightway the mariners took to their oars, and hoisted their sails, and the ship sped on like a strong sea-bird.

When the dawn came the ship was near to the island of Ithaca. The mariners drove to a harbor near which there was a great cave. They lifted out Odysseus, still sleeping, and left him on the sandy shore of his own land. Then they took the gifts which the Phaeacians had given him, and they set them by an olive tree, a little apart from the road, so that no wandering person might come upon them before Odysseus had awakened. Then they went back to their ship and departed from Ithaca for their own land.

Odysseus awakened on the beach of his own land. A mist lay over all, and he did not know what land he had come to. As he looked around him in his bewilderment he saw one who was like a king's son approaching.

Now the one who came near him was not a young man, but the goddess, Pallas Athena, who had made herself look like a young man. She changed from the semblance of a young man and was seen by Odysseus as a woman tall and fair. "Do you not know me, Pallas Athena, the daughter of Zeus, who has always helped you?" the goddess said. "I would have been more often by your side, only I did not

---

semblance: outward appearance

"Do you not know me, Pallas Athena, who has always helped you?"

want to go openly against my brother, Poseidon, the god of
the sea, whose son, Polyphemus, you did blind."

As the goddess spoke, the mist that lay on the land
scattered, and Odysseus saw that he was indeed in Ithaca, his
own country—he knew the harbor and the cave, and the hill
all covered with its forest. And he knelt down on the ground
and kissed the earth of his country.

Then the goddess helped him to lay his goods within the cave—the gold and the bronze and the woven raiment that the Phaeacians had given him. She made him sit beside her under the olive tree while she told him of the things that were happening in his house.

"There is trouble in your halls, Odysseus," she said. She told him about the suitors of his wife, who filled his halls all day, and wasted his substance, and who would slay him. "It would be well for you not to make yourself known for a time," said the goddess, "and so I will change your appearance that no man shall know you."

Then she made his skin wither, and she dimmed his shining eyes. She made his yellow hair gray and scanty. She changed his raiment to a beggar's wrap, torn and stained with smoke. Over his shoulder she cast the hide of a deer, and she put into his hands a beggar's staff, with a tattered bag and a cord to hang it by. And when she had made this change in his appearance the goddess left Odysseus and went from Ithaca.

It was then that she came to Telemachus in Sparta and counseled him to leave the house of Menelaus and Helen; and it has been told how he came to his own ship, also to return to Ithaca.

ODYSSEUS AND THE SWINEHERD

Near the place where Odysseus had landed there lived an old man who was a faithful servant in his house. Eumaeus was his name, and he was a swineherd. He had made for

wither: dry out and shrivel up
scanty: in very small quantity; very little of
swineherd: one who looks after pigs and hogs

himself a dwelling in the wildest part of the island. Old Eumaeus lived in this place tending the swine with three young men to help him. The swine-pens were guarded by four dogs that were as fierce as the beasts of the forest.

As Odysseus came near the dogs dashed at him, yelping and snapping, and he might have suffered foul hurt if the swineherd had not run out of the courtyard and driven the fierce dogs away. Seeing before him one who seemed an ancient beggar, Eumaeus said, "Old man, it is well that my dogs did not tear you, for they might have brought upon me the shame of your death. I have grief and pains enough, the gods know, without such a happening. Here I sit, mourning for my noble master, while he is wandering in hunger through some friendless city. But come in, old man. I have bread and wine to give you."

The swineherd led the seeming beggar into the courtyard, and spread for him a shaggy goatskin. Odysseus was glad of his servant's welcome, and he said, "May Zeus and all the other gods grant you your heart's dearest wish for the welcome that you have given to me."

Said Eumaeus, the swineherd, "A good man looks on all strangers and beggars as being from Zeus himself. And my heart's dearest wish is that my master Odysseus should return."

He went to the swine-pens and brought out two sucking pigs. He slaughtered them and cut them small and roasted the meat. When all was cooked, he brought portions to Odysseus sprinkled with barley meal, and he brought him, too, wine in a deep bowl of ivy wood. And when Odysseus had eaten and drunken, Eumaeus the swineherd said to him:

---

seeming: appearing on the outside to be someone or something (but in fact someone or something else)

"Old man, no wanderer ever comes to this land but that our lady Penelope sends for him, hoping that he will have something to tell her of her lord, Odysseus. But as for Odysseus, no matter what wanderers or vagrants say, he will never return—dogs, or wild birds, or the fishes of the deep have devoured his body ere this. Never again shall I find so good a lord and master."

Said Odysseus, "You say that your master will never return, but I notice that you are slow to believe your own

vagrants: wanderers; hoboes
ere: before

words. Now I tell you that Odysseus will return and in this same year. And as sure as the old moon wanes and the young moon is born, he will take vengeance on those who eat his substance and dishonor his wife and son."

When morning came, Odysseus said, "I am going to the town to beg. I would go to the house of Odysseus, and see if I can earn a little from the suitors who are there. Right well could I serve them if they would take me on."

"Nay, nay," said Eumaeus, "do not go there, stranger. Stay until the son of Odysseus, Telemachus, returns. He will do something for you. Go not near the suitors."

So Odysseus did not go to the town but stayed with Eumaeus, and the old swineherd told of his fortunes and sorrows.

And while they were speaking, Telemachus, the son of Odysseus, came to Ithaca in his good ship. And having come to Ithaca, he bade one of his comrades bring the ship into the wharf of the city while he himself went to another place. Leaving the ship he came to the dwelling of the servant he most trusted—to the dwelling of Eumaeus, the swineherd.

FATHER AND SON

On the morning of his fourth day in Ithaca, as he and the swineherd were eating a meal together, Odysseus heard the sound of footsteps approaching the hut. The fierce dogs were outside and he expected to hear them yelping at the stranger's approach. No sound came from them. Then he saw a young man come to the entrance of the courtyard, the swineherd's dogs fawning upon him.

---

fortunes: lucky and unlucky experiences in the course of life

When Eumaeus saw this young man, he ran to him and kissed his head and his eyes and his hands. While he was weeping over him, Odysseus heard the swineherd saying, "Telemachus, are you come back to us? Like a light in the darkness you have appeared! I thought that never again should we see you! Come in, dear boy, come in."

Odysseus raised his head and looked at his son. As a lion might look over his cub, so he looked over Telemachus. But neither the swineherd nor Telemachus was aware of Odysseus's gaze.

"I have come to see you, friend Eumaeus," said Telemachus, "for before I go into the city I would know whether my mother is still in the house of Odysseus, or whether one of the suitors has at last taken her as a wife to his own house."

"Your mother is still in your father's house," Eumaeus answered.

Then Telemachus came within the courtyard. Odysseus in the guise of the old beggar rose from his seat, but the young man said to him courteously, "Be seated, friend. Another seat can be found for me."

Eumaeus strewed green brushwood and spread a fleece upon it, and Telemachus seated himself. Next Eumaeus fetched a meal for him—oaten cakes and swine flesh and wine. While they were eating, the swineherd said, "We have here a stranger who has wandered through many countries, and who has come to my house as a suppliant. Will you take him for your man, Telemachus?"

Said Telemachus, "For this stranger I will do what I can. I will give him a mantle and doublet, with shoes for his feet

guise: outward appearance; costume
strewed: spread by scattering
fleece: a wooly sheepskin

129

and a sword to defend himself, and I will send him on whatever way he wants to go. But, Eumaeus, I would not have him go near my father's house. The suitors grow more insolent each day, and they might mock the stranger if he went among them."

Then said Odysseus, speaking for the first time, "Young sir, what you have said seems strange to me. Do you willingly submit to insolence in your own father's house? But perhaps it is that the people of the city hate you and will not help you against your enemies. Ah, if I had such youth as I have spirit, or if I were the son of Odysseus, I should go among them this very day, and make myself the bane of each of them. I would rather die in my own halls than see such shame as is reported—strangers mocked at, and servants injured, and wine and food wasted."

Said Telemachus, "The people of the city do not hate me, and they would help me if they could. But the suitors of my mother are powerful men—men to make the city folk afraid. And if I should oppose them I would surely be slain in my father's house, for how could I hope to overcome so many?"

"O Telemachus," said the swineherd, "what would you have me do for you?"

"I would have you go to my mother, friend Eumaeus," Telemachus said, "and let her know that I am safe returned."

Eumaeus at once put sandals upon his feet and took his staff in his hands. He begged Telemachus to rest himself in the hut, and then he left the courtyard and went towards the city.

Telemachus lay down on his seat and closed his eyes in weariness. He saw, while thinking that he only dreamt it, a

mock: to ridicule; to make fun of meanly
bane: a cause of death or destruction

woman come to the gate of the courtyard. She was fair and
tall and splendid, and the dogs shrank away from her
presence with a whine. She touched the beggar, and the
marks of age and beggary fell from him and the man stood
up, tall and noble looking.

"Who are you?" cried Telemachus. "Even a moment ago
you did look aged and a beggar! Now you do look a chief of
men! Are you one of the divine ones?"

Odysseus looked upon him and said, "My son, I am Odysseus, your father. After much suffering and much wandering I have come to my own country." He kissed his son with tears flowing down his cheeks, and Telemachus threw his arms around his father's neck, but scarce believing that the father he had searched for was indeed before him.

But no doubt was left as Odysseus talked to him, and told him how he had come to Ithaca in a ship given him by the Phaeacians, and how he had brought with him gifts of bronze and raiment that were hidden in the cave, and how Pallas Athena had changed his appearance into that of an old beggar.

And when his own story was finished he said, "Come, my son, tell me of the suitors who waste the substance of our house—tell me how many they number, and who they are, so that we may prepare a way of dealing with them."

"Even though you are a great warrior, my father, you and I cannot hope to deal with them. They have come not from Ithaca alone, but from all the islands around. We two cannot deal with such a throng."

Said Odysseus, "I shall make a plan to deal with them. Go you home, and keep company with the suitors. Later in the day the swineherd will lead me into the city, and I shall go into the house in the likeness of an old beggar. And if you should see any of the suitors ill-treat me, harden your heart to endure it—even if they drag me by the feet to the door of the house, keep you quiet. And let no one—not even your mother, Penelope, nor my father, Laertes—know that Odysseus has returned."

Telemachus said, "My father, you shall learn soon what spirit is in me and what wisdom I have."

Eumaeus came back to the hut in the afternoon. Pallas Athena had again given Odysseus the appearance of an ancient beggar, and the swineherd saw no change in his guest.

The Beggar in the Hall of Odysseus

It was time for Telemachus to go to the city. To the swineherd he said, "Friend Eumaeus, I am now going into the city to my mother, to let her hear from my own lips the tale of my journey. And I have an order to leave with you. Take this stranger into the city, that he may go about as he desires, asking alms from the people."

Telemachus then passed out of the courtyard and went until he came into the city. When he went into the house, the first person he saw was his nurse, old Eurycleia, who welcomed him with joy. Then the suitors came into the hall and crowded around him. Then all sat down at tables, and Eurycleia brought wheaten bread and wine.

Just at that time Odysseus and Eumaeus came near, and they heard the sound of the lyre within the house. The suitors were now feasting. And when Odysseus came before his own house, he caught the swineherd by the hand suddenly and with a hard grip, and he said, "Lo now, I who have wandered in many lands and have walked in pain through many cities have come at last to the house of Odysseus. There it is, standing as of old, with its walls and its battlements, its courts and its doors. And lo! unwelcome men keep revel within it, and the smoke of their feast rises up and the sound of the lyre is heard playing for them."

---

alms: charity; money or goods given to the poor
keep revel: to engage in wild partying

Now as they went through the courtyard a thing happened that dashed Odysseus's eyes with tears. A hound lay in the dirt of the yard, a hound that was very old. All uncared for he lay in the dirt, old and feeble. But he had been a famous hound, and Odysseus himself had trained him before he went to the wars of Troy. Argos was his name. Now as Odysseus came near, the hound Argos knew him, and stood up before him and whined and dropped his ears, but had no strength to come near him. Odysseus knew the hound

and stopped and gazed at him. "A good hound lies there," said he to Eumaeus. "Once, I think, he was so swift that no beast in the deep places of the wood could flee from him." Then he went on, and the hound Argos lay down in the dirt of the yard, and that same day the life passed from him.

Behind Eumaeus, the swineherd, Odysseus came into his own hall, in the appearance of a beggar, wretchedly clad and leaning on an old man's staff. Odysseus looked upon the young lords who wooed his wife, and then he sat down upon the threshold and went no further into the hall.

Telemachus was there. Seeing Eumaeus he called to him and gave the swineherd bread and meat, and said, "Take these, and give them to the stranger at the doorway, and tell him that he may go among the company and ask alms from each."

Odysseus ate while the minstrel was finishing his song. When it was finished he rose up, and went into the hall, asking alms from each of the suitors.

Seeing him, Antinous, the most insolent of the suitors, cried out, "O notorious swineherd, why did you bring this fellow here? Have we not enough vagabonds?"

Hearing such a speech from Antinous, Telemachus said, "Antinous, would you have me drive a stranger from the door? The gods forbid that I should do such a thing. Nay, Antinous. Give the stranger something for the sake of the house."

"If all the company gives him as much as I, he will have something to keep him from beggary," said Antinous, meaning that he would do some harm to the beggar.

Odysseus came before him. "They say that you are the noblest of all the suitors," he said, "and for that reason you

notorious: famous for bad deeds
vagabonds: wanderers; vagrants

135

should give me a better thing than any of the others have given me. Look upon me. I too had a house of my own, and was accounted wealthy among men, and I had servants to wait upon me. And many a time would I make welcome the wanderer and give him something from my store."

"Stand far away from my table, you wretched fellow," said Antinous.

Then said Odysseus, "You have beauty, lord Antinous, but you have not wisdom. Out of your own house you would not give a grain of salt to a suppliant. And even while you sit at another man's table, you do not find it in your heart to give something out of the plenty that is before you."

So Odysseus spoke and Antinous became terribly angered. He caught up a chair, and with it he struck Odysseus in the back, at the base of the right shoulder. Such a blow would have knocked another man over, but Odysseus stood steadfast under it. He gave one look at Antinous, and then without a word he went over and sat down again upon the threshold.

Telemachus had in his heart a mighty rage for the stroke that had been given his father. But he let no tear fall from his eyes and he sat very still, brooding in his heart.

THE SCAR

While these things were happening, the wife of Odysseus, the lady Penelope, called to Eurycleia, and said, "This evening I will go into the hall of our house and speak to my son, Telemachus. Bid my two handmaidens make ready to come with me, for I shrink from going among the suitors alone."

---

brooding: thinking dark and gloomy thoughts

Eurycleia went to tell the handmaidens and Penelope
washed off her cheeks the traces of the tears that she had
wept that day. Then she sat down to wait for the
handmaidens to come to her. As she waited she fell into
a deep sleep. And as she slept, the goddess Pallas Athena
bathed her face in the Water of Beauty and took all weariness
away from her body, and restored all her youthfulness to her.
The sound of the handmaidens' voices as they came in
awakened her, and Penelope rose up to go into the hall.

Now when she came among them with her two
handmaidens, one standing each side of her, the suitors were

amazed, for they had never seen one so beautiful. The hearts of all were enchanted with love for her, and each hoped that he might have her for his wife.

Penelope did not look on any of the suitors, but she went to her son and spoke to him. "Telemachus," she said, "I have heard that a stranger has been ill-treated in this house. How, my child, did you permit such a thing to happen?"

Telemachus said, "My lady mother, you have no right to be angered at what took place in this hall."

So they spoke to one another, mother and son. Now one of the suitors, Eurymachus by name, spoke to Penelope, saying, "Lady, if others beheld the beauty you have now, you would have more suitors tomorrow."

"Lord Eurymachus," said Penelope, "speak not of my beauty, which departed in the grief I felt when my lord went to the wars of Troy."

Odysseus stood up, and gazed upon his wife who was standing among her suitors. Eurymachus noted him and going to him, said, "Stranger, would you be my hireling? If you would work on my upland farm, I should give you food and clothes. But I think you would prefer to go begging your way through the country."

Odysseus, standing there, said to that proud suitor, "Lord Eurymachus, you do think yourself a great man. But if Odysseus should return, that door, wide as it is, would be too narrow for your flight."

So angry was Eurymachus at this speech that he would have struck Odysseus if Telemachus had not come among the suitors, saying, "That man must not be struck again in this hall. Sirs, if you have finished feasting, the time has come for you to go to your own homes, I pray you."

All were astonished that Telemachus should speak so boldly. No one answered him back, for one said to the other, "What he has said is proper. Let each man go to his home."

The suitors departed. Then Penelope and her handmaidens went to her own chamber and Telemachus was left with his father, Odysseus.

To Telemachus Odysseus said, "My son, we must now get the weapons out of the hall. Take them down from the walls."

Telemachus and his father took down the helmets and shields and sharp-pointed spears. They carried the armor and weapons out of the hall and hid them. Then when the hall was cleared he went to his own chamber.

It was then that Penelope came back to the hall to speak to the stranger. She spoke to the old nurse who had come with her, and said, "Eurycleia, bring to the fire a bench, with a fleece upon it, that this stranger may sit and tell me his story."

Eurycleia brought over the bench, and Odysseus sat down near the fire. Then said the lady Penelope, "First, stranger, will you tell me who you are, and what is your name, and your country?"

Said Odysseus, "Ask me all you will, lady, but inquire not concerning my name or country, lest you should fill my heart with more pains than I am able to endure. Verily I am a man of grief. But have you no tale to tell me? We know of you, for your fame goes up to heaven."

Then said Penelope, "What excellence I had of face or form departed from me when my lord Odysseus went from this hall to the wars of Troy. And since he went a host of ills has beset me. Ah, would that he were here! The lords of all the islands around have come here and are wooing me against my will. They devour the substance of this house and my son is being impoverished. And now my parents command me to marry one of my suitors. And there is no reason why I should not be wed again, for surely Odysseus, my lord, is dead."

Said Odysseus, "Your lord was known to me. On his way to Troy he came to my land, for the wind blew him out of his course. For twelve days he stayed in my city, and I gave him good entertainment, and saw that he lacked for nothing in cattle, or wine, or barley meal."

When she heard her husband spoken of, the heart of Penelope melted, and tears ran down her cheeks. Odysseus had pity for his wife when he saw her weeping for the man who was even then sitting by her. Tears would have run down his own cheeks only that he was strong enough to hold them back.

Odysseus leaned towards her and said, "Do not waste your heart with endless weeping, lady. Odysseus is near. He has lost all his companions, and he knows not how to come into this house, whether openly or by stealth. I swear that Odysseus himself will stand up here before the old moon wanes and the new moon is born."

"Ah, no," said Penelope. "Often before have wanderers told me such comfortable things, and I believed them. I know now that your word cannot be accomplished. But it is time for you to rest yourself, stranger. My handmaidens will make a bed for you in the vestibule. And here is an ancient woman who nursed and tended that hapless man, Odysseus. She took him in her arms in the very hour he was born. Come,

---

impoverished: made poor
stealth: secrecy
hapless: unlucky

Eurycleia, and wash the feet of this man, who knew your lord and mine."

Thereupon the nurse, old Eurycleia, fetched water, both hot and cold, and brought the bath to the hearth. And standing before Odysseus in the flickering light of the fire, she said, "I will wash your feet, both for Penelope's sake and for your own. The heart within me is moved at the sight of you. Many strangers have come into this hall, but I have never seen one that was so like as you are to Odysseus."

His feet were in the water, and she put her hand upon one of them. As she did so, Odysseus turned his face away to the darkness, for it suddenly came into his mind that his nurse, old Eurycleia, might recognize the scar that was upon his foot. It had been made long ago, when Odysseus was a youth, and a boar's tusk had ripped the flesh of his foot.

And now, as Eurycleia, his old nurse, passed her hands along the leg, she let his foot drop suddenly. The nurse touched the chin of Odysseus and she said, "You are Odysseus."

She looked to where Penelope was sitting, so that she might make a sign to her. But Penelope had her eyes turned away. Odysseus put his hand on Eurycleia's mouth, and with the other hand he drew her to him.

"Woman," he whispered, "say nothing. Be silent, lest my enemies learn what you know now."

"Silent I'll be," said the nurse Eurycleia. "You know me: firm I am, and by no sign will I let anyone know that you have come under this roof."

So saying she finished bathing his feet. Then Odysseus arranged the rags around his leg to hide the scar, and he drew the bench closer to the fire.

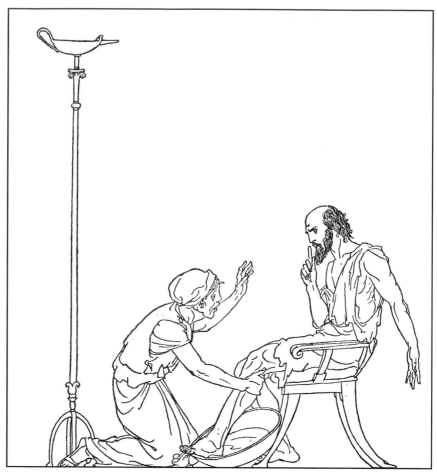

"You are Odysseus."

Penelope turned to him again. "My guest," she said, "the day of my woe is at hand. I am being forced by my parents to choose a husband from the suitors, and depart from the house of Odysseus."

"And how will you choose from among them?" said Odysseus.

"In this way," said Penelope. "My husband's great bow is still in the house. The one who can bend that bow, and shoot an arrow through the holes in the backs of twelve axes set one behind the other—him will I choose for my husband."

Said Odysseus, "Your device is good, Penelope, and some god has instructed you to do this. But delay no longer the contest of the bow. Let it be tomorrow."

"Is that your counsel, O stranger?" said Penelope.

"It is," said Odysseus.

"I thank you," she said. "And now farewell, for I must go to my rest. And do you lie down in the vestibule, in the bed that has been made for you."

So Penelope spoke, and then she went to her chamber with her handmaidens. And in her bed she thought over all the stranger had told her of Odysseus, and she wept again for him.

The Beggar and the Bow

In the treasure-chamber of the house, Odysseus's great bow was kept. Odysseus had not taken it with him when he went to the wars of Troy.

To the treasure-chamber Penelope went. She carried in her hand the great key that opened the doors—a key all of bronze with a handle of ivory. Now as she thrust the key into the lock, the doors groaned as a bull groans. She went within, and saw the great bow upon its peg. She took it down and laid it upon her knees, and thought long upon the man who had bent it.

Beside the bow was its quiver full of bronze-weighted arrows. A servant took the quiver and Penelope took the bow, and they went from the treasure-chamber and into the hall where the suitors were.

When she came in she spoke to the company and said: "Lords of Ithaca and of the islands around: You have come

---

quiver: a case for carrying arrows

here, each desiring that I should wed him. Now the time has come for me to make my choice of a man from among you. Here is how I shall make choice. This is the bow of Odysseus, my lord who is no more. Whosoever among you who can bend this bow and shoot an arrow from it through the holes in the backs of twelve axes, him will I wed, and to his house I will go."

As she spoke Telemachus took the twelve axes and set them upright in an even line, so that one could shoot an arrow through the hole that was in the back of each axe-head. Then Eumaeus, the old swineherd, took the bow of Odysseus and laid it before the suitors.

One of the suitors took up the bow and tried to bend it. But he could not bend it, and he laid it down at the doorway with the arrow beside it. The others took up the bow, and warmed it at the fire, and rubbed it with lard to make it more pliable. As they were doing this, Eumaeus, the swineherd, and Philoetius, the cattle-herd, passed out of the hall.

Odysseus followed them into the courtyard. He laid a hand on each and said, "Swineherd and cattle-herd, I have a word to say to you. But will you keep it to yourselves, the word I say? And first, what would you do to help Odysseus if he should return? Would you stand on his side, or on the side of the suitors? Answer me now from your hearts."

Said Philoetius the cattle-herd, "May Zeus fulfill my wish and bring Odysseus back! Then you should know on whose side I would stand." And Eumaeus said, "If Odysseus should return I would be on his side, with all the strength that is in me."

---

lard: fat (from a hog)
pliable: bendable; flexible

When they said this, Odysseus lifted up his hand to heaven and said, "I am your master, Odysseus. After twenty years I have come back to my own country. If you need a token that I am indeed Odysseus, look down on my foot. See there the mark that the wild boar left on me in the days of my youth."

He drew the rags from the scar, and the swineherd and the cattle-herd saw it and marked it well. Knowing that it was indeed Odysseus who stood before them, they cast their arms around him and kissed him on the head and shoulders. And Odysseus was moved by their tears, and he kissed their heads and their hands.

As they went back to the hall, he told Eumaeus to bring the bow to him as he was bearing it through the hall. He told him, too, to order Eurycleia, the faithful nurse, to bar the doors of the women's apartment at the end of the hall, and to bid the women, even if they heard a groaning and a din, not to come into the hall. And he charged the cattle-herd Philoetius to bar the gates of the courtyard.

As he went into the hall, one of the suitors, Eurymachus, was striving to bend the bow. As he struggled to do so he groaned aloud, "Not because I may not marry Penelope do I groan, but because we youths of today are shown to be weaklings beside Odysseus, whose bow we can in no way bend."

Then Antinous, the proudest of the suitors, said, "Why should we strive to bend the bow today? Nay, lay the bow aside, Eurymachus, and let the wine-bearers pour us out a cupful each. In the morning let us make sacrifice to the Archer-god, and pray that the bow be fitted to some of our hands."

Then Odysseus came forward and said, "Sirs, you do well to lay the bow aside for today. But will you not put the bow into my hands, that I may try to bend it, and judge for myself whether I have any of the strength that once was mine?"

All the suitors were angry that a beggar should attempt to bend the bow that none of their company were able to bend. Antinous spoke to him sharply and said, "You wretched beggar! Is it not enough that you are let into this high hall to pick up scraps, but you must listen to our speech and join in our conversation? If you should bend that bow we will make short shrift of you, I promise. We will have you cut to pieces and give your flesh to the hounds."

Old Eumaeus had taken up the bow. As he went with it to Odysseus, some of them shouted, "Where are you going with the bow, you crazy fellow? Put it down." Eumaeus was confused by their shouts, and he put down the bow.

Then Telemachus spoke to him and said, "Eumaeus, beware of being the man who served many masters." Eumaeus, hearing these words, took it up again and brought it to Odysseus, and put the bow into his hands.

As Odysseus stood in the doorway of the hall, the bow in his hands, and the arrows scattered at his feet, Eumaeus went to Eurycleia and told her to bar the door of the women's apartment at the back. Then Philoetius, the cattle-herd, went out of the hall and barred the gates leading out of the courtyard.

For long Odysseus stood with the bow in his hands, handling it as a minstrel handles a lyre when he stretches a cord or tightens a peg. Then he bent the great bow; he bent it without an effort, and at his touch the bow-string made a sound that was like the cry of a swallow. The suitors seeing

---

make short shrift of: deal with quickly; do quick work

him bend that mighty bow felt, every man of them, a sharp pain at the heart. They saw Odysseus take up an arrow and fit it to the string. He held the notch, and he drew the string, and he shot the bronze-weighted arrow straight through the holes in the back of the axe-heads.

Then he said, "You see, lord Telemachus, that your guest does not shame you through foolish boasting. I have bent the

bow of Odysseus, and I have shot the arrow aright. But now it is time to provide the feast for the lords who woo your lady mother. While it is yet light, the feast must be served to them."

Saying this he nodded to Telemachus, bending his terrible brows. Telemachus instantly girt his sword upon him and took his spear in his hand. Outside was heard the thunder of Zeus. And now Odysseus had stripped his rags from him and was standing upright, looking a master of men. The mighty bow was in his hands, and at his feet were scattered many bronze-weighted arrows.

The Vengeance of Odysseus

He put the bronze-weighted arrow against the string of the bow, and shot at the first of his enemies.

It was at Antinous he pointed the arrow—at Antinous who was even then lifting up a golden cup filled with wine, and who was smiling, with death far from his thoughts. Odysseus aimed at him, and smote him with the arrow in the throat and the point passed out clean through his neck. The wine cup fell from his hands and Antinous fell dead across the table. Then did all the suitors raise a shout, threatening Odysseus for sending an arrow astray. It did not come into their minds that this stranger-beggar had aimed to kill Antinous.

But Odysseus shouted back to them, "You dogs, you that said in your hearts that Odysseus would never return to his home, you that wasted my substance, and troubled my wife,

girt: fastened
smote: struck and killed
astray: off the right path

and injured my servants; you who showed no fear of heaven, nor of the just judgments of men—behold Odysseus returned, and know what death is loosed upon you!"

Then Eurymachus shouted out, "Friends, draw your swords and hold up the tables before you for shields and advance upon him."

But even as he spoke, Odysseus, with a terrible cry, loosed an arrow at him and shot Eurymachus through the breast. He let the sword fall from his hand, and he too fell dead upon the floor.

One of the band rushed straight at Odysseus with his sword in hand. But Telemachus drove his spear through this man's shoulders. Then Telemachus ran quickly to a chamber where there were weapons and armor lying. The swineherd and the cattle-herd joined him, and all three put armor upon them. Odysseus, as long as he had arrows to defend himself, kept shooting at the suitors. When all the arrows were gone, he put the helmet on his head and took up the shield that Telemachus had brought, and the two great spears.

And now he directed Telemachus and Eumaeus and Philoetius to cast their spears. When they cast them with Odysseus, each one struck a man, and four of the suitors fell down. And again Odysseus directed his following to cast their spears, and again they cast them, and slew their men. They drove those who remained from one end of the hall to the other, and slew them all.

The doors of the women's apartment were flung open, and Eurycleia appeared. She saw Odysseus among the bodies of the dead, all stained with blood. She would have cried out in triumph if Odysseus had not restrained her. "Rejoice within your own heart," he said, "but do not cry aloud, for it is an unholy thing to triumph over men lying dead. These men the gods themselves have overcome, because of their own hard and unjust hearts."

Husband and Wife

Eurycleia, the old nurse, went to the upper chamber where Penelope lay in her bed. She bent over her and called out, "Awake, Penelope, dear child. Come down and see with your own eyes what has happened. The suitors are overthrown. And he whom you have ever longed to see has come back. Odysseus, your husband, has returned. He has slain the proud suitors who have troubled you for so long."

But Penelope only looked at the nurse, for she thought she must be mad. Still Eurycleia kept on saying, "Odysseus is here. He is that guest whom all the suitors dishonored in the hall."

Then hearing Eurycleia say these words, Penelope sprang out of bed and put her arms round the nurse's neck. "Ah no!" said Penelope, "ah no, Odysseus has not returned. He who has slain the suitors is one of the deathless gods, come down to punish them for their injustice and their hardheartedness. Odysseus long ago lost the way of his returning, and he is lying dead in some far-off land."

"No, no," said Eurycleia. "I can show you that it is Odysseus indeed who is in the hall. On his foot is the scar that the tusk of a boar gave him in the old days. I spied it when I was washing his feet last night, and I would have told you of it, but he clapped a hand across my mouth to stop my speech. Lo, I stake my life that it is Odysseus, and none other, who is in the hall below."

Saying this she took Penelope by the hand and led her from the upper chamber into the hall. Odysseus was standing by a tall pillar. He waited there for his wife to come and speak to him. But Penelope stood still, and gazed long upon him, and made no step towards him.

Then said Telemachus, "Mother, can it be that your heart is so hard? Here is my father, and you will not go to him."

Said Penelope, "My mind is amazed and I have no strength to speak, nor to ask him aught, nor even to look on him face to face. If this is indeed Odysseus who has come home, a place has to be prepared for him."

Then Odysseus spoke to Telemachus and said, "Go now to the bath, and make yourself clean of the stains of battle. I will stay and speak with your lady mother."

"Strange lady," said he to Penelope, "is your heart indeed so hard? No other woman in the world, I think, would stand so aloof from her husband who, after so much toil and so many trials, has come back after twenty years to his own hearth. Is there no place for me here, and must I again sleep in the stranger's bed?"

Said Penelope, "In no stranger's bed will you lie, my lord. Come, Eurycleia. Set up for him his own bedstead outside his bed-chamber."

Then Odysseus said to her, speaking in anger: "How comes it that my bed can be moved to this place and that? Not a bed of that kind was the bed I built for myself. Know you not how I built my bed? First, there grew up in the courtyard an olive tree. Round that olive tree I built a chamber, and I roofed it well and I set doors to it. Then I sheared off all the light wood on the growing olive tree, and I rough-hewed the trunk with the adze, and I made the tree into a bed post. Beginning with this bed post I wrought a bedstead, and when I finished it, I inlaid

---

aloof: apart; at a distance
sheared: cut
wrought: created; shaped by labor

it with silver and ivory. Such was the bed I built for myself, and such a bed could not be moved to this place or that."

Then did Penelope know assuredly that the man who stood before her was indeed her husband, the steadfast Odysseus—none other knew where the bed was placed, and how it had been built. Penelope fell a-weeping and she put her arms round his neck.

"O Odysseus, my lord," she said, "be not angry with your wife. Always the fear was in my heart that some guileful stranger should come here professing to be Odysseus, and that I should take him to me as my husband. How terrible such a thing would be! But now my heart is freed from all doubts. Be not angry with me, Odysseus."

Then husband and wife wept together, and they told each other of things that happened in the twenty years they were apart, Odysseus speaking of his own toils and sorrows, and Penelope telling what she had endured at the hands of the suitors. And as they told tales, one to the other, slumber came upon them, and the dawn found them sleeping side by side.

SON AND FATHER

And still many dangers had to be faced. The suitors whom Odysseus had slain were the richest and the most powerful of the lords of Ithaca and the islands; all of them had fathers and brothers who would fain avenge them upon their slayer.

Now before anyone in the city knew that he had returned, Odysseus went forth to the farm of Laertes, his old father. As he drew near he saw an old man working in the vineyard,

---

assuredly: with certainty
professing: claiming; declaring
fain: gladly; with desire

digging round a plant. When he came to him he saw that
this old man was not a slave nor a servant, but Laertes, his
own father.

When he saw him, wasted with age, Odysseus stood still,
leaning his hand against a pear tree and sorrowing in his
heart. Old Laertes kept his head down as he stood digging at
the plant, and he did not see Odysseus until he stood before
him and said, "Old man, you do care for this garden well

and all things here are flourishing—fig tree, and vine, and olive, and pear. But, if a stranger may say it, your own self is not cared for well."

"Who are you that do speak to me like this?" old Laertes said, lifting his head.

"I am a stranger in Ithaca," said Odysseus. "I seek a man whom I once kindly treated—a man whose name was Odysseus. A stranger, he came to me, and he declared that he was of Ithaca, and that one day he would give me kindness for the kindness I had shown him. I know not if this man be still alive."

Old Laertes wept before Odysseus. "Ah," said he, "if you had been able to find him here, true hospitality you would have received from Odysseus, my son. But he has perished— far from his country's soil he has perished, the hapless man."

So he spake and then with his hands he took up the dust of the ground, and he strewed it over his head in his sorrow. The heart of Odysseus was moved with grief. He sprang forward and fell on his father's neck and he kissed him, saying, "Behold I am here, even I, my father. I, Odysseus, have come back to my own country. I have slain the suitors and avenged all their injuries and all their wrongful doings. Do you not believe this, my father? Then look on what I will show you. Behold on my foot the mark of the boar's tusk— there it is, from the days of my youth."

Laertes looked down on the bare foot, and he saw the scar, but still his mind was clouded by doubt. But then Odysseus took him through the garden, and he told him of the fruit trees that Laertes had set for him when he, Odysseus, was a little child, following his father about the garden—thirteen pear trees, and ten apple trees, and forty fig trees.

flourishing: prospering; doing well

When Odysseus showed him these, Laertes knew that it was his son indeed who stood before him—his son come back after twenty years' wandering. He cast his arms around his neck, and Odysseus caught him fainting to his breast, and led him into the house.

Within the house were Telemachus, and Eumaeus the swineherd, and Philoetius the cattle-herd. They all clasped the hand of Laertes and their words raised his spirits. Then he was bathed, and, when he came from the bath, rubbed with olive oil, he looked hale and strong. Odysseus said to him, "Father, surely one of the gods has made you younger than you were a while ago."

Said the old hero Laertes, "Ah, my son, would that I had such might as when, long before you were born, I took the Castle of Nericus. Would that, with such might, I stood with you yesterday when you did fight with the suitors."

While they were speaking in this way, news of the slaying of the suitors went through the city. Then those who were related to the slain men went into the courtyard of Odysseus's house, and brought forth the bodies. Those who belonged to Ithaca they buried, and those who belonged to the islands they put upon ships, and sent them with fisherfolk, each to his own home.

Many were wroth with Odysseus for the slaying of a friend, and they put on their armor and went out to avenge themselves upon Odysseus. And as they went through the town they met with Odysseus and his following— Telemachus and Laertes, with the swineherd and the cattle-herd—as they were coming from the house of Laertes.

---

hale: healthy
wroth: very angry

Now as the two bands came close to each other, a great figure came between. It was the figure of a tall, fair, and splendid woman. Odysseus knew her for the goddess Pallas Athena.

"Hold your hands from fierce fighting, you men of Ithaca," the goddess called out in a terrible voice. "Hold your hands." Straightway the arms fell from each man's hands. Then the goddess called them together, and she made them

enter into a covenant that all bloodshed and wrong would be forgotten, and that Odysseus would be left to rule Ithaca as king, in peace.

So ends the story of Odysseus who went with King Agamemnon to the wars of Troy; who made the plan of the Wooden Horse by which Priam's city was taken at last; who missed the way of his return, and came to the land of the Lotus-eaters; who came to the country of the dread Cyclopes, to the island of Aeolus, and to the house of Circe, the Enchantress; who heard the song of the Sirens, and came to the Wandering Rocks, and to the terrible Charybdis, and to Scylla, which no other man had past unscathed; who landed on the island where the Cattle of the Sun grazed, and who was held at the home of the nymph Calypso; so ends the story of Odysseus, who would have been made deathless and ageless by Calypso if he had not yearned always to come back to his own hearth and his own land. And, despite all his troubles and his toils, he was fortunate, for he found a constant wife and a dutiful son and a father still alive to weep over him.

covenant: a formal agreement; a solemn promise
unscathed: unharmed
constant: faithful

Acknowledgments

Text

The text in this volume is adapted from the following sources:

Homer: The Poet for All Ages
from *Everyday Classics Eighth Reader* ed. Franklin T. Baker and Ashley H. Thorndike
(New York: Macmillan, 1918)

What Happened Before the *Iliad*
from *The Merrill Readers: Fifth Reader* ed. Franklin B. Dyer and Mary J. Brady (New York:
Charles E. Merrill Co., 1916); and, "The Fall of Troy" in *Thirty More Famous Stories Retold*
by James Baldwin (New York: American Book Co., 1905)

Stories from the *Iliad*
from *The Iliad for Boys and Girls* (New York: Macmillan, 1907) and *Stories from Homer*
(New York: Thomas Y. Crowell and Co., 1901) by Alfred J. Church

Stories from the *Odyssey*
from *The Adventures of Odysseus and the Tale of Troy* by Padraic Colum (New York:
Macmillan, 1918)

Illustrations

Illustrations in this volume are by Willy Pogany, from *The Adventures of Odysseus and the
Tale of Troy* (New York: Macmillan, 1918)

While every care has been taken to trace and acknowledge copyright, the editors tender
their apologies for any accidental infringement when copyright has proven untraceable.
They would be pleased to include the appropriate acknowledgment in any subsequent
edition of this publication.

Editor: John Holdren

Art Director: Steve Godwin

Designer: Jayoung Cho

ISBN: 1-931728-50-X

Printed by Worzalla, Stevens Point, WI, USA, April 2019